THE
SYNOPTIC
PROBLEM

A CRITICAL ANALYSIS

TO JOHN KNOX
teacher and friend

THE
SYNOPTIC
PROBLEM

A CRITICAL ANALYSIS

William R. Farmer

Western North Carolina Press
DILLSBORO, NORTH CAROLINA

International Standard Book Number (ISBN) 0-915948-02-8

Library of Congress Catalog card number: 76-13764

ACKNOWLEDGMENTS

Grateful acknowledgment is hereby made for permission to quote extensively from the following published works: *The Origin of the Synoptic Gospels* by H. G. Jameson, by permission of Basil Blackwell; *The Four Gospels* by Burnett Hillman Streeter, by permission of Macmillan and Co. Ltd.

Acknowledgment is also made to the editors of *New Testament Studies* and *Biblical Research* for permission to reuse portions of the text of my articles, "Some Notes on a Literary and Form-Critical Analysis of the Synoptic Material Peculiar to Luke" in *New Testament Studies*, April 1962, and "A 'Skeleton in the Closet' of Gospel Research," in *Biblical Research*, vi, 1961.

Printed in the United States of America

Contents

Preface

The purpose of this book is to do something to meet the need for a general renaissance in Gospel studies. If there is to be such a renewal in our time it will come only through a widespread revitalization of the discipline of Synoptic criticism. This book is written out of the conviction that the greatest single contribution to this revitalization that can be rendered at this time is to reopen the question of the Synoptic Problem.

Only after the problem has been convincingly reopened can it be expected that very many scholars will give serious and impartial consideration to alternative solutions to the problem.

For some, but all too few, the problem is regarded as having been reopened already. This book was not written with such readers primarily in mind. Nevertheless, they may, I hope, find it instructive to see the Synoptic Problem treated in a somewhat different perspective.

To those investigators who have preceded me in publishing views calling into question either the priority of Mark or the existence of "Q," I gladly acknowledge my profound indebtedness. Their companionship has been treasured during my own prolonged intellectual pilgrimage, which has been marked first by a questioning of the existence of "Q," and later by a questioning of the priority of Mark to Matthew, and finally by a questioning of the priority of Mark to Luke as well. Without their industry and courage, this book would probably never have been written.

This book seeks to demonstrate that the idea of Marcan priority is highly questionable. The fact that an idea which is highly questionable is nevertheless widely believed or assented to is not new. What may be new to some is the demonstrable fact that ideas which could be grossly false can gain acceptance and credence in the highest intellectual circles and councils of the modern West, under the guise of being the assured results of criticism.

The first five chapters of this book could be regarded as a study in the anatomy of consensus. Whether what is documented in those chapters and in Appendix B, concerning the history of the idea of Marcan priority, has any importance for the history of ideas in general, or the sociology of consensus making, or the theology of the nineteenth century, is for others to decide.

Chapter VI, in due time, in some modified form, may serve as a beginner's manual for a study of the Synoptic Problem.

While writing this book I was sometimes struck by the enormity of my action. I realize that very little attention may be paid to what I have written. And for that eventuality I am fully prepared. But I also know that I have solved for myself a mystifying problem with far-reaching implications, and that in so doing I may have done something that will prove to be helpful to others.

In 1961, while addressing the Chicago Society of Biblical Research, I referred to the "Lachmann Fallacy" to which B. C. Butler had drawn attention. At that time I said: "The number of textbooks and lecture rooms in which this logical fallacy has been perpetrated is legion. I used it in my class lectures for ten years. I estimate that there are at least three hundred intelligent human beings loose in the world who firmly believe in the priority of Mark because of the convincing use I made of that particular *non sequitur*."

The genesis of this book can be traced to the determination to understand how it could be that I once stood before my students and assured them in good conscience that Mark was the earliest Gospel. It was not because of the arguments I then adduced in class. In fact, I distinctly recall feeling that there was a subtlety to the argument from order for Marcan priority which I had never mastered. But the thought never crossed my mind that the argument was itself inconclusive. I used the argument without fully understanding it, because it was an unquestioned part of an unquestioned tradition.

How had my teachers come to pass on to me the view that Mark was the earliest Gospel? This question led me back to investigate the history of the synoptic problem. From one point of view this book can be regarded as an act of *pietas*—a vindication of the integrity of my teachers—for it explains to me how they, like myself, could have done what they did in good conscience.

I trust that the reader will not allow what may appear to be a sensational dimension of this book to obscure the fact that the search has been for truth, not scandal. I personally feel that Chapter V is crucially important in understanding the whole story and would expect the discerning reader to be mindful that we ourselves are children of our times and doubtless influenced in ways that only future historians may make clear.

For those quick to conclude that this book proves that the assured results of criticism are a snare and delusion, it need only be pointed out that criticism itself cannot be shown to be responsible for the false consensus which developed with regard to the priority of Mark. On the contrary, what is demonstrated herein is that consensus on some matters develops in spite of criticism and for reasons over which criticism has little control. Furthermore, were it not for criticism, it would have been impossible to demonstrate the fallacious character of the "assured" results examined in this book. It is not possible for me to find a way to recognize publicly the real contribution my students have made to this book. Their participation in the dialogue through which my stream of consciousness has been channeled into the communicable form given to it in this book has been indispensable.

For one year I also had the benefit of the sympathetic interest of a small group of my peers in Southern Methodist University. Fortnightly, during the academic year 1961–1962, I would meet with the Resident Fellows of the Graduate Council of the Humanities for a discussion of our respective research projects. These colleagues first convinced me that there could be widespread understanding of my problem by men of letters. I am grateful to them and to the many others who have encouraged me to think that what made sense to me could also be made to make sense to others. As a Resident Fellow for that year I was also provided an increased amount of time to devote to research. In these and other ways, this book may be regarded as having been made possible in part through that Fellowship, and for that reason these words of appreciation may be fittingly included in this preface.

A grant from the Bollingen Foundation made it possible to sustain an active program of research during the summers of 1960, 1962, and 1963, and part of the summer of 1961. The summer of 1960 was spent at Göttingen exploring through the holdings of that great University library the history of the synoptic problem in Germany during the nineteenth century. Heinz-Dieter Knigge rendered invaluable aid as a research assistant at that time. During the second half of the summer of 1961 Ed Parish Sanders, as a research assistant, carried forward extensive statistical studies bearing on the problem of the literary relationship between the Gospels. The results of these studies tended to confirm in my mind Augustine's view that Mark was secondary to Matthew, but to call into question his view that Luke was secondary to Mark. This was the first hint that Mark might be secondary to both Matthew and Luke. However, this hint was not recognized at the time, and the results served only to cast doubt on the reliability of such statistical studies. These results have not been included in this book, because until such time as reliable canons of criticism have been adopted by which the significance of such statistical studies may be properly assayed, their probative value remains in doubt. Sanders also assisted in carrying through a detailed redactional analysis of Matthew, the results of which removed all reasonable doubt in my mind that it is possible for one to make as much (if not more) sense out of Matthew on the hypothesis that it was edited without the benefit of Mark and "Q," as it is on the hypothesis that Matthew was written with Mark and "Q" in view. The results of this analysis will be published separately.

The summer of 1962 was spent preparing a polychrome Synopticon, which for the first time enabled me to grasp the totality of the phenomena of verbatim agreement between the Gospels. Those who assisted in the preparation of this Synopticon were Glenn Chesnut, Bryan Forrester, and Mike Thornberry.

With this tool in hand, it was at last possible to proceed in a scientific manner to verify detailed points exhaustively, while at the same time viewing every detail in its widest possible context. The problem was then to consider the various ways in which the different phenomena of verbatim agreement between the Gospels could or could not be explained on alternate solutions of the problem. Finally it was determined that one solution alone seemed to afford an explanation for all the phenomena. It then remained to isolate the phenomena which could be explained on that solution alone. This constituted evidence in favor of that solution as the true solution and led to the formulation of arguments designed to communicate in provable terms the significance of this evidence for the solution of the Synoptic Problem. After that, the next step was one of verification. This was carried out by a new literary analysis of the texts of Luke and Mark designed to test the cogency of the arguments which had been formulated on the basis of the totality of the phenomena of verbatim agreement between the Gospels as abstracted through the aid of the Synopticon.

Further research on the history of the Synoptic Problem was greatly facilitated through the services of the libraries of Southern Methodist University. Mrs. Elizabeth Twitchell, of the Bridwell Library, rendered an indispensable service in her persistent search for rare items through the agency of inter-library loan. For making one or more books available through inter-library loan, I wish to thank the staffs of the libraries of the following institutions: Austin Presbyterian Theological Seminary, Drew University, Duke University Divinity School, Fuller Theological Seminary, Garrett Theological Seminary, General Theological Seminary,

Harvard Divinity School, Oberlin College, Princeton Theological Seminary, State University of Iowa, Union Theological Seminary, University of Chicago Divinity School, Wesleyan University, Yale University Divinity School, and the Cincinnati Public Library.

For microfilming and numerous other courtesies I wish to thank Decherd Turner and other members of the staff of Bridwell Library. Decherd Turner also read the entire manuscript.

Typing and other secretarial assistance in connection with the book have been generously given by Susie Banks, Dorothy Laughbaum, and Clarice Moxley.

William C. Robinson, Jr., read the greater part of Chapter IV and the opening portions of Chapters VI and VII. His invaluable criticisms are gratefully acknowledged.

The complete manuscript was carefully edited by George Wesley Buchanan, who had also a voice in the decision to make the purpose of the book that of reopening the question of the Synoptic Problem, rather than that of attempting to aim at an exhaustive verification of a particular solution.

Others who read parts of the manuscript and made valuable suggestions were Klaus Penzel (Chapters I and II), Heinz-Dieter Knigge (Chapters I and II), Edmund Deane (Chapters III–VII), Gladyce Buchanan (Chapters I–V), and Jane Baker (Chapter I). Edmund Deane also prepared all the Greek texts for the printer. Valuable assistance in the reading of proofs and checking references has been rendered by several students who fittingly remain unnamed as a silent tribute to their many predecessors who have contributed so much to the book in ways that cannot be verified in detail but are not therefore less appreciated.

Finally, I wish to express my appreciation to those New Testament colleagues who have corresponded with me in response to the privately circulated materials on "Q" sent out in 1959, and again in response to my address to the Chicago Society of Biblical Research published in 1961. Without this correspondence there is no way I could have been certain that there exists a widespread disposition on the part of many to have the question of the Synoptic Problem reopened. It is my sincere hope that this book will be received by these scholars, and by all others interested in Gospel criticism, as an acceptable contribution to that end.

WILLIAM R. FARMER

December 18, 1963

CHAPTER I

The Essential
Developments in the
Pre-Holtzmann Period

A. The Eighteenth Century

I. THE EIGHTEENTH CENTURY IMPASSE

In the eighteenth century the central problem facing the student of the Gospels was that of chronology. True chronology was regarded as essential for true history. The conflicting chronologies of the four canonical Gospels cast doubt in the minds of thinking men concerning the reliability of these documents as trustworthy witnesses. Attempts to solve these difficulties were hampered by the confusion caused by irreconcilable traditions in the church. These were chiefly three in number: (1) Clement of Alexandria states that the Gospels with genealogies (Matthew and Luke) were written before the Gospels without genealogies (Mark and John);[1] (2) Augustine held that no Evangelist wrote his Gospel in ignorance of the work of his predecessor or predecessors and that

---

[1] *Hypotyposen*, in Eusebius, *Hist. Eccl.* VI. 14. 5. Eusebius represents Clement as claiming to have received as tradition handed down from the Elders that with regard to the order in which the Gospels were written, "those having genealogies were written first."

the order was Matthew, Mark, Luke, and John. This is in clear conflict with the earlier testimony of Clement of Alexandria. Augustine also regarded Mark as an epitomizer of Matthew;[2] (3) Papias states that Mark was the interpreter of Peter and regards his Gospel as based on the witness of Peter.[3] This is in conflict with Augustine's view that Mark is the epitomizer of Matthew for it is difficult to see why Mark would have been so dependent upon Matthew if he were in such close contact with Peter and had access to Peter's knowledge of the Gospel tradition.

In this situation of impasse and confusion two important developments took place in the second half of the eighteenth century: (1) Investigators attempted to overcome the confusion of church tradition on the origin of the Gospels by going behind the evidence from the church Fathers and developing new hypotheses on the basis of evidence provided by the New Testament writings, especially the Acts of the Apostles, and by reinterpretation of statements made by church Fathers regarding the existence of early Gospels no longer extant. The most important names here are those of Lessing, Herder, and Eichhorn. (2) The older type of Gospel "harmonies" designed to reconcile the accounts of all four Gospels was replaced by a new type of Gospel "parallel," where no attempt

[2] *de Consensu Evangelistarum*, I. 2–3. It may be doubted that Augustine's judgment that Mark epitomized Matthew is truly critical. It seems more likely that the origin of this view flows naturally from his acceptance, on the one hand, of the view that each succeeding Evangelist made use of the work of his predecessor. This latter view was implied in Ammonius' edition of Matthew where sections of the other Gospels were arranged alongside of Matthew's text, which was given in full. Eusebius endorsed the scholarship of Ammonius, and his method of sectioning the Gospels is but an improvement over that of Ammonius. The canons of Eusebius were introduced by Jerome among the Latins, and it is clear that Augustine made the Vulgate of Jerome, furnished with the Eusebian canons and sections, the basis of his *de Consensu Evangelistarum*. Therefore when Augustine wrote that each Evangelist chose not to write in ignorance of what his predecessor had done, he was most likely simply rationalizing a recognition of literary dependence among the Evangelists that probably went back to scholars even earlier than Ammonius. His view that Mark epitomized Matthew is virtually an inevitable conclusion to which one is driven if he holds to the tradition that Mark was written second, and does justice to the clear evidence of literary dependence between Matthew and Mark. It is the tradition that Mark was written second that is yet to be explained.

[3] As quoted by Eusebius, *Hist. Eccl.* III. 39. 15. There is nothing in the words of Papias that throws any direct light on the question of the order in which the Gospels were written, nor is it certain that his words refer to the Gospel handed down in the canon of the church as written by Mark. Nonetheless, in the eighteenth century, the words of Papias were taken as referring to the canonical Mark, and thus were difficult to reconcile with the views expressed by Augustine.

was made to include the Gospel of John, except where in isolated instances there was some evidence of a close connection between John and one or more of the other three. This reflected a consciousness that Matthew, Mark, and Luke were more closely related to one another than they were to John. The most famous and influential of these new Gospel parallels was that of Griesbach, published 1774–1775.[4]

Each of these developments represents a break with tradition; the first broke with the tradition that the canonical Gospels were written before all others; and the second broke with the tradition of attempting to harmonize the chronology of John with that of Matthew, Mark, and Luke. Once these two breaks with tradition were made, the possibilities were virtually unlimited and literally hundreds of new hypotheses were advanced. Not all of these hypotheses are of equal importance, however, and no review of the history of the Synoptic Problem can take them all into account without leaving the reader in a state of confusion and the researcher in a state of frustration. For some hypotheses were never published, and others were out of print and difficult to get hold of even a hundred years ago. A history of the Synoptic Problem is a history of the basic ideas which have influenced men's thinking about this problem. These ideas are limited in number and can be presented in such a way as to provide the reader with a firm grasp of the essentials of the problem and its history. He who would attempt to go beyond this, and attempt to review all the work that has ever been done on this problem, faces an almost limitless task.

2. LESSING'S GERMINAL BREAKTHROUGH

There is no absolute beginning for any history, and if one were to attempt to search out all possible lines of connection between the German scholars with whom we shall begin and their predecessors, he would undoubtedly be led back to the English Deists of the first half and middle of the eighteenth century. But we shall begin with

---

[4] Johann Jakob Griesbach published his synopsis as a part of the first edition of his Greek N.T., *Libri N.T. historici*, Halle, 1774. In 1776 he republished this synopsis separately as *Synopsis Evangeliorum Matthaei Marci et Lucae una cum iis Joannis pericopis quae omnino cum caeterorum Evangelistarum narrationibus conferendae sunt,* Halle; 2nd ed., 1797; 3rd ed., 1809; 4th ed., 1822. The title varied from one edition to another; the exact wording of the title of the 3rd ed. is given here.

Lessing. For with Lessing began the first of the two important developments we have described above, and from him came the single most powerfully fructifying idea in the entire history of the Synoptic Problem, namely the idea of an "Ur-gospel."

Sometime after the death of Hermann Samuel Reimarus in 1767, his daughter Elise placed in the hands of Lessing her father's unpublished manuscript on the Gospels. In 1770, Lessing became librarian at Wolfenbüttel in Brunswick. There, during the years 1774–1778, he published passages from this manuscript of Reimarus under the title "Wolfenbüttel Fragments." These published materials, which dealt critically with the Gospels, evoked great public interest and occasioned severe opposition from orthodox theologians. Lessing did not publicly defend the views expressed in these "fragments," but rather sought to vindicate freedom of discussion of such issues as were raised by the "fragments."

Meanwhile, he was himself preparing a work dealing critically with the Gospels; a work which was not to be published until 1784, three years after his own death.[5] In this work, actually composed in 1778, Lessing pointed out that, in Acts 24:5, the early Christians were called Nazarenes. He conjectured that they would have produced a written Gospel based on oral tradition from the Apostles. This purely hypothetical Gospel he sought to identify with a Gospel now lost, but known to the church Fathers sometimes as the Gospel of the Hebrews, and sometimes as the Gospel of the Nazarenes. This hypothetical Gospel was written in Aramaic and originated soon after Jesus' death.

In the light of this hypothesis, the later testimony of Eusebius concerning the origin of Matthew (*Hist. Eccl.* III. 24. 6) was reinterpreted so as to justify the conclusion that Matthew produced a Greek version of this earlier Aramaic Gospel, so that our canonical Matthew is indeed the work of the Apostle, though only in this secondary sense. Similarly, Papias' testimony was interpreted so as to justify the view that numerous individuals translated this Aramaic Gospel into Greek just as Matthew had done, only from different viewpoints and with different purposes. Naturally this original

[5] Gotthold Ephraim Lessing, "Neue Hypothese über die Evangelisten als bloss menschliche Geschichtschreiber betrachtet," *Theologischer Nachlass*, Berlin, 1784, pp. 45–72. An English translation by Henry Chadwick is included in *Lessing's Theological Writings*, Stanford, 1957; "New Hypothesis Concerning the Evangelists Regarded as Merely Human Historians."

Gospel underwent modifications in the early church so that different translators could have made use of different versions of the original Aramaic Gospel, which, along with the respective differences in viewpoint and purpose of the Evangelists, would go far in accounting for the differences which we now perceive between Matthew, Mark, and Luke. John is accepted in traditional fashion as a "Gospel of the Spirit."

This hypothetical reconstruction contains the seeds for an infinite variety of growth. And the flowering of hypotheses that followed during the next one hundred years can, in large measure, be traced back to the seedbed of Lessing's new and highly original synthesis. Here is the idea of "oral tradition" beginning with the Apostles. Here is the implicit notion that where our Gospels agree we have a double or triple witness to the apostolic and eye-witness Gospel. Here is the idea that the original Gospel was modified during the eye-witness period, which justifies the notion that our canonical Evangelists could all have faithfully reproduced apostolic models. Here is bold interpretation of the Papias testimony. Here is the idea of an Aramaic original. Here, indeed, one is in touch with the paternal ancestor of a great and important family of hypotheses with which the nineteenth century was to be populated. Indeed, almost every subsequent development in the history of the Synoptic Problem is indebted in one way or another to the work of Lessing.

3. GRIESBACH'S CONTRIBUTIONS

Prior to the publication of Lessing's views in 1784, other developments had taken place, the importance of which it is essential to grasp. We have already mentioned the emergence of a new type of Gospel harmony, specifically the famous "Synopsis" of Griesbach. While Griesbach printed some passages of John, he included the entire texts of only Matthew, Mark, and Luke. Therefore, these three Gospels, which were featured in his "Synopsis," came to be known as the "Synoptic" Gospels.

In the beginning of this work, which in its successive editions was to become a handbook for subsequent scientific investigators, Griesbach confessed to "the heresy" of doubting the possibility of harmonizing even the closely related but conflicting chronologies of Matthew, Mark, and Luke. In other words, Griesbach's harmony, if a harmony at all, was a harmony to end harmonization. Henceforth, those who followed in his footsteps would no longer seek to reconcile the conflicting chronologies of the Gospels, but rather would seek to understand the relationships between the Gospels in terms of their direct literary dependence, or in terms of their indirect literary dependence through the mutual use of earlier hypothetical sources.

It is important to recognize the fact that all previous authors of Gospel harmonies had been wrestling with the problem created by chronological differences between Gospels believed to have been written by authoritative witnesses who would not deliberately have differed from one another without good cause. The frank and shocking admission of Griesbach that he confessed to the "heresy" of doubting that this problem could be solved paved the way for widespread theological interest in Lessing's solution. For with Lessing's hypothesis, scholars were provided with an explanation of the reasons why the canonical Evangelists, who frequently agreed verbatim, sometimes differed from one another. Because on this hypothesis each Evangelist could be thought of as following faithfully an apostolic model preserved in the particular modified form of the original Nazarene Gospel available to him.

To the extent to which this was recognized as no true solution to the problem, but one which only served to project the problem back into an earlier stage in the history of the primitive Church where the investigator had no way of knowing what actually transpired, scholars were inclined to hold to a solution which recognized some kind of direct literary dependence between our Gospels. But by then it was no longer possible simply to retreat to the traditional view of Augustine, for in 1782 Koppe had published his programmatic *Marcus non epitomator Matthaei*.[6]

Koppe's attempt to prove that Mark was no epitomizer of Matthew had important consequences. First, it drew attention to the fact that Mark sometimes deviates from Matthew both in order and in content in a way no epitomizer would, and that when he did so

---

[6] J. B. Koppe, professor at Göttingen, published this short Latin dissertation in that city. Quite independent of Lessing, but in the tradition of LeClerc and Michaelis, Koppe thought in terms of the Evangelists copying from more ancient sources such as those of which Luke writes in his preface. In this way he accounted for the verbatim agreement among the first three Gospels, and at the same time he asserted that none of the Evangelists copied from the work of another.

deviate from Matthew, he rather consistently agreed closely with Luke—almost always in order and frequently in content. Such a close relationship between Mark and Luke could be accounted for on the Augustinian hypothesis by allowing that Luke, having both Matthew and Mark before him, followed Mark's order and frequently Mark's content whenever Mark deviated from Matthew. But no reason could be given to account for Luke's preference for Mark in his deviation from Matthew, which did not at the same time lend credence to the view that Mark must have had good authority, well understood by Luke, for his deviations from Matthew, i.e., which did not tend to give weight to Papias' testimony connecting Mark's Gospel with the apostolic witness of Peter.

But once the Papias testimony is taken seriously, it raises the question as to whether our Mark was in any sense dependent on our Matthew. Two names are important in this regard, G. Ch. Storr and G. Herder, both of whom connected our Mark with the testimony of Peter and both of whom held our Mark to be the earliest of the extant Gospels.[7] Their views, published in 1786 and 1797 respectively, seem to have had relatively little importance at the time. Meanwhile, however, another development of great importance had taken place which in fact stimulated Storr in his efforts to establish Marcan priority. This was the view that Mark was a late compilation or conflation made from Matthew and Luke.

In 1783 Griesbach published his own solution to the Synoptic Problem.[8] Holding to Augustine's view that no one of the Evangelists

---

[7] Gottlob Christian Storr, *Über den Zweck der evangelischen Geschichte und der Briefe Johannis*, Tübingen, 1786, pp. 274 ff., 287 ff.
Johann Gottfried Herder, *Christliche Schriften*, Riga, 1797, Vol. III. pp. 303–416. Herder's Christian Writings are available in 19th cen. eds. of his collected works, such as *Sämtliche Werke, Zur Religion und Theologie*, Stuttgart and Tübingen, 1830. *See especially* "Regel der Zusammenstimmung unserer Evangelien aus ihrer Entstehung und Ordnung."

[8] Briefly stated in "Inquisitio in fontes, unde evangelistae suas de resurrectione domini narrationes hauserint," Jena, 1783 (Griesbachii *Opusc. Acad.*, ed. Gabler, Vol. II, pp. 241–256); developed in detail in "Commentatio qua Marci Evangelium totum e Matthaei et Lucae Commentariis Decerptum esse monstratur," Jena, 1789–1790, which in revised form appeared in *Commentationes Theologicae*, edited by J. C. Velthusen, C. Th. Kuinoel, and G. A. Ruperti, Vol. I, Leipzig, 1794, pp. 360 ff. (Reprinted in Gabler, *op. cit.*, pp. 358–425.) The idea that Luke copied Matthew, and that Mark used both Matthew and Luke, was first expounded by the Englishman Owen in his *Observations on the Four Gospels*, London, 1764. Büsching in his *Harmonie der Evangelien*, Hamburg, 1766, pp. 109–119, held that Mark made use of both Matthew and Luke, but he thought Luke was written first, and was used by Matthew. Others as

did his work in ignorance of that of his predecessor or predecessors, but taking into account the fact that Mark could not be understood simply as an "epitomizer" of Matthew, Griesbach proposed that Mark was written later than Luke and was dependent on both Matthew and Luke. The advantages of Griesbach's solution at that time were striking. It enabled the investigator to explain the phenomenon of agreement among Matthew, Mark, and Luke. The very extensive agreement between Matthew and Luke, then, was due to Luke's use of Matthew; and the peculiar agreements between Matthew and Mark in order and content combined with the peculiar divergencies from Matthew by Mark in both order and content was explained by holding that Mark almost never diverged from Matthew in order and seldom in content unless he was following the order and content of Luke.

The fact that Griesbach was a competent textual critic and well acquainted with the literary phenomenon of conflation of related texts no doubt prepared him to see the plausibility of this solution. Griesbach's solution was anathema to the Orthodox, however, for it seemed to them to remove any ground for Mark's having been written at all, since there are only between twenty and thirty verses of Mark's text which have no parallel in either Matthew or Luke. Nor was it welcomed by those conservative scholars who, wishing to accept the historico-critical approach to the Gospels, were, nevertheless, quick to see that Griesbach's hypothesis offered no solution to the problem of finding a satisfactory basis for the history of Jesus, since the order of events given in the two earliest Gospels still remained hopelessly irreconcilable. But for many critics Griesbach's hypothesis was by far the best so far advanced, since it explained the literary phenomenon of agreement between the Gospels without an appeal to hypothetical sources. And while it was hardly consonant with the testimony of Papias, it was the first hypothesis to do justice to Clement of Alexandria's tradition from the elders to the effect that Matthew and Luke were written before Mark and John.

The Griesbach hypothesis was adopted by the leading critical scholars of Germany. This was especially true at Berlin and

---

well seem to have favored the idea that Mark had used both Matthew and Luke, but it was Griesbach who first brought this idea into the main stream of Gospel criticism with sufficient power to gain for it a widespread acceptance as a solution to the Synoptic Problem.

Tübingen. The Berlin school, led by Schleiermacher, de Wette, and Bleek, was more conservative. De Wette and Bleek combined Griesbach's idea about Mark with the idea of an early Ur-gospel used by Matthew and Luke.[9] The Tübingen school, led by F. C. Baur, was more radical and tended to regard all the canonical Gospels as of questionable historical value.[10] It is important to note that the placing of Mark after Matthew and Luke had a wide appeal, and was by no means restricted to the Tübingen school. It dominated critical thinking about the Gospels during the first half of the nineteenth century.

B. The Göttingen-Cambridge Tradition

I. EICHHORN

Meanwhile, however, a new development, which was to have far-reaching consequences, was taking place at the University of Göttingen. The creative agent in this development was J. G. Eichhorn.

Earlier, in 1777, the great Göttingen professor, John David Michaelis, founder of the science of New Testament introduction, in the third edition of his famous work, revived an idea which had lain dormant for sixty years, ever since it was first published by LeClerc in 1716.[11] This idea was that our Evangelists had made use of earlier sources. However, at the same time, Michaelis continued

9 Wilhelm Martin Lebrecht de Wette, *Lehrbuch der historisch-kritischen Einleitung in die kanonischen Bücher des Neuen Testaments,* Berlin, 4th ed., 1842; 5th ed., improved and enlarged, 1848; Eng. tr. by F. Frothingham, Boston, 1858. See also *Kurzgefasstes exegetisches Handbuch zum Neuen Testament,* Vol. I, Parts 1 and 2, being detailed notes on the texts of "Matthew" and "Luke and Mark" respectively.

Friedrich Bleek, *Einleitung in das Neue Testament,* published posthumously in 1862; 2nd ed., revised by his son Johannes Friedrich Bleek, and Eng. tr. by William Urwick, Edinburgh, 1869; 3rd ed., 1875 and 4th ed., 1886, revised by W. Mangold. Bleek had held that Mark was secondary to both Matthew and Luke since 1822; *cf.* his *Beiträge zur Evangelienkritik,* 1846, pp. 72–75, and his *Synoptische Erklärung der drei ersten Evangelium,* published posthumously by Heinrich Holtzmann in 1862.

Die Quellen des Evangelium des Marcus, Berlin, 1825, by H. Saunier, also contains a noted defense of the idea that Mark used Matthew and Luke.

10 Ferdinand Christian Baur, *Kritische Untersuchungen über die kanonischen Evangelien, ihr Verhältniss zu einander, ihren Charakter und Ursprung,* Tübingen, 1847.

11 LeClerc, *Historia Ecclesiastica,* Amsterdam, I. 64. 11, p. 429. Johann David Michaelis, *Einleitung in die göttlichen Schriften des Neuen Bundes,* Göttingen, 3rd ed., Vol. II, par. 125; 4th ed., 1788, Vol. II, par. 129; Eng. tr. by Herbert Marsh, *Introduction to the New Testament,* 1801, Vol. III, Part I, chapt. 3.

to adhere to the Augustinian tradition that Mark knew Matthew, until in the year 1782, another Göttingen scholar dissuaded him from this view. This was accomplished by Koppe in his previously mentioned *Marcus non epitomator Matthaei*.[12]

By the early nineties Eichhorn was attracting students to his lectures on the problem. In 1793 the theological faculty at Göttingen made the Synoptic Problem a subject for competition. There were two prize winners.[13] Both had attended Eichhorn's lectures. Both endeavored to trace back the origin of the Gospels to earlier sources. One conjectured a plurality of such sources, as had LeClerc and Michaelis. The other conjectured a single primitive Gospel, as had Lessing.

A year later Eichhorn first published his views.[14] He argued for a plurality of sources behind our canonical Gospels, all going back to a single Aramaic Gospel. Eichhorn further postulated that the original Aramaic Gospel had been revised. Eichhorn designated one revised edition, A, and held it to be the basis of Matthew, and another revised edition, B, the basis of Luke; then a new edition of the original made out of A and B, designated C, the basis of Mark; and finally another revision, D, used by Matthew and Luke where they agree with one another but differ from Mark. In the original form of his hypothesis, Eichhorn imagined all these revised editions of the original Gospel to have been written in Aramaic.

One can see the synthetic quality of Eichhorn's hypothesis. Like Lessing, he began with a single primitive Aramaic Gospel. But like LeClerc and Michaelis, he held to a plurality of sources earlier than our canonical Gospels. These sources he conceived of in the form of revised editions of the earliest Gospel. Furthermore, Eichhorn seems to have tried to do justice to Griesbach's insight into the relationship of Mark to Matthew and Luke. Otherwise, how are we to understand his idea that Mark is based on a source which had been drawn from the two sources lying immediately behind Matthew and Luke respectively?

The completely new feature of Eichhorn's hypothesis was his idea

---

[12] 4th ed., 1788, Vol. II, par. 144; Eng. tr. Vol. III, Part I, pp. 216–220.

[13] Halfeld and Russwurm. These works cannot be shown to have exercised any influence on the history of the Synoptic Problem. Marsh, *op. cit.*, Vol. III, Part II, p. 191 gives the most detailed bibliographical data.

[14] Johann Gottfried Eichhorn, *Allgemeine Bibliothek der biblischen Literatur*, "Über die drey ersten Evangelien," Vol. V, 1794, pp. 759–996.

of an early revised edition of the original Gospel used only by Matthew and Luke but not by Mark, which enabled him to explain passages where Matthew and Luke agree with one another but differ from Mark. Twentieth century scholars may be bewildered by the complexity of Eichhorn's hypothesis, but in the nineteenth century it was well understood that any hypothesis which denied that the Evangelists had direct access to one another's work must of necessity be somewhat complex. Otherwise, it would not be possible to account for all the phenomena of agreement and disagreement among the Gospels.

The abiding contribution of Eichhorn, however, was not his particular synthesis, but a peculiarly attractive methodological idea he put forth. For he was the first to popularize the notion that it was possible to reconstruct from Matthew, Mark, and Luke the form and content of the original apostolic Gospel from which they are all ultimately derived, by confining oneself to those passages where all three agree. In spite of the fact that the reconstructed form of the original Gospel resulting from Eichhorn's procedure was not convincing, the apparent plausibility of this procedure led subsequent investigators to rely upon it with fateful consequences.

2. MARSH

Both Eichhorn's procedure and his basic hypothesis were taken over and refined by the English scholar Marsh of St. John's College, Cambridge. Marsh, who resided for a period in Germany, was well acquainted with German Gospel criticism. He translated the fourth edition of Michaelis' *Introduction to the New Testament* into English and published it in two parts.[15] His translation of the second part

---

15 *Op. cit.*, Marsh added many notes to his translation of Michaelis' Introduction, and in his dissertation on the Synoptic Problem he included criticism of Eichhorn principally at the point where Eichhorn posited mediating editions of the Ur-gospel which were not in Greek. Marsh's additional notes were translated into German by E. F. C. Rosenmüller. Eichhorn revised his hypothesis under the influence of Marsh's criticisms, and other German critics like de Wette worked closely with the text of Marsh's notes. This was a time when German and English biblical scholarship was closely interrelated. Michaelis himself attributed a decisive influence to his sojourn in England. Griesbach had worked in England as well as France. This healthy interchange between European scholars lasted up through the first quarter of the nineteenth century. Its high point in England was reached in the career of Connop Thirlwall, whose translation of Schleiermacher's essay on Luke, published in 1825 after his return from Germany, has been regarded as epoch-making in the history of English theology. Thirlwall included with his translation of Schleiermacher's essay an

which dealt with the Gospels was completed in 1795. But before publishing this he went on to compose a work of his own entitled "Dissertation on the Origin in Our Three First Canonical Gospels," which he completed in 1798, and included at the end of Volume III of his translation of the second half of Michaelis' *Introduction* (published sometime after 1801). This dissertation includes a systematic review of the situation in Synoptic studies at the end of the eighteenth century and deserves detailed consideration.

In the first chapter, Marsh analyzed the Synoptic Problem and indicated that the phenomena of agreement and disagreement required either a hypothesis that each succeeding canonical Evangelist made use of the preceding canonical Gospel or Gospels, or a hypothesis that all three drew from a common source.[16]

In the second chapter Marsh notes that the phenomena of agreement and disagreement require the admission that if we attempt to explain the problem on the hypothesis that one Evangelist has copied another, we must recognize that the second copied the first and the third copied *both* the first and second. This is because there are agreements between Matthew and Mark against Luke, between Matthew and Luke against Mark, and between Mark and Luke against Matthew. In other words, there are agreements between any two of the Evangelists against the third. And there is no way this could happen (excluding the mutual use of hypothetical sources) unless there was direct literary dependence among all three.[17]

Marsh then notes that this limits the investigator to six possible cases. Thereupon he lists the six cases and cites names of scholars who defend each case. But of these six, only one comes in for serious

---

account of what had transpired in Synoptic criticism since the time of Marsh. It represents an intimate acquaintance with Synoptic criticism in Germany for the period covered. Political and ecclesiastical reaction in Europe hindered the normal development of this scholarly interchange. By the third quarter of the century, when a conscious effort was made by English New Testament scholars under Sanday's leadership, to reestablish responsible academic mutuality with German scholars, the gap was too great for either side really to understand what the other was doing. (*See* Chapter III, pp. 52–60.)

[16] *Op. cit.*, Vol. III, Part II, p. 170. "Either the succeeding Evangelists copied from the preceding; or, all the three drew from a common source."

[17] Marsh's own words are as follows: "If we attempt to account for the verbal harmony of the Evangelists on the supposition that the one copied from the other, we must necessarily assume, not only that one of them copied from the other two, but that these two likewise copied the one from the other: for otherwise we shall not be able to explain the verbal harmony of all three." *Op. cit.*, p. 171.

consideration, namely, that which makes Matthew first, Luke second and dependent on Matthew, and Mark third and dependent on both Matthew and Luke. To this, the Griesbach hypothesis, he devoted the following chapter.

In Chapter Three, Marsh noted that Griesbach departed from the usual procedure and began with the text of the Gospels, rather than with historical arguments to determine which Gospel was written first, second, or third. He did not object to this procedure of Griesbach and admitted the plausibility of his hypothesis. However, Marsh noted certain objections—chief among them being the argument from omission. Of course, on any hypothesis, one must ask why a particular Evangelist would have omitted anything another Evangelist had included.

But the problem of omission is particularly noticeable when Mark is placed third. For, in that case, the phenomenon of omission is maximal. The Augustinian hypothesis had also involved Mark in omitting large parts of Matthew. But the Augustinian hypothesis enjoyed an important advantage which compensated for this difficulty. For alongside the notion that each Evangelist attempted to give as full and complete a report of matters concerning Jesus as he was able (which notion lies behind any attempt to take seriously the so-called "argument from omission"), was the idea that each succeeding Evangelist wrote in order to supplement the work of his predecessor. In fact, this idea may explain the common order in which our Gospels are arranged in the majority of our early codices— i.e., Matthew, Mark, Luke, John. For if one follows the unanimous tradition of the church that Matthew was written first, then he must place Mark second if the principle of the "supplementary" character of the Gospels is to be maintained. If Mark is placed either third or fourth, there really is no justification for its having been written, according to this "supplementary" view of Gospel origins.

Those who adhered to the Griesbach hypothesis in spite of such difficulties did so because it offered the best explanation of the phenomenon of agreement and disagreement among the Gospels. But Marsh hoped to be able to demonstrate another solution "equally as satisfactory." This solution involved the idea of an "Ur-gospel."

In Chapter Four, Marsh deals with the body of scholars who suppose that our Evangelists made use of a common document, or common documents, beginning with LeClerc and ending with Eichhorn.

In the next chapter, Marsh takes up Eichhorn's hypothesis in particular. He notes with approval that Eichhorn rejects the idea that the last Evangelist copied from the two preceding on the grounds that in this case we would have no explanation as to "why one or both of those two Evangelists have matters which the third has not . . . ," i.e., the argument from omission. But he finds Eichhorn's hypothesis inadequate in that the use by the Evangelists of Aramaic sources cannot account for the agreement in the Greek texts of Matthew, Mark, and Luke. Therefore, Marsh introduces Greek translations of the Ur-gospel where Eichhorn had posited various Aramaic versions.

Marsh himself begins with an Ur-gospel, which he thought of as a relatively short narrative, beginning with the baptism of Jesus and ending with his death. This conforms closely to a reconstruction of Matthew, Mark, and Luke, based on passages where all three agree. But in addition to this primitive narrative source which he designated א, Marsh hypothecated a second primitive sayings source which he designated ב. This second source contained both the sayings material common to Matthew and Luke and also the parables unique to each. These two sources were purely hypothetical, and Marsh did not connect either of them with the name of any particular Apostle.

Since, however, Marsh agreed with Eichhorn that one could reconstruct the form and content of א by confining oneself to those parts of Matthew, Mark, and Luke where all three agree, he was of course reconstructing his primitive narrative source more in accordance with the form and content of Mark than of Matthew and Luke.[18] The procedure, then, that was first introduced by Eichhorn and later refined by Marsh leads directly to the idea of the Ur-gospel being an Ur-Marcus. The important point to note here is that once one follows the methodological procedure of reconstructing an Ur-gospel from sections common to all three Gospels he is left with a great body of teaching material common to Matthew and Luke

[18] For if one confines himself to passages where all three Evangelists have the same material in reconstructing a source utilized by Matthew, Mark, and Luke, the reconstructed source will have no birth narratives, and relatively little sayings material and only a few parables. It will begin with the baptism of Jesus and differ from Mark less than from Matthew or Luke.

which would naturally suggest their use of a second source largely consisting of nonnarrative material useful for teaching purposes.

Before this idea of two primitive sources lying behind our Synoptic Gospels could gain wide acceptance, however, it was necessary for other developments to take place.

C. From Schleiermacher to Weisse

I. SCHLEIERMACHER'S *Logia*

In 1832 Schleiermacher published his famous examination of the Papias testimony which he understood as referring to two primitive sources.[19] According to Schleiermacher, Papias refers on the one hand, to a Gospel written by Mark (but not to be confused with our Mark), and on the other hand, to a collection of sayings drawn up by Matthew. It was this conception that the *Logia* of Matthew did not, as others held, constitute a Gospel, but was a collection of Jesus' sayings, which was Schleiermacher's revolutionary contribution.

The moment this conception of a primitive apostolic collection of Jesus' sayings burst on the scene of Synoptic criticism, it at once became theoretically possible to join this idea with that of the Ur-gospel as reconstructed by Eichhorn and Marsh and to identify this Ur-gospel as an Ur-Marcus or even as Papias' Mark, and then it was possible to explain the sayings material common to Matthew and Luke by reference to their dependence upon the Matthean sayings source. This is the ideological genesis of the two-document hypothesis. Schleiermacher, however, never thought in such terms. He regarded the Griesbach hypothesis as the best scientific solution to the Synoptic Problem. Our Mark, therefore, he regarded as a later Gospel with definite affinities to the apocryphal Gospels.[20] Furthermore, although our canonical Matthew drew from the *Logia* of Papias, our Luke did not. Where Luke has a text identical with that of Matthew, it is best explained by Luke's copying Matthew.

[19] Friedrich Ernst Daniel Schleiermacher, "Über die Zeugnisse des Papias von unsern beiden ersten Evangelien," *Theologische Studien und Kritiken,* 1832, pp. 735–768; *Sämtliche Werke,* I. 2, 1836, pp. 361 ff.

[20] *Einleitung ins Neue Testament* (the manuscripts of Schleiermacher's lecture notes as edited by G. Wolde, and published posthumously in 1845); *Sämtliche Werke,* I. 8, sec. 79.

2. LACHMANN

Three years later, in 1835, Lachmann followed Schleiermacher in his interpretation of Papias' *Logia*, and combined this idea with that of Lessing's Ur-gospel.[21] Matthew he regarded as a combination of the Ur-gospel and the *Logia* of Papias. Therefore, Lachmann took a step forward toward the two-document hypothesis. But he did not go all the way. For in his view, as in that of Schleiermacher, Luke did not draw from the *Logia* of Papias. Lachmann, however, did make an additional contribution in an argument he developed to prove that the Ur-gospel was best preserved in the canonical Mark.[22] This argument is based on the phenomenon of order.

On the Griesbach hypothesis, it had already been noted that Mark's order follows the order common to Matthew and Luke, and, when they deviate from one another, Mark almost always follows the order of one or the other. In other words, Mark seems to have no independent order of his own, but seems to follow closely either the order of Matthew or of Luke and when they agree, which they frequently do, Mark almost always follows their common order. In fact, one of the chief advantages of the Griesbach hypothesis is that it enables one to explain the phenomenon of order, which on any other hypothesis involving copying between all three Evangelists is more difficult to explain.

But considering the same phenomenon on the hypothesis of all three Evangelists copying an Ur-gospel, Lachmann was led to quite a different conclusion. Instead of Mark's being secondary to Matthew and Luke, Mark seems to have preserved best the presumed original order of the Ur-gospel. One would reason as follows in arriving at this conclusion: where all three Evangelists independently give their material the same order, one may be confident this was probably the order of the Ur-gospel. And where one departs from the order common to the other two, since they are not copying one another, we must presume that their agreement is due to their following the order of a common source. Since Mark almost never deviates from both Matthew and Luke, but almost always agrees with one or both the other Synoptics, it seems reasonable to conclude that the order

---

[21] Karl Lachmann, "De ordine narrationum in evangeliis synopticis," *Theologische Studien und Kritiken*, 1835, pp. 570 ff.
[22] *Op. cit.*, pp. 574–577.

of the Ur-gospel is best preserved in Mark. Since this is so, it seems further reasonable to think that the Ur-gospel is best represented by the Gospel of Mark.

3. CREDNER

One year later, in 1836, Credner made a similar proposal, only he went one step further.[23] Credner suggested that Papias' Mark was in fact the Ur-gospel copied by our Matthew, Mark, and Luke. Thus, for the first time, the witness of Papias was understood to testify to two primitive sources lying behind our Gospels; an Ur-Marcus and a collection of sayings. Two such hypothetical sources had already been conceived as early as Marsh. But now, for the first time, they were connected with the Apostles Peter and Matthew respectively, through the testimony of Papias.

4. WEISSE

It was not for another two years, however, that the final ideological step was taken. It entailed the idea that both Matthew and Luke were the result of combining the narrative of the Ur-gospel with the primitive sayings source. This step, also, had already been anticipated by Marsh. What Marsh had not done, however, as we have noted, was to connect either of these two hypothetical sources with the Mark of Papias or the *Logia* of Matthew. This final achievement was made by C. H. Weisse in 1838.[24] Although Weisse's new synthesis did not win approval at the time, we must deal with it in some detail because of its importance to Holtzmann's epoch-making synthesis of 1863.

D. Sieffert, Strauss, and F. C. Baur

The same year that Lachmann published his work, 1835, marked the first appearance of D. F. Strauss's *Life of Jesus*, and two works by F. C. Baur—one on Gnosticism, the other on the .Pastoral Epistles.[25] These works signaled the beginning of the Tübingen

---

23 C. A. Credner, *Einleitung in das Neue Testament*, Halle.
24 Christian Hermann Weisse, *Die evangelische Geschichte kritisch und philosophisch bearbeitet*, Leipzig, pp. 28 ff.
25 David Friedrich Strauss, *Das leben Jesu kritisch bearbeitet*, Tübingen. Ferdinand Christian Baur, *Die Christliche Gnosis, order diem, Die sogenannten Pastoralbriefe des Apostels Paulus aufs neue kritisch untersucht*, Tübingen.

school of New Testament criticism, which was to dominate German theology for the next thirty years. Both Strauss and Baur accepted the Griesbach hypothesis. But since the time that Griesbach had first propounded his hypothesis, a further development of great importance had taken place that was to affect seriously the understanding of Christian origins on the part of any historian or theologian who accepted the idea that Mark was dependent upon both Matthew and Luke. This concerned the date of Matthew. Luke, according to his own prologue, was not an eyewitness to the Gospel history. Matthew and John traditionally were so understood.

From the beginning of the nineteenth century onward, critical opinion on the historical value of John was divided. But it was possible to give up John as a historical source and still retain a high opinion of his work as a "spiritual gospel." Matthew, however, was another matter. Once the eye-witness character of the first Gospel was denied, serious consequences followed. Eichhorn had denied that Matthew was an eye-witness Gospel, and Schleiermacher had hinted as much in his work on Luke published in 1817.[26]

But it was in 1832 in Sieffert's work that the matter was settled in Germany once and for all on critical grounds.[27] Sieffert proved beyond reasonable doubt that Matthew was written after the eye-witness period. This did not disturb Schleiermacher, since, for him, John was theologically normative. Nor were those theologians who, like Eichhorn, held to the Ur-gospel hypothesis, perturbed by this development. Their hypothetical Ur-gospel was, after all, from the eye-witness period and they could reconstruct this apostolic source from Matthew, Mark, and Luke. In this way they had access to what they regarded as reliable historical testimony concerning the origins of Christianity.

Such testimony in the nineteenth century was a matter of the greatest dogmatic interest, for it concerned the problem of the historical foundations of the Christian faith. Public confidence in the reliability of the Gospels as historical sources for the understanding of these foundations had been profoundly shaken by the publication

---

[26] *Ueber die Schriften des Lucas, ein kritischer Versuch,* Berlin, 1817; Eng. tr. by Connop Thirlwall, *A Critical Essay on the Gospel of St. Luke,* London, 1825, containing an account of the controversy respecting the origin of the first Gospels since Bishop Marsh's dissertation.

[27] *Ueber den Ursprung des ersten kanonischen Evangeliums, eine kritische Abhandlung,* Königsberg.

of the "Wolfenbüttel Fragments." And Lessing's Ur-gospel may be viewed as an ingenious, constructive contribution to meet that doctrinal crisis. In 1820, Eichhorn had pointed out the advantage of his modification of the Ur-gospel hypothesis for the purposes of that "simplification of Christian doctrine for which German theology has been zealously laboring for fifty years."[28]

Once Matthew was acknowledged to have been written after the eye-witness period, the Ur-gospel hypothesis was well designed to serve the dogmatic interests of Christianity in a new way. For this reason, it is certain that at this point in the history of Protestant Christianity, the Ur-gospel hypothesis offered a distinct service to liberal theologians, which could not be equaled by that of Griesbach. For Griesbach had never broken with the tradition that Matthew was the first of the Gospels, and once it was dated after the eye-witness period, with Luke and Mark later still, the critic who adopted this solution (and questioned the historicity of John), seemed to have no reliable point of contact with the historical foundations of Christianity.

At Tübingen, Baur and Strauss posited some connection between the primitive gospel of the Hebrews and our Matthew. But they followed radically the implication of Sieffert's work and dated all the canonical Gospels quite late. Baur dated Matthew around 130, with the others still later. Strauss, in his famous *Leben Jesu*, faced brilliantly, but without ecclesiastical success, the problem of how one can understand the stories and legends in the Gospels if the Gospels were not written by eyewitnesses. This he does by recourse to the concept of myth.

E. De Wette and Bleek

De Wette and Bleek saw their work in conscious opposition to the Tübingen school. They, like the Tübingen scholars, continued to hold that Mark conflated Matthew and Luke. But Matthew and Luke were dependent upon an Ur-gospel which provided access to historically reliable tradition concerning Christian origins. Therefore, their work never occasioned the same doctrinal anxiety which that of the Tübingen school excited. It should be noted, however,

---

[28] *Einleitung in das Neue Testament*, Göttingen, 2nd ed., Vol. I, p. 445.

that their Ur-gospel was nothing like an Ur-Marcus, since they reconstructed it from the material common to Matthew and Luke, including, of course, all the sayings material that Weisse and his followers attributed to a second source identified with Papias' *Logia*. Essential to this view of de Wette and Bleek is Lessing's notion that Matthew and Luke were unknown to one another—an idea that was to be conclusively disproved in 1880 by Simons.[29]

Meanwhile, however, this idea of no direct literary dependence between Matthew and Luke was to help pave the way for the two-document hypothesis, which by 1880 had achieved such a hold on the minds of its proponents, that when Simons convinced them that Luke did use Matthew, they persisted in their belief that Matthew and Luke had nonetheless independently copied the *Logia* of Papias. Such a notion was critically vulnerable in that it acknowledged direct literary dependence between Luke and Matthew, yet failed to appeal to this direct literary dependence as the simplest and most natural explanation for the extensive agreement between the Gospels in the sayings material they contained in common.

Such a curious state of affairs is explained by the fact that, even as late as 1880, proponents of the two-document hypothesis still thought in terms of the Papias testimony as referring to two actual primitive sources; one narrative, the other a collection of sayings. For these critics the *Logia* was not a purely hypothetical source needed in order to account for phenomena for which there was otherwise no explanation, as tended to be the case for later critics like Streeter. For Holtzmann and his generation the *Logia* was a real collection of Jesus' sayings attested by the witness of Papias. For these men, since they did not doubt that there was such a primitive collection, it seemed natural that Luke would have preferred to copy from it wherever he could, even when he had the same material in Matthew. To have done so would seem to have been a reasonable procedure for Luke, from what he tells us in his prologue, providing, of course, that there ever was such an apostolic collection.[30]

The sublime confidence in the correctness of a particular interpretation of Papias' *Logia* first introduced by Schleiermacher, and later modified by Weisse, was a powerful factor in winning and sustaining

---

[29] Edward von Simons, *Hat der dritte Evangelist den kanonischen Matthäus benutzt?*, Bonn.

[30] Luke 1:3.

support for the two-document hypothesis during the nineteenth century. William Sanday, in "A Plea for the Logia," written at the end of the century, puts the point very nicely when in reference to Matthew and Luke's use of common sayings material he writes: "We have the definite statement of Papias that such a source did exist, and that it had for its author one of the twelve Apostles, so that it could not easily be neglected."[31]

It is very important to understand the contribution of de Wette and Bleek to the history of the Synoptic Problem. Holtzmann depended heavily upon their work.[32] We may say that their crucial importance for subsequent developments was their unique combination of Lessing's Ur-gospel hypothesis with that of Griesbach. This new creation did not endure, but it facilitated the new synthesis which was to be achieved by Holtzmann. It represents a transitional stage in the thinking of critics. Whereas, formerly, critics were divided as to whether the phenomenon of literary dependence called for direct access of one Evangelist to the work of another, or whether this phenomenon could be satisfied by the notion that they independently copied an earlier Gospel; now one and the same critic could combine both ideas in a single hypothesis.

This represents a new mood in literary criticism of the Gospels and sets the stage for the otherwise curious element of flexibility which is found among adherents of the two-document school. They can shift from the notion that Matthew and Luke copied Mark to the notion that this was not the case, but that all three copied an Ur-gospel—so Weisse. Or they can affirm that Luke did not use Matthew and later decide that he did—so Holtzmann. Or they can say that it is clear that Mark made extensive use of "Q" and later change their minds considerably on the point—so Streeter.[33]

And all this shifting around is done with an ease of critical conscience that can mean but one thing. The critic has lost his bearings with reference to the Gospels themselves and the totality of the phenomenon of agreement and disagreement. The Synoptic Problem has now become a great jigsaw puzzle, and the critic is busy trying to fit all the pieces together. Eventually the critic will

---

[31] *Expository Times*, Vol. IX, 1901, pp. 471–473.

[32] Holtzmann was still in his twenties when he was commissioned to prepare the posthumous edition of Bleek's *Synoptische Erklärung der drei ersten Evangelien* for publication.

[33] *See* Chapter III, p. 94.

actually begin to refer to the "Synoptic-tradition," meaning the total mass of the Gospel materials making up Matthew, Mark, and Luke. Thus, the integrity of the Gospels as literary wholes is dissolved, and the distinctive intentions of the Evangelists tend to become obscured.

None of this is true with de Wette or Bleek. That is why their work merits careful consideration by contemporary critics concerned with recovering the purpose and characteristic points of view of the individual Evangelists. But their easy affirmation that Matthew and Luke were unknown to one another (Lessing), and their notion that one could reconstruct an Ur-gospel from material Matthew and Luke held in common (Eichhorn), combined with their literary analysis of Mark as a conflation of Matthew and Luke (Griesbach), set off their work as the beginning of a new trend in Synoptic criticism which can only be described as eclectic. In accordance with this eclecticism, incommensurate elements of originally divergent wholes are combined. Of course, there were traces of this even in Eichhorn's synthesis.

F. Weisse

Compared to original thinkers like Lessing, Herder, and Schleiermacher, such men as Eichhorn, de Wette, and Bleek are of lesser stature. The same can be said for Weisse. For though he was a philosopher, he could in no sense have been compared with his great contemporary, Schleiermacher. Nor had he the critical powers of Baur or Strauss, whose work was characterized by him as "negative-criticism," and set in contrast to that of his own, which he endorsed as "essentially positive."

It is clear from the opening paragraphs of his book that Weisse wants to take account of Strauss's *Leben Jesu*, and at the same time, the work of critics like Sieffert who had shown the secondary character of Matthew. His solution is, therefore, to be viewed as a constructive attempt to enable Christianity to lay claim to eyewitness accounts through Mark and the *Logia*. Weisse notes that on the Griesbach hypothesis, which he recognizes as the prevailing hypothesis, almost all tradition in Matthew and Mark is traced back to a single noneyewitness source—namely, Matthew.[34]

[34] *Op. cit.*, pp. 4 ff.

By comparison, the advantages of his hypothesis are obvious. Instead of the Gospel Matthew, which is secondary to the eye-witness period, being the earliest and most reliable record of Christian beginnings, this Gospel is dependent on two primitive and apostolic sources: Mark and the *Logia*, both of which belong to the eye-witness period. Luke is likewise dependent upon the same two eye-witness documents. This is the famous two-document hypothesis.

It is clear that Weisse consciously drew upon Schleiermacher's idea of the *Logia* as developed by Lachmann. But he himself said that it was "the originality and priority of Mark" more than anything else that was the main point in the development of his hypothesis.[35] He noted that Herder and Storr held a similar view at an earlier period. But he himself seems to have been influenced more by the work of Lachmann, whose argument from order he cited favorably. Against Schleiermacher, Weisse argued that the canonical Mark is identical with Papias' Mark, and had been copied by Matthew and Luke. He appears to have been the first to slip unconsciously into the fallacy of thinking that Lachmann's argument from order had any validity on these terms. Actually Lachmann's argument gains plausibility only when Matthew, Mark, and Luke independently copy an Ur-gospel.

In a subsequent form of his two-document hypothesis, Weisse abandoned the idea that Matthew and Luke copied Mark, and he modified his hypothesis to claim that Matthew, Mark, and Luke were dependent on an Ur-Marcus.[36] In this form Weisse's hypothesis could claim limited support from Lachmann's argument from order. It was the two-document hypothesis thus modified, that is, with Matthew, Mark, and Luke copying an Ur-Marcus, and with Matthew

[35] *Op. cit.*, pp. 29–45. By conceding that the first two chapters of Matthew and Luke are drawn from legends or myths, Weisse handed Strauss an empty victory—because, in his view, these materials were added later by Matthew and Luke, and could not be expected to have any historical value. Thus, the Marcan hypothesis had a certain tactical advantage vis-à-vis the Gospel criticism of Strauss. One could afford to give up certain indefensible ground, in order to make a stronger stand behind a shorter line. Weisse's entire second book (Vol. I, pp. 139–232), is taken up with a discussion of the birth narratives in such a way that no one could say that he had ignored Strauss. The materials are classed as sagas. But Weisse has merely sidestepped the issue, for the legendary and mythical materials in the Gospels are by no means confined to these chapters. In his third book, Weisse takes up history, and in the fourth, stories and sayings in Mark.

[36] i.e. in a later edition of his *Die evangelische Geschichte*.

and Luke copying the *Logia*, that was actually taken over by Holtz-mann in 1863.

Meanwhile, however, Weisse's simple solution to the Synoptic Problem was not taken very seriously in either form. In 1856, eighteen years after he first introduced his idea, Weisse complained that not a single scholar was following him in going the way opened up by the research of Schleiermacher and Lachmann.[37] Apparently Holtzmann, in including Weisse's contribution in his famous synthesis seven years later, was in a sense rescuing Weisse's hypothesis from a fate which its inventor regarded as an undeserved oblivion.

It is evident that the popularity of the two-document hypothesis developed only after it had been worked into the larger synthesis of Holtzmann's work. Another point is also clear: in the view of Holtzmann, it was Weisse who for the first time "scientifically established the Marcan hypothesis."[38] This is a very significant value judgment on the part of Holtzmann and deserves analysis. If true, it would indicate that the priority of Mark, from the time it was regarded as scientifically established by Holtzmann, was intimately bound up with the two-document hypothesis. This is a very important point.

One clear reason why the priority of Mark could not have been established without reference to the *Logia* would be the difficulty of imagining Matthew and Luke being derived from either Mark or an Ur-gospel like Mark, unless there was, at the same time, some way of accounting for the great body of sayings material they held in common, which were not in Mark. This is the ideological function of Papias' *Logia* in the history of the Synoptic Problem.

In those parts of their Gospels where Matthew and Luke have identical material not found in Mark, they were probably copying the *Logia*. Where their material was not sayings material, as for example in the case of the story of the healing of the Centurion's servant, found only in Matthew and Luke, Holtzmann simply attributed that to the Ur-Marcus. So the Marcan hypothesis was first regarded as "scientifically established" only in connection with

---

[37] *Die Evangelienfrage in ihrem gegenwärtigen Stadium*, p. 85.
[38] Heinrich Julius Holtzmann, *Die Synoptischen Evangelien. Ihr Ursprung und ihr geschichtlicher Charakter*, Leipzig, 1863, p. 29.

an Ur-gospel, on the one hand, and Papias' *Logia*, on the other. Without these two ideological presuppositions, pure products of the creative imagination of Lessing and Schleiermacher, the Marcan hypothesis, in the nineteenth century, would have had to bear a very heavy burden of proof, indeed, and would probably never have been accepted by New Testament scholars acquainted with the realities of the Synoptic Problem.

G. Ewald

Before taking up Holtzmann's synthesis in detail, it is necessary to deal with two more developments. The first has to do with the work of the energetic Göttingen Semitist and theologian, Heinrich Ewald.[39] Ewald, like de Wette and Bleek, exhibited the eclectic spirit of the time, and his synthesis decisively paved the way for that of Holtzmann. His nine-document hypothesis was dismissed by his contemporaries as hopelessly complicated. But it remains one of the most ingenious of the nineteenth century. Ewald began with an Ur-gospel. In his student days he had been a faithful interpreter and enthusiastic defender of his teacher Eichhorn, and it is clear that he was carrying on the Göttingen tradition in his attempt to reconstruct this Ur-gospel from passages found in Matthew, Mark, and Luke. Following Schleiermacher, Lachmann, and Weisse, Ewald thought in terms of Papias' *Logia* as a second early source made up of sayings of Jesus. After the Ur-gospel and *Logia* comes Mark—the earliest of the canonical Gospels.

At this point Ewald depends heavily on the work of Herder. Herder had argued that Mark was the earliest of our written Gospels because of its simplicity, its artlessness, and its freshness.[40] The logic of the argument is that the simplest Gospel comes before the more complex. It is the idea of development from the simple to the more complex, applied to the dating of our Gospels. For Matthew and Luke seem more developed and complex Gospels than Mark.

This idea of Herder's had largely been ignored for over half a century until Ewald popularized it. Through him it was passed on to

---

[39] *Jahrbücher der biblischen Wissenschaft*, Göttingen, 1848–1849.
[40] *Op. cit.*

Holtzmann and later to Ewald's student Wellhausen. Through Holtzmann and Wellhausen, this idea was to have a profound influence on the subsequent history of the Synoptic Problem. Meanwhile, of course, critics like Schleiermacher and Strauss read the same phenomena as due to an effort on the part of the Evangelist Mark to achieve "vividness" and "verisimilitude."[41] In Ewald's view, Mark is dependent on the first two sources, though primarily, of course, upon the Ur-gospel rather than the *Logia*. After Mark, in Ewald's hypothesis, comes his unique "book of higher history," through which he is able to explain some agreements between Matthew and Luke against Mark.[42] Then comes Matthew, which is mainly drawn from Mark and the *Logia*, but the author also had access to the Ur-gospel as well as to the "book of higher history." Next come three later works, and, finally, ninth in the series, comes Luke, who made use of every one of the eight earlier sources except Matthew!

The merit of Ewald's complex hypothesis is that it enabled him to explain all the phenomena of agreement and disagreement between Matthew, Mark, and Luke. But the notion that Luke had access to seven earlier sources, but not to Matthew, only shows to what extreme lengths investigators would go at that time in order to explain data which, in the traditional view, had been explained simply by presuming that Luke was dependent on Matthew. The reader must understand, however, that this traditional view had been radically affected by Sieffert's proof that Matthew was not an eye-witness Gospel. After 1832 in Synoptic criticism, the noneyewitness character of Matthew meant that if one were to get back behind Matthew into the eye-witness period, he needed to use the verbal agreement between Matthew and Luke as a sign that both were dependent on an earlier source or sources. If one were to take the position that this verbal agreement could be as well or better explained by holding that Luke copied Matthew, as did scholars of the Tübingen school, one thereby, in the nineteenth century, after 1832, methodologically shut himself off from any systematic procedure whereby he might distinguish between possible early

---

[41] Schleiermacher, *Einleitung*; Strauss, *Leben Jesu.*

[42] What Eichhorn had been able to explain through his single revised edition of the Ur-gospel, "D," Ewald now explains through the *Logia* and his "book of higher history."

tradition from the eye-witness period and composition of the later church.

Not until the twentieth century did the discipline of form-criticism provide a solution to this problem. And by that time Holtzmann's simplified version of Ewald's hypothesis had gained such a firm hold on the collective mind of New Testament scholars that form-critics like Dibelius and Bultmann and all their students continued to work within the limits of Holtzmann's synthesis, without raising any questions about the adequacy of the two-document hypothesis. In other words, they continued to work within the presuppositions of a hypothesis which came into being to solve a problem that form-criticism can solve as well or better on the traditional view that Luke copied Matthew.

But the influence of Ewald's hypothesis will not be fully appreciated until an examination is made of the importance of the man himself and his part in the history of nineteenth century German theology.

In Ewald's student days, eager and devoted young theologians were challenged to become Semitists because the church needed defenders of the faith to combat the reckless and damaging speculation of those scholars who had found striking parallels to the Old Testament materials in the Babylonian and Assyrian texts.[43] Ewald was the perfect type for such a vocation. Years later as a professor at Göttingen his fighting qualities were demonstrated in a secular matter in a most dramatic way. In 1734, King George II founded the famous Georgia Augusta University in Göttingen. From the beginning it enjoyed great fame as a center of learning and academic freedom. After Ewald became a professor at Göttingen, in a period of political reform King William gave his sanction to a constitutional statute for Hannover to which Ewald and his colleagues at Göttingen swore allegiance. But in 1837 King Ernest Augustus, upon ascending the throne, refused to recognize it as binding. Whereupon Ewald and six other professors at the University took the position that their oath to the constitution was nonetheless still

---

[43] The life of the Oxford Semitist, Edward Bouverie Pusey, who studied with Ewald's teacher, Eichhorn, and who became a friend of Ewald's, is a case in point. He spent long and painful hours mastering Arabic, not because he loved the language, but because it was an important weapon against the rationalists who were attacking the Christian faith through Old Testament criticism. *Cf. Life of Edward Bouverie Pusey*, by H. P. Liddon, London, 1893, Vol. I, chap. 5.

binding upon them. This was tantamount to saying that the King had exceeded his rights. These famous "Göttingen Seven" thereupon became *personae non gratae* in Hannover. Ewald responded to a call from Tübingen, where he soon got involved in a feud with F. C. Baur. A few years later, however, in 1848, Ewald was permitted to return to Göttingen.

The circumstances under which he returned seem to have been quite favorable to him, for he immediately began publishing his own scientific journal. This was the famous *Jahrbücher der biblischen Wissenschaft*, and in the first year of its publication Ewald launched his infamously bitter attack on the Tübingen school.[44]

Because of the consequences of this attack upon the history of Synoptic criticism it will be necessary to give the reader some impression of the nature and purpose of Ewald's onslaught. In the first part of an article entitled "Ursprung und Wesen der Evangelien" in the first volume of his *Jahrbuch*, he damns the Tübingen school, charging that Baur and his associates do not take the trouble to understand Christ and the Bible, "still less to take Him to their hearts."[45] Whatever Ewald's intentions, the effect of such charges from so eminent a man was to aggravate mistrust toward the Tübingen school in ecclesiastical and university circles which were under the influence of pietism. Baur's book on the four Gospels published in 1847 is criticized by Ewald. He associates the work of Strauss and Schwegler with that of Baur and laments the effect of their work. There is also a conservative note of nationalism in Ewald's biting criticism. Revolutionary movements for German union and liberty had broken out in 1848, and patriotic feeling at this time was at a high pitch. Ewald speaks of *deutsche Wissenschaft* and the shame it suffers. He points to the danger that German scholarship might become ridiculous in the eyes of the rest of the world. Ewald feels that in contrast to the reigning Tübingen view of the Gospels, it is high time that a correct understanding should be established. He has an interesting argument about the reliability of the Gospel witness based on his knowledge of Mohammed's life. And he concludes this astonishing piece of writing with the observation that Mark is the earliest Gospel because it is free from features which are present in Luke and Matthew and which are late according

44 *Op. cit.*
45 *Op. cit.*, 1848, pp. 113–154.

to his view. There is no reference to Griesbach or Weisse or any other writer—only to Baur whose work seems constantly to be in Ewald's mind.

Later in the same volume in a review of a book by one of Baur's associates, Friedrich Schultheiss, he calls for an end to the "unscientific" results of the "Strauss-Baur school." The inappropriateness of such use by an editor of a scientific journal to press his private attack on other scholars is heightened by Ewald's reference to personal experiences he had while at Tübingen. The yearbook for 1849 contains an evaluation of the Tübingen school with detailed objections to it.[46] This evaluation includes a very vicious personal attack on Baur. Ewald calls him a liar, charges him with immorality, and notes that he has a bad effect on the church. Even the political troubles of Württemberg, according to Ewald, can be traced to the malevolent influence of Baur and his associates.

The yearbook for the same year also includes the second part of his "Ursprung und Wesen der Evangelien" in which he sets forth his nine-document hypothesis.

It is not possible to assess the full effect of Ewald's attack on the Tübingen school. Later writers like Wellhausen give Ewald credit for the defeat of the Tübingen school.[47] Wellhausen calls especial attention to a famous article by Albrecht Ritschl, then a member of the Tübingen school. This article, published in 1851, is referred to by Holtzmann in 1863 as "epoch-making."[48] In it Ritschl goes over to the priority of Mark. Wellhausen refers to Ritschl's article as evidence that Ritschl was "converted" to the Marcan hypothesis by Ewald. Actually, Ritschl is very critical of Ewald in the article. Nonetheless he does agree with Ewald at the crucial point of the priority of Mark to the other Gospels.

There were similar defections in other directions. The brilliant, young contemporary of Ritschl, Hilgenfeld, adopted the order Matthew, Mark, and Luke, but bitterly opposed to the end of his life the notion that Mark could have been written before Matthew.[49]

---

[46] pp. 16–25.

[47] Julius Wellhausen, *Heinrich Ewald, Beiträge zur Gelehrten-geschichte Göttingens,* Berlin, 1901, p. 66.

[48] Albrecht Benjamin Ritschl, "Über den gegenwärtigen Stand der Kritik der synoptischen Evangelien," *Theologische Jahrbücher,* Tübingen, pp. 480–538. Holtzmann, *op. cit.,* p. 39.

[49] Adolf, Hilgenfeld, *Das Marcusevangelium,* Leipzig, 1850.

The established leaders of the Tübingen school, however, stood firm. Both Baur and Strauss were unconvinced by evidence and arguments brought forth both inside and outside the school against the Griesbach hypothesis, and they held to that hypothesis as the best critical solution through the entire controversy.[50] The same was true of certain scholars who were critical of the Tübingen school, such as Bleek.[51] They too were unconvinced by the arguments for Marcan priority and continued to think of Mark as the latest of the three Synoptics.

H. Herder's Oral Gospel

There remains but one more important idea in the pre-Holtzmann period necessary for an understanding of Holtzmann's synthesis and post-Holtzmannian developments. This was Herder's idea of a primitive oral Gospel.[52] In one sense it is only a development of Lessing's hypothesis. For Lessing had conjectured that the Ur-gospel had been formed out of the oral narratives of the Apostles and other eyewitnesses. Herder asked whether this oral tradition might have reached a fixed form before it was written down. Why he was impelled to ask this question will be brought out shortly.

Herder began with the "ministers of the word" in Luke 1:2 and conjectured that they would have found useful a compendium of material for their guidance in preaching. Then on the basis of the words credited to Peter in Acts 1:22 Herder imagined that this compendium of preaching material began with the baptism of John and ended with the ascension of Jesus. Mark with its longer ending begins and ends exactly in this way. Had Herder been defending rather than attacking the Griesbach hypothesis he would have noticed that this striking similarity between Mark and Acts 1:22 is quite well explained by the view that the Evangelist, Mark, faced

---

[50] Baur answered Hilgenfeld in his *Das Marcusevangelium*, Tübingen, 1851, and the two carried on the debate for years in the *Theologische Jahrbücher*. This debate is a worthy subject for thorough analysis and evaluation. That Strauss's adherence to the Griesbach hypothesis continued to be based on what he thought were sound historico-critical grounds can be seen from his *Das Leben Jesu für das deutsche Volk bearbeitet* 1864; Eng. tr. *A New Life of Jesus*, London, 1865.

[51] Bleek, *op. cit.*, *Cf.* writings of F. Delitzsch, Kahnis, and K. F. Nosgen.

[52] *Op. cit.*

with the problem of where to begin and end his Gospel since his prototypes did not agree, did something quite understandable. He followed apostolic precedent in conforming his Gospel to the temporal limits set for Jesus' ministry in Peter's speech in Acts 1. In fact this could also help explain the origin of the early tradition connecting the Gospel According to Mark (which in the beginning had no such ascription) with the Apostle Peter. Once this Gospel was thus associated with Peter it would have been natural on the basis of I Peter 5:13 to have named the author as Mark.

As it was, Herder was combating the Griesbach hypothesis. According to this hypothesis Mark was based on Matthew and Luke and had little in it that was not derived from these two sources. Therefore, its value to the church seemed negligible and its reason for being unintelligible. It was this particular feature of his hypothesis that was most disturbing to Griesbach's contemporaries. For this reason most of his critics attempted to find some more satisfactory place for Mark in their reconstruction without returning to Augustine's idea that Mark was an epitomizer of Matthew, which idea had already been shown to be unlikely by Koppe. Herder's work must be seen in this context of the history of Gospel criticism. Therefore, the fact that Mark began and ended in conformity with the words of Peter in Acts 1:22 would only have confirmed the thought that this Gospel was indeed close to the earliest preaching of the primitive church.

For this purpose and in this form, therefore, the earliest oral tradition was structured into an Aramaic oral Gospel in Palestine sometime between A.D. 35 and 40. The "ministers of the word" communicated this Gospel orally to those whom they engaged to assist them in preaching. These helpers in turn committed this oral Gospel to writing for their own convenience. One of these helpers was the Mark mentioned in Acts. He later took his copy of the Gospel with him to Rome, where he published it in Greek. At about the same time a somewhat expanded form of the original oral Gospel was written out in Aramaic in Palestine and published immediately. In a modified form this work survived in the Gospel of the Nazarenes, and in Matthew. Luke also used it, as well as his own outline of the original oral Gospel which, like Mark, he had made for his own convenience as an aid to preaching. In addition Luke had access to information which he gathered from people who had heard and seen

Jesus. This last idea is, in germinal form, the idea of oral tradition as a means of accounting for the transmission of information about Jesus from the earliest eye-witness period down to the latest period of Gospel composition. It should be noted, however, that there is no interval of time separating the Gospel writers from the living witnesses of those who had heard and seen Jesus. This means that Jesus' deeds and teachings were, at a later period, handed directly to the Evangelists. Oral tradition, as far as it affected the composition of the Gospels, was for Herder confined strictly within the time limits of Evangelists who had had direct contact with eyewitnesses. An important part of this early oral tradition had been codified in the form of a fixed oral Gospel. But in addition there was always the information which could have reached the Evangelist through direct oral communication with eyewitnesses.

The reader should now be prepared to see in retrospect the vast differences as well as the essential kinship between this reconstruction of Gospel origins made by Herder and that made by Lessing. Both agree in beginning with the earliest testimony, that found in the New Testament writings themselves, rather than with early tradition from the church Fathers. Lessing begins with the Acts reference to the Christians as Nazarenes and identifies the Gospel of the Nazarenes as the original apostolic parent of all our canonical Gospels. On this reconstruction Matthew continues to hold the place of primacy among the surviving Gospels, because of its obvious kinship with Jewish Christian and Palestinian origins. Lessing held that the Apostle Matthew was responsible for rendering the Aramaic Gospel of the Nazarenes into Greek. Luke, it seemed to him, made a different selection and arrangement than did Matthew; while Mark appeared to have had a less perfect copy of the original Gospel. This reconstruction does not violently disturb traditional belief in the order and reliability of the Gospels. But it has one severe disadvantage which defenders of the idea of an oral Gospel emphasized.

This was the difficulty created by the disappearance of the original apostolic Gospel. How could such a written Gospel, made by the Apostles themselves, ever have been allowed to disappear?[53] On the

---

[53] The poignancy of this question is felt keenly in the plea of Arthur Wright, of Queen's College, Cambridge, for his readers not to accept uncritically the two-document hypothesis. ". . . it is impossible that these pristine documents should have so completely perished, that there is no mention of them in the church Fathers." *A Synopsis of the Gospels in Greek*, London, 3rd ed., 1906, p. x.

other hand, if the earliest Gospel was not written out in documentary form but was only fixed in oral form, it is understandable that such an original Gospel might have disappeared gradually through disuse once the written forms of the Gospel came more and more to the fore and especially after the Church moved out of its original Jewish environment into the wider Gentile world where it was necessary to communicate in Greek, in which language there probably never was an oral Gospel. For this reason Herder was constrained to ask whether the oral tradition behind Lessing's Ur-gospel might not have reached a fixed form before it was written down.

But once one begins to search for the probable form of this earliest oral Gospel, he is led to the testimony of Acts and encouraged to think that it began with the baptism of John and ended with the ascension of Jesus, according to Acts 1:22. This certainly does not conform to the shape of Matthew or of Luke, though it diverges only a little from the shape of John. How then can one account for Matthew and Luke? It is necessary to think of these Gospels as being related to the original oral Gospel which began with the baptism of John and ended with the ascension of Jesus, only through a secondary expanded version of the oral Gospel. Mark, in contrast, conforms closely in shape to that of the oral Gospel, and one can imagine it to be indeed a reliable representation thereof. Here then is the ideological genesis of the notion of Marcan priority. Here is the way in which one could in the archaic, i.e., creative, stage of Synoptic criticism reason about the origin of Matthew, Mark, and Luke. Lessing and Herder provide the ideological essentials of all later developments.

It is important to grasp firmly the crucial difference between the status of Mark in the views of Lessing and Herder. On Lessing's hypothesis Mark seems based on a less perfect copy of the original Gospel, whereas Matthew and Luke are closer to the original itself. But the reverse is true in Herder's reconstruction. There Mark is the Gospel directly representing the original oral Gospel, whereas Matthew and Luke are based on a later expanded secondary written form of that oral Gospel. In Herder's hypothesis, therefore, Mark has an implicit priority which that Gospel had never enjoyed before in the known history of the church.

Furthermore, Herder's hypothesis was more complex than that of

Lessing. Instead of regarding a Gospel now lost but once definitely known in the early Church as the immediate parent of the canonical Gospels, as Lessing had done by identifying the Ur-gospel with the Gospel of the Nazarenes, Herder made the Gospel of the Nazarenes, along with Matthew and Luke, dependent upon a purely hypothetical Aramaic Ur-gospel which in turn was a later and expanded version of the original oral Gospel. Little wonder then that Herder's idea never had as much influence upon subsequent investigators as did that of Lessing—that is, until after it was convincingly shown in 1832 that Matthew was not written during the eyewitness period. Once the full implications of that fact sank into the minds of critics, then the possibility of Marcan priority, and the more complicated reconstructions, like that of Herder, began to seem somewhat more plausible to men like Ewald, whose nine-document hypothesis must be viewed as a development of Herder's.

In retrospect it is clear that Ewald's hypothesis was an eclectic combination of the ideas of Herder with those of Lessing as developed by his teacher Eichhorn, all modified to take into account the contribution of Schleiermacher's idea about Papias' *Logia*, as this idea had in turn been developed and modified by Lachmann and Weisse. Holtzmann's hypothesis, in turn, is basically an oversimplified version of that of Ewald, in which all hypothetical documents but two are either eliminated or regarded as problematical.

This completes the survey of the pre-Holtzmann period of Synoptic criticism. Many works which might have been mentioned have been passed over in silence, such as those of Wilke and Gieseler, etc.[54] Their work deserves the attention of the specialist interested in the results of earlier research. But such works have been ignored because they do not seem to embody demonstrably significant contributions to the ideological history of the Synoptic Problem.

Scholars like Wilke and Gieseler were working with the ideas of

---

[54] Christian Gottlob Wilke, *Der Urevangelist oder exegetisch-kritische Untersuchung über das Verwandtschaftverhältniss der drei ersten Evangelien*, Dresden and Leipzig, 1838. Wilke thought that Matthew and Luke copied Mark, and that Matthew also copied Luke. Wilke's main contribution was in refuting the oral hypothesis of Gieseler.

Johann Carl Ludwig Gieseler, *Historisch-kritischer Versuch über die Entstehung und die frühesten Schicksale der schriftlichen Evangelien*, Leipzig, 1818. Gieseler took Herder's ideas concerning an oral Gospel and worked them out more thoroughly in opposition to Eichhorn's idea of a written Ur-gospel.

earlier or contemporary investigators: either by way of refinement or refutation. An understanding of their contribution would deepen but not essentially alter the insights gained from a knowledge of the contribution made by those scholars whose ideas have come into view in this survey.

CHAPTER II

The Holtzmannian Synthesis

Holtzmann's synthesis was essentially programmatic. There was in his day, as he himself says, practically no consensus.[1] At the beginning of the century Eichhorn had praised the Ur-gospel hypothesis because in the reconstructed form of this apostolic source German theologians could find the more simplified basis for theology for which they had been seeking. Nevertheless the majority of critics continued to prefer the Griesbach hypothesis simply because it offered a solution to the Synoptic Problem without introducing any hypothetical source or sources. However, in the hands of the Tübingen scholars this hypothesis had come to be

[1] *Op. cit.*, pp. 63–67. The only consensus he could find was the notion that all the Synoptic Gospels go back to a common *Grundschrift*. "Das einzige positive Resultat [of all Synoptic research], das sich uns bisher ergeben hat, ist Dies, dass die Verwandtschaftsverhältnisse der Synoptiker auf eine gemeinsame Grundschrift zurückweisen" (p. 66).

identified with a kind of radical criticism that seemed to threaten the citadel of Faith. Weisse's alternative, in the form of the two-document hypothesis, was not followed by a single investigator, as he himself later complained. Ewald recognized the acute need for scholarly agreement on this fundamental problem for Christian theology, and his hypothesis represents a step in the direction of a new synthesis. However, even for critics like Ritschl, who, under the influence of Ewald, were "converted" to the priority of Mark, Ewald's nine-document hypothesis was hopelessly complex.[2] Let us review the major alternatives in Holtzmann's day. There was on the one hand the Griesbach hypothesis as expounded by the Tübingen scholars. Holtzmann was against this hypothesis and he was able to cite the objections brought against it by younger members of the Tübingen school like Hilgenfeld and Ritschl. His most weighty point, however, was the scientifically gratuitous but powerfully apologetic fact that it was conceded by all contemporary critics that Matthew was secondary to the eye-witness period.[3] This meant that the Griesbach hypothesis, as well as the Augustinian and all others which made Matthew the earliest of the Gospels, simply could not provide a viable solution to the source problem. This is an important key to the proper understanding of later developments in Synoptic criticism.

The secondary character of Matthew was in fact the only real consensus in Holtzmann's day. It was a consensus which united even the Tübingen school with all others. But leaving the Tübingen school aside, there was another consensus shared by all other investigators. In this group Holtzmann was able to include such diverse criticism as that of de Wette and Bleek, with that of Eichhorn and Ewald, and, more important, with the Schleiermacher-Lachmann-Weisse *Logia* criticism. This is basically a mechanical grouping. For except for one point the hypotheses of these scholars were mutually self-contradictory. The one common denominator which Holtzmann was able to trace through all these hypotheses was the idea of a *Grundschrift* lying behind the canonical Gospels.[4] How unreal this consensus actually was is apparent when the nature of this

---

[2] So Ritschl, *op. cit.*, pp. 508 ff.

[3] *Op. cit.*, p. 56. "Heutzutage argumentieren wir nur ex concesso, wenn wir von dem secundären Charakter des ersten Evangeliums ausgehen. Auch die Tübinger Kritik ist darin mit uns einverstanden."

[4] *Op. cit.*, p. 66.

Grundschrift in the different hypotheses is considered. The *Grundschrift* in question in the case of de Wette and Bleek was conceived to be in the shape of what is common to Matthew and Luke. Neither of these scholars doubted that Mark was a late and unhistorical conflation of Matthew and Luke. The *Grundschrift* in the case of Eichhorn and Ewald, on the other hand, was conceived to be in the shape of Mark, whose Gospel was thought by Ewald to be the most primitive and historically reliable.

In the case of Schleiermacher, Lachmann, and Weisse the situation was confused because the views of these three were in turn mutually contradictory, Schleiermacher thinking Mark to be late and of little historical value and Weisse at one time affirming that Mark was the earliest Gospel and at another time that it was only a later recension of an Ur-Marcus. But, nonetheless, to the mind of one like Holtzmann who was searching for some solid ground of scholarly consensus on which to base his reconstruction, it was possible to perceive even here the presence of the idea of written material lying behind and utilized in our Gospels.

Herein lies a fundamental fault of all subsequent Gospel criticism indebted to the work of Holtzmann. It is based not upon a firm grasp of the primary phenomena of the Gospels themselves, but upon an artificial and deceptive consensus among scholars of differing traditions of Gospel criticism.

The root of the matter is a logical problem. How should the importance of consensus be evaluated? If two scientists working on the same problem propose different hypotheses which nonetheless agree at one or more points, what importance does the agreement have? It cannot constitute proof that those parts of the respective hypotheses are true, for such agreement may proceed from a common presupposition made by both investigators that in fact is false.

But what if the number of investigators be increased to ten and once again differing hypotheses are proposed which nonetheless continue to agree at the same point or points as the original two? Should this predispose the impartial observer to think that this agreement represents a consensus that can be scientifically relied upon in a way the diverging parts of the respective hypothesis cannot be relied upon? Once again the answer is, "No," because the agreement could have proceeded from a single presupposition shared by all the investigators. And if that presupposition is false it might even be the prime reason why the respective investigators are proposing conflicting hypotheses. Therefore, as the number of investigators increases, and no one hypothesis emerges as the best solution to all the various aspects of the problem concerned, the presence of a small point of agreement common to the many diverging hypotheses should be examined as a possible clue to some commonly held false presupposition, which is, in fact, putting every investigator who accepts it on the wrong track in his search for a solution.

In the case of the German critics whose work Holtzmann held in Synoptic view, this common presupposition may have been nothing other than Lessing's germinal idea of an apostolic Ur-gospel copied by the Evangelists; an idea which never influenced German criticism until it entered the head of Lessing, and about which he himself wrote to his brother in a letter, "I myself am often astonished to see how naturally everything proceeds from an observation which I found I had made, without rightly knowing how I came by it." The observation Lessing made was that in Acts the Christians are called Nazarenes and since the early Fathers knew a Gospel of the Nazarenes, this Gospel could have been written by the Apostles, and this apostolic Gospel of the Nazarenes could have been copied by our Evangelists. Both the agreements and disagreements of the canonical Gospels seemed then to proceed naturally from such a reconstruction. This is Lessing's idea of the Ur-gospel. Any agreement among subsequent investigators as to the existence of a fundamental *Grundschrift* lying behind and utilized by the Gospel writers may simply reflect the common acceptance of this idea, perhaps consciously, perhaps in some cases unconsciously. If this idea itself is false, if there was no such Ur-gospel, then the kind of consensus which existed among such critics as de Wette, Bleek, Eichhorn, Ewald, and Weisse provided no secure foundation upon which Holtzmann or anyone else could or should construct a new synthesis for Gospel criticism. In fact, instead of reasoning as Holtzmann did, a critic might readily have reached an opposite conclusion. He could have taken the fact that there was widespread disagreement among those critics who held to one form or another of the Ur-gospel hypothesis, as an indication that this very presupposition could have been a factor contributing to their widespread divergence. For if in fact one of the canonical Gospels, however secondary to the eye-witness period it might be, was the first of its kind, then the historian of the Synoptic Problem can say, without hesitation, that the greatest single source of divergence among investigators in the nineteenth century was their openness to the suggestion of Lessing that the agreements among Matthew, Mark, and Luke should be explained not by one Evangelist copying another, but by all three independently copying an earlier source—a fundamental *Grundschrift*, to use Holtzmann's term.

A second structural fault in Holtzmann's synthesis was the idea that Luke did not know Matthew. Holtzmann had little or no evidential basis for this notion and after Simons' work of 1880 he gave it up. But meanwhile this idea of complete independence of Luke and Matthew played an essential ideological role in preparing the way for the acceptance of the idea that Matthew and Luke drew the sayings material they hold in common from an early collection of Jesus's *Logia*. The independence of Luke and Matthew, like the idea of an Ur-gospel, was implicit in the notion of a *Grundschrift* lying behind the canonical Gospels, which Holtzmann took to be a matter of common consent among most investigators.

A third fundamental fault in the synthesis of Holtzmann concerns his method of reconstructing the original form of the *Grundschrift*. Here he followed the procedure first introduced by Eichhorn, who reconstructed the Ur-gospel from passages where two or more of the Gospels agree. De Wette and Bleek realized results not fundamentally dissimilar by confining themselves to what could be reconstructed from passages common to Matthew and Luke. But Holtzmann, under the influence of Weisse, thought not in terms of one primitive source, but two. The first was a narrative source which he designated Alpha. It is clear that he thought of this narrative source as an Ur-Marcus, for he put Ur-Marcus in parentheses immediately after the designation A. The second is a sayings source to which he gave the name Lambda, signifying it with Λ, the first Greek letter of the *Logia* of Papias. Holtzmann then in a largely arbitrary manner, and with a result confirmed by no other critic before or since, reconstructed these two primitive sources.[5] Holtzmann's Alpha included items

---

[5] Some idea of the agreement and disagreement between the reconstructed form of Holtzmann's two primitive documents and those of other German critics can be obtained from the comparative table drawn up by William Sanday, showing the analysis of the first three Gospels by Holtzmann, Weizsäcker, Weisse, Wendt, and Beyschlag arranged in parallel columns, in his article for Smith's *Dictionary of the Bible*, 1893.

which do not occur in Mark (such as the story of the healing of the Centurion's servant, as well as such sayings material as the beatitudes). And his Lambda like Marsh's ב included parables unique to Matthew and Luke. Nonetheless, since Alpha is given no birth narratives and since most of the sayings material common to Matthew and Luke are attributed to Lambda, Holtzmann's Alpha finally looks more like an Ur-Marcus than anything else. Such a literary procedure as was followed by Holtzmann is absolutely unjustified without well established grounds for thinking that behind the existing Gospels there were in fact two such primitive documents. Holtzmann, however, thought that there were such grounds.

These grounds he believed had been firmly established by Weisse. "We may say that it was really Weisse . . . who for the first time scientifically established the Marcan hypothesis."[6]

At first sight this seems to reflect little credit upon the critical acumen of Holtzmann. For Weisse, though he argued against Schleiermacher's view that Papias could not have referred to the canonical Mark, offered no new argument for the priority of the canonical Mark. What he did was to propound a two-document hypothesis which involved the notion that Matthew and Luke had independently copied those sayings materials they had in common from Papias' *Logia*, which through Schleiermacher's work Weisse had learned to think of as a primitive collection of sayings. This enabled Weisse and anyone who agreed with his hypothesis to think in terms of another primitive source which could account for the many narrative and discourse passages held in common by Matthew, Mark, and Luke. Since any source reconstructed primarily from passages found in all three Synoptics, *ipso facto*, will be conformed in extent and content to the shortest of the three, and since Mark is considerably shorter than Matthew and Luke, the Ur-gospel on Weisse's hypothesis inevitably has the shape and content of Mark and therefore is naturally thought of as an Ur-Marcus.

If Holtzmann did not realize this, he might think that Weisse's contribution scientifically established the view that Mark is our most reliable source for a life of Jesus. Holtzmann evidently did not realize this because otherwise his statement about the scientific importance of Weisse's work would be unintelligible. One further

---

[6] *Op. cit.*, p. 29. "Man kann sagen, das Weisse die Marcushypothese eigentlich neu entdeckt und zum erstenmal wissenschaftlich begründet hat."

point of some historical importance should be kept in mind in this connection. It has been noted how Holtzmann was able to refer to Weisse as having established the "Marcan hypothesis," whereas in this review Weisse's theory has consistently been referred to as the "two-document hypothesis." This is conventional twentieth century usage. But in the nineteenth century the "Marcan hypothesis" was understood to be inclusive of and dependent upon the idea of the *Logia* of Papias as interpreted by Schleiermacher.

In fact, the Marcan hypothesis, as Schweitzer points out, was really less of a source theory than it was the theoretical life of Jesus based upon Holtzmann's reconstruction of Ur-Marcus.[7] This liberal life of Jesus, unencumbered by embarrassing birth legends and contradictory resurrection stories, provided the historical basis on which liberal theologians could ground their faith while they pressed with devastating effect their historico-critical attack on the two most vulnerable pillars of nineteenth century orthodoxy—the Virgin Birth and the physical Resurrection. It was, therefore, the "Marcan hypothesis" which provided the liberals a critical basis for their defense of the citadel of Faith against the attack of nineteenth century radicals like Bruno Bauer from the left, while they themselves carried on their battle with the Orthodox to the right.

When Emanuel Hirsch in the twentieth century can complain that all other contemporary German theologians have gone astray in abandoning Mark as the correct basis for their theology, he is giving expression to a theological position which owes its origin to the critical synthesis of Holtzmann and ultimately to Holtzmann's mistaken notion that the Marcan hypothesis had been scientifically established by Weisse.[8]

The reader is well advised to recall that Weisse himself complained

---

[7] Albert Schweitzer, *Von Reimarus zu Wrede. Eine Geschichte der Leben-Jesu-Forschung*, Tübingen, 1906; Eng. tr. *The Quest of the Historical Jesus*, New York, 1948, pp. 203 ff. In the preface to the latest edition of this book, Schweitzer writes: "The decisive point in the quest of the historical Jesus is not which of the two oldest Gospels (Matthew and Mark) is a trifle older than the other. That, moreover, is a literary question which is scarcely possible to answer. The historical problem of the life of Jesus cannot be recognized, much less solved, from the fragmentary record of Mark. The differing narratives of the two oldest Gospels are equally valuable, but Matthew's fullness gives it greater importance, and Baur and his school rightly gave it preference." *The Quest for the Historical Jesus*, London, 1950, p. xi (*Geschichte der Leben-Jesu-Forschung*, Tübingen, 1951, p. xii).

[8] This criticism of contemporary German theology by Hirsch was made during an interview in Göttingen in 1960.

only a few years before his work was so highly praised by Holtzmann, that throughout a period of almost two decades no one had followed him in building on the way opened up by Schleiermacher and Lachmann. If Weisse really established the Marcan hypothesis as Holtzmann thought, then for a period of over twenty years this fact went unnoticed—and that at a time when there was great scientific interest in the question, and at a time when there was a great hunger among German theologians for a sound historical foundation on which to base theology. Important scientific achievements sometimes do go unnoticed for long periods of time. But in such cases there is some explanation for this, as, for example, no public or professional interest in the matter. However, no such explanation is forthcoming in the case of Weisse. It seems evident, then, that Holtzmann attributed a scientific value to the work of Weisse that others had missed or did not acknowledge. And that evaluation rests on a fundamental fault—namely, the failure of Holtzmann to recognize that the Ur-gospel will always have the shape of an Ur-Marcus once its reconstruction in general is based on passages common to Matthew, Mark, and Luke.

This point is so obvious that it is necessary to say in defense of Holtzmann that its pertinence is reduced to insignificance by one simple consideration—that is, the powerful and captivating influence of Schleiermacher's idea of the *Logia* of Papias as a primitive collection of sayings. If there were this collection, and that this was so seemed plausible to many at that time, then that collection could have served Matthew and Luke as a source for the sayings material they have in common. Therefore, for Holtzmann to reconstruct Alpha out of what is left of the materials common to two or more of the Synoptic Gospels once he has abstracted what he thought Luke and Matthew likely took from Lambda, is really not implausible. All that is really required in addition to the *Logia* is the assurance that there was an Ur-gospel—some common *Grundschrift* behind our existing Gospels. This assurance Holtzmann thought he had in the minimal consensus he found among all investigators except those of the Tübingen school. But here again it is clear that this assurance was ill-grounded for it may have had no more foundation than the common presupposition of an Ur-gospel, an idea which since the time of Lessing had exercised even greater fascination for the minds of critics than that of Schleiermacher's *Logia*.

These two creative ideas: a hypothetical Ur-gospel on the one hand, and a hypothetical collection of sayings on the other, when taken together, constitute the historical and ideological genesis of the two-document hypothesis. Scholars lived with the idea of Lessing's Ur-gospel for more than half a century without reaching a consensus that Mark was the earliest Gospel. For on this hypothesis of Lessing, Mark was not a likely candidate for being the most complete form of that Ur-gospel since it did not contain the great body of Jesus' sayings doubly authenticated by the clearest literary evidence in Matthew and Luke. But with Schleiermacher's *Logia* in view all kinds of new possibilities opened. One of these was the two-document hypothesis. It proved to be the most attractive, both because it was simple, and because it commended itself as a scientific basis upon which the liberal quest for the historical Jesus might be pursued. Holtzmann took this hypothesis and made it the basic presupposition of one of the most careful and painstaking analyses of the "Synoptic tradition" to be found in all the literature of the nineteenth century.

From the sheer critical point of view Holtzmann's analysis of the material in the Gospels is on the same high level as that of de Wette and Bleek. The advantage of Holtzmann's reconstruction over all earlier efforts is more evident when compared with theirs. Bleek and de Wette followed Griesbach in considering Mark a late and historically worthless conflation of Matthew and Luke. Their reconstructed form of the fundamental *Grundschrift* behind the Gospels was therefore mostly made up out of passages common to Matthew and Luke, but without any advantage from Mark. This reconstructed *Grundschrift* had in one single source most of the material which Holtzmann was able to attribute to his two sources. Therefore, from this point of view there was nothing radically new in what Holtzmann was able to offer to the liberal theologian as well-attested, early, and reliable tradition. From this vantage point Holtzmann's results, compared with those of de Wette and Bleek, seemed basically conservative.

The genius, however, of Holtzmann's method of reconstructing this *Grundschrift* behind the Gospels as compared with that of de Wette and Bleek is evident in the circumstance that it allowed him to utilize Mark as a historically reliable Gospel without this use of Mark seriously affecting the actual content of the "scientifically" reconstructed *Grundschrift* with which historians and theologians would henceforth work in their quest for the historical Jesus. This provision appealed to the interests of such pietistic and conservative theologians as Ewald had been able to influence, and enabled Holtzmann's work to ride with the resulting wave of reaction against the radical Tübingen scholars without appearing to concede a retreat from the use of rigorous scientific method, which by then had become a *sine qua non* in German theology. The point is that those who thought Mark early and historically reliable could see that Holtzmann's procedure allowed for its proper use, while those who thought it was historically worthless had to admit that Holtzmann's use of it really made little difference in the end result. This is the reason it was possible for so many liberal theologians to embrace Holtzmann's "Marcan hypothesis," in spite of the absence of any compelling evidence or argument for the priority of Mark.

Furthermore, two primitive sources seemed better than one even if the combined reconstructed content of the two added nothing new. And finally this apparently innocuous use of Mark was enough to satisfy the traditionalist who wished to regard the canonical Mark as identical with Papias' Mark, or as a more or less direct descendant of Papias' Mark. This allowed such scholars to imagine that Holtzmann's reconstruction of his Alpha (Ur-Marcus) had the apostolic sanction of Peter just as his reconstruction of Lambda had the apostolic sanction of Matthew.

For reasons such as these, the effect of Holtzmann's careful linguistic analysis and of his painstaking reconstruction of his two primitive sources, was to establish indelibly in the minds of many the impression that he had soundly grounded the two-document hypothesis upon a firm scientific basis.

Charles M. Mead, an American theologian, in residence in Berlin at that time, gave Holtzmann's book the lead review in his survey of "Recent German Theological Literature" for the then widely respected scientific journal *Biblica Sacra*.[9] Mead wrote: "That his [Holtzmann's] peculiar theory, however, can be considered as proved, is not conceded. . . . On the whole the book before us may be considered as important, not only as a contribution to biblical science, but as representing the tone of a very large, perhaps an increasing party of German theologians."

[9] 1864, pp. 887–888.

Coming within one year of the date when Holtzmann's book was published Mead's review is an honest and perceptive evaluation of the work. Honest in that the reviewer admits that Holtzmann has proved nothing, perceptive in that he recognizes the remarkable degree to which Holtzmann has succeeded in producing a work which "represents the tone" of a large and rising party of German theologians. Mead apparently had a firm grasp of trends in contemporary German theology—for by the end of the century this "party of German theologians" was dominant, and at the beginning of the twentieth century nearly all Gospel criticism was being carried on within the limits of Holtzmann's synthesis, and the Marcan or two-document hypothesis was regarded by most as one of the assured results of nineteenth century criticism. In 1900 in a revised edition of his *Einleitung* Adolf Jülicher gave expression to a mood and judgment of his time, which after World War II came to be the orthodox view of nineteenth century criticism, when he wrote with reference to the work of Holtzmann, Bernhard Weiss, Godet, and Zahn: "But only one of these four, Holtzmann, follows the good tradition of German criticism—and moreover, without any school preconceptions—in pointing out the very different degrees of certainty with which we can proceed to formulate decisions within its domain."[10] This concept of "the good tradition of German criticism" was first forcefully utilized by Ewald in his attack on the Tübingen school which threatened to damage *deutsche Wissenschaft* in the eyes of the rest of the world. Holtzmann's writings, free of the spirit of personal polemics which had characterized Ewald's attack on Baur, were like a breath of fresh air after a long night in foul

---

[10] *Einleitung in das Neue Testament*, Freiburg and Leipzig; Eng. tr. *An Introduction to the New Testament*, London, 1904, p. 26. The measure of the extent to which Holtzmann's work of 1863 is believed to have firmly established the two-document hypothesis for many New Testament scholars is given in the words of Werner Georg Kümmel in his excellent volume *Das Neue Testament: Geschichte der Erforschung seiner Probleme*, Freiburg/München, 1958: "Wenige Jahre danach jedoch (1863) wies Heinrich Julius Holtzmann in seinem die ganze bisherige Forschung souverän zusammenfassenden Werk über die 'Synoptischen Evangelien' nicht nur ganz überzeugend auf Grund des primitiveren Charakters der Erzählungsart und Sprache das Markusevangelium als Quelle der beiden anderen Synoptiker nach, sondern zeigte ebenso überzeugend die Notwendigkeit der Annahme einer hauptsächlich aus Reden bestehenden zweiten Quelle hinter Matthäus und Lukas. Dadurch dass dieser Nachweis ganz besonders auch die sprachliche Eigenart der Quellen und den Zusammenhang der Berichte ins Auge fasste, wurde die Zweiquellentheorie durch Holtzmann so sorgfältig begründet, dass die Jesusforschung von da an diesen festen Boden nicht mehr aufgeben konnte" (p. 185).

quarters, and it is no wonder that he, rather than Ewald, became the acknowledged founder of a new historico-critical school to replace that of Baur.[11]

After Holtzmann, the initiative in Synoptic criticism began to shift from Germany to England. If the first half of the history of the Synoptic Problem can be surveyed as a development from Lessing to Holtzmann, a development taking place largely in German universities, then the second half can be surveyed as a development from Holtzmann to Streeter, a development which took place largely in the Universities of Cambridge and Oxford.

[11] Sometimes the names of Weizsäcker and B. Weiss are associated with those of Weisse and Holtzmann as influential in establishing the two-document hypothesis. The fact that Weizsäcker, within a year after the publication of Holtzmann's work published a work of his own in which he too adopted the two-document hypothesis no doubt had some part in contributing to the growing consensus. Simons' very important work which convincingly demonstrated to Holtzmann and Weizsäcker that Luke did use Matthew, ought to have raised serious questions about the two-document hypothesis. But it clearly had no such effect. Again, the development of "form-criticism" after World War I should have opened up a new era of Synoptic source-analysis. But instead this development itself remained to a considerable extent within the limits of the Holtzmannian synthesis.

CHAPTER III

The English Endorsement and Modification of the Two-Document Hypothesis

A. Introduction

The history of the Synoptic Problem subsequent to Holtzmann's epoch-making synthesis of 1863 is mainly the history of the triumph of the two-document hypothesis and the transformation of that hypothesis into the form in which Streeter explained and defended it.[1] The historical problem that must be faced is how

---

[1] The main developments in Synoptic studies in England in the pre-Holtzmann period can be covered in a few sentences. Marsh's views were criticized in an "Examination of Mr. Marsh's Hypothesis" by Veysie, who proposed as an alternative theory that the Evangelists used several written documents, which in turn had no common written source. Schleiermacher in his essay on Luke had criticized Eichhorn from the same point of view. So when Thirlwall translated this essay into English in 1825, it served to strengthen this general position among English scholars. Thirlwall further entered into a criticism of Marsh's hypothesis from this same perspective in his review of the developments in Synoptic criticism since Marsh. There is a reliable firsthand report on the situation in England in 1830 in a letter from E. B. Pusey to Dr. Tholuck. In this letter Pusey complies with a request from his friend Professor Tholuck of Halle, Germany, for information on what had recently been done in English theology. Pusey

to account for the triumph of this hypothesis in the absence of any conclusive demonstration of its validity, and in spite of serious scientific objections which can be and have been raised against it.

It will be well, therefore, in beginning a critical review of the history of the Synoptic Problem from Holtzmann to Streeter to define the nature of the change which the two-document hypothesis underwent during this sixty-year period. This can be done most simply by comparing the two-document hypothesis as Holtzmann expounded it in 1863 with Streeter's exposition of it in 1924. The decisive difference concerns the status of Lessing's idea of an Ur-gospel. Holtzmann regarded some kind of fundamental *Grundschrift* as basic to his hypothesis, whereas Streeter did not. This meant that whereas according to Holtzmann, Matthew and Luke independently copied an Ur-gospel which he called Ur-Marcus; according to Streeter, Mark is the earliest Gospel and Matthew and Luke are directly but independently dependent upon Mark.[2]

The serious consequences of this transformation of the two-document hypothesis was twofold: (1) If Matthew and Luke copied Mark (or, as Streeter would say, "a document for all practical purposes identical with our Mark"), then the argument from order

---

admits that in the field of "Scriptural Interpretation and Criticism" scarcely anything had been done since the work of Marsh, except for the work of Veysie, and Thirlwall, and writes that their view "is, I imagine, likely to be the predominant opinion in England." Pusey noted, however, that Hug's *Introduction* had just been translated into English at Cambridge, and Greswell's *Harmony of the Evangelists* had just been published at Oxford. Both of these works endorsed the Augustinian hypothesis. The Tübingen developments were bypassed by scholars at both Cambridge and Oxford, and the only matter of importance was the favorable reception of the oral hypothesis at Cambridge in the second half of the nineteenth century, especially by Westcott (*Elements of the Gospel Harmony*, 1851; revised as *Introduction to the Study of the Gospels*, 1860, 7th ed., 1887), and later by A. Wright. It cannot be shown that any of these scholars were important precursors of Streeter, and, therefore, while each would have an honorable place in a full account of the history of the study of the Gospels in England, their work is not vital to an understanding of the development of the Synoptic Problem. That is, they seem to have produced no new ideas and no new arguments, which in turn influenced the history of the Synoptic Problem. For that reason their work is passed over in this survey. It is a curious fact that except for the way in which Herder's idea of oral tradition was taken up by Holtzmann, the oral hypothesis cannot be shown to have made any lasting contribution to the history of the Synoptic Problem. This may be due to the fact that to move in the direction of the oral hypothesis, is to move away from the Synoptic Problem. As A. Wright has ingenuously stated: "The oral hypothesis is chiefly valuable, because it gives the critic the liberty which he requires. A document is a rigid thing; oral teaching is flexible." (*Op. cit.*, p. x.)

2 For Holtzmann Ur-Marcus was real. For Streeter it was a "phantom" (*The Four Gospels*, A Study of Origins, London, 1924, 8th impression, 1953, p. 331).

in behalf of the priority of Mark which was the main pillar on which Streeter rested his "fundamental solution" loses its cogency and gives way. (2) If Matthew and Luke independently copied Mark, how can scholars account for their agreements against Mark ?

This latter difficulty Streeter recognized, and his proposed solution in terms of textual assimilation satisfied the majority of critics for thirty years until the subject was reopened by N. Turner at Oxford in 1957.[3]

To the former difficulty, however, Streeter seems to have been completely oblivious. In 1951, B. C. Butler called attention to the fallacy of the argument from order when taken on Streeter's terms, and Butler's analysis of the fallaciousness of Streeter's reasoning at this point was cogently reiterated at Cambridge by G. M. Styler whose *excursus* on "The Priority of Mark" was published in 1962.[4]

But neither Butler nor Styler explained why Streeter and his contemporaries failed to perceive this fundamental and elemental logical fallacy in their basic argument for the priority of Mark. No review of the history of the Synoptic Problem will be adequate that does not help the critic understand this oversight of an entire generation of New Testament scholars, and that does not explain why

---

[3] "The Minor Verbal Agreements of Mt. and Luke against Mk." *Studia Evangelica,* Texte und Untersuchungen, Berlin, 1959.

[4] B. C. Butler, *The Originality of St. Matthew, A Critique of the Two-Document Hypothesis,* Cambridge, 1951. G. M. Styler, "The Priority of Mark," in C. F. D. Moule's *The Birth of the New Testament,* New York, 1962. The argument from order in behalf of Mark rests on the fact that the order of material in Mark is in general the same as the order in Matthew or Luke or both. Almost never is the order of Mark different from both Matthew and Luke. This fact suggests, on the Ur-Marcus hypothesis, that Mark has preserved fairly faithfully the true order of the earlier Gospel which all three Evangelists have copied. The cogency of this suggestion rests on the probability that the agreement of two Evangelists or three, always working independently of one another, is most simply explained by their connection through their common source— i.e. Ur-Marcus. But if there were no earlier Gospel, then the same phenomena of agreement and disagreement in order could be explained by any hypothesis which gave to Mark some kind of middle position between Matthew and Luke. Thus, if Luke were first, and Mark second, and Matthew third, the phenomena of agreement could be achieved if Matthew sometimes followed Mark where Mark had followed Luke, but always followed Mark where Mark had deviated from Luke. This hypothesis requires the further explanation as to why Matthew would always follow Mark where Mark had deviated from Luke. But the conventional notion that Matthew and Luke independently copied Mark is fraught with a similar difficulty in that it requires the further explanation as to why Matthew would never deviate from Mark where Luke had deviated from Mark. (*See* Chapter VI.) Even the Ur-Marcus hypothesis requires the further explanation as to why Mark, working independently of Matthew and Luke, would never deviate from that common order of Ur-Marcus to which Matthew and Luke bear concurrent testimony.

conscientious investigators even today are reluctant to entertain seriously the thought that the two-document hypothesis might be less than an assured result of nineteenth-century criticism. When Styler referred to Streeter's work as "the classical statement and defence" of "the Two-document Hypothesis," and to the "shock" occasioned by the publication of Butler's attack on the hypothesis, he was giving expression to a state of mind shared to one degree or another by the vast majority of New Testament critics who today take a serious interest in Gospel criticism.[5]

Nothing relieves this state of shock for the New Testament scholar as does an understanding of the development of the two-document hypothesis, and an account of the main factors contributing to the "consensus" that this hypothesis was an assured result of nineteenth-century criticism. This "consensus" had its roots in the ready and ever wider acceptance in Germany of Holtzmann's fundamental work of 1863.

B. Sanday's Mediating Role

Holtzmann's book was never translated into English, but there can be no doubt that the two-document hypothesis was brought to England originally from Germany. The name of William Sanday is to be closely identified with the importation. He certainly was one of the earliest to endorse the two-document hypothesis as a majority opinion among the best German critics.[6] In the preface to his first book, published in 1872, the young Sanday revealed his analysis of the needs of the times, and hinted at the programmatic character his career was to take. Since Sanday, within twenty years, was to become a very influential figure, and since his words disclose the historical context in which the two-document hypothesis was first endorsed in England, it is best to quote him:

I cannot think that it has not been without serious loss on both sides, that in the great movement that has been going on upon the continent for the last forty years covering the rise and fall of the Tübingen school and the rise of the mediating Theology, the scanty band of English theologians should have stood almost entirely aloof, or should only have touched the

---

[5] *Op. cit.*, pp. 223–224.

[6] *The Authorship and Historical Character of the Fourth Gospel, Considered in Reference to the Contents of the Gospel Itself. A Critical Essay*, London, 1872, p. ix.

outskirts of the questions at issue, without attempting to grapple with them at their centre. . . . There is no limit to the efficacy of scientific method if it is but faithfully and persistently applied. . . . I propose . . . to carry on the same method of enquiry, first, to investigate the origin and composition of the Synoptic Gospels, and finally, to the subject of New Testament theology. . . . With regard to the Synoptists, provisional conclusions have been taken from the elaborate work of Dr. Holtzmann (*Die Synoptischen Evangelien.* Leipzig, 1863). It should be remembered that Dr. Holtzmann does not stand alone, but that for the greater portion of his results (e.g. as to the documentary origin of the Synoptic Gospels, the priority of St. Mark, the existence of two main documents and the independent use of them by the Evangelists) he has the support of a majority of the best critics during the last ten or fifteen years, including among these Weizsäcker, Meyer, Ritschl, Weiss, Wittichen, and practically also the veteran Ewald. These conclusions I accept temporarily, but I hope to be able to approach the subject myself with sufficient independence.[7]

Six years later, 1878, Sanday wrote: "We do not think the synoptic problem has yet been solved. . . ."[8] But his memorial in the *Journal of Theological Studies* in 1921 carried these words: "He had in his first book (1872) anticipated the present solution of the synoptic problem; he had worked through it year after year in his seminar. . . ."[9] Though written by Walter Lock, and not by Sanday's greatest protégé, Streeter, these words give self-confident expression to the same consensus. The "present solution" to which Lock refers is the two-document hypothesis. Three years later Streeter called it the "Fundamental Solution," and gave it its "classical statement and defence."[10] Streeter's definitive work, in which this statement and defense are made, appropriately carries the following dedication:

IN MEMORIAM
GULIELMI SANDAY, S. T. P.
INSIGNISSIMI APUD OXONIENSES
HORUM STUDIORUM FAUTORIS

In his famous Bampton Lectures, Sanday said: "I yield to no one in admiration for the Germans or in gratitude to them for their great

[7] *Op. cit.,* pp. 7–9.
[8] *Academy,* Vol. 14, September 21, 1878, pp. 296–297.
[9] Vol. 22, January 1921, p. 102.
[10] *Op. cit.,* Chapter VII, pp. 151–198. Because of frequent reference Streeter's *The Four Gospels* will hereafter be referred to as *F.G.*

services, of which I have continually availed myself both in these lectures and elsewhere. . . ."[11]

And yet it is clear that Sanday did not at that time think the Germans, or anyone else, had solved the Synoptic Problem—for in an earlier lecture in the same series, in connection with the literary analysis of the Synoptic Gospels, he said:

> That analysis has been going on more or less upon its present lines for quite thirty years, and yet I cannot take upon myself to say that any completely acceptable result has been arrived at. The latest researches have in fact had rather the effect of opening up new questions than of closing old ones. The problem is indeed one of extraordinary difficulty and complexity. I do not of course mean that there are not some conclusions which seem to disengage themselves, but even these to one who tries to look at the whole subject impartially are so crossed by conflicting indications, that I should not in my present responsible position and with my present degree of knowledge and insight like to propound them for your acceptance.[12]

In a footnote to the published form of the lectures Sanday refers his readers to his article on the "Gospels" in Smith's *Dictionary of the Bible*. This article was written in 1891 and opens with a "History of the Criticism of the Synoptic Gospels," which Sanday significantly begins in 1863. The first three sentences of that history constitute an important introduction to the historical context within which Sanday attempted to come to terms with the Synoptic Problem.

> The year 1863 . . . might be said to mark a turning-point in the history of Synoptic criticism. For some twenty years up to that date, in the land in which criticism generally was most active, the Tübingen School had been in the ascendent. This school owed its characteristics to the remarkable talent for speculative and historical combination possessed by its founder, F. C. Baur.

The following points are of importance in gaining a firm grasp of the history of the Synoptic Problem as it developed in England under the influence of Sanday: (1) The year 1863 clearly refers to the date of publication of Holtzmann's *Die synoptischen Evangelien*. Although the Tübingen school "always had a declared and uncompromising antagonist in Ewald," wrote Sanday, and even though

---

11 *Inspiration, Eight Lectures on the Early History and Origin of the Doctrine of Biblical Inspiration*, London, 1893, p. 320.
12 *Op. cit.*, p. 281.

"the seeds of the theory which was to receive fuller development in the next period had already been laid simultaneously by Weisse and Wilke in 1838," nonetheless, he continued, "the publication of Holtzmann's *Die synoptischen Evangelien* in 1863 was practically a new departure." Holtzmann's work was "more thorough and searching than any that had preceded it." Its publication represents the "threshold" of a new period.

(2) The older period, brought to an end in 1863, was dominated by the Tübingen school, and especially its founder, F. C. Baur. In his discussion of the Tübingen school Sanday was preoccupied with its methodological faults: "The speculative, dogmatic reconstruction came first in order of time, and the literary criticism had to follow in its train. It was a theory impressed from above downwards." In contrast, Holtzmann rightly approached the problem "from below." His method began, "not with broad general conceptions, but with a close and searching examination of the language of the Gospels and of their relation to one another." This analysis of the differences between the work of Holtzmann and that of the Tübingen school is both oversimplified and misleading.

The suggestion that Baur held to the idea that Mark was written after Matthew and Luke because this suited his historical theories concerning Christian origins cannot be proved. Furthermore, Sanday seemed unaware of the fact that the Griesbach hypothesis continued to seem cogent and had a history of its own—quite apart from the connection it had with the Tübingen school. Sanday made no reference to the work of de Wette or Bleek. This is curious since Sanday knew that Bleek's *Introduction to the New Testament* had been translated into English and had been generally available as one of the volumes in Clark's *Foreign Theological Library* since 1869. Sanday did acknowledge very briefly the existence of Samuel Davidson's *Introduction to the New Testament*, in the revised edition of which (1868), Davidson adopted the Griesbach hypothesis.[13] But Sanday regarded Davidson's work to be under the influence of Baur and therefore of no independent importance.[14] This is all strange indeed, since both Bleek and Davidson set forth in clear and rational terms the evidence and arguments which led many critics outside

[13] *An Introduction to the Study of the New Testament, Critical, Exegetical, and Theological*, London.
[14] "Gospels," Smith's *Dictionary of the Bible*, p. 121 8b.

the Tübingen school to think that Griesbach's solution to the Synoptic Problem was the one that best answered the questions which arose on the grounds of literary criticism.

David Friedrich Strauss's new *Leben Jesu* had been generally available in English since 1865.[15] This book, unlike his first *Leben Jesu*, contains a discussion of the various solutions of the Synoptic Problem, and makes clear the grounds on which a member of the Tübingen school was led to think Mark to be later than Matthew and Luke. Strauss wrote:

Between two Gospels [Matthew and Luke], which with many coincidences exhibit also many marks of independence of each other, each having whole sections peculiar to itself, and even the matter common to both to a certain extent in a different order, there stands a Gospel [Mark] which, in point of matter, has scarcely anything exclusively its own, and of its sixteen chapters, only about as much as would fill half a chapter not common to the one or the other of its adjacent Gospels, coinciding likewise in point of arrangement sometimes with one of these, sometimes with the other, and seeming sometimes to compile the form of expression from both the others together. The supposition then spontaneously forces itself upon us, that a Gospel like this does not, in point of time, stand between the two others (as Augustine has held), but was afterwards made up from them as its already existing sources. This view has been brought forward by Griesbach, and by the clear explanation which seemed to result from it was held to be so convincing, that up to the latest period it was able to hold its ground as the really popular one among theologians.[16]

Strauss wrote this in 1864, by which time the breakup of the Tübingen school was well under way. The ecclesiastical authorities in Würtemberg had united with the civil authorities to ban students of Baur from holding academic posts in the University of Tübingen. Baur was replaced by Weizsäcker who, like Holtzmann, had adopted Weisse's two-document theory. When Strauss wrote ". . . up to the latest period it [the Griesbach hypothesis] was able to hold its ground as the really popular one among theologians," he witnessed to the fact that by 1864 Synoptic criticism had indeed entered a new period. But the reader of Sanday's "History of the Criticism of the Synoptic Gospels" would certainly be misled by Sanday's suggestion that this

---

15 *Op. cit.*
16 *Op. cit.*, pp. 109–110. See also Strauss's views of Mark: pp. 169–183. [Eng. tr.].

period had been ushered in by "a new departure" among New Testament scholars working on the Synoptic Problem. In point of fact, Holtzmann's "close and searching examination of the language of the Gospels and of their relation to one another" is easily matched by the critical work of de Wette and Bleek. Furthermore, in assessing the weight of influence of theological considerations upon German Synoptic criticism at this time, it would be necessary to consider the extent to which Holtzmann's method of reconstructing his *Grundschrift* was indebted to that of Eichhorn, who openly drew attention to its patent theological advantages. It further would be necessary to take into account Albert Schweitzer's report in his *Quest of the Historical Jesus*. Schweitzer was dealing with the works of Schenkel and Weizsäcker:

> What attracted these writers to the Marcan hypothesis was not so much the authentification which it gave to the detail of Mark, though they were willing enough to accept that, but the way in which this gospel lent itself to the *a priori* view of the course of the life of Jesus which they unconsciously brought with them. They appealed to Holtzmann because he showed such wonderful skill in extracting from the Marcan narrative the view which commended itself to the spirit of the age as manifested in the 'sixties.
>
> The way in which Holtzmann exhibited this characteristic view of the 'sixties as arising naturally out of the detail of Mark, was so perfect, so artistically charming, that this view appeared henceforward to be inseparably bound up with the Marcan tradition. Scarcely ever has a description of the life of Jesus exercised so irresistible an influence as that short outline—it embraces scarcely twenty pages—with which Holtzmann closes his examination of the Synoptic Gospels. This chapter became the creed and catechism of all who handled the subject during the following decades. The treatment of the life of Jesus had to follow the lines here laid down until the Marcan hypothesis was delivered from its bondage to that *a priori* view of the development of Jesus. Until then anyone might appeal to the Marcan hypothesis, meaning thereby only that general view of the inward and outward course of development in the life of Jesus, and might treat the remainder of the Synoptic material how he chose, combining with it, at his pleasure, material drawn from John. The victory, therefore, belonged, not to the Marcan hypothesis pure and simple, but to the Marcan hypothesis as psychologically interpreted by a liberal theology.[17]

17 *The Quest of the Historical Jesus,* London, 1950, pp. 203 ff.

In other words, the decisive factor in the triumph of the Marcan (or two-document) hypothesis was not any particular scientific argument or series of arguments, however important some of these may have been. The decisive factor in this triumph according to Schweitzer was theological.

The unavoidable conclusion to which the historian of the Synoptic Problem is led is that Sanday, for all his acquaintance with the contemporary German scene, did not have a firm grasp of the history of Synoptic criticism, nor an adequate understanding of the subtle psychological and theological factors in the situation to which Schweitzer draws attention. This does not mean that Sanday was unaware of some of the dynamics operative in Germany in his own day. On the contrary, he seemed to have been fairly knowledgeable concerning the situation, which for some time had been dominated by the increasingly successful struggle of an alliance of conservative and liberal forces against the radical remnants of the Tübingen school to the left and the reactionary forces of Lutheran confessionalism to the right. The eventual theological leader of this new historico-critical school was Albrecht Ritschl, a former pupil of Baur, and once a member of the right wing of the older Tübingen school, but by the 1860's Ritschl had shifted from New Testament criticism to systematic theology, and the historical groundwork which was regarded as basic to this new school had been firmly fixed by Holtzmann, Weizsäcker, and B. Weiss—all of whom were committed in one form or another to Weisse's two-document hypothesis.

The members of this school are known in German church histories as the "mediating" theologians. Holtzmann was the most famous and most highly regarded scholar of the school.

An autobiographical note by Albert Schweitzer indicates that in his student days in Strassburg, Holtzmann's reputation and status as a scholar was such that no student dared to dispute his views. This was an honor which Schweitzer himself was disinclined to bestow on any professor. But he admitted that he could not help standing in awe of this great man.

Although Holtzmann, Weizsäcker, and B. Weiss were themselves primarily New Testament critics, the struggle in which they were regarded as scriptural authorities was essentially ecclesiastical and theological. Weizsäcker's appointment to succeed Baur at Tübingen was a sign of the real forces at work at that time. Therefore, the "popularity" of a particular solution to the Synoptic Problem among German theologians was especially likely to be influenced by the extent to which its advocates were allowed to teach in the universities, and the extent to which it could legitimately advance the cause of the current life-and-death church struggle. The real enemy was the Tübingen school and only incidentally the Griesbach hypothesis, which Baur had accepted. But there can be no doubt that the Griesbach hypothesis lost "popular" support with the collapse of the Tübingen school.[18]

Sanday was acquainted with the situation in Germany and he was aware of that contemporary scholarship which was considered by the Germans to be important. But there is no evidence that he had a firm grasp of earlier German Gospel criticism.[19] The German literature that he reviewed for the benefit of English readers came from the pens of scholars who belonged chiefly to the "mediating" school.[20] As a student at Oxford in the early sixties Sanday had already been alerted to the dangers of the radical and destructive criticism of German theology for English theology and church life. The question raised by conservative Evangelicals at Oxford at that time was whether historico-critical research should be applied to the Scriptures at all, in view of the results which were coming from the German universities. Sanday's trips to Germany and his contacts with the new "mediating" forces in German theology made him intimately aware of the fact that the historico-critical method was a two-edged sword which could be made to cut for, as well as against, the Church. Among the "mediating" theologians of Germany he

[18] The importance of the collapse of the Tübingen school for an understanding of the history of the Synoptic Problem was first brought out sharply by John H. Ludlum, Jr., in his article "New Light on the Synoptic Problem," published in two parts in *Christianity Today*, Vol. III, Nos. 3 and 4, November 10, and November 24, 1958.

[19] In his article in Smith's *Dictionary of the Bible*, in 1893, Sanday went back no further than the Tübingen school in his survey of the history of the Synoptic Problem. In his brief survey of the history of the Synoptic Problem in his first article in the series "A Survey of the Synoptic Question," for the *Expositor*, Vol. III, 4th series, 1891, pp. 88–91, Sanday seems to be completely dependent upon the information given in B. Weiss's *Einleitung* for what he relates about the pre-Tübingen period. B. Weiss's account is not a complete history of the Synoptic Problem, but primarily a chronicle of the development of the two-document hypothesis. While it contains valuable information, it is like those accounts which pass for histories of Philosophy and which make it appear that the Greek atomists were men who anticipated modern science, and that history is a chronicle of such transhistorical relationships, instead of the story of the inner dynamics of a matter which can only be laid bare by writers who have a firm grasp of the problems involved.

[20] *Op. cit.*, pp. 90–91.

found a *modus vivendi* in which his critical interests could be given free reign, without his feeling that they would lead him away from the church. The exact causal relationship between Sanday's later theological orientation and his early experiences in Germany has as yet to be defined. But it cannot be denied that there is a basic and sympathetic kinship between the "mediating" theology of Germany and the fundamental theological and ecclesiastical operational stance of Sanday and of every young English scholar over whom he exercised any considerable influence, including Sir John C. Hawkins and B. H. Streeter. Lock in his memorial to Sanday wrote:

England has lost the theologian who formed the greatest present link between her scholars and those of America and the continent of Europe. . . . Through the whole of his life he was attempting to mediate between traditional ideas and the claims of modern criticism. . . .[21]

Leaving aside the genetic question it is evident that Sanday, despite his occasional criticisms of its members, psychologically identified himself throughout his life with the mediating school of German criticism. And in so doing he would seem to many to have been amply vindicated. For in his own lifetime men were to watch the radical criticism of Baur flower out into the Christ-myth school which in Germany, Holland, England, and America went so far as to deny the historical existence of Jesus. And at the other extreme, the right wing of conservative Evangelicalism, especially in Holland, England, and America, developed into a reactionary antimodernist movement which in an obscurantist manner tended to sever all connection with "higher" criticism.

The only way it is possible to understand Sanday's attitude toward the two-document hypothesis is to recognize that for him it was the single most important presupposition of that historico-critical school of German criticism, which he believed to be right on the essential theological problems. Actually Sanday's attitude toward the two-document hypothesis was perplexingly ambivalent. When he spoke as a student of the Synoptic Problem he was appropriately cautious, and readily acknowledged that there were serious critical objections to this hypothesis.[22] But at other times he endorsed it simply on

---

[21] *Op. cit.*, pp. 97–98.
[22] *Inspiration*, p. 281; *Expositor*, 1891, p. 426.

the grounds that an increasing number of scholars were accepting it.[23]

Sanday's interest in the solution of the Synoptic Problem was clearly practical. Following the statement he made during his Bampton Lectures in 1893 concerning the difficulties that prevented him from propounding a solution to the Synoptic Problem for the benefit of his hearers, he said:

It must not be thought that I despair of a solution. I greatly hope that before very long a sustained and combined effort, for which the circumstances are now particularly favorable, may be made to grapple at close quarters with the difficulties and wring from them a better result than has been obtained hitherto. If we do not do it, others will, because attention is being very much directed to the subject, I would however lay stress on the hopes which I entertain from combination. I feel sure that more could be done in this way than by individual efforts however skilful.[24]

This is Sanday's apologia for his famous Oxford seminar, which he began the year following in 1894. This seminar met more or less regularly nine times a year over an extended period of sixteen years. It is the most sustained literary-critical project on record.[25] And the

[23] In 1893, with regard to the priority of Mark Sanday wrote: "It is, if not an assured result of criticism, yet rapidly becoming so." (Smith's *Dictionary of the Bible*, p. 1224b.) In 1902 he expressed himself as follows: ". . . speaking broadly it may be said that on what is called the *priority of St. Mark* there is an imposing amount of agreement among scholars of all nationalities . . . there is also considerable agreement in the view that there was a second primitive document. . . . Taken together these two assumptions . . . constitute what is known as the two-document hypothesis . . . [which] is at the moment more largely accepted than any other . . ." (*Criticism of the New Testament*, St. Margaret's Lectures, 1902, pp. 12 ff.). Five years later in 1907 Sanday wrote: "Quite recently two of Germany's foremost scholars have come to grapple at close quarters with problems of the Gospels, Wellhausen and Harnack. . . . It is also interesting and also important that Wellhausen and Harnack without any connection with each other as well as all the other writers I have mentioned agree in postulating these two documents (Mark and Q) as at the base of the Synoptic tradition. So far as consent can prove anything—and it is to be remembered that in this case the consent is of scholars of the highest competence who have all worked together and closely upon the facts—we may really, I begin to think, take the second document as well as the first as practically assured." (*The Life of Christ in Recent Research*, Oxford, 1907, pp. 154 ff.) However, between 1893 and 1907 no new arguments and no new evidence had been discovered to support the two-document hypothesis. And Sanday's own Oxford seminar, after over a decade of continuous research, had not been able to reach any new consensus, but rather had achieved results which called the two-document hypothesis into question. This, however, was not to be made obvious for another four years with the publication of essays from members of the seminar. (*See* Chapter V.)

[24] *Inspiration*, p. 282.

[25] *Studies in the Synoptic Problem*, edited by W. Sanday, Oxford, 1911. Rev. Sir John C. Hawkins, *Horae Synopticae, Contributions to the Study of the Synoptic Problem*, Oxford.

fruits of this seminar are fully worthy of the time and effort which were put into it. In addition to the essays which were contributed by its members to the volume *Oxford Studies in the Synoptic Problem*, published in 1911, Hawkins' famous *Horae Synopticae*, published in 1898 and revised in 1909, should be closely identified with this seminar, and Streeter's *The Four Gospels*, published in 1924, should be regarded as the final legacy of the Oxford Seminar, where the young Streeter got his start.

For convenience's sake, but not without real justification, one may think of this seminar as having created an "Oxford school" of Synoptic criticism. And in this sense, it would be fair to say that the influence of this "school" of Synoptic criticism has been greater than any other in the English-speaking world.

Indeed German critics, although they generally stand aloof from Streeter's four-document hypothesis, and especially his theories on Proto-Luke, have never challenged the classical defense of the two-document hypothesis which he gave in his "Fundamental Solution," and Hawkins' *Horae Synopticae* has been singled out by them for the highest praise. Of course the twentieth century German New Testament critics who have cited respectfully the careful work of these Oxford scholars were themselves only later members of the same historico-critical school with which the younger Sanday identified himself from the beginning. So they really have only recognized the later fruit of the seeds of a particular school of criticism transplanted from German to English soil.[26]

The very fact that English scholars have ignored the Cambridge scholar Marsh who anticipated by forty years the "two-document" hypothesis with his primitive א and ב is an indication of the extent to which this English school of Synoptic criticism is but a phase of the historico-critical work going on in the German universities after the collapse of the Tübingen school. In some instances the Oxford scholars went into greater detail than did the German scholars as, for example, in the statistical studies of Hawkins. But where the "Oxford" school went beyond the two-document hypothesis, as in the idea of a Proto-Luke, no new consensus was formed.

There is no convincing evidence that Sanday ever abandoned his

[26] It may be doubted that many German critics have been fully aware of the indebtedness of the "Oxford school" to Holtzmann and his contemporaries. In any case it is notable that neither Hawkins nor Streeter makes reference to Holtzmann's epoch-making work.

belief in the essential validity of the two-document hypothesis, all his cautious reservations notwithstanding. And his own statement about the procedure of his seminar indicates that he was pre-occupied with settling the residual problems created by the acceptance of this hypothesis.

The Gospels, he tells us, were taken up section by section as they are arranged in a synopsis. Different synopses were used, but the same method was followed. The views of one or two of the leading commentators were reported "usually beginning with the very close and careful treatment of Dr. Bernhard Weiss," then the passage was discussed freely by the members of the seminar.[27] Such a method encouraged preoccupation with the views of the commentators consulted—chiefly Bernhard Weiss, whose particular solution of the chief problem for the two-document hypothesis (i.e., agreements between Matthew and Luke against Mark) was finally vindicated in the young Streeter's proof that Mark knew "Q." Streeter accomplished this in a brilliant manner. He began by noting that

There are several places where Matthew, Mark, and Luke are all three substantially parallel, but where the variations in detail and additions in which Matthew and Luke agree against Mark are so striking that it is clear they must have derived their versions in part, if not wholly, from some other source than Mark.[28]

This "other source" of course was assumed to be "Q." Streeter then examined these passages and found that Mark's text was dependent on and posterior to that of Matthew and Luke. This is shown, he claimed, "by two constantly recurring sets of phenomena." These are:

(a) The Marcan version is almost invariably the shorter, but the brevity is caused by the omission of features in the Q version which are obviously original. The Q version is not an expansion of the Marcan, the Marcan is a mutilation [sic] of the Q version.

(b) It frequently happens that Mark conflates [sic] into a single saying portions of what appear as two separate sayings in Q, or combines [sic] into one context sayings which appear apart and in what appear to be more appropriate contexts in Q.

This led the young Streeter to the following conclusion: "The *cumulative* effect . . . is irresistible, and must establish beyond

---

[27] *Studies in the Synoptic Problem* (hereafter referred to as *Oxford Studies*), p. viii.
[28] "St. Mark's Knowledge and Use of Q," *Oxford Studies*, p. 166.

reasonable doubt that Mark was familiar with Q."[29] This is right, but only if all possibilities, except the two-document hypothesis, are precluded from consideration. For most of the phenomena to which Streeter called attention can be explained better on the Augustinian hypothesis—and all the phenomena which he considered can be explained better on the Griesbach hypothesis. Indeed the evidence noted by Streeter that Mark "mutilates," "conflates," and "combines" texts which are found in their more original form in Matthew and Luke, is strikingly supportive of the Griesbach hypothesis. De Wette and Bleek found evidence pointing in the same direction throughout the entire text of Mark, and this led them to the view that Griesbach's hypothesis offered the best critical solution to the Synoptic Problem.

It seems evident that the excellent commentaries of de Wette and Bleek were not among those regularly reported on in Sanday's seminar. In any case there must have been some overriding consideration that blocked out from view any serious concern for either the Augustinian or the Griesbach hypothesis. Otherwise it is difficult to understand how Streeter could have refrained from including some reference to the bearing of his findings on the merits of the Griesbach hypothesis at least.

In fact there were such considerations. Among them were certain arguments advanced in behalf of Marcan priority. The most important of these was first presented in a paper read at Oxford in 1886 by F. H. Woods, tutor of St. John's College. Sanday realized the importance of Woods' work and encouraged him in it. In 1890 this paper was published in a volume of essays by members of the University of Oxford of which Sanday was a chief editor.[30]

C. Woods' Argument in
Behalf of Marcan Priority

Although Woods' essay was published several years before Sanday opened his seminar on the Synoptic Problem, it may be regarded as a proleptic contribution of the Oxford school. First of all it had deeply impressed Sanday. In his own words he described it as a "very

[29] *Op. cit.*, p. 176.
[30] "The Origin and Mutual Relation of the Synoptic Gospels," *Studia Biblica et Ecclesiastica. Essays chiefly in Biblical and Patristic Criticism*, Vol. II, Oxford, pp. 59–104.

careful and elaborate essay."[31] The essay is in fact a detailed argument for the priority of Mark. And Sanday's early judgment of its merits is very revealing: ". . . I believe that it will retain a permanent and even classical value."[32]

But of even greater consequence for the history of the Synoptic Problem was Hawkins' estimate of Woods' essay. In his influential treatment of the Gospel of Mark in the second edition of his *Horae Synopticae*, Hawkins refers to "the theory now very generally held, that a source corresponding on the whole with our present Gospel of Mark was used by the other two Synoptists as a basis or *Grundschrift* [*sic*]. . . ." And he adds:

For English readers this view is clearly explained and effectively supported by Mr. F. H. Woods in *Studia Biblica*: his arguments seem to me to lead irresistibly to the result which he thus expresses, "we conclude, therefore, that the common tradition upon which all the three Synoptics were based is substantially our St. Mark as far as *matter, general form,* and *order* are concerned."[33]

Then with regard to this conclusion of Woods, he further says

[31] *Expositor*, 1891, p. 181.

[32] *Op. cit.,* footnote 2. In this footnote, Sanday apologizes for not having given Woods' essay a more conspicuous place, and explains that "the point with which it deals is one as to which I have long been convinced." It is not clear whether the "point" Sanday has reference to is the priority of Mark or the argument from order. *See also* his statement "The argument from 'order' has been very neatly and effectively stated by Mr. F. H. Woods in *Studia Biblica*." ("A Plea for the Logia," *Expository Times*, Vol. IX, 1900, p. 472.)

[33] p. 114. In a footnote Hawkins adds: "The same view is well expressed and illustrated by Jülicher, *Introd. to N.T.*, E.T., pp. 348 ff." Jülicher, however, recognized clearly that the Synoptic Problem cannot be satisfactorily explained on the terms of the Ur-Marcus hypothesis: ". . . for in that case it would be equally extraordinary that he [Mark] should, practically without exception, have appropriated to his own use precisely those portions which had also been selected thence by the other two." Jülicher, having previously eliminated from consideration the possibility that Mark drew from Matthew and Luke, concluded: "Mark, then, served as the source both for Matthew and Luke." This is not a logical conclusion based upon an impartial consideration of all hypothetical possibilities, else it would be a *non sequitur*, as Butler and others have shown. It is an historical judgment, based upon a consideration of the three major alternatives of the nineteenth century: (1) Griesbach, (2) Ur-Marcus, and (3) a modification of the Ur-Marcus hypothesis, by which it is envisioned that Mark was a direct source for Matthew and Luke. Jülicher objected to the view that Mark drew from Matthew and Luke on the grounds that: ". . . then we should be forced to assume that with an extraordinary partiality he always chose out those portions which were common to *both* his predecessors, while to explain the origin of those portions we should have to resort to some entirely new hypothesis." This objection is not convincing, because (a) it is conceivable that a writer would choose not to deviate significantly from a text to which his sources bore concurrent testimony (*see* p. 78), and (b) the origin of the agreements between Matthew and Luke is susceptible of a satisfactory explanation

that this "may now (1909) be called a practically certain result of modern study of the 'Synoptic Problem.'"[34] It is apparent that one reason members of Sanday's Oxford Seminar never gave serious thought to either the Augustinian or Griesbach hypothesis could have been the fact that the priority of Mark was taken for granted as a methodological presupposition of the work of the seminar, and that Woods had provided "irresistible" arguments leading to that conclusion.

The irresistible character of Woods' logic resolves itself into an elaborate presentation of the old argument from order first set forth by Lachmann. It is not clear whether Woods realized this or not. He acknowledged that his results "contained little" that was "absolutely new." But he made no specific reference to Lachmann. The important point is that his entire case falls to the ground unless Matthew, Mark, and Luke all independently copied some Ur-gospel. This point is obscured in Woods' essay by the fact that he goes on to argue against Holtzmann's view that Ur-Marcus was more extensive than our Mark. He believed that his arguments "prove conclusively that the original basis [*Grundschrift*] of the Synoptic Gospels coincided in its range and order with our St. Mark."[35]

It further seemed to Woods

a priori probable, though not a necessary consequence, that if the common basis of the Synoptics can be found to have coincided in range and order almost exactly with our St. Mark, it did so also in language.[36]

The effect of Woods' essay, therefore, was to narrow the gap between Ur-Marcus and Mark to practical insignificance—and to pave the way for Streeter's logical fallacy of thinking that the argument from order still held after the idea of an Ur-Marcus had been completely abandoned and Matthew and Luke were conceived to be directly dependent on the text of Mark. Here is a germinal seed of one of the most calamitous misconceptions in the history of the Synoptic Problem.

---

on the assumption that there was direct literary dependence of one upon the other, or of both upon a common source. And in any case Jülicher's solution, which, like that of Streeter, posited direct literary dependence of Matthew and Luke upon Mark, faced serious difficulties. As these difficulties are delineated in this chapter the reader should understand that they are quite as real for the Holtzmann-Jülicher tradition of Synoptic criticism, as they are for the Holtzmann-Streeter tradition.

[34] p. 115.
[35] *Studia Biblica*, p. 61.
[36] *Op. cit.*, p. 95.

The plausibility of Woods' proof of the practical originality of Mark was strengthened by the fact that at the end of it he was able to append the following note:

Unfortunately it was not till this essay was in the press that I had an opportunity of seeing Dr. Holtzmann's new work *Die Synoptiker*, Freiburg, 1889. It is gratifying to find that he has given up I believe all the opinions which I have ventured to criticize, especially that fundamental theory of an Ur-Marcus larger than our Synoptical Gospel. He now holds that St. Mark itself was the main source of both St. Matthew and St. Luke. In fact the argument on which he lays the greatest stress is just what it has been my chief object to point out, the continuity of the Marcan order traceable in these two Gospels.[37]

To Woods, this work of Holtzmann gave "important additional support" to his arguments. But more important, it had the effect of converting Woods' essay into a kind of *Magna Carta* of Oxford Synoptic criticism. For it indicated that Woods' independent research which led him to criticize Holtzmann's famous work of 1863, was in fact being vindicated by independent developments going on in Germany. With Woods' essay in hand, it was possible to feel that here were results completely free from any dependence upon German scholarship. In fact, however, without the hypothetical concept of Lessing's Ur-gospel, independently copied by Matthew, Mark, and Luke, Woods' essay is quite inconclusive. Woods, however, may never have fully realized this. For in his appended note just quoted, he represented Holtzmann as holding at one and the same time the notion "that St. Mark itself was the main source of both St. Matthew and St. Luke," and the notion that the argument from order supported this view. But if Matthew, Mark, and Luke are directly related to one another rather than being indirectly related through some earlier source which all three have independently copied, then the phenomenon of order no more supports the priority of Mark than priority of Matthew or Luke. Here is the earliest evidence of an error that B. C. Butler sixty-five years later was to term the Lachmann fallacy (a fallacy of which Lachmann himself, however, was never guilty).[38] When Streeter structured this logical *non sequitur* into his "Fundamental Solution" in 1924, he was

---

[37] *Op. cit.*, pp. 94–95.
[38] "The Lachmann Fallacy," *op. cit.*, pp. 62–71.

merely making explicit a notion which had been implicitly held in the "Oxford school" from the beginning.

In part, then, Streeter's oversight of the fundamental logical fallacy in his basic argument for the priority of Mark was the result of a developing tradition which began with a plausible form of the argument from order and then moved almost imperceptibly to Streeter's form of the argument. The period of time it took for this tradition to develop extended from 1890, the date of publication of Woods' essay, until 1924 when Streeter wrote his *The Four Gospels*.

D. The Fate of the

Griesbach Hypothesis

I. WOODS' ARGUMENT AGAINST GRIESBACH

Woods' essay was primarily conceived to prove the originality of Mark, but it also discredited the Griesbach hypothesis. He wrote:

> It might be argued that the results arrived at by our examination would be equally accounted for on the hypothesis that the whole of St. Matthew and St. Luke existed previously to St. Mark, and that he compiled his Gospel from them, adopting now the order of one, now the order of the other. But the following objections seem fatal to such a view.[39]

The objections which Woods then set down were not fatal to the Griesbach hypothesis, though to one convinced of the originality of Mark on other grounds, they no doubt "seemed" weighty. Woods' objections are four in number and are worthy of comment.

(1) We cannot reasonably account for the remarkable omissions which St. Mark must continually have made, such as the Birth and Childhood of our Lord, the details of the Temptation, the Sermon on the Mount, the full ministerial directions to the Apostles or the Seventy, and above all the accounts of our Lord's appearance after His Resurrection. All these are topics which would have become of increasing interest and importance as the Church grew; and it is extremely unlikely that we should find them in the earlier Gospel, and not in the later.[40]

[39] *Studia Biblica*, pp. 66–67.
[40] p. 67.

It would suffice to point out that this is no real objection to Mark's having been written after Matthew and Luke, since such considerations equally well lead to the conclusion that John also could not have been written after Matthew and Luke, which notion to the impartial critic is a patent absurdity, even if on other grounds he thought John was written before the others. But the argument from omissions is inconclusive at best, and there is no hypothesis which does not face this problem in some form. As Streeter demonstrated by his proof that Mark was familiar with "Q," the problem of omission is also serious on the two-document hypothesis. For if Mark knew "Q" how it is possible to explain his omission of so much of the material that was in "Q"? And even if Mark did not know "Q," as Streeter decided later was more probable, what explanation can be given for the omissions Matthew and Luke made from Mark? Streeter listed the various considerations influencing writers to omit material from their sources, but then observed: "But even when we can detect no particular motive, we cannot assume that there was none; for we cannot possibly know, either all the circumstances of Churches, or all the personal idiosyncrasies of writers so far removed from our own time."[41]

(2) It is almost impossible to suggest any method by which St. Mark could have made his selection.[42]

To the extent that a critic personally felt this way, after having made a careful analysis of Mark, this would be a weighty objection indeed. But it cannot be regarded as a fatal objection to the Griesbach hypothesis by the impartial critic who has himself as yet made no effort to rethink the redactional method of each Evangelist, and then made the further effort to compare the relative difficulty of understanding their respective editorial practices on alternate hypotheses.

(3) This view would not account for the order of St. Mark in several passages, especially in [the] section [of Mark 3:7–6:13], and would certainly not explain how it is that the parallels with St. Matthew and St. Luke so frequently over-lap.[43]

Woods did not specify the passages for which the Griesbach hypothesis would not account, so that it is difficult to comment on his third objection, except to note that the chief merit of the

41 *F.G.*, p. 169.
42 p. 67.
43 p. 67.

Griesbach hypothesis for all its adherents was its ready explanation for the phenomena of order. As for the overlapping to which Woods refers, it is true that Mark's conflation of Matthew and Luke would not of itself account for this. But according to Griesbach, Luke first used Matthew and then Mark combined Matthew and Luke. This means that Mark was combining two Gospels between which there already existed a relationship of literary dependence.

Therefore, the redactional process envisioned by Griesbach was neither simple nor mechanical. The comment made with reference to the preceding objection would be equally relevant here.

(4) Lastly, this view leads us into greater difficulties than those it proposed to solve. The relation between St. Matthew and St. Luke, which the views argued out in this paper at least partially explain, become an almost hopeless enigma, at which we can only guess. We seem therefore forced to adopt the opposite alternative, viz., that St. Matthew and St. Luke both made use of a Gospel very nearly agreeing with our present St. Mark in its subject matter and the order of its contents.[44]

Woods is correct in noting that on the Griesbach hypothesis one is still obligated to account for the relationship between Matthew and Luke, and it is true that adherents of that hypothesis never reached a consensus on this point. But all these objections together fall short of "forcing" the impartial critic into adopting Marcan priority. At most they should lead him to suspend judgment until the relative merits of each hypothesis have been weighed carefully. Woods' essay certainly did not accomplish this.

It is difficult to know to what extent these four objections might have influenced members of Sanday's Oxford Seminar to make no reference to the Griesbach hypothesis—not even when their results, as in the case of Streeter cited above, supported that particular solution.

From a completely different direction, however, there were similar developments which would have operated against any serious consideration of the relative merits of the Griesbach hypothesis. These developments are associated with the names of two Cambridge trained scholars, Abbott and Rushbrooke, whose collaboration produced results which had a wide and extensive influence on the history of Synoptic criticism.[45]

[44] p. 67.
[45] *See* Chapter V, pp. 190 ff.

2. ABBOTT, DAVIDSON, AND THE THEOLOGICO-CRITICAL CLIMATE

Edwin A. Abbott was a student at Cambridge in the early sixties, at about the same time Sanday was studying at Oxford. Like Sanday he developed an early and abiding interest in the Synoptic Problem. He was in his thirties when he was selected by the editors of the *Encyclopaedia Britannica* to write a major article on the "Gospels," which, in its published form in the 1879 edition, turned out to be a book-length essay of 75,000 words. This article exercised a profound influence upon the history of the Synoptic Problem in England. Reliable chroniclers of biblical criticism give it a prominent place.

In his book, *The Bible in the Nineteenth Century*, after indicating the progress of Marcan priority in Germany, Holland, and France, J. Estlin Carpenter wrote with reference to England:

In this country Dr. Abbott securely established it in his article on the "Gospels" in the *Encyclopaedia Britannica* (1879).[46]

Abbott's article began with an argument against the Griesbach hypothesis. The "method" by which he was to disprove the Griesbach hypothesis, he claimed would at the same time enable one to "establish" on an immovable [*sic*] basis, the originality of Mark. Abbott concludes his argument thus:

We may, therefore, regard it as absolutely certain that by far the greater part of Mark is not borrowed from Matthew and Luke, and that the duality of phrase, which is undoubtedly a characteristic of Mark, must be explained by other causes.[47]

Carpenter reviews Abbott's argument with approval and then notes: "The hypothesis that Mark was only an abstract of Matthew and Luke has never been revived."[48]

This is a strange report in view of the fact that three years after Abbott's article was published, Samuel Davidson, in the second edition of his *Introduction to the Study of the New Testament*, held that the Griesbach hypothesis was still the best solution to the Synoptic Problem, and set forth in detail the evidence which led him to adopt this hypothesis and to abandon the very elaborate version

[46] London, 1903, p. 302.
[47] All citations of this article will be made from the R. S. Peal Reprint, Chicago, 1892, of the 9th ed. of *The Encyclopaedia Britannica*, p. 791b.
[48] *Op. cit.*, p. 303.

of the oral hypothesis which he had worked out in the first edition of his *Introduction* in 1848.[49] Davidson's work had been highly regarded by the best critical minds of England and Germany. No British scholar since Marsh enjoyed as favorable an international reputation as he. Davidson was credited with having been the first to introduce effectively to the English-speaking world the science of New Testament introduction as espoused by the Germans. A few years after the first version was published Davidson resigned his academic post at the Lancashire Independent College, because the authorities of the college, alarmed at his views, passed resolutions concerning the dangerous character of his teaching. The ostensible reason for their alarm was his espousal of a documentary view of the Pentateuch. When Davidson requested them to specify their objections the committee declined the task "as unnecessary," and he was left no choice but to resign.

In his preface to the final edition (1894), Davidson reflected on the popularity of Salmon's *Introduction*.

In a country so ecclesiastically conservative as this, orthodox books are naturally greeted with a favour denied to productions of another stamp. But minds look at evidence differently, especially when the evidence is varying and doubtful. I need hardly say that I have tried to state it fairly and to deduce from it such conclusions as appear just. Bound by no dogmatic creed, I am free to follow wherever truth leads; having no sect, denomination, or church to please, I am subject to no temptation to conceal my real sentiments or to play the hypocrite for the sake of fame and gain. As to religion, it does not consist in theological science, and allows intellectual freedom when the heart is right.

Perhaps we hear overtones of pique and envy in these words from an old man. But these are also the words of a pioneer biblical scholar who sacrificed academic preferment in the interests of truths, many of which the twentieth century critic espouses with impunity.

Davidson's work may still be consulted with profit, especially by those interested in being exposed to the full range of New Testament criticism as it had developed up to 1882, the date of the second

---

49 2nd ed., *op. cit.*, pp. 352–584. Davidson's first *Introduction* had as its title: *An Introduction to the New Testament, Containing an Examination of the Most Important Questions Relating to the Authority, Interpretation, and Integrity of the Canonical Books, with Reference to the Latest Inquiries*, London. This *Introduction* was thoroughly revised in 1868 and published under the title *Introduction to the Study of the New Testament*. This revised edition was republished in a 2nd ed. in 1882, and again in a 3rd ed. in 1894.

edition. In contrast to the preoccupation with the work of members of the "mediating" school, as became increasingly the case among English scholars like Sanday and Abbott, Davidson's critical interests were more inclusive and less negative toward the Tübingen school. His comments on the work of Reuss reveal quite well the situation as Davidson saw it in 1882, just after Abbott's article was published in the *Encyclopaedia Britannica*.

Professor Reuss's recent publications on the New Testament are somewhat disappointing, savouring as they do of the Vermittelungs-Theologie ["mediating" school], and influenced to some extent by a reactionary spirit towards the Tübingen school. Though this school as represented by Baur and Schwegler has carried its speculations too far, the important advance it has made in the criticism of the New Testament cannot be reversed. Modified it may be; but its mark upon [the study of] early Christian literature is deep and permanent. In correcting its excesses moderation must be carefully preserved. . . .[50]

But Davidson's appeal went generally unheeded. At the suggestion of the influential Harvard professor, J. H. Thayer, the translation of Reuss's "History of the New Testament," had already been undertaken by Edward L. Houghton, a student in Andover Theological Seminary. It was published under the title *History of the Sacred Scriptures of the New Testament* in 1884, by T. and T. Clark of Edinburgh.

The same publishing house which in 1884 published Reuss's work fifteen years earlier had published an English translation of Bleek's *Introduction*. This fact of publishing history corresponds to a change in the critical climate of Western Europe. This change, which did not take place everywhere at the same time nor anywhere all at once, is the single most important fact of nineteenth century intellectual history affecting the theological and critical context within which the discipline of biblical studies was to find its *raison d'état*, and it may be described as a shift of the locus of theological initiative from the left to a point more toward the center. There was also a corresponding change in the role of criticism. In the earlier period criticism had a liberating influence. It was used as a tool by which thinking men could extricate themselves from an enslavement to a literalistic theory of inspiration on the one hand, and from the suffocating

[50] 2nd ed., p. v; 3rd ed., p. vii.

influence of an a-cosmic Pietism on the other. In the later period, however, criticism and Pietism were joined together in a new force. The change was only one of degree, but it was nonetheless noticeable and widespread. In the Roman Catholic Church, for example, there seems to have been no New Testament critic in the second half of the nineteenth century to match the critical brilliance and spirit of free inquiry which was found in the first half of the century in the work of a critic like Hug.

The turning point seems to have come in the reaction against the Tübingen school in both political and ecclesiastical circles in Germany. This reaction effected a realignment of liberal and conservative forces in German theology out of which emerged a great central party—the *Vermittelungs-Theologie* or "mediating" school.

The older Berlin school of Schleiermacher, de Wette, and Bleek, in which there was a remarkable spirit of free inquiry, nurtured by the theological and philosophical presuppositions of Schleiermacher's thought and writing, was not a direct party to this conflict, except as its members had been broadly critical of some of the theoretical procedures and results of Baur and his pupils. But though not directly involved in the reaction against the Tübingen school, men like de Wette and Bleek were certainly eclipsed by the new generation of Holtzmann, Weizsäcker, and B. Weiss. Although the works of de Wette and Bleek continued to be reissued in Germany, certainly by the eighties the future of New Testament criticism was firmly in the hands of the new "mediating" school. And the publication in Edinburgh of an American translation of Reuss's *Introduction* suggests that the strong points of the "mediating" school were appreciated not only in Germany, and the universities of Oxford and Cambridge, but elsewhere in the English-speaking world as well.

These strong points were brought out very clearly in the words of Marcus Dods, written in 1891 in his review of Sanday's Bampton Lectures:

> That the faith of the Christian should be healthy enough to find nutriment in every discovery of criticism goes without saying. That all truth must help and not hinder the cause of Christ is an axiom. But recent averments of criticism regarding Scripture have certainly disquieted many minds, and some re-assuring voice is greatly needed. No man seems better fitted than Professor Sanday to utter such a voice. He

is thoroughly informed, he is singularly fair-minded, he is sober, reverent, devout. Probably no man would be so naturally chosen to arbitrate between the traditionalists and the critics. Instinctively drawn to mediate in the present disquietude, Professor Sanday has delivered nine lectures. . . .[51]

Although these words were written in reference to Sanday's lectures on inspiration of the scriptures—they both describe the vocational character of Sanday and the practical needs of the times as understood by leading men.

Once it is recognized that responsible men like Sanday ignored the views of de Wette and Bleek and dismissed a critic like Davidson in a peremptory manner along with the members of the Tübingen school it is easier to understand how it became possible by the end of the century for Carpenter to say that Abbott's article in the *Encyclopaedia Britannica* "securely established" the priority of Mark in England and that thereafter the Griesbach hypothesis was "never" revived. He should not be taken literally. He was speaking in general terms about the way events actually developed. He might more accurately have said: "Abbott's argument against the Griesbach hypothesis was effective in persuading many, including myself, that Mark was not an abstract of Matthew and Luke." Even so, the historian must ask, "To what extent was there a widespread disposition, because of the theologico-critical climate, to receive uncritically arguments against the Griesbach Hypothesis?" The answer to this question may best be ascertained after examination of Abbott's argument. This argument is of considerable interest. It is based upon a phenomenon which Morton Scott Enslin thinks is "confessedly the most baffling and probably the crux of the whole problem of the relationship of our gospels," namely the minor agreements of Matthew and Luke against Mark.[52]

3. ABBOTT'S ARGUMENT AGAINST GRIESBACH

Abbott printed in full the Greek texts of all three Synoptic accounts of the Parable of the Wicked Tenants. The various kinds of verbal agreements between the Gospels were marked for the

[51] *The Expositor*, 4th series, Vol. IV, 1891, pp. 147–149.
[52] *Christian Beginnings*, New York and London, 1938, p. 430.

convenience of the reader. Abbott then observed that besides the matter common to all three, Mark and Luke have a good deal of additional matter in common, as do Mark and Matthew. But, in striking contrast, Matthew and Luke have no additional matter in common, except that in verse 3 of Mark they insert οἱ γεωργοὶ for clearness; in verse 7 they insert ἰδόντες; and in verse 9 they insert οὖν (Mk. 12:1–11∥Mt. 21:33–42∥Lk. 20:9–17).

Abbott then dismissed "The three trifling words" which Matthew and Luke "agree in adding" to the tradition common to all three, by accounting for their insertions as due to independent editorial alteration and improvement of the common text. He then claimed that "it can be proved by *reductio ad absurdum* that Mark did not copy from Matthew and Luke." Abbott's argument is as follows:

For suppose that he did so copy, it follows that he must not only have constructed a narrative based upon two others, borrowing here a piece from Matthew and here a piece from Luke, but that he must have deliberately determined to insert, and must have adopted his narrative so as to insert, every word that was common to Matthew and Luke. The difficulty of doing this is enormous, and will be patent to anyone who will try to perform a similar feat himself. To embody the whole of even one document in a narrative of one's own, without copying it *verbatim*, and to do this in a free and natural manner, requires no little care. But to take two documents, to put them side by side and analyse their common matter, and then to write a narrative, graphic, abrupt, and in all respects the opposite of artificial, which shall contain every phrase and word that is common to both—this would be a *tour de force* even for a skilful literary forger of these days, and may be dismissed as an impossibility for the writer of the Second Gospel.

Actually the agreements between Matthew and Luke against Mark in this parable are more extensive than Abbott has noted. There are additional agreements in omission, word order and case. But these agreements do not seriously affect the essence of Abbott's argument. Its plausibility depends upon the degree to which the reader experiences a sense of absurdity when he is asked to envision a writer with two documents before him, writing out "a narrative, graphic, abrupt, and in all respects the opposite of artificial, which shall contain every phrase and word that is common to both." But this would not seem absurd, if the writer intended to do exactly that.

Abbott has sought to heighten the sense of absurdity by contrasting Mark with a contemporary "skillful literary forger." Leaving aside the pejorative element introduced by the comparison of the Evangelist with a "forger," the more substantive contrast that Abbott presumably intends is that between the author of our Mark and a skillful writer. Abbott presumes that the reader understands that Mark is not a skillful writer. But how is that to be determined ? The best evidence would be the pleonasms with which Mark's text is replete. On the assumption that Mark's text reflects the author's best literary style critics usually conclude that it is cumbersome and by comparison with that of Matthew and Luke, unskillful. But if, in fact, Mark did conflate the texts of Matthew and Luke, then his skill or lack of skill would need to be judged in the light of that fact. Abbott's unjustified assumption that Mark was not a skillful writer and that he could not have performed the task of carefully conflating the two texts is obscured by the gratuitous introduction of forgery into the comparison. The sense of absurdity is thus heightened, but the argument, which at best is circular in character, is not really strengthened thereby.

It might well be an inhuman expectation of any writer to require that in conflating two such texts he should incorporate *every* word, i.e., not to omit an unnecessary subject, or particle—always to keep the exact word order—never to insert an unnecessary pronoun— never to change the case or number of a noun—never to allow his own style to influence his version of the combined text even when it did not affect its sense—that would be an inhuman expectation indeed, for it would reduce the writer to a mere literary mechanic and rob him of any creativity whatever, not to speak of eliminating the element of human fallibility. But this is precisely not the case in point and herein Abbott's argument contains a false proposition of some consequence. For the text of Mark is *not* exactly the same as that of Matthew and Luke when they agree. There *are* differences— minor differences to be sure. But the fact that they are minor in extent does not necessarily mean that they are minor in importance.

These minor differences of agreements of Matthew and Luke against Mark, instead of suggesting the plausibility of the Griesbach hypothesis to Abbott, as they might well have done, since they are consonant with that hypothesis, were explained by him in a way consistent with Marcan priority (but not without dependence on the notion of a common *Grundschrift*). Once having dismissed these agreements from view, Abbott felt free to ask the reader to think that on the Griesbach hypothesis one would be required to imagine that Mark conflated the texts of Matthew and Luke in such a way as never to deviate in a *single* word from the text they had in common. But of course this is not true, as may be seen from the very specimens of text he had printed for the convenience of the reader.

If on other grounds the reader were disposed to think Mark the earliest Gospel, then Abbott's argument, if read uncritically, might be taken as weighing against the Griesbach hypothesis. In fact, under just these circumstances, it did become a very powerful influence working not only against the Griesbach hypothesis, but for Marcan priority, and must be counted as one of the most important contributing factors to the eventual consensus that the priority of Mark was firmly established by nineteenth-century criticism.

But to one who was not disposed to think one way or the other about Mark, and was objectively attempting to weigh the evidence as impartially as possible, Abbott's argument is far from conclusive, and the objective critic would recognize that the claim to have established by this argument the originality of Mark on an "immovable basis" is unfounded, and that Abbott's recommendation to "regard it as absolutely certain" that the Griesbach hypothesis was false on the basis of his argument was ill advised.

In 1884 Abbott in collaboration with Rushbrooke republished this argument. Now, however, it was prefaced by a supporting propositional argument:

> *In the case of three narratives* A, B, *and* C (e.g. Mark, Matthew, and Luke), *if* A *contains much that is common to* A *and* B *alone, and much that is common to* A *and* C *alone, and* all that is common to B and C, *it follows generally that* A *contains the whole of some narrative from which* B *and* C *have borrowed parts.*[53]

At the end of the century F. C. Burkitt, at a lecture in Cambridge, paraphrased this argument, then added that the conclusion was "extremely important," that it was "the one solid contribution which the scholarship of the nineteenth century has made toward the solution of the synoptic problem," and that there was "no escape from the logic" of Abbott's "singularly lucid statement."[54]

---

53 Edwin A. Abbott, and W. G. Rushbrooke, *The Common Tradition of the Synoptic Gospels*, London, 1884, p. vii.
54 F. Crawford Burkitt, *Two Lectures on the Gospels*, London, 1901, pp. 46–47.

Burkitt then explained that there was no escape, because the only real alternative, namely "that Mark borrowed from Matthew and Luke," is ruled out by Abbott's argument against the Griesbach Hypothesis, which argument Burkitt then quoted in full. In ways such as this the consensus of Marcan priority was formed by later scholars who uncritically and at face value took over arguments which were actually inconclusive, and endorsed them as "solid" contributions of nineteenth-century scholarship.

In the text of Abbott and Rushbrooke, however, there is an explanatory transition between the propositional argument and the argument *reductio ad absurdum* which Abbott had previously used in his original article in the *Encyclopaedia Britannica*. This explanatory transition reads as follows:

The important clause in this proposition is that "A contains all that is common to B and C," in other words, that Mark contains (as happens in some passages) *all that is common to Matthew and Luke*. For how could this happen (to the extent to which it occasionally happens, not amounting to a word or phrase or two, but to a considerable part of the whole) on the supposition that Mark borrowed from Matthew and Luke? Mark could only have achieved such a result *by carefully underlining all the words common to Matthew's and Luke's narratives*, and by then writing a narrative of his own, which should *include all these words* and yet preserve the natural style of an original composition.

To the reader who has followed carefully Ernest De Witt Burton's definitive monograph on *Principles of Literary Criticism and the Synoptic Problem*, the suggestion that Mark could not have proceeded in the way Abbott describes in conflating the narratives of Matthew and Luke is not convincing.[55]

Burton considered the situation where a writer had before him two documents, where the author of one had copied the other, and recognized the fact that such a writer "might conceivably depart from either or both of his sources, when they were not in agreement, but avoid departing from them in that to which they bore concurrent testimony."[56] This is indeed conceivable, in which case it would not have been unnatural for such a writer to have prepared the texts of his two sources in some such way as Abbott had described—though this

[55] Published in 1904 in *The Decennial Publications* of the University of Chicago, Vol. V.

[56] Burton's recognition of this redactional possibility is found in a footnote p. 9 (p. 201). He does not use it as it is now suggested it can be used.

need not have been done by the writer, but could have been achieved by someone else for any one of several reasons. Once the texts of Matthew and Luke had been so prepared, it would not have been an impossible or even an unnatural task to have conflated them in some such manner as Mark is imagined to have done on the Griesbach hypothesis. In fact no such underlining need necessarily have taken place. All that is required is to imagine that the Evangelist thought in terms of meeting a need for a form of the Gospel which deviated in no significant sense from the narrative to which the texts of Matthew and Luke "bore concurrent testimony." Under these circumstances the author of such a Gospel would have incorporated the common text of his sources into his own work whenever he followed the text of the one or the other where the second had copied the first. So that on the Griesbach hypothesis, whenever Mark copied Luke where Luke had copied Matthew, Mark was thereby incorporating into his Gospel the text common to Matthew and Luke. And whenever Mark copied Matthew where Matthew had been copied by Luke, Mark was likewise thereby incorporating into his Gospel the text common both to Matthew and Luke. It is true that he might have deviated more often than he did from the texts of Luke and Matthew respectively in these passages, which on the Griesbach hypothesis would suggest that he was mindful of his task and that he was guided by some such purpose as Burton regards to be conceivable for a writer in his situation. It would follow from this that where the texts of such a writer's sources did not bear "concurrent testimony," that is, where they deviated, he would then be free to follow the one or the other, or to make use of other sources if he had access to them, or to compose his text in such a way as to combine their differing accounts, or even to exercise his own creative imagination. None of this is self-evidently incompatible with the kind of result that exists in Mark.

4. STANTON'S ARGUMENT AGAINST GRIESBACH

Burkitt was not alone at Cambridge in taking the view that the Griesbach hypothesis had been "ruled out" of consideration. Three years after Burkitt's inaugural lectures, the Cambridge University Press published the second volume of Vincent Henry Stanton's three-volume work, *The Gospels as Historical Documents*. Stanton was at that time the Ely Professor of Divinity in Cambridge University, and through his lengthy and scholarly survey of the Synoptic Problem in Hastings' *Bible Dictionary*, he enjoyed the reputation of being an authority on this subject. That dictionary article in the Hastings *Bible Dictionary* published at the beginning of the century, and the second volume of his *magnum opus* published in 1909, strengthened the Cambridge professor's influence in giving to successive student generations and to the general reading public strong reassurances that the priority of Mark was "one of the most widely accepted results of modern criticism of the Gospels."[57]

Stanton's references to the Griesbach hypothesis disclosed insights in relation to the question both of the merits of its proposed solution and the manner in which these merits were countered by an adherent of Marcan priority. Stanton opened his discussion of the Griesbach hypothesis as follows:

It was a merit in Griesbach's Hypothesis that it brought the relations between St. Mark and the two other Synoptics into view together. And consequently in any attempt to deal comprehensively with the evidence bearing on the origin of the Gospels this hypothesis can hardly fail to appear on the scene, as an alternative explanation, *albeit one to be rejected.*[58] [Italics mine, W.R.F.]

Stanton then proceeded to outline the nature of the phenomena of agreement in subject matter, order, etc., between the Gospels in a way that reflects the influence of Abbott and Burkitt on his formulation. Then he made an interesting admission of some importance for the history of the Synoptic Problem.

First Stanton assumed (mistakenly of course) that the Griesbach hypothesis concerned only the relationship of Mark to Matthew and Luke. Then he noted that the "parallelism between St. Luke and St. Matthew in Marcan contexts is left altogether unexplained by Griesbach's theory." "That theory," he continued, "calls for another besides itself to complete it, and such a supplementary theory is not forthcoming."

[57] *The Gospels as Historical Documents*, Part II, "The Synoptic Gospels," Cambridge, pp. 30–31. In tracing the history of the Synoptic Problem at this point, Stanton, as is also true of his article in *H.D.B.*, shows dependence upon the survey of the matter in Weiss's *Einleitung*. The major difference is in the greater importance given to Holtzmann. (The same can be said for Sanday's survey. *See* footnote 19.)
[58] *Op. cit.*, p. 33.

The supplementary theory Stanton had in mind was that there must also have been some kind of literary relationship between Matthew and Luke. But of course this was always a part of the Griesbach hypothesis in all forms. As held by Griesbach himself and members of the Tübingen school, the Griesbach hypothesis entailed Luke's use of Matthew. As modified by de Wette and Bleek, it entailed the use of an Ur-gospel by Matthew and Luke. Stanton continued: "We should not, indeed, be at a loss for one (i.e., a supplementary theory), if we could hold that either our first or our third evangelist had used the work of the other as one of his principal sources. . . ." "But," concluded Stanton, "that possibility has already been excluded." A footnote refers the reader to an earlier discussion where the proposition is set forth: *"Our third evangelist was not to any considerable extent dependent upon the first (or the first upon the third) for the common contents of their gospels."* This was followed by a reference to Simons' view that Luke knew Matthew, which view Stanton admitted had been accepted by "a certain number of critics," but which he had "sufficiently allowed for" in saying that Luke *"was not to any considerable extent* dependent upon St. Matthew." This was followed by certain objections to the view that Luke knew Matthew, the chief one being: "the task of separating the various portions of the matter (matter common to Matthew and Luke) from the context in which they stand in St. Matthew and putting them together and introducing them again as they appear in St. Luke would have been a very troublesome one, and there could be no good reason, so far as we can see, for undertaking it."

Such objections as this are largely gratuitous, though they draw attention to the fact that in the history of the Synoptic Problem the redactional process followed by Luke in his use of Matthew seems never to have been effectively set forth by the adherents of the Griesbach hypothesis. Nonetheless, Stanton is prepared to grant that the Griesbach hypothesis is viable in some instances.

It is true that in some instances phrases, or whole sentences, occurring separately in St. Matthew and St. Luke but conjointly in St. Mark, might have been intentionally combined in the way that Griesbach's theory assumes.

In a footnote Stanton added:

E.g., at Mk. 1:32 // Mt. 8:16 // Lk. 4:40, it would not have been difficult to combine ὀψίας δὲ γενομένης (Mt.) δύνοντος δὲ τοῦ ἡλίου (Lk.) into ὀψίας δὲ γενομένης ὅτε ἔδυσεν ὁ ἥλιος (Mk.) Moreover, early and medieval writings in which more than one source has been drawn upon would supply not a few illustrations of patchwork of this kind. The conflate readings of which there are many in manuscripts of the Gospels may likewise be compared.[59]

It would seem that the recognition of such support for the Griesbach hypothesis would issue in a full-scale investigation of its relative merits as compared to that of Marcan priority. Instead Stanton counters these arguments in favor of the Griesbach hypothesis with certain objections.

Stanton's first objection amounted to the claim that it was possible to explain this same phenomenon on the Marcan hypothesis. He wrote: "But, in the first place, those who hold that a document most nearly represented by our St. Mark lay before the two other Synoptics are not precluded from supposing that an editor of the former has here and there introduced into it touches from the two other Gospels." This seems to be an original idea to account for the pleonastic character of Mark's text. According to Stanton's idea, whenever there are duplicate phrases in the text of Mark where one-half occurs in Matthew and the other half in Luke, it is legitimate for adherents of Marcan priority to imagine that an editor of Mark, under the influence of either Luke or Matthew (which Gospels according to this idea must be presumed to be known to this editor), has introduced into his text, from one of these Gospels, a duplicate phrase, thus converting a nonpleonastic text of Ur-Marcus into the pleonastic text of the canonical Mark. According to this idea all the manuscripts of Mark are descendent from this edited text, since these pleonasms are well attested in the best manuscripts of Mark.

Stanton's idea cannot be disproved. But it would hardly occur to a critic to think of an idea like this if he were not predisposed to some notion of Marcan priority which he was seeking to defend in the face of evidence more readily explicable on some rival hypothesis. According to the Griesbach hypothesis the Evangelist Mark, rather than some later editor, was held responsible for the same pleonastic text, but through the more normal (i.e., well known) process of combining or conflating two closely related texts.

Stanton's second objection to the Griesbach hypothesis was in substance that it would have been a "troublesome" or "impossible"

[59] *Op. cit.*, pp. 35-36.

task for Mark to combine Matthew and Luke. He concluded his objection categorically: "Their different expressions [those of Matthew and Luke] have not been fitted together in St. Mark, but can reasonably be regarded as recastings of St. Mark." Two passages were cited in a footnote to illustrate the objection. The first is Mark 1:30,31 // Matthew 8:14,15 // Luke 4:38,39. Stanton discussed the passage from the perspective of Marcan priority and concluded: "Mark's words might well have suggested the form either in St. Matthew or in St. Luke; but it is inconceivable that any rational being would have set himself to fuse the two and thus have produced what Mark has written."

A careful study of the passage concerned, however, does not bear out Stanton's judgment. For assuming the conceivable situation that Mark was working with Matthew and Luke and did not wish to depart from the text to which they bear concurrent testimony, but was free when they depart from one another to follow one or the other or to combine the two or to improvise—under these circumstances the text of Mark is not self-evidently a text which a rational being might not have produced.

The chief differences between Matthew and Luke in the first part of the story of "The Healing of Peter's Mother-in-Law" is that in Luke the incident was introduced by a transitional phrase concerning Jesus' leaving the synagogue and entering Simon's house, whereas in Matthew there is no reference to the synagogue and it is Peter's house Jesus enters. In the second part of the story the chief difference has to do with the action of Jesus. In Matthew Jesus touched the woman's hand, but in Luke Jesus did not touch her hand but stood over the woman and rebuked the fever. On the Griesbach hypothesis the text of Mark was explained as a combination of the account in Matthew and Luke, in which Mark had not departed from that text to which Matthew and Luke bear concurrent testimony.

In verses 29 and 30 Mark followed Luke's account at those points where Luke differed from Matthew, and in verse 31 Mark followed Matthew's account at those points where Matthew differed from Luke. For the critic unaccustomed to think of Mark's Gospel as having been composed in this way, a conflated text might well seem inconceivable. But Stanton has already acknowledged that "it would not have been difficult for Mark to have combined" Matthew 8:16

with Luke 14:40 to produce Mark 1:32.[60] The two cases are somewhat different, but it is unclear on what basis Stanton regarded the one as explicable on the Griesbach hypothesis, but not the other.

The second passage which Stanton cited to illustrate his objection to the Griesbach hypothesis was Mark 2:24 ‖ Matthew 12:2 ‖ Luke 6:2. The text of Matthew reads: "But when the Pharisees saw it, they said to him, 'Look, your disciples are doing what is not lawful to do on the sabbath'." Luke reads: "But some of the Pharisees said, 'Why are you (pl.) doing what is not lawful to do on the sabbath?'" The text of Luke is such that the antecedent of the plural "you" may refer back only to the disciples of Jesus or may be taken to refer to Jesus and his disciples together. In any case, the difference between the accounts is twofold: (1) In Matthew the Pharisees addressed Jesus about the conduct of his disciples, whereas in Luke they addressed the disciples directly. (2) In Matthew the rebuke of the Pharisees was put in the form of a direct assertion, whereas in Luke the rebuke was cast into the indirect form of a question.

On the Griesbach hypothesis the text of Mark would be explained as follows: Mark combined Matthew and Luke without departing from that text to which they bore concurrent testimony except in his stylistic substitution of καὶ for the postpositive δέ (verse 24); and the historic present λέγει for the aorist εἶπεν (verse 25), neither of which alterations affects the sense of the text. He followed Matthew in showing the Pharisees addressing Jesus concerning the conduct of his disciples, and then he followed Luke in casting their rebuke into the form of a question.

After observing that "it cannot be supposed that anyone would have tried to give what the first and third evangelists have written in Mark's form," whereas on the Marcan hypothesis the explanation of the text is "natural enough," Stanton stated as his departing comment on this entire matter: "Such cases are innumerable." If this is true, the conclusion is that there are innumerable cases where agreements and differences between Matthew, Mark, and Luke can be explained on the Griesbach hypothesis. The historian of the Synoptic Problem is led to ask anew, "how could it have been possible for the Griesbach hypothesis to have received no more serious attention than was afforded to it by the leading students of the synoptic problem at both Oxford and Cambridge, even granting

[60] *Op. cit.*, p. 35, footnote 2.

the powerful influence of the arguments of Woods and Abbott against this hypothesis?"

E. Preliminary Observations

The objection against the Griesbach hypothesis that there is no proof that the need ever existed in any Church for a Gospel like Mark to be produced out of Matthew and Luke, and that such a procedure "may be dismissed as an impossibility" for the Evangelist Mark, are nicely met by the previously cited twofold dictum of Streeter: "We cannot possibly know, either all the circumstances of churches, or all the personal idiosyncrasies of writers so far removed from our own time."[61] Though Streeter used these words in a different context, they call attention to the fact that available knowledge of the needs of the Churches for which the Gospels were produced, and knowledge of the purposes and literary methods of the Evangelists is largely derived from inferences based upon a critical study of the Gospels themselves, and not vice versa.

If knowledge concerning the time and circumstances under which Mark was written were available, Mark could be viewed against the background of the situation of the Church at that time and possibly some statements could accurately be made about what needs did or did not exist or what literary methods would or would not have been appropriate. But even then, available knowledge of the Church in the first two centuries is such that in most cases this still would be somewhat precarious. Meanwhile, so long as the question at stake is that of the time and circumstances under which Mark was written, it is methodologically unsound to rule out any hypothesis which

---

[61] *See* footnote 41. Nor can those who so object deny that the original defenders of Marcan priority were actually aware of this same problem on the Marcan hypothesis. "The ultimate difficulty felt by so many modern critics about the Gospel of Mark is not the minor discrepancies in the narrative, though they are present, or the tales of miracle, for it is always possible to allow for unscientific description or exaggeration. The difficulty lies in its presentation of the actual contents of the 'Gospel' itself and the career of Jesus." F. Crawford Burkitt, *The Earliest Sources for the Life of Jesus*, New York, new and revised ed., 1922, pp. 49–50. The mystery of the purpose of Mark on the Marcan hypothesis has been heightened by the results of "form-criticism," in that Mark is further removed from the earliest tradition, in the total impact it makes as a Gospel, than is either Matthew or Luke. There is much late material in all the Gospels, but the proportion of material that is recognized on the basis of "form-criticism" to be early or authentic, is much greater in Matthew and Luke than in either Mark or John. Nor can this fact be explained by appeal to the use of "Q" by Matthew and Luke, for much of the earliest tradition is found in the material peculiar to these gospels.

satisfactorily explains the literary phenomena of the Synoptic Problem, merely on the basis of a presumed knowledge of the history of the Church or a history of the development of Christian doctrine, especially when such presumed knowledge is in fact based on a reconstruction which has been in part formed by a particular solution of the Synoptic Problem (i.e., Marcan priority) which is in conflict with the hypothesis being tested (that of Griesbach, or any other). To proceed in such a way would be to argue in a circle, which is exactly what Abbott (and a host of others since) did in arguing that certain passages in Mark were earlier than their parallels in Matthew or Luke, on the basis of an assumed theory of doctrinal development in the primitive Church.

None of this is meant to suggest that such considerations as have been reviewed above are to be construed as arguments *for* the Griesbach hypothesis. The point to be emphasized, however, is that an analysis of those formative or germinal arguments of Woods and Abbott which are cited by later authors as decisive in establishing Marcan priority in England, indicate that the general debate over the Synoptic Problem did not issue in a full and impartial testing of alternative hypothesis such as that of Augustine or Griesbach, but rather concentrated on resolving the residual difficulties inherent in the two-document hypothesis as imported from Germany. There has been no definitive treatment of the question of Marcan priority. Yet the one thing that was needed above all by those who adopted the work of critics like Holtzmann was some compelling reason to believe in the priority of Mark. That was the single most unlikely feature in the two-document hypothesis. That there were early collections of sayings material antedating the time when the Gospels were written was altogether plausible. For the sayings material in the Gospels themselves indicated as much. But the view that Mark was the earliest Gospel was in conflict with the best external evidence scholars could adduce, and far from self-evident on the basis of internal evidence.[62] Sanday's seminar was a sustained sixteen-year

[62] Holtzmann brought this out clearly in 1863 in his recognition that Matthew is not infrequently more original than Mark, and that sometimes Mark has in only a shorter form what Matthew and Luke have more fully. He lists thirty-six significant agreements between Matthew and Luke against Mark, and concludes that Mark cannot be the earliest Gospel: "In der That steht es fest, dass unser kanonischer Marcus kein Originalwerk sein kann." *Op. cit.*, pp. 60–67. It was not until after 1880 that Holtzmann was free to change his mind and pronounce Mark as the earliest Gospel, used as a source by both Matthew and Luke. This change was made possible because by then

"combined" effort to mount a successful assault on the Synoptic Problem—but so far as the historian can determine, this effort seems to have been carried out *within* the general boundaries of one form or another of the two-document hypothesis. This is candidly the position of Sanday even at the very end, when other members of the seminar were producing results which raised questions about "Q."

The opening words of his essay in *Oxford Studies* are as follows:

> We assume what is commonly known as the "Two-Document Hypothesis." We assume that the marked resemblances between the first three Gospels are due to the use of common documents, and that the fundamental documents are two in number.[63]

This sounds very much like an introductory formula, not only for the opening essay, but for the work of the seminar so far as Sanday was concerned. It is a precise formulation of the minimum but essential common ground shared by Holtzmann, Weizsäcker, and B. Weiss ever since Sanday's early visits to Germany. It was still the common ground even more widely held in Germany by 1894 when Sanday first opened his seminar. Since then five student generations had come and gone, and Sanday had been throughout that period the undisputed leader of the seminar.

In 1878 Sanday had reviewed B. Weiss's "Das Matthäus—Evangelium und seine Lucas—Parallelen," in *The Academy*. At that time he simply noted that there were three rival theories: (1) that of Griesbach, which he significantly referred to as "the Tübingen

---

he had become convinced that Luke had used Matthew, and in this way he was able to reduce the difference between Ur-Marcus and Mark to the point of practical insignificance. But Holtzmann at no time would have been able to agree with the position of Jülicher and Streeter—that Luke did not copy Matthew *and* that there was no Ur-Marcus. For Holtzmann, nurtured in the Synoptic criticism of Bleek and other pre-Holtzmann critics, knew well that there were secondary features in the text of Mark which created serious difficulties for any such view. There was, however, one ingredient in Holtzmann's synthesis, which could be exploited in such a manner as to obviate the necessity of both an Ur-Marcus and Luke's use of Matthew, and still allow for Marcan priority, namely "oral tradition." Without the concept of oral tradition it is doubtful that the idea of Marcan priority would have survived the nineteenth century testing of the two-document hypothesis. Because oral tradition allows the critic such flexibility, it is not easy for the post-Jülicher-Streeter critic to recognize as serious difficulties, secondary features in the text of Mark, which, when faced by Holtzmann, forced him to posit either an Ur-Marcus, or Luke's use of Matthew.

[63] "The Conditions Under Which the Gospels Were Written, in Their Bearing Upon Some Difficulties of the Synoptic Problem," p. 3.

Theory," (2) the "Two-Document" theory, and (3) the "Oral" theory. Sanday's mediating tendencies were apparent even then, for he expressed the sanguine view that: "These three theories, however, have of late shown an increasing tendency to approximate to each other." This hopeful prophecy was picked up the year following and cited with favor by Abbott in his article in the *Encyclopaedia Britannica*.

But at that time Sanday was not willing to go farther than to concede that he agreed to the priority of Mark in "a general sense." The chief problem, as Sanday saw it, centered in those cases where Mark could best be explained as being in some sense secondary. All advocates of the two-document hypothesis at that time agreed that there were such passages—many of them in fact. Sanday observed: "Two ways—and, as it would seem, only two—are open. The one has been adopted by Dr. Holtzmann, the other by Dr. Weiss."

These two ways were: first, the idea of an Ur-Marcus that was more extensive than canonical Mark and which Matthew and/or Luke sometimes preserved more faithfully than Mark—held by Holtzmann (and Weizsäcker); and second, the idea of an overlap between Mark and the *Logia*. Mark combined the Petrine tradition with material drawn from the *Logia*, which was conceived of as more than a collection of sayings and having the form of a Gospel. Matthew and Luke then copied both Mark and the *Logia*, drawing more fully from the sayings material in the *Logia* than had Mark—so B. Weiss.

Sanday raised objections against both alternatives, but chiefly against the view of Weiss. He thought that the Synoptic Problem had not yet been solved and it seemed to him that unless the view of Holtzmann (and Weizsäcker) could be established, it would be as well to fall back upon the traditional Augustinian hypothesis as to embrace Weiss's solution. This is very interesting, for in 1911 in his Introductory essay in *Oxford Studies*, in which he commented upon the essays of the other contributors, he wrote:

> It is not without reluctance that I have come round to the conclusions advocated by Mr. Streeter in Essay V, that St. Mark already possessed the knowledge of Q. This involves the complication, so often laid to the charge of the theory of Dr. Bernhard Weiss, that it implies the use of Q by the later evangelists twice over, once through the medium of Mark, and a second time independently. This is a complication that one would gladly

avoid if one could. But I have for some time had before my mind arguments similar to those put forward by Mr. Streeter, and in the form in which he states them they seem to compel assent.[64]

It is very important that the reader grasp the full significance of Sanday's admission. For he assented to the essential feature of Weiss's hypothesis, which thirty-three years earlier he had on critical grounds counted as "little better" than that of Augustine.

There is a note of irony in the fact that thirteen years later, Streeter altered his previous position and concluded his discussion of the overlapping of "Q" and Mark with the observation: "On the whole then, the evidence is decidedly against the view that Mark used Q."

For a period of forty-six years, and until today, a central problem confronting the advocates of the two-document hypothesis, as that problem was formulated by Sanday in 1878, has not been satisfactorily resolved—namely the instances where on critical grounds Mark has been acknowledged to be secondary. The need to resolve this problem was for all practical purposes obviated, however, by the developing consensus that Matthew and Luke had copied Mark and not some Ur-Marcus. After that consensus had become final the fundamental difference between Holtzmann and B. Weiss became academic. Scholars could disagree with little practical consequence about the extent and form of "Q" and its overlapping with Mark. These were questions incapable of proof in any case since "Q" itself was not available. But the consensus that Matthew and Luke copied Mark has never been firmly established.

It is helpful to delineate several distinguishable stages in the development of this consensus. First came the two-document hypothesis as imported from Germany. Then came logical arguments by Woods and Abbott claiming to disprove the Griesbach hypothesis and to prove the priority of Mark. But both men thought in terms of a *Grundschrift* behind the Synoptics, i.e., some kind of Ur-Marcus. The arguments of Woods and Abbott tended to reduce the gap between Ur-Marcus and the canonical Mark. Next came the acceptance of these arguments as proof of Marcan priority by scholars like Sanday, Hawkins, and Burkitt. Then further arguments were advanced against Ur-Marcus by Hawkins, Abbott, and

[64] P. xvi.

Burkitt, and finally came Streeter's "Fundamental Solution" where Matthew and Luke were held to be dependent on the canonical Mark and not on an Ur-Marcus.

This whole process presupposed something at the beginning that was later believed to be disproved, i.e., Lessing's idea of an Ur-gospel, a *Grundschrift*, or Ur-Marcus in Holtzmann's terms. Also essential to the process were the arguments of Woods and Abbott. But the argument of Woods is of no value without Ur-Marcus, and that of Abbott is logically inconclusive. Therefore, the confidence of men like Sanday, Hawkins, and Burkitt that such arguments had securely established the priority of Mark, was ill-founded, as was Streeter's "Fundamental Solution," which presupposed this whole development.

F. Burkitt's Lectures of 1906
and Streeter's Fatal Omission

In 1906, T. and T. Clark published ten lectures by F. C. Burkitt under the title, *The Gospel History and Its Transmission*. These had been delivered both in London, as the Jowett Lectures for 1906, and in Cambridge, as inaugural lectures on the occasion of Burkitt's becoming Norrisian Professor of Divinity. In his second lecture Burkitt copied verbatim large parts of his lecture on the Synoptic problem delivered in 1900, with one significant omission—that of Abbott's argument against the Griesbach hypothesis. He repeated verbatim his paraphrase of the propositional argument which had been introduced into the text of Abbott and Rushbrooke's *The Common Tradition of the Synoptic Gospels*, but inserted into that paraphrase the following proposition:

Moreover, the common order is Mark's order; Matthew and Luke never agree against Mark in transposing a narrative. Luke sometimes deserts the order of Mark, and Matthew often does so; but in these cases Mark is always supported by the remaining Gospel.[65]

From these facts, Burkitt drew the same conclusion he did in 1900—i.e., that the priority of Mark is the "one solid contribution made by the scholarship of the nineteenth century toward the solution of the Synoptic Problem." There was no reference to Abbott's name in 1906, which was not unfitting since he had by then

[65] *The Gospel History and Its Transmission*, Edinburgh, p. 36.

apocopated Abbott's argument so as to make its authorship almost unrecognizable, nor was there any reference to the name of Woods, who had first introduced the English public to the argument of order. Instead, having learned from Wellhausen about Lachmann, Burkitt wrote concerning the argument he had just reviewed: "And I think it will not be out of place to pause for a moment to pay a tribute to the memory of the great scholar Lachmann, who was the first clearly to formulate it as long ago as 1835." The antecedent of "it" in this statement is not the statement about the phenomenon of order, but the entire argument which is an illogical conflation of two different arguments. This indicates that Burkitt was not able to recognize that Abbott's propositional argument, which was formulated without reference to the phenomenon of order, was never previously connected with Lachmann's argument until in Burkitt's lecture of 1906.

Abbott's original argument, however, was not completely forgotten by Burkitt, and later in the same lecture, making use of the same terms, he was able to convert it into an argument against the idea of an Ur-Marcus. Burkitt wrote:

Suppose for a moment that the common source was not S. Mark, but some earlier document, the greater part of which has been incorporated in our S. Mark—a document, in fact, such as the Germans call *Ur-Marcus*. Well, then, we have Matthew, Mark, and Luke all basing their work upon this *Ur-Marcus*. What will be the result? As long as they all copy *Ur-Marcus* exactly, they will all agree. That is, indeed, what we often find. Sometimes one of the three, say Matthew, will not copy exactly: either he will drop something out, or add something fresh, or make some change or correction. In that case, if Mark and Luke still go on copying exactly, they will still agree, but Matthew will be different. That also is what we find, and the same is true if it was Luke who did not copy exactly. But if it was Mark that did not copy exactly when Matthew and Luke did, we should find Matthew and Luke agreeing against Mark; and this we do not find. Either, therefore, Mark always copied this hypothetical *Ur-Marcus* exactly, or we must suppose that wherever he did not copy exactly, Matthew and Luke also did not copy exactly.[66]

Here exists the same false proposition that was present in Abbott's original form of the argument, i.e., the statement that Matthew and Luke do not agree against Mark. This allows Burkitt to ridicule the

[66] *Op. cit.*, pp. 40–41.

only two conceivable alternatives he can imagine. Either "Mark always copied this hypothetical Ur-Marcus exactly"—which apparently Burkitt reasonably enough expected the reader to recognize as not likely, "or we must suppose that wherever he did not copy exactly, Matthew and Luke also did not copy exactly"—the unlikelihood of which coincidence actually taking place being itself quite obvious.

Although Burkitt's form of the argument entails the inaccurate proposition that there are *no* agreements between Matthew and Luke against Mark, these agreements are frequently so minor in extent as compared to the agreements between Matthew and Mark against Luke and Luke and Mark against Matthew, that as an argument against the idea of an Ur-gospel it does not necessarily lose *all* its force even when these minor agreements are considered.

Nonetheless, it could hardly be considered a compelling argument against Ur-Marcus, certainly not in the form in which Burkitt put it. Indeed, Burkitt did not claim that it was compelling.

The "most convincing" argument against an Ur-Marcus was, according to Burkitt, an argument completely original to himself— which he had first put forward in his Cambridge lecture in 1900. "The hypothesis of an Ur-Marcus," claimed Burkitt, "presupposes an interest in the biographical details of the public life of Jesus Christ, of which there is little trace elsewhere."[67] An examination of early Christian literature as a body, excluding the Gospels, discloses an interest in the rudiments of the Creed, together with an interest in Christian ethics. "But the details of the Galilean ministry of Jesus Christ are hardly mentioned." Burkitt concluded that Matthew and Luke represented far more nearly than Mark "the temper and preferences of the early churches." Whereas, "It is the peculiar merit of St. Mark's Gospel, from the point of view of the historical investigator, that it deals mainly with a cycle of events foreign to the life and interest of the growing Christian communities." That there are comparable characteristics of Mark which suggest for it a second century origin, Burkitt did not mention. But with the objections against Ur-Marcus weighing heavily in his mind, Burkitt asserted that there were only two categories of evidence which required the hypothesis of an Ur-Marcus: (1) passages where Matthew and Luke agree against Mark; (2) passages where "all

67 *Op. cit.*, pp. 60 ff.

three Synopticists being different, the differences cannot be explained from the text of Mark as it stands."

Burkitt then passed in review twenty passages of the first category, i.e., "where Matthew and Luke may be said to have minor agreements against Mark." These he took from the compilation of these agreements made by Hawkins in *Horae Synopticae,* and which indeed include some of the passages which are very difficult to explain on the Marcan hypothesis. But none of these passages were of the second category, and therefore, when, after discussing them, Burkitt concluded, "It appears to me that the evidence is extremely weak, and that we are not compelled by it to imagine a hypothetical *Ur-Marcus . . .,*" the antecedence of "it" is the evidence from the first category alone, and his conclusion did not touch the evidence for Ur-Marcus from the second category. In fact, Burkitt made no further reference to the evidence from the second category.

A careless reader might conclude that Burkitt's treatment of the evidence requiring an Ur-Marcus covered all the evidence that was relevant, and that only the minor agreements of Matthew and Luke against Mark were important in this connection. But that was clearly not the case, nor did Burkitt think it was. There is, however, an ambivalent character to Burkitt's treatment of the matter. And he clearly leaves the reader with the impression that the case for Ur-Marcus is unconvincing.

That there is a causal relationship between the ambivalent character of Burkitt's discussion of the case against Ur-Marcus and Streeter's treatment of the same subject cannot be proved. But it is significant that Streeter did not deal with the evidence of an Ur-Marcus from the second category. In fact, Streeter completely ignored the existence of any such evidence. He treated in great detail the problem of the minor agreements of Luke and Matthew against Mark, and also the problem of the major omissions Matthew and Luke have made from Mark which some regarded as requiring an Ur-Marcus. But there was no consideration of the very significant evidence for Ur-Marcus from passages where all three have material in common, but where there are differences between their accounts which cannot be explained on the assumption that Matthew and/or Luke copied Mark.

This fatal omission on the part of Streeter is all the more damaging to his "Fundamental Solution" in view of the fact that by 1924 he had been led to reverse himself and to take the position that: "On the whole . . . the evidence is decidedly against the view that Mark used Q."[68] For Mark's use of "Q" was, and still is for all conscientious adherents of the two-document hypothesis who reject the idea of Ur-Marcus, a necessary presupposition by which passages in Mark secondary to Matthew and Luke are believed explicable.

G. A Survey of the Pre-Streeter Treatment of the Minor Agreements of Matthew and Luke against Mark

In order to understand why Streeter was misled into thinking that if he could explain the minor agreements of Matthew and Luke against Mark he would have removed the only real ground for holding on to the concept of Ur-Marcus, it is necessary to review the history of the discussion of these minor agreements and to note the way in which they became the focal point of Synoptic criticism, so that right up to 1924, the date of Streeter's first edition of his *The Four Gospels*, C. H. Turner in the *Journal of Theological Studies* could write:

So long as it is supposed that there is a residuum of agreements between Matthew and Luke against Mark in matter taken from Mark . . . , so long will research into the Synoptic question be hampered and final solution be delayed. . . .[69]

I. ABBOTT

These agreements also featured prominently in Abbott's opening argument in his famous article in the *Encyclopaedia Britannica* in 1879. At that time Abbott was prepared to dismiss them as "trifling."

---

[68] *F.G.*, p. 191. It should be added that Streeter did take account of the fact that Matthew seems to have preserved a text more original than Mark in three instances. This phenomenon Streeter explained by the idea that Matthew's M source overlapped with Mark, and that in these three passages the more original form of the tradition was preserved in M and that Matthew in these three passages copied M rather than Mark. *Cf. F.G.*, p. 259.

[69] "Marcan Usage: Notes Critical and Exegetical, on the Second Gospel," *J.T.S.*, Vol. XXV, 1924, p. 377.

They could easily be explained as the kind of editorial changes Matthew and Luke would have introduced independently into their text of the *Grundschrift* behind the Gospels. In this way Abbott was able to identify the text of Mark with that of the *Grundschrift* in many passages, and thus by implication to narrow the difference between Ur-Marcus and Mark to insignificance.

By 1901, however, after an exhaustive study of all these minor agreements (about 230 of them), which he painstakingly compiled and printed as an appendix to his book, *The Corrections of Mark*, Abbott reversed his position on the grounds that these agreements were of such a nature as to lead him to the conclusion that they could not be due to the coincidental modifications made by two independent editors (Matthew and Luke), but must be due to the conscious effort of a single mind.[70] Fifty years earlier, such painstaking results would have been widely accepted as but one more indication that Mark was indeed working together the narratives of Matthew and Luke. From the point of view shared by adherents of the Griesbach hypothesis, when Mark was conflating Matthew and Luke, his own peculiar stylistic preferences, especially when they did not affect the sense of the text, would naturally have influenced his account of the Gospel narratives in just such a way as this.

But Abbott himself had closed that door by his "irresistible" argument against the view that Mark was secondary to Matthew and Luke. Thereby, he had shut himself up with but one escape. If the single editorial source of the characteristics of these minor agreements could not be traced to two independent editors (Matthew and Luke), nor to Mark, they must have been made by a single editor working on the text of Mark, making improvements or, as Abbott termed them, "corrections" in Mark's text. Matthew and Luke then could have used this "corrected" version of Mark, and canonical Mark would then appear not as a lineal descendant of the later edition, but of the original uncorrected text of Mark. This was an ingenious idea. And lest the reader dismiss it too hastily as an example of eccentric criticism, it will be well to allow a sympathetic critic to explain his understanding of the significance of Abbott's idea:

I reject the idea of an *Ur-Marcus*, or older form of the Gospel, because the great majority of the coincidences seem to me to belong to a later form

[70] *Diatessarica Part II, The Corrections of Mark Adopted by Matthew and Luke,* London, 1901, pp. 300 ff.

of text rather than an earlier. And I call this form of text a recension, because there is so much method and system about it that it looks like the deliberate work of a particular editor, or scribe exercising to some extent editorial functions.

This appears to come out clearly from Dr. Abbott's classification of the corrections. We may give this in Dr. Abbott's own words:

"They are, almost entirely, just such modifications of Mark's text as might be expected from a Corrector desirous of improving style and removing obscurities.

"(i) In about twelve instances Matthew and Luke adopt corrections defining subject or object. For example, where Mark omits the subject (leaving it to be understood as 'they,' 'people,' etc.) Matthew and Luke supply 'the disciples,' etc. . . .

"(ii) In about fifteen instances they correct in Mark the abrupt construction caused by the absence of a connecting word. . . .

"(iii) In about thirteen instances they correct Mark's historic present. This number does not include the corrections of Mark's use of 'says' applied to Jesus (see (v)).

"(iv) In about twelve instances they substitute the participle (e.g., 'saying') for the indicative with 'and' (e.g., 'and he says') or for the relative and for the subjunctive, e.g., 'whosoever has,' which is changed to 'those having,' etc.

"(v) In about twenty-three instances they substitute for Mark's 'says' ($\lambda\acute{\epsilon}\gamma\epsilon\iota$)' the word 'said ($\epsilon\hat{\iota}\pi\epsilon\nu$),' or correct Mark's imperfect 'used to say' or 'began to say' ($\acute{\epsilon}\lambda\epsilon\gamma\epsilon\nu$, more rarely $\mathring{\eta}\rho\xi\alpha\tau o\ \lambda\acute{\epsilon}\gamma\epsilon\iota\nu$). . . .

"(vi) In at least thirty instances Matthew and Luke agree in adopting the idiomatic Greek connecting particle ($\delta\acute{\epsilon}$)—commonly and necessarily (though most inadequately) rendered by the English 'but'—instead of the literal translation of the Hebrew 'and,' i.e., $\kappa\alpha\acute{\iota}$. . . .

"(vii) Another class of corrections includes improvement of Greek construction or style, by softening abruptness, of a different kind from that mentioned above . . . changing interrogatives into statements, introducing $\mu\acute{\epsilon}\nu$ . . . $\delta\acute{\epsilon}$, $\grave{\alpha}\lambda\lambda\acute{\alpha}$, or other particles, and altering Hebraic or vernacular words or phrases. In a few instances the correction may be made in the interests of seemliness, rather than of style. . . .

"(viii) In some cases, and notably in the use of the exclamatory 'behold,' Matthew and Luke appear to agree in returning to the Hebrew original (*Op. cit.*, pp. 300–304)."

The number and the recurrence of these phenomena is evidently due to design, and not to accident. What appears to have happened is something of this kind. Neither our present Gospel, even in the best text, nor the copies used by St. Matthew and St. Luke were exactly what St. Mark wrote. All our extant copies, whether of the Received Text or of those constructed upon the most highly critical principles, are descended from a single copy which, although very near to St. Mark's autograph, is not to be identified with it. A few mistakes or slight modifications had already crept in. In like manner, the copies used by Mt Lk were not St. Mark's autograph. Into them, too, changes had been introduced, and that with considerable freedom. And it happens that, while these two copies—the copies used by Mt Lk—were closely allied to each other, indeed we may say probably sister MSS., they belonged to a different family or different line of descent from that other important copy from which the great mass of our extant authorities is descended.

This is easily exhibited in the form of a diagram.

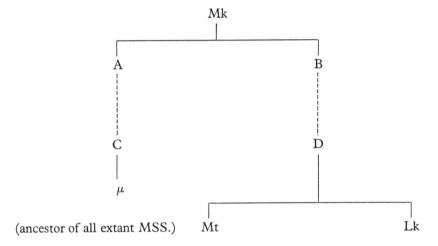

The question may be asked how it came about that these copies which were used by St. Matthew and St. Luke have not (like the A group) left descendents that have survived to the present day. It is never difficult to account for a MS. of this period perishing, and perishing without off-spring. The books of this date were almost all written upon papyrus, and papyrus is a frail material; and the Christian book must have been much used and exposed to accidents of many kinds. But there was a special reason why those two copies should perish unregarded. The moment the two longer Gospels of St. Matthew and St. Luke were written, the shorter Gospel of St. Mark was at a discount. In early times it was always the Gospel least used and least quoted. The two longer Gospels incorporated the greater part of St. Mark; and therefore the possessor of either of them possessed practically the substance of St. Mark as well: and so that Gospel fell into comparative, though of course not complete, disuse.

This is the way in which Abbott's new contribution affected the thinking of Sanday.[71]

2. SANDAY

Sanday apparently had never been persuaded of the plausibility of Abbott's original suggestion in 1879 of the way to account for these minor agreements. For Sanday saw them as part of a larger question: Why if Mark is the original Gospel is it in many passages clearly secondary to Matthew and Luke? This was the fundamental problem for the two-document hypothesis and, as Sanday made clear in his review of B. Weiss's work in *Academy* in 1878, the two best known solutions were championed respectively by Holtzmann and B. Weiss. Sanday in 1878 preferred Holtzmann's idea of an Ur-Marcus to Weiss's notion of Mark's use of the *Logia* in order to resolve this fundamental problem.

Thirteen years later, in 1891, Sanday published "A Survey of the Synoptic Problem" for the *Expositor*, in which he once again dealt with the question of Ur-Marcus.[72] This time also he was engaged in reviewing certain contemporary work on the Synoptic Problem. The context in which Sanday came to grips with the matter is worth reviewing for the light it throws on the historical conditions within which the minor agreements of Matthew and Luke against Mark were discussed at that formative period.

Sanday first disassociated himself from those who sought a solution to the Synoptic Problem on the basis of the oral hypothesis and identified himself with those "who are constrained to seek for the foundation of our Gospels in a written document," i.e., Holtzmann's *Grundschrift*. The first question to be answered, according to Sanday, was: What was its extent? He then noted that the consensus of those writers whose work he had reviewed was that "the fundamental document approached most nearly in its character to our present St. Mark." The question as to its extent, therefore, "is really a question as to its relation to our St. Mark." Sanday then explained to his readers that the view that there was an Ur-gospel like our St. Mark, "but not exactly to be identified with it," was based on the fact that there are instances where the preference for

<hr />

[71] *Oxford Studies*, pp. 21–23. J. P. Brown followed Sanday in "An Early Revision of the Gospel of Mark," *J.B.L.*, Vol. LXXVIII, 1959, pp. 215–227.

[72] *Expositor*, 4th series, Vol. III, pp. 180 ff.

originality must be given to one or both the other Gospels. As far as order was concerned he thought that without exception the order of Mark is the original since "there is no case in which the order of a section common to all three is supported by St. Matthew and St. Luke against St. Mark." This seemed also to be true, on the whole, he added, for the *language* of the Synoptic Evangelists. Earlier Woods' argument from order had been followed by a note in which he had argued that it was a priori probable that the language of Mark was also most original. But Sanday here for the first time spelled out this argument in a logical form, which had significant affinities with Abbott's argument for Marcan priority in the *Encyclopaedia Britannica.* Sanday wrote:

> If we take the sections common to the three evangelists, there is a vast number of expressions in which St. Mark coincides with one or other of his fellows against the third. Rather more often he coincides with Matthew against St. Luke; but the instances are also very numerous in which he coincides with St. Luke against St. Matthew. On the strength of this phenomenon, we say that he is *prior* to both.
>
> But here the facts are not quite so uniform as they are in regard to the order. The rule is certainly a rule which has the immense preponderance of instances in its favour throughout the Gospel. Still it is not without exceptions.[73]

Sanday then cited for purposes of illustration, the text of Mark 1:12–13 with the parallel texts from Matthew and Luke and noted:

> It will be observed that St. Mark has the double expression, "into the wilderness," and "in the wilderness." St. Matthew has the one, St. Luke has the other. Again, both St. Mark and St. Luke have the expression "being tempted," implying that the temptation was spread over the days. These are the kind of coincidences—though not nearly so strong or so numerous as in many sections—which suggest the use of a written document; and that document would be in these respects most nearly represented by St. Mark.

Although such coincidences in language might be construed as difficulties for the oral hypothesis, they cannot be so construed for any theory that envisions direct literary dependence. In fact, the double expression in Mark concerning the wilderness is taken by the adherents of the Griesbach hypothesis as a sign that the text of

[73] *Op. cit.,* p. 189.

Mark has been conflated from Matthew and Luke. Clearly by 1891, Woods and Abbott had prevailed in their view that the Griesbach hypothesis was no longer viable.

Sanday next cited the agreements of Matthew and Luke against Mark and noted that: "by the same criterion by which in a multitude of other instances we infer the priority of St. Mark, we should infer here his posteriority; we should infer that there was a common original which the other two Gospels represented better than he did."

Of course, the inference of a "common original" is forced upon the critic only if he is prepared to deny any direct literary relationship between Matthew and Luke, which was a cardinal principle of the two-document hypothesis as it was first conceived in Germany. In any case, according to Sanday, the phenomena to which he had brought the attention of his readers constituted "*prima facie* indication . . . of priority and posteriority side by side." Sanday continued:

It is this double aspect of the Gospel which has led many critics to think that, although our Gospel is very like the original document, it is still not identical with it; that behind our St. Mark there was an original or proto-Mark slightly different from it. There are obvious difficulties and improbabilities in this view. Foremost among them is the question, how it can have entered into the head of anyone to alter a document which lay before him just in these small respects and no more.[74]

And then Sanday concluded: "The student of the Synoptics is brought here face to face with a real problem; and he will do well to set steadily before him all the possible hypotheses he can think of for its solution."

On the basis of Woods' essay, however, and on the basis of Abbott's article it is doubtful whether Sanday would have regarded those hypotheses purported by them to be ruled out by their arguments as belonging to the category of "possible" hypotheses. In any case, there is no evidence that Sanday himself ever looked with favor upon any theory which questioned the basic premises of the two-document hypothesis.

Sanday's own contribution to the solution of this residual difficulty for the two-document hypothesis remained strictly within the limits set by its basic presuppositions:

[74] *Op. cit.*, p. 191.

One hypothesis, which I am myself inclined to keep in sight, though I should not venture to say that it was adequate to explain the facts, is, that these facts were not so much editorial as textual, that they did not mark any deliberate recension of the Gospel, but were only incidental to the process of copying. This I think we can prove, that as we approach nearer to the autographs, the freedom of the copyists increases. In the first two or three copies, especially of the Gospel of St. Luke, it must have been very considerable indeed. Here we have a *vera causa*, which may be introduced if we want it. I hope some day to test more exactly how far it will carry us, but I doubt if it will carry us far enough.[75]

The point of importance for the history of the Synoptic Problem is the idea that the differences between the Gospels might be explained as "only incidental to the process of copying." Its plausibility rests on the fact that in textual criticism the later manuscripts tended to conform more closely to one another than the earlier. Sanday reasoned that the very first copyists might have introduced considerable changes into their copies of the Gospels. His idea would seem to account most simply for a particular minor agreement of Matthew and Luke against Mark on the theory that in this case the texts of Matthew and Luke preserve the true text of the Ur-gospel, and that some early copyist of Mark felt free to introduce a change into the text of his copy, and that this change has been preserved in the best extant manuscripts of Mark. Like Lessing's idea of the Ur-gospel this idea of Sanday's can neither be proved true or false. Therefore, it could be taken up and modified indefinitely by subsequent critics as indeed it was.

3. STANTON 1893

Two years later, V. H. Stanton took up the same problem. His general position in relation to that of Sanday is quite interesting. Like Sanday he rejected the oral hypothesis and accepted one part of the two-document hypothesis, i.e., the priority of Mark (on the Ur-Marcus hypothesis); at that time he was skeptical of the second part, i.e., that Matthew and Luke both copied the *Logia*. Stanton was also quite conscious of the minor agreements of Matthew and Luke against Mark, but was not concerned about their importance for the question of the relationship between Ur-Marcus and our Mark as was Sanday, but for quite another reason. Stanton wrote:

[75] *Op. cit.*, p. 191.

It must probably have occurred independently to many students of the Synoptic problem, as it had to the present writer, that the cases of which I am now speaking must be the crucial ones for deciding whether St. Luke was directly dependent upon our St. Matthew. And it is upon these cases mainly that Simons bases his argument in his thesis entitled *Did the third Evangelist use the canonical Matthew*?[76]

Then Stanton noted that Simons' thesis was directed against two other explanations of the same phenomena: (1) Holtzmann's appeal to the idea of Ur-Marcus; (2) Weiss's appeal to the idea of Mark having knowledge of the *Logia*, and then he concluded: "Against both of these Simons' argument appears to be very telling." Stanton praised Simons' work and noted that Simons made significant use of agreements in omission as well as positive agreement between Matthew and Luke against Mark. By themselves agreements in omission did not seem very important. But when "taken in conjunction with more positive features" where there was a concatenation of agreement between two gospels against the third, then "they are worthy of being noted." This is an insight which unfortunately Streeter ignored in his classic treatment of these agreements. For he regarded all such agreement in omission as insignificant.[77]

Stanton next noted, however, that Simons did not really grapple with certain difficulties in the way of the view that Luke knew Matthew—the chief of which seems to have been the difference between the two Gospels. Simons' explanation of these differences was that where Luke differed from Matthew he was following the *Logia*. But this explanation did not satisfy Stanton who himself was unconvinced of this aspect of the two-document hypothesis.

Therefore, Stanton asked whether there might not be some other way of explaining the minor agreements of Luke and Matthew against Mark, which would not require Luke to have known Matthew. He answered by saying that he believed that the operation of three causes was sufficient to account for this.

(a) In adapting St. Mark's narrative some of the changes would naturally suggest themselves to both writers. Many coincidences between them might occur, which it would not be fair to call the result of accident; for the same general principle would in part guide both evangelists in dealing

---

[76] "Some Points in the Synoptic Problem. III. Some secondary Features," *Expositor*, 4th series, Vol. VII, London, 1893, p. 263.

[77] *F.G.*, pp. 295-296.

with the same authority. (b) Tradition as known to both may have been marked by these forms of expression in which they differ from St. Mark. (c) For some of the similarities, copyists may be responsible. A process of assimilation of the texts of the Gospels may have been going on at a time prior to the earliest of which textual criticism can give us any information, like that which we know to have taken place at a later time.[78]

Stanton's first cause was essentially the same as that of Abbott in his article in the *Encyclopaedia Britannica*. The second was new, unless "Tradition" here were understood in the form of the *Logia*, in which case this would be but a version of B. Weiss's explanation for these agreements. As for Stanton's third cause, a footnote referred the reader to Sanday's article in the *Expositor*, where he first suggested the process of copying as a *vera causa* to explain these same phenomena. However, Stanton had either misunderstood or radically developed Sanday's idea. For Sanday said nothing about textual "assimilation." His idea of freedom on the part of the earliest copyist explains why one out of the three is different from the other two. Stanton's idea seems to be quite another, though it is clear from his reference to Sanday in his footnote where the source of his idea was to be found. Stanton had in mind the fact that later copyists sometimes conformed their text of one Gospel to the parallel text of another. And he conjectured that this may have been going on at a date prior to that of the earliest manuscripts. In this way, a particular agreement between Matthew and Luke against Mark could be explained in the following manner: (1) all three Evangelists copied a particular passage of the Ur-gospel faithfully; (2) some early copyist (for the sake of the example, say a copyist of Matthew), introduced a change into the text of his copy of Matthew; (3) this copy then became the parent of the best manuscript tradition of Matthew for this passage; (4) some later copyist in possession of one of these altered copies of Matthew, while copying Luke, conformed the text of the copy of Luke he was making to that of this particular altered text of Matthew; (5) then this "assimilated" text of Luke became the parent of the best manuscript tradition of Luke for this passage; (6) meanwhile, the text tradition of this passage in Mark was not similarly altered nor affected by corresponding assimilating tendencies. Accordingly, the way to approximate most nearly the true text of Ur-Marcus and of the autograph of both

[78] *Op. cit.*, p. 265.

Matthew and Luke would be by following the single reading of Mark and ignoring the double-attested reading in Matthew and Luke. It cannot be proved that this idea was not implicit in the mind of Sanday when he first introduced the notion that such agreements against Mark could be accounted for by the process of copying. But it can be shown that Stanton was the first to make the idea explicit.

The importance of all this for the history of the Synoptic Problem is that Sanday's idea as modified by Stanton, and applied first by Hawkins and under his influence by Burkitt and then Turner, finally, in the hands of Streeter, developed to the point that the whole procedure was reversed, and instead of the process of copying being used simply as a cause to explain a difficulty for the two-document hypothesis, the priority of Mark was made the basis of an "objective criterion" by which, in some cases, the text critic could decide which of alternate readings was the best.[79]

4. HAWKINS

In 1899, three years before Abbott's exhaustive study of the minor agreements, Hawkins had published the results of his own careful study of the same phenomena in his *Horae Synopticae*, under the title "The Alterations and small Additions in which Matthew and Luke agree against Mark." This title makes clear that Hawkins presupposed the Holtzmannian *Grundschrift* as basic to his methodological procedure.[80] Hawkins' method also presupposed "Q," and his study of these phenomena was structured by a questionable methodological procedure, which was taken over by Streeter with devastating results. This has to do with the idea of dividing the phenomena of agreements between Matthew and Luke against Mark into separate categories according to the way the phenomena can most simply be explained on the two-document hypothesis.

Hawkins began by noting that out of the 183 sections into which Tischendorf had divided his *Synopsis Evangelica*, 68 afforded opportunities for comparing parallel passages of all three. Out of these 68, there are 10 "in which a considerable amount of matter,

---

[79] The questionable character of this procedure has not gone unnoticed. *Cf.* N. A. Dahl, "Die Passionsgeschichte bei Matthäus," *New Testament Studies*, Vol. II, 1955, p. 21.

[80] *Cf.* ". . . a source corresponding on the whole with our present Gospel of St. Mark was used by the other two Synoptists as a basis or *Grundschrift* . . ." Hawkins, *Horae Synoptica*, 2nd ed., p. 114.

chiefly consisting of discourse, is found in Matthew and Luke, while it is absent from Mark." Hawkins' solution for these passages was "to suppose that . . . the editors of Matthew and Luke turned to the Matthaean Logia, or some other such document ('Q'), in search of additional matter which should contain more of the teaching of Jesus than was supplied by Mark." The methodological question to be asked is this: On what critical basis are these particular agreements of Matthew and Luke against Mark segregated from all others? If Hawkins' appeal to "Q" to explain agreement in *these* passages is valid, why not in the others? The critical answer to this methodological question within the two-document school had always been: "there is no justification for such a separation." Either explain them all as B. Weiss had done, which leads one to the conclusion that the *Logia* was in the form of a Gospel, or explain none of them this way in which case one is forced to resort to the idea of an Ur-Marcus of greater extent than our Mark, as was true of the earlier Holtzmann. But why "either-or"? Why not "both-and"? Why not do as Hawkins had done, and separate these passages from those where the agreements were less extensive, and which, therefore, could be considered, as they were later so termed by Burkitt, as "minor" agreements? It then would be possible to appeal to other causes, such as those which Abbott and Sanday had first suggested, to explain these "minor" agreements.

But so to proceed is to adjust methods to preconceived conclusions. It is to argue in a circle. The real question at issue is whether the two-document hypothesis is valid, i.e., whether this residual problem for the two-document hypothesis can be resolved. If reliable tests should be applied, they would need to be applied impartially to all the phenomena of a given category without preferential treatment to any particular subcategory of phenomena where the phenomena in the subcategory do not have some common characteristics differentiating them from the phenomena in the category as a whole. The agreements of Matthew and Luke against Mark constitute a legitimate category of phenomena. But Hawkins has here set up a subcategory for these ten passages. If asked what common characteristics differentiate these ten passages from the other fifty-eight, where there are agreements between Matthew and Luke against Mark, the only answer is that the extent of the agreements between Matthew and Luke against Mark is greater in these passages. But this difference is only one of degree. Why stop at ten; why not make a separate category for the top five or the top fifteen?

The very idea that here motivates Hawkins is lethal to the science, not to speak of the art, of literary criticism. It is impossible to make progress in the attempt to understand the literary relationship between two documents when the literary phenomena are analyzed into categories on the basis of their compatibility with a particular solution to the problem in view. The categories must be formed on the basis of some objective criterion, independent of any pre-conceived hypothesis. After this has been done, theories may be hypothecated to account for the existence of the categories. In scientific work categorizing is only for the convenience of simplifying the problem of grasping the totality and variety of the phenomena themselves. This means that identical or similar phenomena must be grouped carefully on the basis of the nature of the phenomena. Otherwise, categorizing makes the task of comprehending the true nature of the totality of the phenomena more difficult, and in some cases virtually impossible. This is precisely what has happened to the phenomena of the agreements of Matthew and Luke against Mark at the hands of Hawkins, and later Streeter.

Hawkins says that the ten passages he put in his first category and which he then explained by appealing to the idea of an overlap between Mark and "Q" are "chiefly" made up of discourse. But in fact these ten passages cannot be legitimately separated from all others as a group on that basis. If the sixty-eight passages where Matthew, Mark, and Luke have parallel material are taken and on a completely objective basis the top ten or eleven passages where there is a maximum amount of agreement between Matthew and Luke against Mark are singled out, they include narrative, mythology, gnomic material, an exorcism story, parables, a healing story, an Old Testament quotation, and Apocalyptic material. Of what significance is it to be told that in these passages there is a con-siderable amount of matter, "chiefly consisting of discourse" which is found in Matthew and Luke but is absent from Mark? What is the significance of "discourse" in this context? It must not be taken to mean that these passages are homogeneous as to any literary classification—for they obviously are not. "Discourse" here is a broad nonspecific term which encourages the reader to associate these passages with one of the two basic sources of the two-document hypothesis, namely, the *Logia* or "Q" which is popularly considered to be a collection of "discourses" of Jesus. To say that: "It seems reasonable, therefore, to suppose that in these sections, or in most of them . . . the editors of Matthew and Luke turned to the Matthaean Logia, or some other such document (Q), in search of additional matter which should contain more of the teaching of Jesus than was supplied by Mark," is to draw attention away from the really interesting characteristic of these passages—namely, their diversity. An objective test designed to ascertain the significance of these passages for the understanding of the agreements of Matthew and Luke against Mark would, therefore, take into account the fact of the very real disparity among these passages as well as any apparent similarity they may have to one another. Their classification into a single category on the basis of extent of agreement alone is unwarranted, since they themselves vary from one another enormously as to length and as to the amount of agreement between Matthew and Luke against Mark, all the way from the most extensive kind of agreement down to agreement which is hardly distinguishable in extent from the most extensive of the so-called "minor" agreements. There is no ground on which to base a justification for treating them separately from all other agreements.

However unsatisfactory may have been B. Weiss's insistence that all these agreements between Matthew and Luke against Mark were to be explained by hypothecating that Matthew's *Logia* was an Ur-gospel known to all three Synopticists, and however unsatisfactory may have been Holtzmann's theory that they were to be explained by the notion that Matthew, Mark, and Luke all used an Ur-Marcus, these solutions seem to have an integrity of method which is denied to that of Hawkins. The best way to expose the bankruptcy of such a method of literary criticism is by showing its results to be false or misleading. This shall be done in the detailed analysis to be given to the end results of this methodological development as it finally expressed itself in Streeter's classical treatment of the minor agreements of Matthew and Luke against Mark.

But before turning to Streeter's work it will be necessary to complete the exposition of Hawkins' study of these phenomena, and also to take notice of subsequent developments in the history of this important problem up to 1924.

Having separated the ten sections with the most extensive agreement between Matthew and Luke against Mark, Hawkins next separated seven sections in which he stated that there was no instance of such agreement. This left him with 51 sections which he further divided into separate groups of 30 and 21 respectively. The basis for this division has little if anything to do with the nature of the phenomena themselves. Hawkins noted that in these 51 sections there was a total of about 240 agreements to be considered. About 218 could be explained by one of three causes: (1) some were words "so ordinary and colourless and so nearly synonymous with Mark's that the use of them may be merely accidental"; (2) others were "such obvious amplifications or explanations as it would be natural for any writers to introduce"; (3) still others were "changes to a more smooth and usual Hellenistic vocabulary and style from the comparative harshness and 'unusualness' of Mark."

Out of the 51 sections under consideration, Hawkins found that in 30 it was possible for him to account for all the agreements in any one section by one or more of these three causes. Therefore, these 30 sections constitute Hawkins' third group. Hawkins' fourth and final group was simply composed of the 21 sections left, which were characterized by each having at least one agreement "as to which it seems almost impossible that Matthew and Luke could have accidentally concurred in making them." Hawkins thought that in such cases: "the changes seem to be owing to some influence, direct or indirect, of a common source, and not to the independent judgment of two compilers." Hawkins thereupon appended the list of the 21 such agreements.

After having done this, Hawkins posed the familiar twofold question: "What was the nature of this source?" Was it an Ur-Marcus?, or was it some other early non-Marcan document ("Q")? There were difficulties with both these solutions, and so Hawkins considered also the solution of Simons: "Or was one of these compilers able to consult the work of the other . . . ?" This solution seemed also unsatisfactory to Hawkins. The most probable explanation for the 21 residual difficulties for the two-document hypothesis Hawkins found in Sanday's *vera causa* as developed by Stanton. In each case, reasoned Hawkins, we should imagine that first some copyist changed his text of Matthew or Luke, and that later this change was carried across (either intentionally or unconsciously) to the other, i.e., the said agreement between Matthew and Luke against Mark was due to the combined process of textual corruption and assimilation.

In 1906 Burkitt in his second inaugural lecture published the results of his attempt to carry out Hawkins' suggestion for these 21 agreements.[81] And in 1909 C. H. Turner in the *Journal of Theological Studies* published the results of his effort to push this line of investigation even further.[82] Turner's specific suggestion was to "allow more weight than has hitherto been given to the old Latin and old Syriac evidence."

This was in January, 1909. Meanwhile, however, Sanday himself had come around to the view presented by Abbott in 1901. And Hawkins under Sanday's influence had also adopted the same view. The modified text of Hawkins' treatment of this subject in the second edition of his *Horae Synopticae* published later the same year (1909), reflected this change in Hawkins' thinking. He did not give up the idea that the process of textual corruption and assimilation accounts for some of these arguments. "But," he wrote, "it appears to me now that others of them, and perhaps the majority, may be best accounted for by Dr. Sanday's suggestion that they are due to the use by Matthew and Luke of 'a recension of the text of Mark different from that from which all the extant MSS. of the Gospel are derived.'" This is an exact quotation from the text of Sanday's essay as it appeared in 1911, and indicates that Hawkins apparently had access to Sanday's manuscript sometime prior to 1909.

In a footnote, however, Hawkins noted in connection with his list of the 21 agreements:

There is a full discussion of this list in Prof. Burkitt's *Gospel History* . . . , and a reference to it by Mr. C. H. Turner in J.T.S. . . . (Jan. 1909), to which I would call attention. I quite agree that textual criticism has diminished, and is likely to diminish further, from the force of several of these instances. . . .

It is clear, therefore, from the foregoing developments, that the eclectic attitude toward the possible *vera causa* of the minor agreements, which was first made explicit by Stanton in 1893 and espoused by Hawkins in 1899, was further sanctioned by the ambivalent character of the modifications and additions Hawkins

[81] *The Gospel History and Its Transmission*, pp. 42–58.
[82] "Historical Introduction of the Textual Criticism of the New Testament," Part II, *J.T.S.*, Vol. X, 1908–1909, pp. 174 ff.

introduced into his discussion of these agreements in the second edition of his influential *Horae Synopticae* in 1909.

5. STANTON 1909

V. H. Stanton's second volume of his three-volume work, *The Gospels as Historical Documents*, published in the same year (1909), contained a lengthy treatment of these minor agreements, which he termed "coincident differences from St. Mark in the First and Third Gospels." These "coincident differences" could be adequately accounted for, thought Stanton, by the joint appeal to four causes: (1) "Differences between the text of the Marcan document used by the first and third evangelists and our St. Mark." Stanton's idea was that there were different copies of Ur-Marcus. The original copy of Ur-Marcus from which canonical Mark is descended was altered. For example, "the use of the term τὸ εὐαγγέλιον absolutely (Mk. 1:1; 1:14,15; 8:35; 10:29), which is peculiar to this Gospel, is to be explained this way." So also ὁ τέκτων in Mark 6:3; καὶ πάντων διάκονος in Mark 9:35; and πᾶσιν τοῖς ἔθνεσιν in Mark 11:17 were all probably insertions or glosses of this kind. Also the "erroneous" ἐπὶ 'Αβιαθὰρ ἀρχιερέως in Mark 2:26 may have been an addition by a "badly informed copyist." This is really Sanday's original idea of textual corruption due to the process of copying. Stanton made use of it to explain agreements in omission between Matthew and Luke against Mark. Unlike Streeter, Stanton realized that these agreements were important. In fact, Stanton held them to be "the most important class of agreements." Why he held them to be *most* important is not clear, unless it was that they seemed to him to disprove Simons' idea that the minor agreements between Matthew and Luke against Mark were to be explained by Luke's acquaintance with Matthew. Stanton reasoned, "If Luke had noticed that something contained in one of his principal sources had been omitted by a writer who, like himself, had used those sources, his most natural impulse would have been to include it all the more carefully in his own work, lest it should be forgotten." In this way, of course, Luke would have removed all similar agreements in omission. This is not a convincing argument, but it is possible to agree with Stanton in his recognition that agreements in omission are significant.

The three remaining causes are identical with those Stanton first proposed in his article in *The Expositor* (1893). Stanton, then, showed the same tendency toward eclecticism in dealing with these agreements as Hawkins.

6. LUMMIS

In 1915 Cambridge University Press published a small book by Lummis entitled *How Luke Was Written*. Lummis claimed that there were agreements between Matthew and Luke against Mark which none of Stanton's four causes would explain. There were also categories of agreements, where taken singly the phenomena were not significant, but taken as a whole they were significant and "cannot be explained at all except by an acquaintance of Luke with Matthew."[83] For example, Stanton had cited the use by Matthew and Luke of δέ where Mark has καί, as an "Undesigned agreement between the first and third evangelists in revising their Marcan document." On the basis of mathematical probability, however, taking into account the total number of times they used δέ and καί respectively, Lummis calculated that the coincidental substitution of δέ for καί by Matthew and Luke could on the basis of chance be expected to occur less than half as many times as in fact it did. The chief merit of this first-rate little book is its penetrating analysis of the "Q" hypothesis.[84]

[83] E. W. Lummis, *How Luke Was Written* (Consideration affecting the Two-document Theory with special reference to the Phenomena of Order in the Non-Marcan Matter common to Matthew and Luke), Cambridge, 1915, p. 23.

[84] The degree of openness with which Lummis approached the study of the Synoptic Problem may be gauged from his recognition of the implications of the view of Simons, Jacobsen, Holtzmann, Stockmeyer, Wendt, Soltau, Spitta (he could have added Weizsäcker), that Luke was dependent upon Matthew: "When once it is conceded, even hypothetically, that Lk. was acquainted with Mt. as well as with Mk. the assumption that any notice which is common to all three gospels was derived, by Lk. and Mt., from Mk. no longer holds good. It may be that Lk. took the passage from Mt., and that Mk. is secondary to Mt., or to Lk., or to both Mt. and Lk. (Here the arguments of Griesbach, and those of the Tübingen critics, may well be considered.) A few passages in Mk. which, in my view, are secondary to Lk., or conflate, will be noticed in the course of the essay." Contrast Lummis' openness to the Griesbach hypothesis with the attitude expressed in the words of James Moffatt with reference to Griesbach's work: "The first vigorous appearance of this unlucky and prolific dandelion, which it has taken nearly a century of opposition (led by Storr, Knobel, Lachmann, Wilke, Weisse, B. Weiss, Holtzmann, Weizsäcker, and Wendt) to eradicate." (*An Introduction to the Literature of the New Testament*, Edinburgh, 1911, p. 177.) It was the fact that since 1880, the very scholars whom Moffatt cites as *eradicators* of the Griesbach hypothesis, themselves had been led to concede that the evidence indicated that Luke used Matthew, that led Lummis to see that it was needful to reconsider "the arguments of Griesbach and those of the Tübingen critics."

The assignment for making the all-important review of this book in the *Journal of Theological Studies* was entrusted to a young Oxford scholar, who by then, thanks to Sanday's commendation of his contributions to *Oxford Studies*, had gained recognition as an important authority on the Synoptic Problem. To appreciate fully the weight men like Sanday and those who had a high regard for the work of his Oxford Seminar would be likely to place on Streeter's judgment even in 1915, it is necessary to read and digest Sanday's words in his introductory essay in *Oxford Studies*. Sanday had just commented on the essays which concerned "Q" by Hawkins, Streeter, Allen, and Bartlet:

... I confess that to myself the earlier group [the essays by Hawkins and Streeter] comes with great and cumulative force. If Sir John Hawkins lays the foundation, the fabric erected upon it by Mr. Streeter seems to be very solid and compact, clamped together (I might say) by iron bands throughout its whole extent. I do not think that I need go further into the details of this; I would invite the reader to work through the essays at close quarters for himself.

But I feel it to be at once a duty and a pleasure to call attention to what seems to me to be the remarkable excellence of Mr. Streeter's summarizing essay (VII) on "The Literary Evolution of the Gospels." I do not remember to have seen, within anything like the same compass, a picture at once so complete, so sound, and (to my mind) so thoroughly scientific, of the whole course of development in the Apostolic and sub-Apostolic age in its bearing upon literary composition in general and the composition of the Gospels in particular. It is real evolution, and an evolution conceived as growth, in which each stage springs naturally, spontaneously, and inevitably out of the last. I shall in future always refer to this essay when I desire either to refresh or to correct the picture present to my own mind.[85]

Streeter's review of Lummis' book is politely negative. "The book shows a great deal of careful work and much ingenuity, but though it is not impossible that Luke had seen Matthew, the objections to the view that he derived the so-called 'Q matter' from him are so insuperable that it is difficult not to feel that it is labour and ingenuity wasted."[86]

[85] *Oxford Studies*, pp. xv–xvi.
[86] *J.T.S.*, Vol. XVII, 1915–1916, p. 124.

7. JAMESON

Seven years later Basil Blackwell of Oxford published H. G. Jameson's book *The Origin of the Synoptic Gospels*, "a Revision of the Synoptic Problem" (1922). Like Lummis, Jameson too believed that the agreements of Matthew and Luke against Mark constituted positive evidence for Luke's use of Matthew. Jameson did not think that such causes as mere chance, the use of "Q," the recension of Mark, or textual assimilation were adequate to account for the phenomena.

Jameson's book was reviewed in *The Journal of Theological Studies* by F. C. Burkitt, who complained that Jameson throughout treated "the synoptic problem as if it were an Oxford idiosyncracy, almost as the creation of Oxford scholars."

This charge was unjustified. Jameson, in the course of his small book of 132 pages, recognized the work of Abbott, Lightfoot, Lummis, Stanton, Wright, and Burkitt from Cambridge, and Harnack, Hilgenfeld, Schmiedel, B. Weiss, and Zahn from Germany. He made more frequent reference to the work of Burkitt's colleague, Stanton, than to that of Hawkins or Sanday. His three references to the views of Burkitt were not particularly complimentary, and his citation of Stanton's views on the relative unimportance of the phenomenon of textual assimilation was an occasion for pique on Burkitt's part since Burkitt had appealed to this as the primary cause for explaining the minor agreements, and since Jameson did not refer to Burkitt's important chapter on the subject in his book, *The Gospel History and Its Transmission*. Burkitt's review of Jameson's book is devoid of any reference to Jameson's evaluation of the significance of the agreements between Matthew and Luke against Mark.

Jameson's solution for the Synoptic Problem was to return to the classical Augustinian hypothesis in which Mark used Matthew and Luke used both Matthew and Mark. As with Streeter's review of Lummis' work, so Burkitt's review of Jameson's is politely negative. "I don't think for a moment that Mr. Jameson is right, nor will my readers in this *Journal* expect me to think so, but he has considered some objections to the 'Two-Document Theory' in a scholarly way and his work demands some notice." As may be seen from Appendix B, pp. 287 ff., Jameson's work deserved more notice than it was given. Burkitt's closing comment reflects his attitude toward any radical "revision" of the Synoptic Problem: ". . . Mr. Jameson supposes that Mark wrote with Matthew before his eyes. I find it frankly incredible."[87]

It is a fact of considerable significance that at both Cambridge and Oxford, by 1922, serious students of the Synoptic Problem, working responsibly within the context of their respective university literary-critical traditions, were not only led to the view that the literary evidence indicated that Luke had used Matthew but were successful in having their work published under unquestionable auspices and promptly reviewed in the *Journal of Theological Studies* by recognized critics.[88]

It is true that both reviewers, Streeter and Burkitt, were negative in their evaluation of any departure from the two-document hypothesis. But neither challenged the view of Lummis or Jameson that the agreements of Matthew and Luke against Mark constituted positive evidence that Luke had used Matthew. At that time, therefore, the best critical minds at both Oxford and Cambridge were acutely aware of the evidence which in Germany had led competent scholars like Simons, Jacobsen, P. Ewald, Stockmeyer, Wendt, Soltau, and Spitta to conclude that Luke knew and used Matthew. This evidence had led the veterans of the two-document hypothesis, both Holtzmann and Weizsäcker, to the same view.

It was with good reason, therefore, that C. H. Turner as late as 1924 drew attention to the fact that so long as it was supposed that there was a residuum of agreements between Matthew and Luke against Mark in matter taken from Mark, so long would research into the Synoptic question be hampered and final solution delayed.

8. TURNER

In 1920 in his inaugural lecture as the Dean Ireland's Professor of Exegesis in the University of Oxford, Turner had admitted that the most important obstacle to the recognition that Mark was used by Matthew and Luke was the phenomenon of agreement between Matthew and Luke against Mark. At that time he concluded,

[87] *J.T.S.*, Vol. XXIV, July 1923, p. 443.
[88] It would be unnecessary to call attention to this fact if it were well recognized that the tradition of Synoptic criticism in England as well as in Germany is much richer and more inclusive than is suggested by the textbooks written during the last decades. The recovery of this tradition in all its richness will facilitate that new birth of freedom in Synoptic criticism by which both the university and the church will have their intellectual life quickened, whatever be the consequences for faith.

". . . those who assert that for the matter common to all three Synopticists St. Mark is the source of the other two, have of course to give some explanation of what looks like a fatal bar to their claims."[89] Turner's solution was to postulate an overlapping of Mark and "Q." He admitted, however, that this would not account for all the agreements—which otherwise were explained by Sanday and Hawkins as due to Matthew and Luke having used a revision of the text of Mark different from that from which all the extant manuscripts of Mark are derived. Turner justly rejected this solution, however, on the ground that it introduced a new factor, a special recension of Mark, concerning the existence of which there was otherwise not the slightest indication. At that time Turner preferred, if necessary, the simpler hypothesis that Luke had at a later stage of the composition of his gospel come across Matthew and then introduced from it "a new touch here and there."

During the years 1924 and 1925 Turner published a series of studies on "Marcan Usage" in the *Journal of Theological Studies*. These studies all have as their purpose to show that Mark could be original even in the face of evidence to the contrary. The final study on "the use of numbers in St. Mark's Gospel" is representative of the series. Turner began:

It is my firm conviction that the Mark which lay before the later Synopticists, St. Matthew and St. Luke, was no other than the Mark which we possess. . . . In the book which is the starting point of all detailed criticism of the Synoptic problem, Sir John Hawkins' *Horae Synopticae* (ed. 2 p. 152) this conclusion is nearly but not quite reached. . . .[90]

Turner noted that Hawkins listed nine passages where the hand of a later editor was very probably to be seen. Of these nine, three were cases of large numbers, 2,000 (Mk. 5:13), 200 (Mk. 6:37), 300 (Mk. 14:5). The fact that these numbers were not found in either Matthew or Luke created the presumption in Hawkins' mind that they were inserted by a later editor. But not so Turner, who proceeded to make a painstaking analysis of Mark's use of numbers.

Turner summarized his results as follows: ". . . it is more common for both of them (Matthew and Luke) to omit than for both of them

---

[89] Cuthbert H. Turner, *The Study of the New Testament*, 1883–1920, Oxford, 1920, pp. 40–41.

[90] *J.T.S.*, Vol. XXVI, 1924–1925, "Marcan Usage: Notes, Critical and Exegetical, on the Second Gospel, Part VI," pp. 337 ff.

to retain a number given in Mark: and it is vastly more common (about three times in four) for one or other of them to omit a number than for both of them to retain it." Then he concluded:

As the result of our enquiry, it is not too much to say that the suggestion that some of the numbers in Mark are not original because both Matthew and Luke omit them cannot maintain itself in face of the argument from Marcan usage. One more nail has been driven into the coffin of that old acquaintance of our youth, Ur-Marcus. He did enough harm in his time, but he is dead and gone: let no attempts be made to disinter his skeleton.[91]

Apparently Turner had only limited alternatives in mind, for the same facts were easily susceptible to quite a different explanation. If the frequency of Mark's usage of numbers indicates "that Mark is fond of numerals" as Turner claims to have proven, then what is so surprising if, on the Griesbach hypothesis, for example, Mark tends to prefer to incorporate numerals into his text from the texts of Matthew and/or Luke whenever he finds them there, and on other occasions to introduce them into his text even when he does not find them in either Matthew or Luke? In fact, Turner's evidence could be turned into an argument in favor of Schleiermacher's view that Mark exhibited characteristics which marked it as having affinities to the later apocryphal Gospel literature, where there was a noted tendency to make the Gospel tradition more specific: Mark's use of numbers being an example of this tendency.[92]

It would appear that Turner was so preoccupied with getting rid of Ur-Marcus that he had little time or inclination to evaluate the bearing of his careful linguistic studies on the relative merits of alternative solutions to the Synoptic Problem.

This closing reference to Ur-Marcus by Turner, made just the year following the publication of Streeter's *The Four Gospels*, was remarkably reminiscent of Streeter's equally impassioned closing plea: "Renounce once for all the phantom Ur-Marcus. . . ."[93] These words are found in the last sentence of the crucial chapter in Streeter's book where he dealt with "The Minor Agreements of Matthew and Luke against Mark." This plea reflects the historical context within which Streeter worked, and indicates the limited nature of the orientation of his treatment of these disturbing phenomena.

[91] *Op. cit.*, p. 346.

[92] Schleiermacher, *Begriff, Inhalt, Methode der Einleitung im Neue Testament*, Para 79, *Sämmtliche Werke*, Vol. 8, Berlin, 1845, p. 315.

[93] *F.G.*, p. 331.

Streeter, like Burkitt and Turner, wanted to get rid of the ghost of Ur-Marcus. Which is to say that he was preoccupied with disproving the need for an Ur-gospel as a *Grundschrift* behind Matthew, Mark, and Luke. In the nineteenth century, Lessing's idea of an Ur-gospel had been made the essential basis of Holtzmann's epoch-making presentation of the two-document hypothesis. At the hands of Streeter this enlivening, but troublesome spirit of the nineteenth century was at last effectively exorcized from twentieth century studies, as a demon from a dead past. But the nineteenth century was to have its vengeance upon scholars who did not take the trouble to make its acquaintance, for, like the proverbial unclean spirit, Lessing's Ur-gospel returned to the house from which it had been cast out, in the form of Streeter's Proto-Luke; and with him Proto-Luke brought other spirits more evil than himself, M and L, "and the plight of that household became worse than before."

This survey of the pre-Streeter history of the treatment of the minor agreements of Matthew and Luke against Mark is now completed. The position and arguments of all those Oxford and Cambridge scholars who influenced Streeter have been reviewed. There was in Streeter's day no consensus concerning these phenomena, except as to their importance. Everyone recognized that a final solution of the Synoptic Problem awaited a definitive treatment of these agreements. Streeter succeeded in bringing order out of chaos—or so it seemed at the time. The magnitude of his achievement is measured by the remarkable success his work had in dispelling doubts as to whether the two-document hypothesis would weather the disintegrating effects of continuing research from men like Lummis and Jameson, or whether it would be shipwrecked on the sharp edges of these almost imperceptible rocks of resistance jutting up from the subterranean depths of unresolved critical tension to protest against a hypothesis according to which they ought not to exist.

In achieving this result Streeter followed the eclectic method of drawing upon the various causes which had been put forward by different scholars to explain these agreements, without entering into a critical discussion of these causes, and without regard for their mutually self-contradictory character in some instances. Streeter seems to have taken no account of the arguments of either Lummis or Jameson.

IV

An Analysis of Streeter's Contribution to the Two-Document Hypothesis

A. Streeter's Treatment of the Minor Agreements

I. THE ATOMIZATION OF THE PHENOMENA

Because of the great importance of the minor agreements of Matthew and Luke against Mark, and because Streeter's treatment of them exercised such a profound influence upon the subsequent history of the Synoptic Problem, it will be appropriate to examine the foundation which he laid for his investigation of these agreements, and to analyze the methods he followed in explaining them.

Streeter laid bare the structural plan of his argumentation in a "Synopsis" at the beginning of each chapter. In this case the plan was fivefold. First came four categories of the minor agreements of Matthew and Luke against Mark, followed by a conclusion. The four categories of agreement were arranged in the following order: (1) Irrelevant Agreements; (2) Deceptive Agreements; (3) Agreements due to the overlap of Mark and "Q"; (4) Agreements due to Textual Corruption.[1]

[1] In this chapter all further references to Streeter's work, *The Four Gospels*, will be by page number inserted in the text in parentheses.

This procedure tends to atomize the phenomena. And if one restricts the discussion of these phenomena to one group at a time, as Streeter did, there is a danger that the total concatenation of agreements in a given Synoptic passage will never be impressed upon the mind of the reader of such a discussion. For example, if a particular passage exhibits a web of minor but closely related agreements of Matthew and Luke against Mark, there is the prospect that these different agreements will be divided into two or more of Streeter's different categories, thus dissipating the full impact which these same agreements would make on the mind of the reader if he were to have them all brought to his attention at the same time, and discussed together in the concrete wholeness of the particular context which they have in the passage concerned.[2]

The arrangement and procedure which Streeter followed had exactly this misleading effect, as can be seen from an examination of Streeter's justification for his different categories.

In the opening paragraph, following the introductory Synopsis, Streeter wrote:

Many years ago Dr. Sanday expressed the opinion that the solution of this problem would be found in the sphere of Textual Criticism; and from time to time Professors Burkitt and Turner have called attention to facts pointing in this direction.

But, writes Streeter, "no consistent attempt" seems to have been made to bring this line of investigation up to date in the light of the latest research. Streeter continues:

Before, however, attempting to do this, I must elaborate the point . . . that the majority of these agreements do not require any explanation at all. Matthew and Luke . . . were not mere scribes . . .; they were historians combining and fully rewriting their authorities, and . . . consistently *condensing* them.

"From this," writes Streeter, "certain consequences follow," which are two in number, both having to do with what he calls "Irrelevant Agreements."

2 *See* especially Finley Morris Keech, *The Agreements of Matthew and Luke Against Mark in the Triple Tradition*, 1962 (unpublished thesis, Drew University Library, Madison, New Jersey), pp. 38–41.

2. THE IRRELEVANT AGREEMENTS

(a) Compression can only be achieved by the omission of details. Matthew and Luke have abbreviated "practically every paragraph in the whole of Mark" and therefore would naturally have concurred "in a very large number of their omissions. . . ." Streeter concludes: "Coincidence in omission proves nothing as to the source used."

In response to this argument two points should be considered: (1) It presupposes that the priority of Mark has been firmly established by the five arguments for Marcan priority in Streeter's "Fundamental Solution." Therefore, if these reasons are shown to be invalid, this argument as stated loses its cogency. (2) It completely ignores the valid observation found in Stanton's discussion of the phenomena of agreement in omissions, where the point was made that agreements in omission may be significant if they occur in conjunction with other more positive agreements. That is to say, it is conceivable that a particular agreement in omission between Matthew and Luke against Mark could occur in the context of a major web of interrelated minor agreements where it would lend credence to the over-all impression that there is some kind of literary dependence between these two Gospels. Therefore, contrary to the judgment of Streeter, and in accord with that of Simons and Stanton, agreements in omission should be studied, and not dismissed throughout the entire discussion of all other agreements simply on the basis of this argument, as Streeter consistently does.

(b) The second consequence that follows from Streeter's point that Matthew and Luke were not "mere scribes" concerns the assertion that "Mark's native tongue was Aramaic and his Greek is quite the most colloquial in the New Testament." Since Matthew and Luke use a less colloquial Greek, in copying Mark they will naturally coincide accidentally from time to time in introducing the same "correction of style and grammar." As an example Streeter cites the use of the "historic present."

The "historic present," for example, a fairly common idiom in Latin, is comparatively rare in Greek, as it is in English; but Mark uses it, apparently as the equivalent of the Aramaic "participle," 151 times. Matthew cuts these down to 78, Luke to 4. Obviously, then, Matthew and Luke cannot but concur in the alteration of tense upwards of 60 times. . . .

This argument, in a somewhat different form, is the same as was used by Abbott in 1879 to prove that Mark was earlier and more primitive than Matthew and Luke. It was later rejected by Abbott on the grounds that one is left with the impression that these stylistic and grammatical agreements come from a single editorial hand and cannot be explained as due to the accidental concurrence of two independent editors. Sanday in 1911 concurred in this judgment of Abbott, and Hawkins tended to go along with Sanday. Both Lummis and Jameson had pointed out the unlikelihood on the basis of mathematical probabilities that the number of some of these agreements would be as high as in fact they are. It is strange, therefore, that Streeter would persist in adhering to a view that was critically dated long before 1924.

It is not enough, however, for the purpose of a critical review of the history of the Synoptic Problem, simply to note that Streeter's approach to this problem was out of date even before his work was published. For the climate of critical opinion since 1924 has been heavily influenced by the successive reprintings of Streeter's work, and it will be necessary to subject the logic of Streeter's argumentation to careful analysis so that the reader may see its practical consequences, and be in a better position to evaluate the trustworthiness of that quadrant of critical opinion which has been structured and informed by Streeter's work.

In the first place this stylistic argument presupposes that Mark's Greek can be proved to be "crude" and "vulgar" in comparison with that of Matthew and Luke, rather than merely "different" in some way to be defined after the question of literary dependence has been settled. For if Mark were "epitomizing" Matthew or conflating the texts of Matthew and Luke his editing policy would need to be taken into account in a critical evaluation of his Greek. This would be especially true in the latter case.

In order to prove that Mark's Greek was "crude" and "vulgar," Abbott, in his article in the *Encyclopaedia Britannica*, which is the fountain source of this idea in English literature and which profoundly influenced English critical opinion on this point, listed nine expressions or words used by Mark which were expressly forbidden by the grammarian Phrynichus.[3] Of these nine, Abbott stated that

---

3 *Op. cit.*, p. 802a.

Luke used none, though in a parenthesis he noted that Matthew used some. This left the reader with the impression that Mark was grossly insensitive to the correct literary standards of his time as compared to other early Christian writers.

The facts are that of the nine instances of bad Greek cited by Abbott only one is not used by at least one other New Testament writer such as John, or Paul, or the author of Acts. Furthermore, three of the nine words may have been copied by Mark directly from Ur-Marcus on Abbott's terms, or from Matthew on the Augustinian or Griesbach hypothesis, since they occur in Matthew in parallel passages where there is evidence of copying. If allowance is made for the possible common authorship of Luke-Acts, of Abbott's list of nine instances of bad Greek in Mark, seven are also used by the authors of either Matthew or Luke-Acts. The facts seem to indicate that all the Evangelists on occasion used words condemned by the Atticistic grammarians. But so presumably did many contemporary writers. Otherwise the critical lists compiled by these purists would have had no point.

If it is true that one Evangelist wrote better Greek than another it probably indicates more about his private education or that of his intended readers than it does about the date of composition of his Gospel, or its relationship to the other Gospels.

In literary criticism there is no canon by which questions of literary dependence can be settled on the basis of good or bad grammar, for the simple reason that there is no basis for establishing a correlation between good or bad grammar and originality of authorship. There are too many instances in the history of literature where the original work is a superior literary creation compared to those works which are dependent upon it, and vice versa.

In addition to the nine instances of "rude" or "vulgar" Greek in Mark which are expressly forbidden by Phrynichus, Abbott lists two "barbarisms": (1) the use of ὅταν with the indicative, and (2) the use of ὅτι to ask a question. He then adds that both these "idioms are common in the *Acta Pilati*, and perhaps indicate Latin influence."

But this is a double-edged sword which can also cut against the notion that Mark is primitive and original to Matthew and Luke, because these "barbarisms" suggest that Mark has interesting affinities with later Apocryphal Gospel literature (both in its bad grammar and in its Latinisms), notably the *Acta Pilati*, which is clearly dependent on the earlier Gospels.[4]

Abbott's suggestion that these "barbarisms" may indicate a Latin influence upon Mark is of special interest in view of a particular example which Streeter cited to illustrate his idea that some of these minor agreements are irrelevant. For Streeter noted that the "historic present," which is a stylistic characteristic of Mark, is a fairly common idiom in Latin. Therefore, there are no obvious grounds for turning from the possibility of influence from Latin usage upon Mark's Greek in preference for the suggestion that Mark used this idiom "as the equivalent of the Aramaic 'participle.'"

The pertinency of this question is heightened by the fact that there were critics well-known to Streeter who were keenly conscious of the influence of Latin usage on Mark's Greek. C. H. Turner, in his discussion of the question of the influence of Latin upon Mark asked the question: "Whence did Mark derive his occasional use of an order of words so fundamentally alien to the Greek language?" Turner continues:

Greek puts the emphatic words in the forefront of the sentence, and the verb therefore cannot be left to the last. Latin, on the other hand, habitually closes the sentence with the verb. The conclusion seems irresistible that just as Jerome in the Vulgate introduces a Graecizing order, ... Mark introduces in the Greek of his Gospel a Latinizing order.[5]

Turner did not dispute the notion that the Evangelist Mark had come to Rome originally from Palestine. "The Greek he had picked up in his boyhood at Jerusalem was, we may assume, wholly nonliterary and colloquial." This, however, is just the point. Turner and Streeter and apparently the readers for whom they wrote were prepared to *assume* that the "non-literary" and "colloquial" Greek of Mark was to be explained by his boyhood in Jerusalem. In Streeter's case, for example, there is the assumption that Mark's use of the "historic present" was an Aramaism rather than a Latinism.

---

[4] The evidence of literary dependence between the *Acta Pilati* and Matthew, Luke and John is unmistakable. That the dependence is of the Gospels upon the *Acta Pilati* is highly unlikely. There is no clear evidence of literary dependence between the *Acta Pilati* and Mark.

[5] *Journal of Theological Studies*, Vol. XXIX, July, 1928, p. 355.

This is an understandable assumption for those convinced that Mark is primitive and close to the Palestinian origins of the Church. To think otherwise might create difficulties. For it is one thing for Streeter's readers to be asked to imagine Matthew and Luke cutting down on Mark's *Aramaisms* for the sake of their Greek speaking Gentile readers. It is quite another thing, however, to ask them to imagine Luke and Matthew cutting down on Mark's *Latinisms*, since their readers were used to a Greek upon which the influence of Latin had long been felt. At least this is a presumption that would follow naturally from the historic and cultural realities of the times, and one which is supported by the fact that neither Matthew nor Luke are free from Latinisms. Matthew also has more authentic Aramaisms, for that matter, than does Mark.

In the light of this excursus into the background of Streeter's arguments concerning the significance of Mark's use of the historic present, it should be clear that there is little or no proof in this whole line of reasoning in which Streeter was engaged. Therefore, the twenty agreements cited by Streeter of Matthew and Luke against Mark, where they both have εἶπεν and Mark has the historic present λέγει, may or may not be irrelevant. Possibly all twenty instances of this particular agreement are irrelevant. In each case, however, it is necessary to see this particular agreement in the context of all other related phenomena in the concrete passage in which the agreement occurred. Only in this way can one put himself in a reliable position to weigh the evidence for and against a decision to regard this particular agreement as relevant or irrelevant. To declare in advance all twenty of these agreements irrelevant simply because, on the basis of the argument which Streeter sets forth, they can be subsumed under a category which he terms "irrelevant," is methodologically unsound.

Streeter concluded the discussion of his "Irrelevant Agreements," with the following statement: "The above constitute considerably more than half the total number of the Minor Agreements we are discussing, and it goes without saying that they have no significance whatever (298)."

Such a preemptory judgment as Streeter's prompts the notation that in so proceeding he has uncritically followed the early, untested suggestion of Abbott as developed by Stanton, Hawkins, and Turner, and has turned his back on the later Abbott's justifiably skeptical attitude toward this idea, an attitude which was subsequently shared by Sanday.[6]

The point is not that Streeter completely ignored Abbott's and Sanday's later judgment. In fact, although he wrongly credited Sanday alone with Abbott's solution, he acknowledged this later explanation of the phenomena as the one "accepted by the majority of the authorities as the most probable." Streeter's error was in ignoring the basis for this explanation, which if valid, as Streeter granted by implication it might be, cut the ground out from under his explanation for the majority of the agreements between Matthew and Luke against Mark. For Streeter to have proceeded with his discussion of these agreements as if neither Abbott nor Sanday had expressed his considered judgment that "by far the greater number" of them look like "the deliberate work of a particular editor," and that "the number and recurrence of these phenomena is evidently due to design, and not to accident," and for him to have ignored the implications of such published statements of seasoned students of the Synoptic Problem, is difficult to explain. Abbott and Sanday may have proposed an unacceptable solution for the evidence of "design" they noted in these agreements, but that does not remove the evidence itself. And that evidence stands in the way of any attempt to explain these phenomena as "coincidental" or "accidental" and therefore "irrelevant." This means that in the judgment of critics like Abbott and Sanday, Streeter's assertion that "it goes without saying" that "considerably more than half the total number of the Minor Agreements . . . have no significance whatever" because of "coincident" omissions and "accidental" corrections of style and grammar, is without support from their own study of the phenomena, and that far from having in this manner legitimately removed from consideration these agreements, Streeter still has them to explain. This means that on Streeter's own count, from Abbott's and Sanday's point of view, he has left unexplained

---

[6] Sanday in 1911 wrote in response to Turner's views in *J.T.S.* for January, 1909: "It might well be thought that some of the agreements are so slight and easy to account for that they might be set down as accidental . . . But I believe that by far the greater number of the coincidences of Mt. Lk. against Mk. are due to the use by Mt. Lk. . . . *of a recension of the text of Mark* . . . I call this form of text a recension, because there is so much method and system about it, that it looks like the deliberate work of a particular editor . . . In about twenty-three instances they substitute for Mark's 'says ($\lambda \acute{\epsilon} \gamma \epsilon \iota$)' historic present the word 'said ($\epsilon \mathring{\iota} \pi \epsilon \nu$)' . . . The number and the recurrence of these phenomena is evidently due to design, and not to accident."

"considerably more than half the total number of Minor Agreements. . . ." Unfortunately, however, by 1924 both these veterans of Synoptic criticism had died and their cries from the grave were muffled by Streeter's equivocal deference to their view, on the one hand, and effectively nullified by a eulogistic endorsement from Cambridge for Streeter's work, on the other:

> It is impossible to begin to write about this work called *The Four Gospels* without praise, praise for the justice of its proportions, for the security of its conclusions, for the learning it shows on every page, and the ingenuity and persuasiveness of its argumentation. I venture to think *The Four Gospels* the most important book that has been written on this august subject for half a generation. . . . The book will be for a long time an excellent advanced base from which a future generation of students can start for the further investigation of the Gospels.

These words are exactly those abstracted from Burkitt's review of *The Four Gospels* in the *Journal of Theological Studies*, April, 1925, by the publishers for use as advertisement to go on the book's commercial jacket.

Ironically enough, that same review began: "In Canon Streeter's most important new book the long labours of Dr. Sanday at Oxford have really borne fruit, better perhaps than they ever could have done while that venerable figure was still overshadowing the field."

Burkitt went on to express the judgment that Streeter's book represented "a great advance on the *Oxford Studies in the Synoptic Problem*, published in 1911." The opinion of a reviewer has seldom been more wrong, for exactly the opposite is true at every point where an intelligible comparison can be made. For example, Streeter's essay on "St. Mark's Knowledge and Use of Q" in *Oxford Studies* is qualitatively more substantial than the corresponding section of his work in 1924.[7] And Hawkins' essay "Three Limitations to St. Luke's Use of St. Mark's Gospel" represents a more secure literary-critical achievement than does Streeter's idea of Proto-Luke which took one of its points of departure from this essay.[8]

---

[7] *Oxford Studies*, pp. 165–183; *The Four Gospels*, pp. 186–191.
[8] *Oxford Studies*, specifically the section: "The Disuse of the Marcan Source in St. Luke ix.51–xviii.14," pp. 29–59; *The Four Gospels*, "Proto-Luke," pp. 201–222.

In the closing section of this unprecedentedly exhaustive review of seventeen pages, Burkitt wrote:

A few words must be said in conclusion about Dr. Streeter's treatment of the minor agreements of Matthew and Luke against Mark. . . . The treatment of residual small differences is always a thorny subject, and students of the Synoptic Problem hold very divergent views in the matter [*sic*]. In what is after all the main issue I am in very near agreement with Streeter. The majority of these agreements do not require any explanation at all. . . .

It is only in the case of twenty or thirty of the agreements which Streeter explains as due to textual corruption that Burkitt finds some instances where he has reservations. This means that in about 200 instances of agreement Burkitt thinks Streeter has given an adequate account of the phenomena. This is enough to break the back of any widespread resistance to that idea which Streeter's detailed treatment of these agreements promotes, namely, that all agreements which remain unexplained probably could be easily explained if only our knowledge of the history of textual transmission was greater than it is.[9]

---

[9] Jameson's references to the work of Burkitt were few and unflattering. In contrast, Streeter made more references to the works of Burkitt than to the combined works of Abbott, Sanday, Stanton and Turner. The significance of these references is enhanced by their tone: "The Old Latin and the Itala . . . by the same author (Burkitt) must be read by all students of the Latin versions." With reference to Burkitt's edition of the Syrian text of Syr. S. and Syr. C., Streeter wrote: "The Introduction and Notes of this edition form a contribution to textual criticism the value of which to the advanced student cannot be over-estimated." With specific reference to Burkitt's views on the Synoptic Problem Streeter wrote: "Further advance, however, towards a satisfactory solution of the Synoptic Problem has been, in my opinion, retarded by the tacit assumption of scholars that, if Matthew and Luke both used Mark, they must have used it in the same way. To Professor Burkitt, I believe, belongs the credit of first protesting against this assumption. . . ." At not a few points Streeter took exception to the views of Burkitt, but always with unfailing respect and restraint. In all Streeter referred to Burkitt's work twenty-five times. Burkitt's work had never before received such flattering recognition from Oxford. It would be inhuman to think that he was not both gratified and grateful. It is within this context that the eulogistic character of the almost unrestrained endorsement Burkitt gave to Streeter's book can be understood best: It was impossible, Burkitt had said, to begin to write about Streeter's work without praise for the justice of its proportions, the sanity of its conclusions, the learning it shows on every page, and the ingenuity and persuasiveness of its argumentation. Streeter was not being facetious, therefore, when in the following issue of *J.T.S.* he wrote in reference to Burkitt's review of his book: "The remarks which Prof. Burkitt makes about my book as a whole are couched in terms of approbation far more generous, I am sure, than I deserve, and it is therefore in no sense to defend myself or my book, that I write this article." There may be, however, an element of gamesmanship in

After claiming to have accounted for the majority of the minor agreements as "irrelevant," Streeter added: "But there remain quite a number of cases where the coincidence of Matthew and Luke does at first sight appear significant, but where further scrutiny shows this to be a mistake." This led Streeter to a discussion of his second category, that of "Deceptive Agreements."

3. THE DECEPTIVE AGREEMENTS

When it came to the cause of his "Deceptive Agreements," Streeter appealed to the same idea he used in the first category— namely, the idea that two editors working independently upon the text of the same document would naturally concur sometimes in introducing the same improvements. The proof which Streeter offered at this point was such as to bear careful scrutiny. He continued:

Thus frequently, when Mark uses a word which is linguistically inadmissible, the right word is so obvious that, if half-a-dozen independent correctors were at work, they would all be likely to light upon it. For example, Mark 4 times uses the verb φέρειν of animals or persons, and every time Matthew and Luke concur in altering this to ἄγειν or some compound of ἄγειν. φέρειν like its English equivalent "carry," is properly used of inanimate objects which one has to lift; when speaking of a person or an animal that walks on its own legs the natural word to use is ἄγειν, the equivalent of the English verb "to lead" (298–299).

Streeter's words in answer to a criticism made by Burkitt: "Now in regard to the Old-Antiochian text I am a humble disciple of Prof. Burkitt. Practically everything I know about the Old Syraic is derived from his works. . . . The arguments which I adduce in support of this theory are avowedly, in the main, a summary of his. Has Prof. Burkitt abandoned this view of his? If so, I wonder why?" To this note was appended an answer by Burkitt, in which he patiently explained in detail his reservation with regard to "Canon Streeter's Caesarean text," but which made no further reference to *The Four Gospels*. Both men emerged from the encounter with enhanced reputations. Streeter's work had come through substantially unscathed, and Burkitt's authority as a text critic had been impressively vindicated. It is a corollary of this development that the work of Lummis and Jameson should be further disregarded at Oxford and Cambridge. Burkitt first paved the way for Streeter to ignore Jameson's work by his negative review of Jameson's book. Then he further sanctioned this *scandalous* omission by Streeter by a *eulogistic* seventeen-page review in which the omission was never mentioned. The power to review, especially in an influential journal, is very great. Burkitt as much as any single individual bears the responsibility for the uncritical acceptance of Streeter's formulation of the "Fundamental Solution" to the Synoptic Problem.

On the surface this explanation sounds plausible. The fact is, however, that in Hellenistic times φέρειν was encroaching upon ἄγειν by taking the meaning "lead" or "bring," of animals or persons. This usage, therefore, is not unnatural when found in the Gospels.

Streeter's statement that "every time" Mark uses φέρειν in this way, "Matthew and Luke concur in altering this to ἄγειν," suggests that neither of these writers could tolerate such a usage. This is simply not true since both Matthew and Luke do use φέρειν in this way. It is true that there is some indication that Luke may have preferred the use of ἄγειν or one of its compounds where both Matthew and Mark use φέρειν (Cf. Mt. 17:17 ǁ Mk. 9:19 ǁ Lk. 9:41). But φέρειν is found where ἄγειν might have been used in Luke 15:23. This suggests that whereas the Evangelist Luke himself may have preferred the use of ἄγειν rather than φέρειν, he was perfectly capable of copying φέρειν when used in place of ἄγειν directly into his text if he found it in his source. Therefore, even granting for the sake of Streeter's argument, the theory of Marcan priority, there is no support for his notion that Luke would have consistently introduced some form of ἄγειν in place of φέρειν in these four passages.

Furthermore, in the case of Matthew, as well as Luke, there is clear evidence that the Evangelist was prepared to use φέρειν where other writers would use ἄγειν (17:17). If judgment were suspended with regard to Marcan priority and attention given to the phenomena Streeter mentioned, it would appear that all three Evangelists reflect the fact that φέρειν was encroaching upon ἄγειν in Hellenistic times, since all three use φέρειν in the same way. But Matthew and Luke more often follow the older usage and have ἄγειν rather than φέρειν. Mark, however, uses φέρειν where ἄγειν would have done as well ten times. In one of the ten cases Matthew also has φέρειν, but in four of the ten, both Matthew and Luke have some form of ἄγειν. It would appear, therefore, that Mark's Greek at this point is clearly more under the influence of the later tendencies in Hellenistic Greek than is that of either Matthew or Luke.

On either the Augustinian or the Griesbach hypothesis this data would seem to represent a stylistic preference of Mark not shared by Matthew or Luke, and indicate that in epitomizing Matthew or in combining Matthew and Luke, Mark four times allowed his stylistic preference to influence his text. In so doing he did not alter the sense of his text, but simply allowed it to reflect the usage that was presumably current for him.

Since, even on the Marcan hypothesis, Streeter's argument has no persuasiveness, his statement, "Equally inevitable are corrections like κλίνη, θυγάτηρ, and ἑκατοντάρχης for the apparent vulgarisms κράββατον, θυγάτριον, and κεντυρίων . . ." will prompt the impartial critic to demur at such preemptory argumentation, and investigate the facts.

The facts are: (1) κράββατον is found in both John and Acts, and was so commonly used for "bed" in the Hellenistic period it was taken over into Latin as the loan word grabatus; (2) θυγάτριον is but the diminutive of daughter and was used as a term of affection in Hellenistic Greek; it is so used, for example, by no less a literary figure than Plutarch (ANT. 33); (3) ἑκατοντάρχης used by Matthew and Luke is not uncommon in Hellenistic literature, including the LXX and the papyri. Mark's κεντυρίων is a loan word in Greek taken over from the Latin centurio, and as such is found in the papyri and interestingly enough in the Apocryphal Gospel of Peter.

There is no way to argue convincingly from these facts to the conclusion that it would have been "inevitable" for either Matthew or Luke to have made a substitution for any one of these three words, let alone for them to have coincided in substituting the same word in each instance.

These cases clearly bear out other indications that have been noted, i.e., that Mark's Greek seems to reflect certain features of later Hellenistic Greek usage at points where the Greek of Matthew and Luke do not, and that Mark at this point shared this characteristic with second century Greek literature in general, and with Latinized Hellenistic Greek literature in particular, and interestingly enough with second century Apocryphal Gospel literature.

In a similar vein Streeter discussed the substitution of τετράρχης for βασιλεύς and the alteration μετὰ τρεῖς ἡμέρας to τῇ τρίτῃ ἡμέρᾳ, and then wrote: "I proceed to consider some further Agreements of a more striking character, which nevertheless I believe are really deceptive."

Streeter then set forth in Greek the immediate context of ten agreements of Matthew and Luke against Mark, each one of which occurred in a passage where it was impossible for Streeter to appeal to the idea of Matthew and Luke independently "compressing" Mark, since one or both of them has a text as long or longer than that of Mark. They are, in order in which Streeter discusses them, Mark 2:12; 16:8; 3:1; 12:9–10; 6:6; 4:10; 4:36; 13:19; 8:29; 15:30–32; 14:47; 15:43.

The treatment of the first passage in the list is typical of Streeter's procedure throughout the other nine and will be given as a sample: Streeter's format is as follows:

Mark 2:12	*Matthew* 9:7	*Luke* 5:25
ἐξῆλθεν ἔμπροσθεν	ἀπῆλθεν εἰς τὸν	ἀπῆλθεν εἰς τὸν
πάντων.	οἶκον αὐτοῦ.	οἶκον αὐτοῦ.

After thus presenting the evidence in what appears to be a completely objective form, Streeter wrote:

A coincidence like this in five consecutive words seems at first sight to belong to a different category from the single word agreements so far discussed. But it is instructive as illustrating the fallacy of merely counting words or considering extracts without a study of the context.

Then follows a discussion in which Streeter argued that "the only *real* coincidence between Matthew and Luke was that both of them were at pains to bring out more clearly than Mark that the man did exactly what our Lord commanded him." He continued:

In Mark this command runs, "Arise, take up thy bed and go to thy house." Matthew proceeds, "And having arisen, he went away to his house." Luke even more precisely: "Having stood up before them, and having taken up what he lay on, he went away to his house." εἰς τὸν οἶκον αὐτοῦ is simply the echo of Mark's εἰς τὸν οἶκόν σου. The change from Mark's ἐξῆλθεν to ἀπῆλθεν is even more inevitable.

In this manner Streeter explained away as merely deceptive an agreement between Matthew and Luke against Mark extending through five consecutive words in the Greek text. Streeter's point about the "fallacy of merely counting words or considering extracts without a study of the context," is well taken. But a full study of the context in which this five word agreement occurs exposes the questionable character of Streeter's basic methodological procedure of dividing up the minor agreements into several different categories and then treating only examples of one category at a time.

For if one turns to the story of the healing of the Paralytic in Mark 2:1–12 and its parallels in Matthew 9:1–8 and Luke 5:17–26, where the five word agreement between Matthew and Luke against Mark is to be found, he will find that this agreement does not occur in isolation from other agreements of Matthew and Luke against Mark, but rather that it is but part of an extensive web of interrelated minor agreements, each of which when considered by itself might appear dismissable as insignificant, but when considered together constitute such a concatenation of agreements of Matthew and Luke against Mark as to seem unlikely to be merely accidental, but rather to point to some kind of literary relationship between Matthew and Luke.

These agreements include the following: "Behold! . . . on a bed . . . [being carried by four men] . . . he said . . . and . . . [in his spirit] . . . he said . . . [to the paralytic] . . . [and take up your bed] . . . upon the earth to forgive sins . . . he went away to his house. . . ."

The words in brackets are found in the text of Mark but have nothing to correspond to them in the text of either Matthew or Luke. They constitute therefore, agreements in omission between Matthew and Luke against Mark. None of these agreements in omission can be explained as irrelevant on Streeter's terms since while Matthew is more concise than the other two, Luke's account is actually slightly more full than that of Mark, and for this reason, in this instance, there is no basis for thinking that he had compressed Mark. On Streeter's terms, therefore, these omissions remain unexplained, and indeed nicely call attention to the inadequacy of Streeter's over-all method since he has definitely left the reader with the impression that he has taken full account of agreements in omission in his discussion of the subject he termed "Irrelevant Agreements" consequent upon editorial "compressing" of Mark's account by Matthew and Luke. Streeter has failed to draw the attention of his readers to the fact that there are the same kind of agreements in omission between Matthew and Mark against Luke in passages where no appeal can be made to the idea of Matthew and Luke compressing Mark, as, for example, the ten passages he discussed under the category of "Deceptive Agreements." Simons held that agreements in omission are significant when they occur, as they do in this case, in connection with more positive agreements.

These more positive agreements call for comment in terms of the way they would be regarded by Streeter when met singly and in isolation from one another:

(1) Streeter treated "Behold!" in his first category as an "Irrevelant Agreement." Abbott's judgment in the case of this particular agreement was that "Matthew and Luke appear to agree in returning to a Hebrew Original," which of course fitted in beautifully with his idea that Matthew and Luke were working with a recension of the Greek text of Mark which had been "corrected" by some editor who had access to the Semitic original behind our Greek Mark.[10] This is why he gave his book the title *The Corrections of Mark.*

Streeter completely ignored the question whether this usage does or does not reflect a Semitic idiom, and wrote: "Mark, for some reason or other, never uses this word in narrative; Matthew uses it 33 times, Luke 16. No explanation, then, is required for the fact that 5 times they concur in introducing it in the same context—for obviously the number of contexts is limited where its use would be at all appropriate." But on Streeter's terms there should not be *any* contexts where it would have been appropriate for Matthew and Luke to introduce this Semitic idiom. For if Matthew and Luke removed the historic present "upwards of 60 times" in order to make the Semitic style of Mark more idiomatically Greek, they should never have frustrated their purpose by introducing this Semitic idiom. This agreement remains inadequately explained on Streeter's terms.

(2) Mark has no *immediate* equivalent of "on a bed," and though the word for "bed" used here is a word never used by Mark, there is no apparent reason why both Matthew and Luke should have independently introduced this particular expression at this particular point into their Gospels. Since, on the Marcan hypothesis, Matthew and Luke tend to compress or condense Mark, Streeter has no explanation for this kind of agreement of Matthew and Luke against Mark. In fact, having based the greater part of his case for considering the majority of the minor agreements as "irrelevant," on the asserted grounds that "both Matthew and Luke consistently compress Mark," this kind of agreement works very much against Streeter, for it is an instance of agreement at a specific point where the text of Luke is fuller than that of Mark. Furthermore, at precisely this point in Mark's text there is an agreement of Matthew and Luke against Mark in their not having anything in their text to correspond to Mark's words "carried by four men." The idea conveyed by Mark's text of a paralytic "carried by four men" is

[10] *Op. cit.*, p. 304.

significantly different from the idea conveyed by Matthew and Luke's text of a paralytic brought to Jesus ":on a bed." They are not mutually exclusive ideas, but the agreement of Matthew and Luke cannot be explained as due to concurring stylistic, or editorial alterations or substitutions accidentally made for Mark's phrase "carried by four men." In fact, here again is another example where the tradition as preserved in Mark's text is more specific than that in either Matthew or Luke. To have a paralytic "carried by four men" is a more specific description of the mode of his conveyance than to say he was brought "on a bed," because the latter implies that a certain number of persons were involved in transporting his person, without giving their number, whereas, the specific number is given by Mark. The observation that Mark's phrasing is less specific than that of Matthew and Luke in that it does not mention that the man was "on a bed" is immaterial since attention is drawn to that fact in the next verse of Mark's text. That Mark uses a different word for bed from that used by Matthew and Luke, is also not material as to whether Mark's account is more specific than that of Matthew and Luke, though it magnifies the agreement of Matthew and Luke against Mark in this instance. The tradition in Mark's story at this point is clearly more specific in detail. This is a known characteristic of second century Apocryphal Gospel literature. Therefore, this particular conjoining of a positive agreement with an agreement in omission points to a place for Mark on the chronological scale of Gospel literature later in time, and closer to the second century Apocryphal Gospel literature than either Matthew or Luke. It was the great mass of evidence of this kind which enabled Schleiermacher to observe that Mark had certain affinities with the Apocryphal Christian writings. Defenders of the primitivity of Mark in Schleiermacher's day appealed to the same evidence as proof of the "eye-witness" character of Mark's account. Twentieth century critics are undecided on this point. But most scholars who take "form-criticism" seriously follow Bultmann in denying any eye-witness character to the greater part of Mark's narrative, and in holding that the Gospel tradition as it developed into the second century Gospel literature tended to become more specific.[11]

---

[11] It is a curious unresolved contradiction in "form-criticism" as popularly understood, that critics like Bultmann utilized the relatively few places where the above canon of criticism works in favor of Mark's originality to illustrate the value of "form-criticism" on the Marcan hypothesis and tended to ignore the relatively greater number

It is clear, then, that none of the causes to which Streeter appealed in any of his categories explains such an agreement.

(3) The agreement "he said" is paralleled in Mark by the usage of the historic present "he says." On Streeter's terms this is classified as an "Irrelevant Agreement" caused by the accidental concurrence of independent stylistic corrections made by Matthew and Luke. This agreement occurs once more in this passage following the agreement in omission [in his spirit], and eighteen additional times elsewhere. It was one of the eight agreements specifically listed by Abbott as confirming his view that all the minor agreements are from a corrector who aimed to improve the text of Mark by stylistic and other editorial changes. On the basis of the number and recurrence of these phenomena Sanday decided that they were "due to design, and not to accident."

The historic present is found in all the Gospels, but more frequently in John and Mark than in Matthew and Luke. The usage is frequent in Josephus and in the papyri, but not so frequent in the LXX. John uses it 162 times, Mark 151, Matthew 93, and Luke-Acts 22. Considering the relative lengths of the Gospels it is clear that the historic present is a favorite stylistic peculiarity of Mark.

However, it is difficult to imagine Matthew as correcting Mark's more colloquial Greek (to use Streeter's expression) by substituting "he said" for "he says" in numerous instances when he himself frequently used the historic present. In fact, Matthew used the same word in the same form (λέγει) as an historic present, just as Mark did in this passage, no less than 50 times elsewhere in his Gospel. Of these 50 instances, 10 might be explained, on the Marcan hypothesis, as due to Matthew copying Mark, but 40 cannot be so explained. Therefore, on his own terms, Streeter's notion that in

---

of instances where it works against Marcan priority. For example, after Bultmann has finished setting down what in his opinion is secondary in the Marcan forms of the biographical apophthegmata, the more original form of the tradition stripped of these secondary accretions frequently is closer to Matthew and/or Luke than to Mark. Yet Bultmann never notes this interesting fact in the discussions of the passages concerned in his *Die Geschichte der synoptischen Tradition*, Göttingen, 1921. This oversight cannot be excused on "form-critical" grounds since the use of biographical apophthegmata in contemporary literature constitutes the proper standard by which the more original form of the tradition is to be judged, and by this standard for comparison, Mark's form of the tradition in question is generally secondary to that of Matthew and Luke. Cases in point are: Mark 10:13-16; 11:15-19; 12:41-44; 13:1-4; 14:3-9.

these twenty agreements of Matthew and Luke against Mark, Matthew has corrected Mark's more idiomatic Greek is unconvincing. For this notion leaves unexplained the fact that Matthew himself, quite independent of Mark, used the very same idiom 40 times. There is no reason to think that Matthew would correct a particular "colloquialism" in Mark 20 times which he uses elsewhere twice as often. To have so corrected Mark under these circumstances would have been unnatural for most writers, and there is no evidence to support Streeter's suggestion that Matthew did so.

Furthermore, an examination of Luke's usage of the historic present also undermines Streeter's position at this point. A redactional analysis of the Gospel of Luke indicates that the evangelist himself seldom, if ever, preferred to use the historic present (compare Lk. 8:49 ‖ Mk. 5:35; Lk. 11:37, 45). The historic present is used 13 times in Acts, however. More important is the fact that in 6 different instances Luke has copied this usage into his text when he has found it in his special source material (compare Lk. 7:40; 13:8; 16:7; 16:23, 29; 19:22). There is no reason to think, therefore, that Luke would scrupulously avoid the historic present when he found it in his text of Mark. In fact, on the Marcan hypothesis there is one instance where Luke has taken the historic present from the text of Mark (Mk. 5:35 ‖ Lk. 8:49). In this case there is no Matthean parallel. There is no ground for Streeter to expect his readers to imagine that Luke would borrow the historic present from Mark in this one instance, and then accidentally coincide with Matthew in twenty instances in rejecting this usage and in correcting Mark's "colloquial" Greek.

This agreement of Matthew and Luke against Mark is very simply explained on either the Augustinian or the Griesbach hypothesis by imagining that: (1) Matthew wrote "he said" in these twenty cases, having freely used the historic present elsewhere; (2) Luke followed Matthew in these instances, since he often copied a source carefully, and in any case showed no strong personal preference for the historic present; (3) Mark substituted the historic present in all twenty cases. This change introduced by Mark would not have greatly affected the sense of his text, but rather would have reflected his personal style or current usage among his intended readers. Although this would be coming at the problem from a different direction than that advocated by Abbott and Sanday, it would in an inverse manner do justice to the evidence they saw for regarding these minor agreements as stemming from a purposeful and unitary redactional source. That source in the first instance would be the stylistic and grammatical usage of Matthew. On the Augustinian hypothesis, when the style and grammar of Mark's Greek led him to depart from the text of Matthew, Luke in these instances would create an agreement with Matthew against Mark whenever he followed Matthew's text more faithfully than had Mark. These agreements would naturally reflect Matthew's usage. On the Griesbach hypothesis, wherever Luke had copied Matthew's text faithfully, Mark would create an agreement between Matthew and Luke against his Gospel, whenever he permitted the style and grammar of his own Greek to deviate from the text to which Matthew and Luke bore concurrent testimony. Here again the minor agreements would reflect Matthean usage.

On Streeter's terms, even granting Marcan priority, this particular minor agreement is left inadequately explained.

(4) The agreement "and" presents a curious unexplained problem on Streeter's terms. In connection with the discussion of this conjunction found in the section on "Irrelevant Agreements," Streeter wrote: "Another stylistic improvement made innumerable times by Matthew and Luke is the substitution of δέ for καί." But in this passage the phenomenon is reversed, for Matthew and Luke agree in having the conjunction καί against Mark's δέ. Streeter offers no explanation for this agreement. By itself it constitutes only the smallest thread of evidence indicating literary dependence between Matthew and Luke. But when it is joined to all the other threads of agreement between Matthew and Luke against Mark in this passage, it adds strength to an otherwise strong web of evidence. Through the mutual cohesiveness of this web, even this tiny thread of evidence gains enough tenacity to make unwarranted its dismissal as insignificant in this context.

(5) The agreement "upon the earth to forgive sins" is also found in Mark in exactly the same words, but in a different word order. Streeter did not discuss the phenomenon of word order.

When occurring in isolation from other minor agreements between Matthew and Luke against Mark, a small agreement in word order would be of little or no significance. But in the full context of this particular literary unit it assumes a significance it would not have otherwise, and it delicately strengthens the over-all impression of the existence of a literary relationship between Matthew and Luke, either direct, or indirect through some kind of Ur-gospel.

(6) ". . . he went away into his house." This five-word agreement in Greek of Matthew and Luke against Mark must be evaluated within the total context of the web of supportive evidence presented in the discussion of the five positive agreements set forth above. ". . . he went away into his house" does not stand alone in this passage as an agreement of Matthew and Luke against Mark, as Streeter's presentation of it might suggest, but as the last in a series of mysteriously related minor agreements. What is the answer to the mystery of their existence? Is it possible to penetrate this mystery and find the reason for these agreements by the method of classification and analysis Streeter follows? This is the question the reader is asked to consider in evaluating the true significance of Streeter's work.

It should, by now, be clear that before the critic attempts to argue from the context of a particular minor agreement, it is incumbent upon him to note the full concatenation of agreements between Matthew and Luke against Mark within that context. This Streeter never did, and this means that his treatment of these minor agreements is affected throughout by a methodological flaw which renders his results of doubtful scientific value.

Furthermore, in order to appreciate the full impact of the agreement of any two Gospels against the third, it is necessary to join these agreements with those which all three Gospels share in common, and then to note the full extent of this combined agreement. For if one Evangelist copied the work of another, then in order to consider the total extent of verbal agreement between the two, it would be necessary to take into account both kinds of agreement. For example, if, as Simons and others thought, the minor agreements of Matthew and Luke against Mark constitute evidence that Luke used Matthew, it would be further necessary to consider the full extent of agreement between Matthew and Luke in order to evaluate the various ways in which Luke may have used Matthew. Did Luke make major use of Mark and "Q" and then only minor use of Matthew, as Simons thought? Or did Luke make such extensive use of Matthew that it is unnecessary to hypothesize his use of "Q"? If so, where should the line be drawn? Could Luke have been copying Matthew where some critics think he was copying Mark?

In the case of the passage under consideration, the total extent of the agreement between Matthew and Luke reads as follows: "and seeing their faith, he said . . . your sins . . . and . . . this man . . . Jesus . . . their . . . he said . . . in your hearts? Which is easier to say . . . your sins, or to say, 'rise and walk'? But in order that you may know that the Son of Man has authority upon earth to forgive sins . . . to . . . arise and . . . your . . . into your house. And . . . he went away into his house . . . and . . . God."

This represents exact verbatim agreement in Greek. There are additional agreements which have not been included where the same words are used but not in the same form. This extent of exact verbatim agreement, extending to the smallest points of grammar, such as case, number, person, tense, voice, mood, gender, etc., constitutes *prima-facie* evidence for direct literary dependence between Matthew and Luke. And if, as Streeter, Turner, Burkitt, and others thought, the evidence for an Ur-Marcus is not compelling, then the simplest explanation for the totality of this agreement would be the assumption that Luke copied Matthew or vice versa. It would not be possible to imagine Matthew and Luke independently deriving all this agreement through copying Mark, since then there would be no way to explain the assembly of minor agreements of the most varied sort between Matthew and Luke against Mark. Such agreements ought not to exist if Matthew and Luke independently copied Mark. How can they be explained?

If on other grounds there are sound reasons to think that Mark drew from Matthew and Luke, as Griesbach and many other nineteenth century critics held, then the least inadequate explanation for these minor agreements would be the suggestion put forward by Burton as to what a writer in this situation might conceivably do, and to regard Mark as being reasonably concerned to remain faithful to the wording and above all the sense of the narrative to which Matthew and Luke bore concurrent testimony, even frequently following the one or the other rather than departing from both when they departed from one another. The minor agreements between Matthew and Luke against Mark under such circumstances would simply be the residual parts of the text which one of them had copied from the other, but which Mark did not incorporate into his Gospel. Minor agreements would be of unlimited variety: stylistic, grammatical, syntactical, etc. The only thing they would tend to have in common would be their inconsequential effect upon the meaning of the narrative and possibly a certain unitary complexion emanating as they would, under these circumstances, from Mark's conscious or unconscious grammatical usage and stylistic preference freely influencing his adaptation of an essentially Matthean text. This is all entirely commensurate with the actual nature of the minor agreements between Matthew and Luke against Mark, and constitutes their simplest explanation.

The difficulty with this explanation from Streeter's point of view would have been the relationship it envisions of Mark to Matthew and Luke. Streeter thought that the priority of Mark was an assured result of nineteenth century criticism, and therefore, this simple solution was never a live option in his mind.

It is clear that Streeter was not confident that his treatment of his "Deceptive Agreements" would be convincing to those who had read and had been impressed with the arguments of Abbott, Sanday, Lummis, and Jameson against the idea of an accidental coincidence of agreement of Matthew and Luke against Mark in so many instances. Therefore, in a passage which is typical of his whole approach to this question, Streeter concluded his discussion of the "Deceptive Agreements" as follows:

If, however, anyone thinks the proportion [of coincident alterations] too large to be accidental, it is open to him to accept Dr. Sanday's hypothesis that the text of Mark used by Matthew and Luke had undergone a slight stylistic revision. But, I would submit, it is not open to him to account for the phenomena reviewed above by the hypothesis of an "Ur-Marcus," that is, a more primitive edition of Mark. For *in every case* the coincident language used by Matthew and Luke has been shown to be more polished and in every way less primitive than the existing text of Mark. If, therefore, the coincident agreements of Matthew and Luke can only be explained on the theory that they used a different edition of Mark from the one we have, then it is the earlier of the two editions, the Ur-Marcus in fact, that has survived" (304–305).

Two observations are worth making: (1) This concluding paragraph makes it quite evident that Streeter had no clear concept as to the real cause of these minor agreements. Otherwise it would not be possible for him to concede the possibility of Sanday's alternate explanation which is mutually contradictory to the one he has expounded at length in the preceding pages. (2) Streeter's chief purpose seems to have been to deny any grounds for Ur-Marcus, or rather any grounds for a distinction between the text of Mark and that of Ur-Marcus, if there was an Ur-Marcus, rather than to find a satisfactory explanation for these minor agreements. In other words, Streeter's treatment of the minor agreements of Matthew and Luke against Mark is to be regarded, not as a balanced impartial investigation into the most probable cause or causes of these phenomena, but rather as a sustained, but piecemeal attempt to demonstrate that these agreements do not constitute an evidential basis for belief in Ur-Marcus.

4. THE OVERLAPPING OF MARK AND "Q"

Streeter's third category of agreements is constituted by those which may be explained by an overlapping of Mark and "Q". Streeter writes:

It is now realized that Q, as well as Mark, contained versions of John's Preaching, the Baptism, Temptation, Beelzebub Controversy, Mission Charge, parable of Mustard Seed, and that Matthew regularly, Luke occasionally, conflates Mark and Q. Hence agreements of Matthew and Luke against Mark in *these* contexts can be explained by the influence of Q.

The most important point to note here is that on the two-document hypothesis, there are passages in Mark which overlap with corresponding passages in "Q." No defender of the two-document hypothesis has ever denied this, unless at the same time he posited the existence of an Ur-Marcus to account for these passages where Matthew and Luke agree with one another against Mark, and agree in giving a more original form of the tradition than has Mark. This means that Streeter, and all who acknowledge this overlap between Mark and "Q," also acknowledge that both Matthew and Luke are involved in conflating Mark and "Q." This is highly significant for it brings out a point too little appreciated and frequently overlooked entirely, namely, that every hypothesis which in any sense does justice to the phenomena of the Synoptic Problem involves conflation of some kind. It is sometimes assumed that only the Griesbach hypothesis involves conflation. But the Augustinian hypothesis envisions Luke conflating Matthew and Mark, and the two-document hypothesis entails Matthew conflating Mark and "Q" and Luke doing the same.

There is no way in which to escape the conclusion that at least one of the Evangelists was involved in the task of conflating closely related texts.[12]

Streeter warns against appealing to this cause in contexts where there is no clear evidence of an overlap between Mark and "Q." But such warnings, however well intended, are scientifically gratuitous. For there are no satisfactory criteria by which a two-document adherent can decide in advance when the evidence is sufficient to posit an overlap between Mark and "Q." In practice, adherents of the two-document hypothesis consistently appeal to this overlap to explain any case where the text of Matthew and Luke clearly is more original than that of Mark.

This questionable mode of operation was made quite explicit more than once by C. F. Burney in his book, *The Poetry of Our Lord*.[13] For example, in his discussion of the saying:

Whosoever willeth to save his life, shall lose it;
But whosoever shall lose his life for my sake, shall find it.

Burney notes that Matthew (16:25) and Luke (9:24) agree in giving the saying in this form as does Mark (8:35), except that "Mark adds 'and the gospel's' after 'for my sake,' which clearly overweights the clause." Because Matthew sometimes, and Luke frequently, destroys the poetic structure of sayings, Burney reasons: Since it is improbable that both Matthew and Luke improved the form of Mark's parallelism by excision of these words, "we must infer that they depended upon a source of information superior to Mark, i.e., probably Q."[14] This same phenomenon, however, is

---

[12] The relative proportion of the text of a Gospel which is the result of conflation will vary from one hypothesis to another. There is no canon of literary criticism, however, by which this fact alone can be appealed to in settling the question of the order in which the Gospels were written. That is, there is no way to have known in advance whether a document which is found to be the result of conflation would be so throughout the greater part of its length, or only in a relatively few places.

[13] *The Poetry of Our Lord, An Examination of the Formal Elements of Hebrew Poetry in the Discourses of Jesus Christ*, Oxford, 1925.

[14] *Op. cit.*, pp. 74–75. *Cf.* pp. 140–142. In other instances where the Marcan form was found by Burney to be secondary on the basis of his formal analysis, he appealed to other causes. Mark 10:27, for example is explained as follows: "This example offers another instance in which Mark is clearly inferior to the other Synoptists. The typical form of antithesis (as witnessed by numerous other examples) is that given by Matthew: 'With man this is impossible, But with God all things are possible.' This has been somewhat paraphrased by Luke: 'The things which are impossible with men are possible

more simply explained on either the Augustinian or Griesbach hypothesis which presume Luke to be free to copy Matthew faithfully and Mark to be free to follow Matthew or Luke or both, and at the same time add "and of the gospel." This expression is in complete accord with Mark's editorializing style as may be seen by a comparison with Mark 10:29 where the same expression may be seen in the saying concerning the renunciation of property and family for the sake of Jesus *and for the sake of the gospel.* Most commentators agree that this expression comes from the hand of Mark and is secondary to the original form of the tradition since it reflects a usage of the term "gospel" which is accepted as characteristic of the life situation of the church rather than that of Jesus. Matthew and Luke agree against Mark in both passages in not having this secondary expression. In post-Streeter criticism there has been no obligation to discuss the significance of this important sign of the secondary character of Mark's text as compared to that of Matthew and Luke, because of Streeter's dictum that agreements in omission are irrelevant. If there are serious critical objections standing in the way of accepting any hypothesis involving direct literary dependence of Mark upon one or both the other Synoptic Gospels, then some form of the Ur-gospel hypothesis needs to be utilized in order to account for these secondary features of Mark's text. For even appealing to the idea of an overlap between Mark and "Q," it is necessary to make this appeal so frequently and extensively throughout the length of Mark, that "Q," as B. Weiss perceived in the nineteenth century, is to be conceived of in the shape of a Gospel beginning with the baptism of John and continuing on up into the section dealing with the events during the last days of Jesus' ministry.

Before the twentieth century critic revives Lessing's Ur-gospel, however, he should give serious attention once again to those hypotheses which appeal to the concept of direct literary dependence among the Evangelists. For if it is possible to explain the phenomena adequately without hypothecating unknown sources to

---

with God', a form in which the strict parallelism of the two antithetical statements is modified so as to produce a *single* statement—still, nothing is added. In Mark, however, we read: 'With men it is impossible, But not with God; For all things are possible with God.' Here the insertion of 'But not with God', which is really redundant by the side of the following line, has the effect of marring the sharpness and balance of the antithesis. Clearly the addition is a gloss."

account for the agreements between the Gospels, then this would be preferable to any equally satisfactory hypothesis which entailed the appeal to hypothetical documents. There is a distinct prospect that the Synoptic Problem can be explained now without reference to Ur-Marcus or "Q." For the difficulties raised in the nineteenth century against the Augustinian and Griesbach hypothesis, to mention only the best known of those which make no appeal to the use of an Ur-gospel or "Q," need not be regarded as insuperable today.

5. THE "AGREEMENTS DUE TO TEXTUAL CORRUPTION"

Streeter's final category of agreements is constituted by those he believed could be explained by a process of textual corruption. After a section in which he briefly discussed such textual phenomena as assimilation, etc., Streeter, in an extended seventeen-page monograph under the subtitle "The MS. Evidence," discussed ". . . all the minor agreements not already discussed in this chapter which seem to me at all significant." These include, observed Streeter: ". . . those mentioned by Hawkins and by Burton; also all those in Abbott's exhaustive list which are in the slightest degree remarkable, along with certain others I have noticed myself."[15] Then follows a treatment of thirty-one passages, each of which is set forth in the Greek text, and then explained.

Since Streeter's discussion of the first passage (Mk. 1:40–42) is typical of the way he proceeded throughout this section, it will be used here as an example to illustrate his method and evaluate his results.

After printing the Greek text according to the same formula used in his presentation of the "Deceptive Agreements," Streeter discussed five positive agreements. One of these was the familiar use of ἰδού by Matthew and Luke. Another was the familiar correction by Matthew and Luke of Mark's historic present. Both of these agreements were dismissed by Streeter as irrelevant on the basis of his

---

[15] Hawkins, *Horae Synopticae*, 2nd ed. pp. 208–212; Burton, *Some Principles of Literary Criticism*, p. 209; Abbott, *Corrections of Mark*, pp. 307–324. The two most complete published lists of these agreements are by Abbott, and Monsig. de Solages, *A Greek Synopsis of the Gospels, A New Way of Solving the Synoptic Problem*, Toulouse, 1959, pp. 1055–1066.

previous defense. But Streeter's reasoning and evidence at these points has been shown to be unconvincing. Therefore, these agreements stand unexplained. For the remaining three positive agreements Streeter cites manuscript evidence which creates the impression in the mind of the reader that the agreement is no longer certain and may in fact be due to a process of textual corruption of some kind. But Streeter failed to draw attention to three agreements in omission between Matthew and Luke against Mark within the same context of the relatively brief span of text he was considering. The total concatenation of minor agreements in these three verses is as follows: "... and behold ... [to him that] ... Lord ... [being moved with compassion] ... he touched him, saying [to him] ... immediately. ..."

When one takes into account both the positive agreements and the agreements in omission of Matthew and Luke against Mark he finds that these agreements together contribute to a continuous verbatim agreement between Matthew and Luke of eighteen consecutive words in the best critically reconstructed editions of the Greek text. This kind of phenomenon Streeter never discusses.

Is the reader to think that Matthew and Luke in complete independence omitted αὐτῷ ὅτι, added κύριε, omitted σπλαγχνισθείς, transposed the word order of αὐτοῦ ἥψατο, substituted a participle for Mark's historic present καὶ λέγει, omitted αὐτῷ, and then substituted εὐθέως for εὐθύς, all in the compass of three verses? It would be far simpler to account for this series of agreements and the eighteen word consecutive verbatim agreement on the hypothesis that Luke copied Matthew. And if for some reason that simple solution is proved impossible, this passage would constitute evidence for the use of an Ur-gospel, either Ur-Marcus or "Q" in the form of a Gospel with healing stories. It does not significantly change the picture in this instance to be told by Streeter that in the case of κύριε the textual evidence is so uncertain "no text can be relied upon," and that in the case of the word order of ἥψατο αὐτοῦ, "If we accept the reading of D as original all is explained," and that in the case of εὐθέως "scribes as a rule, except in Alexandria," preferred εὐθέως to εὐθύς.

Even if each one of these three positive agreements could be due to textual corruption, that still would not change the fact that eighteen words are in consecutive agreement between Matthew and Luke, and that the texts of Matthew and Luke in these verses are still closer to one another than either is to the text of Mark—even as Streeter proposed to emend Mark's text on the basis of his own textual theories.

Whatever merit some of Streeter's textual theories may have in other contexts, it cannot be gainsaid that after over a quarter of a century during which text critics have had ample opportunity to study the suggested textual emendations Streeter set forth in his discussion of these thirty-one passages, that these suggested changes seldom if ever have been adopted in the construction of new critical editions. Therefore, there is no reason to think that Streeter's treatment of these thirty-one passages represents more than a conscientious effort to explain away residual agreements he was not able to treat satisfactorily under his three previous categories. Streeter never drew attention to the total concatenation of agreement, and all that was said on the importance of this methodological fault in the discussion of his treatment of the "Deceptive Agreements" applies with equal force here.

Further confirmation of the fact that Streeter's treatment of the textual evidence is no impartial attempt to ascertain the true bearing of available knowledge about the process of copying upon the problem of these minor agreements, comes from the disclosure that it is possible to increase the number of agreements between Matthew and Luke against Mark by the same method used by Streeter to decrease these agreements.

In 1863 Holtzmann in his famous *Die Synoptischen Evangelien* noted that it would be possible to increase the instances of agreement between Matthew and Luke against Mark if the most conspicuous variant readings could be regarded as the true ones.[16]

With this suggestion in mind, F. M. Keech in 1962 proceeded to check the texts of the Gospels over about forty per cent of the material they share in common. Keech used Legg's volumes for Matthew and Mark, and Tischendorf's eighth edition for Luke (consulting Nestle's twenty-first edition for more recent notations). From his survey Keech makes the following observations: (1) It is possible to *decrease* greatly (perhaps by half) the number of agreements,

---

[16] J. H. Ludlum drew attention to this fact in a letter to the author (June 23, 1959) in connection with his comments on a compilation of all the agreements of Matthew and Luke against Mark in "triple-tradition" contexts, made by F. M. Keech. The information in turn was given to Keech.

(a) by citing textual variants in Mark to agree with the text of Matthew and Luke, thus removing an agreement against Mark; (b) by citing a variant in Matthew or Luke, once again removing an agreement against Mark. (2) It is also possible to *increase* greatly (perhaps by several times) the number of agreements against Mark, (a) by finding a variant reading in Mark, thus creating an agreement against Mark (as Holtzmann indicates); or, (b) where all three Gospels read differently to find a Matthean variant to agree with Luke's text or a Lucan variant to agree with Matthew's text. (3) It is possible to change the number of agreements by adopting readings of Sinaiticus as against Vaticanus, or vice versa.[17]

This test was not complete, and Keech did not present his evidence over a sample portion of the parallel texts of Matthew, Mark, and Luke. Nonetheless, it is clear that Streeter did not apply his method of emending the texts of the Gospels impartially. If he had he would have drawn attention to examples where instances of agreement between Matthew and Luke against Mark could be added by accepting variants equally well attested as those he cited to reduce these agreements. This he never did. It may be answered that it was not Streeter's purpose to set forth the results of such an impartial investigation. And, if it be asked what his purpose was, the answer is presumably to be found in the words with which he opened the discussion of "Textual Corruption": "I proceed to explore the hypothesis that a large number of the Agreements are due, not to the original authors, but to later scribes. . . ." But how can a hypothesis be explored if careful consideration is not given to the evidence which weighs against it—in this case the evidence from variant readings which suggest that the instances of agreement between Matthew and Luke against Mark can be increased by the same method Streeter followed in decreasing them?

There is no evidence that Streeter laid the careful groundwork which an impartial exploration of this hypothesis entailed. And until such time as all significant variants which might conceivably increase or decrease the agreements between Matthew and Luke against Mark have been identified, analyzed, and thoroughly studied, any presentation like that which Streeter has set forth in this section is at best inconclusive and at worst misleading.

[17] F. M. Keech, *op. cit.*

6. A "RESIDUAL CASE"

Streeter concluded his discussion of the minor agreements between Matthew and Luke against Mark with a topic which he terms "Some Residual Cases." One of these he treats in great detail, namely, Mark 14:65 and its parallels.[18]

It is of the highest importance to grasp firmly the radical character of the proposal Streeter made to explain away the clear and unambiguous positive agreement between Matthew and Luke against Mark in this passage. Streeter proposed to explain the agreement between Matthew and Luke against Mark in including the question: "Who is the one who struck you?" by appeal to a process of assimilation along all Matthean lines of textual transmission. Streeter's proposal cannot be fully appreciated until it is known that textual evidence is unanimous in support of Matthew's reading. Streeter proposed that Matthew's unanimously attested reading be set aside as due to a process of *sporadic* corruption which had affected the text tradition behind all extant copies of Matthew. The source of this total corruption of all extant copies of Matthew was Luke, where this reading was original. Matthew's text, therefore, as restored to its original form would omit the words: "Who is the one who struck you?"

If this procedure were taken seriously by text critics it would revolutionize that discipline, and play havoc with serious historico-critical work on the Gospels. A history of textual corruption like this might be possible theoretically, but before the critic appeals to such a radical emendation, it is important to know whether the texts of the Gospels, as now reconstructed on the basis of the best manuscripts available are susceptible to an intelligible literary and historical interpretation. The answer is, "Yes"—on the Ur-Marcus hypothesis, where Matthew, Mark, and Luke are but three different versions of an independent Ur-text. The agreement between Matthew and Luke against Mark in this case is explained simply by the assumption that they have copied Ur-Marcus more faithfully than Mark. In other words Mark himself omitted these words which Matthew and Luke copied from Ur-Marcus. It is not clear why Mark omitted these words, but that is not a serious difficulty, because it is never

---

[18] Streeter's argumentation in this discussion is so detailed and complex it is best for the reader to have his words represented exactly as he set them down. *See* Appendix A.

possible to know everything that would have influenced a writer so far-removed from our own time and circumstances.

But since Streeter was quite convinced that Ur-Marcus was a phantom, it will be instructive to compare the relative merits of Streeter's explanation of the agreements and differences among Matthew, Mark, and Luke at this point, with the way in which these same phenomena would be explained on some other hypothesis, as for example, that of Griesbach. On Griesbach's hypothesis the history of the redaction of the tradition would be explained as follows: Matthew 26:67 reads, "Then they spat in his face and struck him and some slapped him, saying 'Prophesy to us, you Christ! Who is it that struck you?'" Matthew's form of the tradition calls up an image of a prisoner being tormented, distracted and mocked by his captors. The question "who struck you?" heightens the emphatic quality of the scene, for it pictured Jesus with other men's spittle running down his face and buffeted by their blows, being so distracted by this abuse he could only with difficulty have identified those who had struck him. The text as it stands in Matthew is on all literary, historical, and form-critical grounds unimpeachable. It represents in concise form a creative line of dramatic writing fully consonant with the movement and purpose of the larger literary whole of which it is a part.

Luke's text reads, "Now the men who were holding Jesus mocked him and beat him; they also blindfolded him and asked him, 'Prophesy! Who is it that struck you?' And they spoke many other words against him, reviling him." Since the question "who struck you" presupposed that Jesus had not seen who had just struck him, Luke made Jesus' incapacity quite explicit: he was blindfolded! Luke's narrative gains in verisimilitude at this one point, but it loses in dramatic power elsewhere; first by Luke's omission of the reference to Jesus being spat upon; and second, by the addition of "and they spoke many other words against him, reviling him," which is both repetitive and anticlimactic.

Mark in conflating the texts of Matthew and Luke wrote: "And some began to spit on him, and to blindfold him, and to strike him, saying to him, 'Prophesy!' And the guards received him with blows." Mark omits the taunting question, "who struck you?" verified in the texts of both Matthew and Luke. This omission does not change the narrative in any obvious way, though it points up the secondary character of Mark's text, since he had retained Luke's reference to Jesus being "blindfolded," which detail originally came into the tradition only to make more specific the reason for Jesus' incapacity to see who it was who had struck him. In Mark's text this detail no longer has point.[19] Mark was able to conflate Matthew and Luke down to the point in their texts where he read "Prophesy!" But then he faced the problem of what to do next. Should he include Matthew's "you Christ," or omit it with Luke? And beyond that should he copy Luke's concluding comment, or omit it since there was nothing with which he could combine it in Matthew. Mark's decision is editorially comprehensible. He conflated down to the command "Prophesy!" then he ended the narrative in his own words. Mark had an editor's right to omit the question, "Who struck you!" It was not absolutely necessary to the narrative. But by omitting this question Mark's text has lost the point that the men were taunting Jesus in their demand that he "Prophesy!" Their taunt was to the effect: "If he be the Son of God, he surely will be able to tell us who it is who has struck him!"

From this viewpoint the secondary character of Mark's text is especially clear from the fact that in conflating Matthew and Luke he has inadvertently maximized the now obviated circumstances which accounted for Jesus' incapacity to see who has struck him. For Mark shows Jesus both spat upon (from Matthew) and blind-folded (from Luke)!

The point of these comments is only to illustrate that it is not necessary to accept Streeter's radical proposed emendation. In fact, these words which Streeter would explain away from Matthew's text as due to some process of early sporadic textual corruption, are quite consistent with those which precede them in Matthew's text. There is, therefore, no sound reason for accepting Streeter's emendation, and these words must stand, as with Hawkins and Burton, as a particularly significant agreement of Matthew and Luke

---

[19] Streeter's explanation completely breaks down at this point, since without the taunting question in the text of Mark no copyist would have had any motive to assimilate Mark's text to that of Luke by inserting the detail of "blindfolding." As Streeter himself says: "These two stand or fall together." On Streeter's terms of textual assimilation it would be simpler to explain the omission of the reference to blindfolding and the substitution of τῷ προσώπῳ αὐτοῦ for αὐτῷ in D a f as made under the influence of Matthew's text where there is no reference to blindfolding, and where the men spit εἰς τὸ πρόσωπον αὐτοῦ.

against Mark.[20] Without an Ur-Marcus to explain this agreement, the strict two-document adherent is led to think that here again Mark overlapped with "Q." But this would mean that "Q" contained a passion narrative, which most two-document adherents are reluctant to affirm.

7. CONCLUSIONS

The failure of Streeter's effort to enable his readers to escape from this impasse is commensurate with the failure of his argumentation at all crucial points throughout his discussion of the minor agreements of Matthew and Luke against Mark. Streeter's treatment of these phenomena is inconclusive at best.

Nonetheless, Streeter's highly questionable piece of scientific writing was widely accepted by many knowledgeable readers as a detailed and trustworthy analysis of the phenomena.

The implausibility of the argumentation which Streeter followed in his discussion of this final agreement is to be kept in mind when considering the significance of Streeter's following proposal:

The minor agreements which I have examined above include all that are sufficiently striking to be worth discussing in detail. The residue are agreements still more minute. *Of these textual assimilation is the probable explanation* [italics mine. W. R. F.].

This is the point at which the unwary reader, if he is unconscious of the implausibility of Streeter's argument throughout this part of his book, is led to give or withhold his assent to a final proposition. To give assent seems to entail only a reasonable claim upon one's credulity. But giving assent involves far-reaching consequences. For it means being prepared to think that *any* agreement between Matthew and Luke against Mark is explicable and that the last objection to the notion that Matthew and Luke copied Mark has been effectively removed.

[20] Hawkins listed it as one of twenty agreements of Matthew and Luke against Mark which he thought it "almost impossible that Matthew and Luke could have accidentally concurred in making." Burkitt recognized it as "undoubtedly" the passage which gave more support for Ur-Marcus than any other, and admitted that he did "not think we are in a position entirely to solve this problem. . . ." *The Gospel History and Its Transmission*, p. 52. Burton listed it as one of fifteen agreements of Matthew and Luke against Mark "which affect the sense of the passage further than by the change of tense or an unimportant exchange of prepositions." Burton's eighth conclusion at the end of his essay on *Principles of Literary Criticism and the Synoptic Problem* begins: "The agreements of Matthew and Luke against Mark in the triple narrative which are scattered throughout the gospels are an unexplained remainder."

F. C. Burkitt, who was himself a text critic, in discussing Streeter's treatment of this final "Residual Case," approved Streeter's "critical Judgment" in preferring this "attractive" conjecture. That he did so with some hesitation did not fundamentally call Streeter's work into question. Burkitt's closing paragraph had the effect of reassuring the readers of *J.T.S.* that Streeter's work was essentially trustworthy:

After all, this textual work is only one part of Dr. Streeter's volume, and it would be out of proportion to stress it too strongly either by praise or blame. What is so admirable in his book is the general proportion kept between the parts, and the just emphasis which he lays on things of the first importance, such as in the priority of Mark. . . . Perhaps he has given us few final solutions, but the book will be for a long time an excellent advance base from which a future generation of students can start for the further investigation of the Gospels.

In this way Streeter's work on the Synoptic Problem in his *The Four Gospels* was sanctioned by the single most influential figure in British New Testament circles of the day. The consequence of this endorsement was Streeter's elevation above all contemporary scholars working on the problem. Henceforth, his book was to be regarded as the "advanced base" from which future work would take its point of departure. Any books which departed from the two-document hypothesis as Streeter defined it in his "Fundamental Solution" were no longer to be considered seriously.

B. Jameson's Refutation
of Streeter's Arguments

The works of Lummis and Jameson, of course, were adversely affected by this development. This was especially ironical in the case of Jameson since he had already been made aware of Streeter's views on the Synoptic Problem through Streeter's article in Peake's *Commentary on the Bible*, published in 1920, and had taken Streeter's arguments into account in his book in 1922. In this book Jameson refuted most of the essential arguments which Streeter incorporated into his "Fundamental Solution" in 1924.

Streeter's refusal to acknowledge the serious and responsible work of Jameson, in which the logical fallacy of Streeter's arguments had been exposed, constitutes in the history of the Synoptic Problem the single most unparalleled act of academic bravado on record.

Jameson refuted the argument from order and showed that it could be used quite as well to argue for the Augustinian hypothesis.

Streeter in 1924 made an allusive reference to a recent attempt to revive the Augustinian hypothesis but dismissed the idea on the grounds that only a lunatic would have acted as Mark is assumed to have acted on that hypothesis. Augustine was excused by Streeter because he did not possess a synopsis of the Greek text.

Jameson also refuted Streeter's argument for "Q," which he had originally set forth in 1915 in his review of Lummis' book. This argument presupposed the priority of Mark and asserted the absurdity of thinking that Luke would have reintroduced sayings material taken from Matthew into Marcan contexts different than Matthew had given them. Jameson simply noted that these sayings are not given a Marcan context in Luke. Streeter repeated this argument in 1924 as if the fact that it was a *non sequitur* had never been pointed out.

If Streeter's reference in 1924 to "ingenious persons who rush into print" includes Jameson, and in context it is difficult to know who else Streeter could have had in mind, Streeter's accusation was quite unfair. No one could have written the kind of book Jameson wrote without having studied the Synoptic Problem for years. His solution may have been wrong, but his grasp of many of the essentials of the problem was firmer than that of Streeter or of Burkitt, and compared favorably with that of the best students of the problem. [*See* Appendix B.]

C. Streeter's Misconception
of Hawkins' "Horae Synopticae"

Streeter was prone to an elementary misconception of the qualifications for evidence in his notion that the "immense mass of details" which Hawkins had "collected, analyzed and tabulated" constituted evidence for the priority of Mark (164). Hawkins never made any such claim for his painstaking work. He believed that the arguments of Woods led "irresistibly" to the conclusion that the *Grundschift* behind the Gospels "is substantially our St. Mark as far as *matter, general form,* and order are concerned." Hawkins thought that this conclusion, which in 1909 could be called "a practically certain result of modern study of the 'Synoptic Problem'" suggested a further question: "What is the account to be given of the Marcan matter which neither Matthew nor Luke has incorporated, and which therefore lies before us as peculiar to Mark ?" Hawkins, as a contribution to the study of this question, brought together and classified the "Marcan peculiarities." He personally questioned the idea of an Ur-Marcus, and was interested in showing that most of these "Marcan peculiarities" could have been omitted or altered by Matthew and Luke, so that there was no need to think that the Mark copied by Matthew and Luke was other than canonical Mark.[21]

The "Marcan characteristics" as such, which Hawkins tabulated, no more supported the priority of Mark than Matthew or Luke. Indeed, some of the phenomena he tabulated can be better explained on hypotheses other than that of Marcan priority.

For example, in section V Hawkins tabulated a list of phenomena under the heading "Duplicate Expressions in Mark, of which One or Both of the Other Synoptists use one Part, or its Equivalent."

The list as it stands does not constitute evidence for the priority of Mark. Yet Streeter writes:

... Mark is very fond of "duplicate expressions" such as "Evening having come, when the sun set" (1:32). In these cases one or other of the later Evangelists usually abbreviates by leaving out one member of the pair; and not infrequently it happens that Matthew retains one and Luke the other. Thus in the above example Matthew writes "evening having come," Luke "the sun having set" (163–164).

This example stands first in the list compiled by Hawkins. It also stands first in a list of passages which Bleek thought obligated the critic to regard Mark as secondary to Matthew and Luke. In connection with this duplicate expression Bleek wrote:

If Mark's were the original and primary statement, the inference would be that Matthew and Luke divided his words between them, Matthew appropriating one portion, and Luke the other. But it is improbable that an independent writer would have used two such expressions side by side to designate the eventide, had he not been led thereto by finding them elsewhere. The likelihood clearly is, that Mark has here blended the expressions of the two other evangelists.[22]

[21] *Horae Synopticae*, 2nd ed., pp. 114–153.
[22] *Einleitung*, 2nd ed., paragraph 94; Eng. tr. *An Introduction to the New Testament*, p. 261.

The point is that such duplicate expressions do not by themselves constitute evidence for or against Marcan priority. They are susceptible to different interpretations, and possibly they are better explained on one hypothesis than on another. But it has never been shown that they can be explained best on the Marcan hypothesis, and, until that is done, they cannot justly be considered as evidence for the priority of Mark.

In a case like this a careful linguistic analysis is needed to ascertain whether either part of the duplicate expression is characteristic of any one of the three Gospels. In this case ὀψίας δὲ γενομένης (evening having come) is a rare expression. To begin with ὀψία is not found elsewhere in the LXX or other Greek versions of the Old Testament, including the Apocrypha; nor is it found elsewhere in the New Testament, except twice in John (6:16 and 20:19). The use of ὀψία in a genitive absolute construction with γίνομαι to begin a sentence is found in the whole of biblical literature only in Matthew and Mark. It occurs six times in Matthew and four times in Mark. It never occurs in Mark except in passages where the same expression is found in the Matthean parallel. Furthermore, when it occurs in Matthew it is always in exactly the same characteristic form of one of the redactors of Matthew, quite likely the Evangelist himself. In Mark, on the other hand, this exact form is found only in this passage under consideration. In the other three instances where Mark used this particular expression there are slight variations. The evidence is as follows:

Matthew	8:16 ὀψίας δὲ γενομένης	Mark	1:32 ὀψίας δὲ γενομένης
		,,	4:35 ἐν ἐκείνῃ τῇ ἡμέρᾳ ὀψίας γενομένης
,,	14:15 ὀψίας δὲ γενομένης	,,	6:35 καὶ ἤδη ὥρας πολλῆς γενομένης
,,	14:23 ὀψίας δὲ γενομένης	,,	6:47 καὶ ὀψίας γενομένης
,,	20:8 ὀψίας δὲ γενομένης		
,,	26:20 ὀψίας δὲ γενομένης	,,	14:17 καὶ ὀψίας γενομένης
,,	27:57 ὀψίας δὲ γενομένης	,,	15:42 καὶ ἤδη ὀψίας γενομένης

On the Marcan hypothesis the critic is asked to imagine that Matthew copied this expression exactly as Mark had it the first time he encountered it, but thereafter whenever he followed Mark in the use of this rare expression he consistently deviated from Mark and rigidly restricted himself to this particular grammatical form, even introducing it in 14:15 where Mark had ὥρας instead of ὀψίας, and in 20:8 where there was no Marcan parallel.

If Mark were secondary to Matthew, however, the critic would only be required to imagine that Mark tended to modify this Matthean expression quite freely wherever he found it in his text of Matthew. That is, the critic would simply conclude that if Mark copied Matthew, he apparently had no objection to the expression, but that it was not so much a part of his regular literary usage as to have assumed for him the form of a fixed stylistic introductory formula. He, therefore, copied it when he came upon it, but without any apparent concern to preserve the formula-like character the expression had in Matthew. The one time that Mark used the expression when there was no Matthean parallel, he did not use it as the beginning of a sentence as was characteristic of Matthean usage.

Either of these explanations is possible, though the latter is preferable since it leaves nothing to be further explained, whereas on the former explanation there is the question why Matthew would utilize the exact same form in all six instances. It is easier to explain the phenomena in Matthew as a stylistically fixed introductory formula, which has been freely altered in Mark, than vice versa.

By themselves these facts are not decisive. But if the preponderance of evidence of this kind weighed in the same direction, then facts like this would weigh significantly against Streeter's notion that Matthew copied Mark.

It is important to note that Hawkins elsewhere in his book gleaned from Matthew, Mark, and Luke a long list of similar expressions, which he termed "formulas":

For want of a better word I use the term "formula" to express the short sentences, or collocations of two or more words, which recur mainly or exclusively in one or other of the Synoptic Gospels, so that they appear to be favorite or habitual expressions of the writer of it.[23]

Hawkins listed first those formulas which were confined exclusively to one Gospel. Peculiar to Matthew he listed 15 expressions; to Mark 6; and to Luke 12. Then he wrote:

The above lists are not intended to be exhaustive, but to give specimens of expressions or "formulas" peculiar to each Synoptist. But there is

[23] *Op. cit.*, pp. 168–169.

another class of them which is more important and interesting, because more likely to throw light upon the process of the formulation of the Gospels. I mean those which are used once (or in a few cases twice) by a Synoptist in common with one or both of the others, and are *also* used by that Synoptist independently in other parts of his narrative.

Hawkins then listed seven such formula-like expressions for Luke, nineteen for Matthew, but none for Mark. He recorded none for Mark presumably because he had been unable to find any clear cut instances in that Gospel.

Of the 7 formulas which appeared to Hawkins to be "favorite or habitual expressions" of Luke, 5 are found at least once in Mark in parallel passages, and 2 occur also in Matthean parallel passages.

Of the 19 formulas which appeared similarly to Hawkins to be characteristic of Matthew, 14 are found at least once in Mark in parallel passages, and 10 occur also in Luke.

This means that formulas which appear to be "favorite or habitual" expressions of Matthew are found frequently both in Mark and Luke in parallel passages where there is evidence of copying. Such formulas of Luke also occur fairly frequently in Mark. There seem to be no such expressions characteristic of Mark, however, which show up in either Matthew or Luke. This fact is particularly difficult to understand on Streeter's theory concerning Marcan priority. For if Matthew and Luke copied Mark, presumably they would inadvertently copy at least a few of Mark's characteristic expressions into the texts of their Gospels. This would seem to be especially true in the case of Matthew where the amount of verbatim agreement between Matthew and Mark is so great that if Matthew copied Mark it would seem to be highly unlikely that he would have averted all characteristic expressions of Mark.

There is only one solution that affords a ready explanation for all the facts which Hawkins has tabulated in this connection, namely, the Griesbach hypothesis. On this view the favorite expressions of Matthew would naturally appear occasionally both in Luke and Mark, because Griesbach thought both Luke and Mark copied Matthew. And favorite expressions of Luke would also occur occasionally in Mark since Mark copied Luke. But habitual expressions of Mark would not usually occur either in Matthew or Luke, even less likely in parallel passages alone, because there would be no way in which these earlier authors, when they wrote their

Gospels, could have had direct access to Mark's use of these expressions, since his Gospel was written after those of Matthew and Luke.

Hawkins had no ready explanation for this evidence on the Marcan hypothesis, and since the Griesbach hypothesis was no longer under consideration because of the arguments of Abbott and Woods, Hawkins was constrained to find some other explanation. He noticed that in the case of the 19 favorite expressions of Matthew several occurred first in Matthew at a point where there was no Marcan parallel, and then occurred later where there was a Marcan parallel. Since Hawkins did not doubt that Matthew copied Mark (or an Ur-Marcus almost like Mark), this led him to conclude that in these instances Matthew drew these favorite expressions "from his memory of his sources and not from documents before him." [24] This, of course, is not a very satisfactory solution. The phenomenon is more simply explained on any hypothesis which recognized Mark to be in some sense secondary to Matthew.

Out of the five times that favorite expressions of Luke occur in Mark, the expression occurs earlier in the text of Luke twice. By itself this would not be significant. It is a fact, however, which is fully commensurate with a theory which affirms that Mark copied Luke.

If the favorite expressions of the Synoptists listed by Hawkins as peculiar to each Gospel are added to the others, it brings the total for Matthew to 34, Luke to 19, while Mark remains at 6. Of the 34 favorite expressions of Matthew, 14 are found in Mark only in parallel passages. Of the 19 of Luke, 5 are found in Mark and once again only in parallel passages. No favorite expressions of Mark are found in either Matthew or Luke. Of the 34 of Matthew, 10 are found in Luke, but of the 19 of Luke only 2 are found in Matthew.

This evidence weighs consistently and heavily in favor of Mark's dependence on Matthew. It weighs as consistently but not so heavily in favor of Mark's dependence on Luke. It does not weigh consistently in favor of Luke's dependence on Matthew, but in balance it supports that view. None of this evidence weighs in favor of Streeter's view that Matthew and Luke copied Mark.

Hawkins also tabulated a list of "words and phrases" characteristic of Matthew, Mark, and Luke. A similar analysis of this datum fails to adduce any evidence to support Streeter's view.

[24] *Op. cit.*, pp. 171–172.

D. The Abbott-Streeter Linguistic Argument
for Marcan Primitivity

Why then did Streeter think that anyone who worked through the "immense mass of details" which Hawkins presented on pp. 114–153 of *Horae Synopticae* would be convinced of the originality of Mark? It was because in this section of his book Hawkins was, as he himself acknowledged, dependent upon the pioneer work of Abbott in his famous article on the "Gospels" in the *Encyclopaedia Britannica* of 1879.[25] Abbott repeated his views in the *Encyclopaedia Biblica* in 1902. In both of these very influential works Abbott presented "linguistic" evidence in support of the originality of Mark.

Hawkins may have thought that his refinement and amplification of Abbott's data constituted evidence for the priority of Mark. If so he was cautious enough not to say so. Streeter made no reference to Abbott, but it is clear that he had consulted the *Encyclopaedia Britannica* article by Abbott, and it is to Abbott the historian must go for the germinal as well as the classical exposition of this type of argumentation.[26]

Abbott in his 1879 article, listed nine passages in Mark where he thought expressions occurred "which would be likely to be stumbling blocks in the way of weak believers, so that they are omitted in the later Gospels, and would not have been tolerated except in a Gospel of extreme antiquity."[27]

Streeter utilized Abbott's first entry which he prefaced and presented as follows:

In the same spirit [of reverence] certain phrases which might cause offence or suggest difficulties are toned down or excised. Thus Mark's "he *could* do there *no* mighty work" (6:5) becomes in Matthew (13:58) "he *did not many* mighty works"; while Luke omits the limitation altogether. (162).

Luke, in fact, has no close parallel, and when these expressions in Matthew and Mark are studied in context it is not at all clear that

---

[25] "The Additions and Peculiarities of Mark," pp. 801–803.

[26] *Cf. F.G.*, p. 164. That Streeter had consulted Abbott in *Encyclopaedia Britannica* rather than or in addition to *Encyclopaedia Biblica* is indicated by his use of the qualifying noun "grammarian" and the adjective "vulgar." That he had consulted Abbott in one or both of the encyclopedia articles is seen from his selection of Phrynichus from among the grammarians cited, and above all from his use of the word "Expressly."

[27] *Op. cit.*, p. 802b.

Matthew is secondary to Mark. Matthew's "And he did not do many mighty works there, because of their unbelief," implies indirectly that nonetheless he did do some, so that Mark's "And he could do no mighty work there, *except* that he laid his hands upon a few sick people and healed them" could be another example of Mark's tendency to make the tradition more specific by indicating by way of exception, the specific kind of δύναμις he did do in Nazareth. In any case the passage offers no clear indication that Luke has "excised" or that Matthew has "toned down" a phrase in Mark which "might cause offence or suggest difficulties" as Streeter, following Abbott, suggested.

Streeter added a second example not listed by Abbott, but frequently cited since as evidence of Marcan originality:

"Why callest thou me good?" (Mk. 10:18) reads in Matthew (19:17) "Why asketh thou me concerning the good?"

In fact, Luke's text reads exactly the same as that of Mark so that, if Luke copied Mark as Streeter assumes, this is not a convincing instance of a text in Mark which "might cause offence or suggest difficulty" to the later Evangelists. If it were such a text, why did Luke on the Marcan hypothesis copy it precisely as he found it in Mark? Apparently it caused him no offence at all, otherwise presumably he would have changed it. In any case, it is by no means certain that the text of Matthew is secondary to that of Mark and Luke. As for "good teacher!" such an address is very rare in Jewish literature, and of itself would indicate that the text of Mark and Luke is secondary to Matthew's unqualified "teacher!" which is typically Jewish.

The remainder of Matthew's text presents a difficult problem to the interpreter, but there is no evidence that its solution lies in the direction of imagining that he was altering Mark or Luke. Finally, in the following verse, the list of commandments in the text of Mark has been expanded to include an additional prohibition, "Do not defraud." There is some scholarly opinion in favor of this being a later scribal addition to Mark's text, but the balance of textual evidence supports the view that it belongs to the original text of Mark. On Streeter's view that Matthew and Luke were copying Mark they each independently had decided to omit this prohibition.

But why? Taylor suggests that it may have been because it was not in the Decalogue.[28]

But the fact that the list does not conform to any particular Old Testament list of prohibitions, being rather the result of both selection and compilation, somewhat weakens the plausibility of this suggestion. The prohibition occurs in I Corinthians 7:5 (*compare* also I Corinthians 6:7, 8). It probably was added to Mark's list either by a later scribe or by Mark himself. In balance the presence of this extra command in the text of Mark weighs against the priority of Mark in this passage, and weakens its usefulness to Streeter as an example of the phenomenon he was seeking to illustrate. When this is taken together with the other considerations discussed above, the careful inquirer is left as unprepared to think that he has been given convincing evidence that Matthew and Luke "toned down" or "excised" offensive or difficult Marcan phrases in this second instance as in the first.

Since Streeter wrote as if the evidence supporting this argument were strong and unambiguous, it is necessary to treat the remaining eight passages cited by Abbott in his classical presentation of this argument. In this original form of the argument, Abbott prefaced his citation of these particular passages with the promise that he was going to give his readers "still more cogent proof of the early date of Mark."[29] Under Abbott's aegis these passages passed into subsequent literature on the Synoptic Problem as solid proof of the priority of Mark, and after Streeter they were proliferated and transmuted into evidence that Matthew and Luke had altered the more primitive text of Mark. The argument is in fact very illusive, and in the minds of many in the post-Streeter period who were convinced of Marcan priority on the basis of a received scholarly consensus, it constituted a seemingly impregnable fortress into which one could retreat, and from which he could look down with condescension if not disdain upon all efforts to undermine the established position in Synoptic studies. How secure the foundations of this argument for Marcan priority actually were may be judged best after a consideration of the integrity of the following eight foundation stones which Abbott first laid down for its defense.

All subsequent construction that was erected on this particular

28 Vincent Taylor, *The Gospel According to St. Mark*, London, 1953, p. 428.
29 *Op. cit.*, p. 802b.

foundation in the pre-Streeter period, especially the detailed work of Hawkins, is but the potential debris of a crumbling wall once these foundation stones are weakened.

The eight remaining passages which Abbott presented as potential "stumbling blocks in the way of weak believers" which were, therefore, omitted by Matthew and Luke, will be considered individually in the order he gave them. These were presented by Abbott only as examples of "many" such expressions. Presumably, however, they are typical, and the manner in which they sustain careful examination will provide the reader with some basis for an evaluation of the whole of this argument.

(1) "The statement (Mk. 1:32, 34) that *all* the sick were brought to Jesus, but that he healed only *many*, whereas Matthew (8:16) says that he healed *all*, and Luke (4:40) that he healed *each one* (ἐνὶ ἑκάστῳ)."

The contrast between *all* and *each one* of Matthew and Luke on the one hand, and Mark's *many* on the other, which Abbott brings out by italicizing, is a result of a completely unnecessary and unnatural reading of the respective texts of each Gospel. Mark's *many* has as its immediate antecedent for comparison "the whole city," and not the preceding "all who were sick." Mark's text reads "They brought to him all who were sick or possessed with demons. And the whole city was gathered together about the door. And he healed many who were sick with various diseases and cast out many demons." The graphic detail that "the whole city was gathered together about the door," is not in the accounts either of Matthew or Luke and constitutes a significant agreement in omission between Matthew and Luke against Mark. On form-critical grounds this graphic detail would be regarded as secondary. The respective texts of Matthew and Luke make good sense without it. From this point of view it is reasonable to think of Mark altering the text of one or both the other Gospels, or an Ur-text common to all three, to make his version commensurate with this graphic detail. The logical development of Mark's text is threefold. (1) All the sick were brought. (2) Everyone in town was there. (3) Out of all those people he healed many and cast out many demons. Jesus could not have healed all the people according to Mark's text, for not all the people were sick. The "whole city" was there! If this be regarded as evidence for the priority of Mark, then the impartial investigator is reduced to a highly subjective kind of testimony on the pertinence of which experts can hardly be expected to agree.

(2) "The attempt of His mother and brethren to lay hands on Him on the ground that he was insane (Mk. 3:20–21)."

There is no contextual justification for Abbott's translation of ἐξέστη as "he is insane." This translation would have pejorative connotations which are not consonant with Mark's usage of this term elsewhere, and are not required by the context here.

This word is used by Matthew and Paul only once, but by Luke and Mark several times. Throughout the Gospels and Acts, it is used directly or indirectly with reference to ecstatic revelatory experiences of a religious nature. But, it is not used in the pejorative sense implied by Abbott's translation here. When the same kind of religious experience was unambiguously referred to from a disapproving point of view, some form of μαίνομαι was generally used. This is always the case in Acts. Paul and John also used μαίνομαι in a clearly pejorative sense.

On the basis of these linguistic facts it is not possible to agree with Abbott that this passage would have caused difficulty for either Matthew or Luke. It is not absolutely inconceivable that it might have caused them difficulty, but there is no way of knowing this, and no sound reason for thinking it to be true.

Furthermore, these verses of Mark (19b–21), constitute a distinctly Marcan introduction to tradition which, on the two-document hypothesis, was also in "Q." Certainly the extensive agreement between Matthew and Luke against Mark at this point makes it clear that they were not copying Mark, but that one was copying the other, or that both were copying some other written source. For these reasons, there is even less basis for Abbott's suggestion that both Matthew and Luke had *omitted* these verses. For on the two-document hypothesis it is not even clear that Matthew and Luke knew of their existence. On Abbott's terms, which call for Mark's dependence upon Ur-Marcus, the secondary character of these verses in Mark is clear.

Vincent Taylor wrote:

The use of the historic present ἔρχεται, of πάλιν, and of ὥστε c. acc. and inf. with the double negative [all characteristics of Mark's style], suggests that Mark is writing freely without the aid of a source in vss. 19b–20.

Nonetheless, presumably on the basis of the context of Mark 3:21, Taylor was convinced that Mark 3:19b-21 "is based on the best historical tradition." But that which is distinctive about verse 21 is simply the detail that those close to Jesus, having heard about the crowds pressing in upon him, went out to take him away on the grounds that "he was beside himself"—to use the neutral and colorless translation of Taylor. In the narrative of Mark, however, this constituted but one more example in which Mark had made the tradition more specific. For in Mark 3:31, Jesus' mother and brethren were represented as standing outside the same crowd and calling to him, without any reason being given for their presence or their actions. In Mark's narrative the general function of verses 19b-21 was to introduce the whole of the tradition in verses 22-35, and the special function of verses 20-21 was to provide specific reasons for the presence of Jesus' mother and brethren at the edge of the crowd, and for their concern to reach him in verse 31.

On form-critical grounds, therefore, these details in Mark, unsupported by Matthew and Luke, should be regarded as possible secondary features of his text, owing their origin to Mark's tendency to make the tradition more specific.

The sum of the matter in this case is that linguistic considerations, as well as those of source and form-criticism, conspire to raise a reasonable doubt in the mind of the investigator as to the value of this passage in lending support to Abbott's claim for Mark's priority, let alone Abbott's claim in behalf of Mark's primitivity.

(3) "The imputation of an ambitious petition to James and John, instead of (as Matthew) to their mother (Mk. 10:35)."

It is not unreasonable to think that an Evangelist who could record of *one* disciple that Jesus said to him, "get thee behind me Satan! You are a hindrance ($\sigma\kappa\acute{\alpha}\nu\delta\alpha\lambda\sigma\nu$) to me, for you are not on the side of God but of men (Mt. 16:23)," would be willing to impute "an ambitious petition" to *two*. The inconclusiveness of Abbott's kind of reasoning is perceived the moment the Marcan parallel to Matthew 16:23 is consulted. For the offensive words $\sigma\kappa\acute{\alpha}\nu\delta\alpha\lambda\sigma\nu$ $\epsilon\hat{\iota}$ $\acute{\epsilon}\mu\sigma\hat{\upsilon}$ are not found in Mark's text. Thus on Abbott's terms and following his reasoning it would be Mark, not Matthew, who had softened the harshness of the charge against Peter, and would be, therefore, the less primitive Gospel.

There is no proof in this kind of argument for the simple reason that reliable knowledge of the circumstances of the churches for which the Gospels were written and reliable knowledge of the idiosyncrasies of the Evangelists, is largely dependent upon a correct solution for the Synoptic Problem and not vice versa.

It should be clear, therefore, that until such time as the Synoptic Problem has been solved on the basis of objective literary and historical criteria, all appeal to the kind of evidence Abbott here adduced can only confuse the issue.

(4) "The mention of the marvel of Pilate at the speedy death of Jesus, which might have been perverted to support those who denied that Jesus had really died upon the cross (Mk. 15:44)."

It does not seem reasonable that this possibility of perverting Mark would have constrained or influenced both Matthew and Luke independently to have omitted this detail from their respective accounts of Jesus' burial. And if the danger of docetic perversion of the Gospel accounts was so pervasive and influential as to have led Matthew and Luke to omit this detail at the time they composed their Gospels, then how much more reason for Tatian, writing in the second century, to have exercised an equal caution. Yet Tatian included this detail in his fourfold version of the Gospel. To argue that he would have had to include this because for him Mark was canonical or of apostolic authority is unconvincing, since he omitted innumerable other small details. The fact that Tatian did not omit this detail argues against Abbott's suggestion that Matthew and Luke would have done so. For there is no evidence that there was any abatement in the pervasiveness and dangerous influence of docetism between the time the canonical Gospels were written and the time of Tatian.

This significant agreement between Matthew and Luke against Mark should be regarded as a problem to be explained on the Marcan hypothesis, rather than evidence for that hypothesis.[30]

---

[30] Indeed it carries the historian back to the least unlikely origin of Abbott's ingenious suggestion. On this view Abbott would first have recognized the difficulty for Marcan priority created by this doubly attested witness against the originality of Mark's text. Then, convinced as he was that Mark was the most primitive Gospel, he would have been led to think of some reasonable explanation why Matthew and Luke both independently would have omitted this detail. A particular explanation would then have seemed the most plausible of any he could imagine. Then somehow in his mind this explanation was apparently transmuted from a possible explanation of a difficulty for the adherent of Marcan priority into a positive argument which gave "cogent proof of the early date of Mark."

(5) "The statement that Jesus only gave power to his apostles to cast out devils (Mk. 3:15), and not (as Mt. 10:1) to heal diseases."

In fact, Luke 9:1 is a parallel to Matthew 10:1 and agrees with Matthew against Mark in representing Jesus as giving to the Twelve authority both to cast out demons and to heal diseases. On the Marcan hypothesis, if Matthew and Luke had copied independently an Ur-gospel, as Abbott held they did, then their twofold and independent witness to the text of that Ur-gospel would generally be preferred to the single witness of Mark. And if Matthew and Luke had independently copied the canonical Mark, as Streeter maintained, then an explanation is required for their agreement in a small detail of this sort against Mark.

In fact, Mark tends to emphasize the importance of demons and the authority of the disciples over them. For example, in Mark 6:7 the same concentration on the authority of the Twelve to cast out demons occurs as in Mark 3:15. Apparently this is a characteristic interest of Mark and agrees with his theological purposes in writing the Gospel. Thus, it would be very presumptuous to join Abbott in appealing to it as a sign of the "extreme antiquity" of Mark's Gospel.

(6) "The enumeration of the different stages by which Jesus, at least on one occasion, effected a cure, and the description of the, at first, only partial cure (Mk. 8:24)."

This healing story is unique to Mark. Why would Matthew and Luke both have omitted the same miracle? It can hardly be for the reason Abbott suggested, since they also omitted a second miracle from Mark (7:32–35) in which there is no such initial partial cure. These two miracles in Mark are unique among the healing stories in the Synoptic Gospels in picturing Jesus utilizing saliva in his cures. The use of saliva was a common feature in Hellenistic miracle

---

In a similar way adherents of any hypothesis are always in danger of arguing in a circle by assuming the conclusion they attempt to establish. At best such considerations have only limited probative value. They can legitimately be cited only as evidence commensurate with a particular hypothesis. This, however, is expected of all relevant phenomena before any hypothesis can be advocated as true. To cite such evidence as positive proof for the primitivity of Mark is to be guilty of going beyond the evidence and propounding a *non sequitur*. Abbott has not only gone beyond the evidence in this instance, he has cited as evidence for his view a passage which must be adjudged of doubtful probative value, even if on other grounds it was known with absolute certainty that Matthew and Luke copied Mark.

stories.[31] Mark has ten healing stories. On the Marcan hypothesis one is asked to believe that both Matthew and Luke independently chose to omit the same two miracle stories. They not only omitted these two unique miracle stories, but neither of them omitted any of the remaining eight. That is, each of them copied exactly eight out of ten miracle stories, and incidentally the same eight. Leaving aside the element of choice momentarily, it should be noted that the statistical improbability of such a coincidence is extremely great.

Such coincidences do take place, but when freak accidents happen there is generally some explanation which in retrospect helps explain how the unexpected took place. What explanation can be given in this case? Did both Matthew and Luke have an aversion to the use of saliva in healing stories about Jesus? There is no reason to think so, for so far as is known such stories were not regarded as offensive in any sense.

This phenomenon admits of a credible solution on any hypothesis that acknowledges direct literary dependence among all three Evangelists and does not entail Mark as having been written first. But the simplest explanation comes through the Griesbach hypothesis on which view Luke has taken nine healing stories from Matthew, and Mark has incorporated eight of this number into his Gospel and added two more from a special collection of healing stories having at least one common feature not shared by the healing stories in Matthew and Luke, specifically the use of saliva.

Matthew and Luke's omission of this miracle story, which Abbott here cites in support of the Marcan hypothesis, not only is not satisfactorily explained in the manner he suggests, but its common omission by Matthew and Luke is but one more example of the diversified character of the phenomenon which constitutes the major stumbling block for adherents of the Marcan hypothesis, namely that of agreements between Matthew and Luke against Mark.

---

[31] *See especially* the story of healing recorded both by Tacitus (*Hist.* iv. 81) and Suetonius (*Vesp.* 7), which begins: "While Vespasian was in Alexandria, a blind man approached him and asked to have his cheeks and eyes anointed with the ruler's spittle. . . ." In the Asclepian cult, miraculous healings were sometimes occasioned by the god coming to the ill or injured person in the form of a sacred serpent and touching the part of the body to be healed with his tongue. In one story the god healed a blind boy through one of the sacred dogs in the temple. That the dog licked the blind boy's eyes is not stated but may be presumed. *See Asclepius*, a two-volume work by Emma J. Edelstein and Ludwig Edelstein, Baltimore, 1945. *See also* Laurence J. McGinley's *Form-Criticism of the Synoptic Healing Narratives*, Woodstock, 1944, p. 130.

(7) "The statement that the fig tree, instead of being withered up 'immediately' (as Matthew, παραχρῆμα 21:19), was not observed to be withered till after the interval of a day (Mk. 11:21)."

The critical problems are especially great with respect to Mark's version of the cursing of the fig tree. It is quite possible that Mark deliberately chose to divide the story into two parts in order to have an interval between the actual cursing and the recognition by the disciples that the curse had been fulfilled. This would have turned the attention of Mark's readers to earlier words of judgment from Jesus which had either been fulfilled subsequently in the life of the church, perhaps in the recent past of Mark's readers, or were expected to be fulfilled in the immediate future. The point would have been that while there is sometimes an interval between the pronouncement of judgment by Jesus and its fulfillment, that fulfillment is certain.

In any case, Mark's text in 11:13b and 13d seems to have been expanded by glosses typical of Mark. And the vocabulary of Mark 11:20–21 "is wholly Marcan and suggests, as far as it goes, that the account was composed by Mark himself." [32]

None of these considerations creates confidence in this passage as constituting reliable evidence by which to illustrate convincingly the "early date of Mark," as Abbott so confidently asserted.

(8) "The bare statement (Mk. 16:4) that the women found the stone rolled away from the sepulchre (which might have been used to support the statements of those who maintained that the friends or enemies of Jesus had stolen his body), whereas Matthew (28:2) distinctly meets such an objection by asserting that an angel descended from heaven in the sight of the keepers and rolled away the stone."

The plausibility of this suggestion is as strong as one's confidence in Mark's early date and in Mark's "disposition to record facts as they came, without emphasis or subordination," as Abbott claims.[33] There is no doubt that Matthew 28:2–4 is relatively late and largely legendary if not wholly mythological tradition. But it is not self-evident that Mark's less mythical account is earlier. For which is the earlier of two accounts, that which treats the resurrection in mythological terms, or that which treats the event in a more or less straightforward historical manner ? There really seems no certain way to tell.

32 Vincent Taylor, *op. cit.*, p. 466.
33 *Op. cit.*, p. 803a.

To assume without question that Mark's account is the earlier because it is free from angelic intervention is probably due more to a preference of modern man for a less miraculous or supernatural account of the Resurrection than to the application of objective canons of literary and historical criticism. Once again it is appropriate to remind the reader that there is little or no proof in this line of argument for the reasons which have been given in the treatment afforded the similarly inconclusive examples cited by Abbott.

In conclusion: the nine examples given by Abbott and the one added by Streeter to prove that Mark is prior to Matthew and Luke on the grounds that Mark's text in its primitivity presents difficulties that the later Evangelists would have changed or omitted, all fail to sustain careful analysis. These ten passages are but paternal prototypes of an unending line of progeny thought by many post-Streeter critics to offer positive proof not only of the primitivity of Mark's text, but proof that Matthew and Luke copied Mark. The final verdict of the historian who considers this kind of evidence without any prior commitment to the originality of Mark is simply: "not proved."

This means that the first half of Streeter's fourth reason for accepting the priority of Mark is unconvincing. Streeter stated that reason as follows:

The primitive character of Mark is further shown by (a) the use of phrases likely to cause offence, which are omitted or toned down in the other Gospels, (b) roughness of style and grammar, and the preservation of Aramaic words (151–152).

It citing evidence for Mark's "roughness of style and grammar," Streeter was once again dependent on Abbott. This evidence was analyzed earlier (pp. 120–124) in connection with Streeter's appeal to it in his treatment of the "Minor Agreements," and was found to be inconclusive.

E. Streeter's Remaining Arguments
for the Two-Document Hypothesis

Since Streeter's first three reasons for accepting the priority of Mark were exposed as fallacious by Jameson in 1922 and again by Butler in 1951, there is no need to give them further consideration.

That which remains to be done in analyzing Streeter's essential arguments for his "Fundamental Solution," is to consider certain residual evidence cited in support of his fourth reason, to evaluate briefly his fifth reason, and then to consider his arguments for "Q."

Streeter appealed to two more arguments cited by Abbott in favor of the primitivity of Mark's language, which because they have favorably impressed subsequent generations of New Testament scholars are worthy of critical evaluation.

The first of these is formulated by Streeter as follows:

But the difference between the style of Mark and of the other two is not merely that they both write better Greek. It is the difference which always exists between the spoken and the written language. Mark reads like a shorthand account of a story by an impromptu speaker—with all the repetitions, redundancies, and digressions which are characteristic of living speech. And it seems to me most probable that his Gospel, like Paul's Epistles, was taken down from rapid dictation by word of mouth. The Mark to whom tradition ascribes the composition of the Gospel was a Jerusalem Jew, of the middle class; he could speak Greek fluently, but writing in an acquired language is another matter. Matthew and Luke use the more succinct and carefully chosen language of one who writes and then revises an article for publication. This partly explains the tendency to abbreviate already spoken of, which is especially noticeable in Matthew. Sometimes this leads to the omission by one or both of the later writers of interesting and picturesque details, such as "in the stern . . . on a cushion" (Mk. iv. 38), or "they had not in the boat with them more than one loaf" (Mk. viii. 14) [163].

The whole of this argument is but a series of loosely connected affirmations none of which has much probative value. For example, the statement that the difference between the style of Mark and Matthew and Luke "is the difference which always exists between the spoken and the written language," is seen to be questionable after but the briefest reflection on the concrete nature of spoken and written language. Sometimes written language is very crude, and sometimes it is highly polished. The same can be said concerning spoken language. Sometimes impromptu speech is repetitious, redundant, and digressive, but at other times it is beautifully articulated with a rhythm and balance that defies improvement. The notion that the alleged crudeness of Mark's Greek is due to its close relation to living speech owes nothing to any known scientific study of the problem of the differences between spoken and written language.

Likewise, Streeter's confidence that Mark's Gospel, like Paul's epistles, "was taken down from rapid dictation by word of mouth," is seen to be unjustified on two counts: (1) the kind of parenthetical syntax which may constitute a sign that Paul's epistles were so dictated is not characteristic of Mark;[34] (2) the most distinctive feature of Mark's language, namely, its pleonastic character, is not characteristic of Paul's Epistles, nor is it explained on the theory of rapid dictation.

So also, Streeter's easy acceptance of the tradition that the author of the Gospel of Mark is the John Mark of Acts, is ironically incommensurate with his rejection of the tradition that Matthew was the first Gospel written.

Finally, the "interesting and picturesque" details, such as "in the stern . . . on a cushion" (Mk. 4:38), and "they had not in the boat with them more than one loaf" (Mk. 8:14), are of doubtful historical value. The possibility that these details have come into the tradition in course of time in response to the well-attested tendency in the church to make the tradition more specific by the addition of just such details is at least equal to the possibility that they are historical, or that they are signs of the "eyewitness" or "primitive" character of Mark's text.

Altogether, then, this argument is ill-conceived and has little or no probative value in settling the question of whether Mark's language is more primitive than that of Matthew or Luke.

A second argument for the primitivity of Marcan language, which until now has not been considered, Streeter also took from Abbott. It was Streeter's final argument under this head, and remains one of the most specious in the history of the Synoptic Problem. Streeter writes:

Lastly, there are eight instances in which Mark preserves the original Aramaic words used by our Lord. Of these Luke has none, while Matthew retains only one, the name Golgotha (27:33). . . .

---

[34] C. H. Turner made a careful study of the nearest parallel syntactical phenomena in Mark and did not suggest that they indicate that Mark was taken down from rapid dictation. His study rather suggests that parenthetical clauses in Mark are the result of conscious reflection on the part of a redactor working over written traditions which need to be made more intelligible to his intended readers. "Marcan Usage: Part IV, Parenthetical clauses in Mark." *J.T.S.*, Vol. 26, 1924–1925, pp. 145–156.

This is a misleading statement of the facts, for it creates the false impression that Mark's text preserves more Aramaisms than does that of either Luke or Matthew.

In evaluating the significance of the use of Aramaic words in the Gospels it is necessary to make a distinction between Aramaic words present in the text, but not expected by the Evangelist to be understood by his readers, and Aramaic words used with the expectation that readers would understand them. The former are either translated or explained in Greek for the benefit of the readers, while the latter stand untranslated and unexplained. Only the Aramaic words which stand in the text untranslated and unexplained witness unmistakably to the Semitic provenance of the tradition in which they occur.

The presence in a Gospel of Aramaic terms which are translated for the reader's benefit may be due to one or more of several causes. It is known, for example, that foreign words are sometimes introduced into Hellenistic healing stories.[35] The presence of Aramaic words in the Greek stories of healing attributed to Jesus can be adequately explained by appeal to this known contemporary literary practice. The presence of such terms in a Gospel, therefore, is by no means a guarantee of the primitivity of that Gospel. The fact that Aramaic words were attributed to Jesus in two healing stories in Mark, whereas no such Aramaic expressions occur in the healing stories of Matthew or Luke, is, on form-critical grounds, as well or better explained as a sign of Hellenistic influence on Mark, than it is by Streeter's suggestion that such terms indicate that the language of Mark's Gospel is closer to the language of Jesus than that of Matthew or Luke.

When Mark translated these Aramaic words attributed to Jesus, he implicitly recognized the fact that they would not be understood by most of his intended readers. The possibility that they were inserted for effect, therefore, cannot be discounted.

It is well known that in the second century unintelligible and

---

[35] *Cf.* Bultmann, *op. cit.*, p. 238. Taylor, *op. cit.*, p. 296, notes that both Bultmann and Dibelius recognize that the use of foreign words is a part of the technique of ancient miracle stories. He thinks, however, that this is an improbable explanation for the presence of the Aramaic words in the healing stories of Mark in 5:41, and 7:34, on the grounds that in most cases where Mark's text includes Aramaic words no healing is involved. Taylor concluded that "The retention of the Aramaic words, absent in Mt. and Lk., shows the greater originality of Mk." (*Op. cit.*, p. 297.)

esoteric words were used for effect in some Christian literature. For example, in the Apocryphal Acts of Pilate (XI. 1) at a point where Luke's account of the crucifixion was being copied, after πάτερ in Luke 23:46, the author introduced βαδδαχ ἐφκίδ ρουελ and then wrote: "which being interpreted means"; and then follows the well-known words of Jesus found in the Greek text of Luke: "Into thy hands, I commend my spirit." This proves that words of Jesus as found in the Greek texts of the earlier Gospel writings, at a later date and presumably for some definite literary purpose, were presented first in a language form unknown to the readers, and then given as found in the source being copied in Greek, after being introduced by a formula reading: "which being translated (or interpreted) means." This may be the most probable explanation for the presence of the parallel phenomenon in Mark. But if this be true, Streeter's appeal to these Aramaic words as a sign of the primitive character of Mark's Gospel is very misleading.

Likewise, Irenaeus protested against those who used "Hebrew" words in the churches "in order," he writes, "the more thoroughly to bewilder" the Christian initiates.[36] There is no doubt, therefore, that a select usage of the sacrosanct language of the first Christians and of Jesus himself, made it possible for a writer or speaker to impress the mind of Greek-speaking congregations.

In all these cases, however, as with Mark, these words were translated for the benefit of those for whom they were unintelligible. The words from the cross "My God, my God, why has thou forsaken me," which occur in Matthew and Mark with slight variations in Hebrew and Aramaic, were translated by both into Greek. The point, therefore, is not that Mark is the only Evangelist to use Aramaic or Hebrew words for dramatic effect, nor that he was the first to do so. The point is rather that this practice continued in the Church and that, therefore, such usage affords no reliable criterion either for dating the Gospels or settling the question of priority.

In contradistinction to this usage of Aramaic words it is profitable to compare such unquestionably authentic Aramaisms as ῥακά (fool) in Matthew 5:22 and τὸν κορβανᾶν (the treasury) in Matthew 27:6. The presence of these untranslated and unexplained Aramaic words in Matthew's text is universally recognized as evidence of some close

[36] *Irenaeus Against Heresies*, Bk. I, Chap. 21, Par. 3.

connection between the tradition preserved in Matthew and the Semitic origins of early Christianity. There are no examples of Aramaisms in Mark which are distinctive of that Gospel and which compare to these untranslated Aramaic usages found only in Matthew.[37] In 7:11 Mark uses κορβᾶν, but not without translating it for the benefit of his readers.

Therefore, on the basis of the use of Aramaic words, it is by no means clear that Mark's Gospel is the most primitive. If weight were to be given to evidence of this kind, it would weigh in favor of the primitivity of Matthew rather than Mark.

At all essential points, therefore, Streeter's fourth reason for accepting the priority of Mark is seen upon analysis to be no more convincing than his first three. Like his first three arguments, his fourth as well may be compared to a pillar that from a distance appears to be a sound and stately column, capable of bearing its full share of the weight of the structure erected above it, but which upon close inspection is found to be a top-heavy shaft made from faulty stone precariously mounted upon a crumbling base.

Streeter's fifth reason for accepting the priority of Mark is summarized as follows:

The way in which Marcan and non-Marcan material is distributed in Matthew and Luke respectively looks as if each had before him the Marcan material *in a single document*, and was faced with the problem of combining this with material from other sources.

[37] Mark's use of Rabbi which is never translated as it is in John (1:38), is not an exception to this statement, since it is also found untranslated in Matthew. Mark's use of the expression 'Αββά, ὁ πατήρ is also not an exception. This expression is found in the remainder of the New Testament only in Rom. and Gal., and is presumably a liturgical formula coming from a bilingual situation, where the Aramaic word for father with reference to God is still retained even in Greek-speaking churches. It would be difficult to show that Jesus probably spoke this way. Paul's letters prove that it was used in Christian communications in Gentile circles from Asia Minor to Italy. The agreement of Matthew and Luke against Mark in this instance is especially weighty, since there is no known reason why either Evangelist would have deliberately eliminated such an expression from his Gospel. The most probable explanation for these words on the lips of Jesus, is that they represent a later modification of the more original address to God by the name ὁ πατήρ in the earliest form of the Gospel tradition in Greek, as in Matthew and Luke. This modification would presumably have been made under the influence of current liturgical usage in the churches for which Mark was intended. The incongruity of placing upon the lips of Jesus a bilingual formula of the church is best understood as but an example of the tendency in the church to form the tradition in keeping with the demands of worship for a sense of the contemporaneous character of the revelatory moments of Jesus' passion. This may also be one reason for the frequent use of the historic present in Mark.

This is no reason for accepting the priority of Mark, but rather is a conclusion to which one might come if he were convinced on other grounds of Marcan priority and were concerned to make an observation about the relationship between Marcan and non-Marcan material in Matthew and Luke.

Streeter noted that, in the case of Luke, Marcan and non-Marcan material alternated in great blocks, and he observed:

This alternation suggests the inference that the non-Marcan materials, though probably ultimately derived from more than one source, had already been combined into a single written document before they were used by the author of the Third Gospel. (167)

This inference is valid only on the presupposition of Marcan priority. For if Luke copied Matthew, then in the so-called non-Marcan sections, he simply combined sayings material from Matthew with corresponding material from another source or sources. The probability that Luke did have access to one or more written sources other than Matthew is not in question. The point at issue in Synoptic criticism in this connection is whether, in those parts of their respective Gospels where there is extensive verbatim agreement between them, Matthew and Luke have copied Mark or "Q," or whether one is directly dependent upon the other. This raises the question of the existence of "Q."

Streeter's arguments for the existence of "Q" are two in number. The first was effectively refuted by Jameson in 1922 and deserves no more attention than he gave it.[38] The second was formulated by Streeter as follows:

Sometimes it is Matthew, sometimes it is Luke, who gives a saying in what is clearly the more original form. This is explicable if both are drawing from the same source, each making slight modifications of his own; it is not so if either is dependent on the other. (183)

This is the classical reason brought forward by de Wette and Bleek for their view that Matthew and Luke did not know one another, and which led them to assert that these Evangelists drew this material along with all else they held in common from an Urgospel. In and of itself, therefore, it does not support the existence of "Q" any more than it supports the existence of an Ur-gospel in

[38] See Appendix B, p. 292–293.

the shape of the one hypothecated by de Wette and Bleek. Nor does it constitute a difficulty for their view that Mark was third and the result of a literary process of conflating Matthew and Luke. But it does stand in the way of accepting Griesbach's hypothesis in the form he himself proposed it, since that entailed Luke's use of Matthew. It also stands in the way of accepting the Augustinian hypothesis for the same reason. Until such time as adherents of these hypotheses are able to answer this objection to the view that Luke used Matthew, there will be grounds for reasonable doubt concerning both these views. This is at least true with regard to the problem of the relationship envisioned between Matthew and Luke on these hypotheses.

It would appear, therefore, that Streeter's reasons for accepting the existence of "Q" were far from conclusive, and of very little, if any, probative value. To his credit it should be noted that with regard to "Q," Streeter was both circumspect and cautious. He concluded:

We are justified, then, in assuming the existence of Q, so long as we remember that the assumption is one which, though highly probable, falls just short of certainty. (184)

Critical opinion will vary as to just how far short of certainty the assumption of the existence of "Q" on Streeter's terms actually was. But no one will complain that Streeter's language at this point is inordinately uncritical. However, his statement with regard to Marcan priority is in notable contrast:

How anyone . . . can retain the slightest doubt of the originality and primitive character of Mark I am unable to comprehend. (164)

F. Streeterian Dogmatism

The chief evidence which Streeter cited in defense of the "original and primitive character of Mark" has been reviewed in detail. The result of this critical review leaves the historian with one overwhelming impression, namely that by Streeter's time the priority of Mark was uncritically accepted in the absence of convincing evidence in its favor, and in spite of its serious residual difficulties. Chief among these difficulties was the phenomenon of agreement of Matthew and Luke against Mark. Streeter's major contribution in behalf of the two-document hypothesis was his attempt to remove this difficulty. It is clear that in trying to do so Streeter did not conduct an impartial scientific investigation into its nature and cause, but rather made an honest, though inconclusive, effort to explain these agreements on the basis of a pre-established conviction that Mark was "original and primitive." The reasons he gave for believing Mark was the earlier Gospel are not convincing and, therefore, do not account for the inordinate degree of certainty he expressed in his statements on the matter. There is a marked absence of tentativity in Streeter's attitude toward Marcan priority, and a strong note of impatience with those who questioned it. This is the dominant attitude in the post-Streeter period of Synoptic criticism and distinguishes it from the pre-Streeter period. Adherents of Marcan priority in the pre-Streeter period were probably no less convinced of this view than was Streeter, but they were more tentative in their published statements concerning the Synoptic Problem and seldom expressed in print any impatience with those who raised questions about Marcan priority. This shift in the climate of critical opinion toward an attitude of impatient dogmatism on the question of Marcan priority is reflected in the closing words of Burkitt's review of Jameson's book in 1922, and is only implicitly to be found, if indeed it is there at all, in Streeter's review of Lummis' book in 1915. It is completely absent from Streeter's essays published in *Oxford Studies* in 1911. This would appear, therefore, to be a postwar development.

The arguments of Abbott and Woods had become conventional by the end of the century and no doubt contributed to the accepted view that the priority of Mark was an established result of nineteenth-century criticism. But the acceptance of these conventional arguments by Streeter in turn requires explanation since they were all either fallacious or inconclusive. Streeter demonstrated that he had a competence for Synoptic criticism in his early essays published in the *Oxford Studies* in 1911. Therefore, it is not possible to attribute his acceptance of these arguments to a complete inaptitude for Synoptic studies. Other factors must be called into consideration in order to understand why the priority of Mark was widely accepted by Streeter and a host of competent scholars in the absence of any compelling proof and in the face of serious scientific difficulties.

V

Other Factors
Contributing to
the Twentieth Century
Consensus

A. The Intellectual Climate

One very important factor contributing to the too-ready acceptance of evidence and arguments advanced in behalf of the Marcan hypothesis had strong psychological and theological dimensions which are difficult both to define and to assess. This factor was the intellectual climate at the turn of the century. It is not generally appreciated that the Marcan hypothesis was peculiarly well-suited to the intellectual tastes of men who shared the late nineteenth-century optimism in the progress of science in all its expressions. The fact that Mark was relatively simple, without legendary birth narratives and mythological post-Resurrection appearance stories, has been noted.[1] But equally important is the

[1] Cf. Chapter I, p. 25. The words of Abbott in the *Encyclopaedia Britannica*, in 1879 disclose the intellectual temper of the times: "It might be expected that when we come to the additions peculiar to each of the three synoptists we should find some increase to the amount of supernatural events. Now it seems to be a striking proof of the antiquity of the Second Gospel (Mark) that we find in it no additions of this kind. Not that

fact that the few parables of Jesus found in Mark included the so-called parables of growth, which fit beautifully the philosophical scheme of development which dominated late nineteenth century thought. Under this norm, the kingdom of God was conceivable as a developing social reality which rendered theologically credible a theory of social progress leading to higher and higher forms of communal existence corresponding to the evolutionary development of biological realities from simple forms of life to higher and higher forms of intelligence, culminating in man.

The point is not that there was any conscious connection between the two-document hypothesis and developmental and evolutionary social theories, but that the Marcan hypothesis exhibited features which commended itself to men who were disposed to place their trust in the capacity of science to foster the development of human progress.

It must not be concluded, however, that in the nineteenth century

---

Mark does not lay stress on what appears to be supernatural; on the contrary . . . ; but we find in Mark no mention of our Lord's birth or childhood, and only the barest prediction of His resurrection. As an explanation of the deficiency of information on the resurrection, it has been frequently suggested that the later part of the Gospel may have been lost; . . . It seems far more probable that Mark ends his Gospel here (16:8) because the common tradition ended here, and because he scrupled to add anything to the notes and traditions which he knew to rest upon a higher authority than his own. If this be the true explanation, it stamps with the seal of a higher authority such traditions as have been preserved to us by so scrupulous an author. We proceed therefore to an investigation of the peculiarities of Mark, with a confidence in him increased rather than diminished by the fact that he has neither the introductions nor the appendices which are found in the rest of the Gospels." (Pp. 801b–802a.) First editions of works frequently carry both introductions and appendices, so Abbott's point rests not on the analogy of literature, but on the assumption that the earliest Gospel would have been relatively more free of the supernatural element which predominates in the opening and closing sections of Luke and Matthew. The fact is, however, that verse for verse, the supernatural element predominates over the greater part of Mark's Gospel, whereas in Luke and Matthew the legendary and mythological material is frequently relieved by long sections of material of a nonlegendary and non-mythological character, and which provide the critic with the most reliable information available as to what Jesus was actually about and what he said, which is what Abbott and his generation were interested in and thought Mark could best tell them. Once it is recognized how the mythological predominated over the historical in some Christian circles as early as the first generation of the Church (*cf.* Paul), it will be seen that by the second generation when the Gospels were written, there is no solid basis for the view that "it seems to be a striking proof of the antiquity" of Mark that it contains no "supernatural" birth stories or Resurrection accounts. And if one were to argue that the Gospel which contained the highest percentage of reliable historical tradition were the earliest, then, on "form-critical" grounds, the choice would be between Luke and Matthew, with John and Mark coming chronologically between Luke and Matthew and the second century Apocryphal Gospel literature.

the Synoptic Problem lacked specific interest for men of science and letters working outside conventional theological circles of University and Church, nor that they were ignorant of its importance. Quite to the contrary.

In 1889 Thomas Huxley wrote:

I do not call to mind any problem of natural science which has come under my notice which is more difficult, or more curiously interesting as a mere problem, than that of the origin of the Synoptic Gospels and that of the historical value of the narratives which they contain. The Christianity of the Churches stands or falls by the results of the purely scientific investigations of these questions.[2]

Huxley himself understood and approved the method and results of contemporary Synoptic criticism. After pointing out the futility of looking to tradition for a solution to the problem of Gospel origins, Huxley wrote:

It is otherwise if we make the documents tell their own story: if we study them, as we study fossils, to discover internal evidence of when they arose, and how they have come to be. That really fruitful line of inquiry has led to the statement and discussion of what is known as the *Synoptic Problem*.[3]

Huxley was persuaded of the essential correctness of the Marcan hypothesis, especially as it had been championed by Abbott.[4] Though he recognized that the Synoptic Problem had not been solved with finality, his confidence that it would be solved was unqualified:

... considering how recent the really scientific study of that problem, and how great the progress made during the last half century in supplying the conditions for a positive solution of the problem, I cannot doubt that the attainment of such a solution is a mere question of time.[5]

Huxley expressed this optimistic view in 1893. Here the nineteenth

[2] *Science and Christian Tradition*, New York, 1896, p. 270.
[3] *Op. cit.*, p. xviii.
[4] "... at the present time, there is no visible escape from the conclusion that each of the three [gospels] is a compilation consisting of a groundwork [*sic*!] common to all three ..." *op. cit.*, p. 221. In a footnote Huxley added: "See, for an admirable discussion of the whole subject, Dr. Abbott's article on the Gospels in the *Encyclopaedia Britannica*; and the remarkable monograph by Professor Volkmar, *Jesus Nazarenus und die erste christliche Zeit* (1882). Whether we agree with the conclusions of these writers or not, the method of critical investigation which they adopt is unimpeachable." Volkmar was a member of the Tübingen school who adopted the priority of Mark.
[5] *Op. cit.*, xxxii.

century faith in science as a redemptive instrument guaranteeing progress in human affairs is clearly at the base of Huxley's confident prediction that a final solution to the Synoptic Problem was inevitable. Within a half century this confident prediction that a final solution *would be* found was replaced by an equally confident assertion that a final solution *had been* found. The conviction with which the prediction was made was rooted in the same religious faith which structures and nourishes the conviction with which the assertion is made. Both are expressions of a misplaced faith in the inevitable progress of science. To men nourished by this faith it is inconceivable (a) that a satisfactory solution would not be forthcoming eventually and (b) that once it had been found it might be wrong.

Darwin's epoch-making *Origin of Species* had been published during Sanday's student days at Oxford and there is no doubt that in the years following, like many of the best minds of his generation, he drank deeply from the cup of salvation offered by the cult of "scientism," that is, faith in science. This faith in the scientific method, and in the possibilities of combining the efforts of numerous investigators inspired him in organizing and leading his Oxford seminar on the Synoptic Problem. His eulogistic blessing of Streeter's work in *Oxford Studies* in 1911 reflects the fact that Sanday's intellectual apparatus was impregnated with non-Biblical, nontraditional, nontheological and nonliterary thought categories taken over from the quasi-scientific jargon of the late nineteenth century. With specific reference to Streeter's essay "The Literary Evolution of the Gospels" Sanday wrote:

I do not remember to have seen, . . . a picture at once so complete, so sound, and (to my mind) so thoroughly *scientific*, of the whole course of *development*. . . . It is a real *evolution*, and an *evolution conceived as growth*, in which *each stage springs naturally, spontaneously, and inevitably out of the last*.[6] [Italics mine. W. R. F.]

One more example may be cited to illustrate the fact that these quasi-scientific ideas of the late nineteenth century were not only on the lips of Sanday but determinative of his critical judgment. In 1891, when discussing the question whether Matthew or Luke

---

6 *Oxford Studies*, p. xvi.

preserved the more original form of "Q" he sided with Luke in the following terms:

On the one side we have unity, aggregation, compactness, which has very much the appearance of being artificial (Matthew). On the other hand we have dispersion, disorder, confusion, which looks more like the *state of nature* (Luke).[7] [Italics mine. W. R. F.]

Leaving aside the question of the accuracy or adequacy of Sanday's conception of the "state of nature," here is found a naïve assumption that modes of argumentation appropriate in natural sciences may be simply applied in literary criticism. Precisely this same naïve assumption was found in Huxley's dictum that the Gospels should be studied as fossils are studied. In retrospect this seems crude, and it is difficult to imagine men like Sanday allowing such extraneous considerations to influence their critical judgments. But the intellectual atmosphere men breathed in the nineties was charged with a virtual apocalyptic expectation of long-awaited scientific break-throughs. The Synoptic Problem was conceived of as a scientific problem, and at that time the success of the physical sciences led men to think that the application of the same methods appropriate to geology or biology would inevitably, sooner or later, also bring progress at every point along the frontiers of knowledge. The possibility that the true solution of the Synoptic Problem had already been discovered a century earlier and was being overlooked was as inconceivable as that the sun rotated around the earth or that every creature was created *de novo* on a particular day by a special act of God. To think in such terms as these would be to deny the inevitable progress of science. According to this concept, each scientific investigator was obliged to acquaint himself with the most recent stage in the advance of his particular science, and then to assist his colleagues in making the next advance.

To criticize a man like Sanday for not really giving serious consideration to the Augustinian or Griesbach hypotheses is to miss the mark. The temper of the times was not conducive to reconsideration of hypotheses which were believed to have been tested and found inadequate. The demands of progress led men to press forward confident that the final solution was yet to be found and when found

7 "A Survey of the Synoptic Question," *The Expositor*, 4th Series, Vol. III, Part III, p. 307.

would be in the form of an amplification or at most a modification of the "fundamental solution," that is, the priority of Mark and the existence of "Q."

Sanday conceived himself to be more than an individual research scholar. His vocation was to be a scholar-statesman within the church and university. He gave clear expression to this fundamental idea in his Bampton lectures.

I greatly hope that before long a sustained and combined effort, for which the circumstances are now particularly favourable, may be made to grapple at close quarters with the difficulties and wring from them a better result than has been obtained hitherto. If we do not do it, others will, because attention is being very much directed to the subject. *I would however lay stress on the hopes which I entertain from combination. I feel sure that more could be done in this way than by individual efforts however skilful.*[8] [Italics mine. W. R. F.]

Sanday's individual contribution was to discover trends toward consensus among scholars working on the problem, and then to provide the inspiration and administrative genius for a "sustained and combined effort" to solve the residual problems on which consensus was yet to be achieved. Sanday's Oxford seminar was the practical result of this eminently practical plan of attack.

Unfortunately, Sanday's operational idea was itself faulty in that it misconstrued the nature of consensus among literary critics. The fact that German critics like Holtzmann, Weizsäcker and B. Weiss all adhered to some form of the two-document hypothesis was no sound foundation upon which to build a seminar on the Synoptic Problem. Especially was this true after 1880 when Simons convinced these same German critics that Luke knew Matthew. After that the possibility that Luke copied Matthew extensively was sufficiently real so as to render any consensus among these critics on the priority of Mark or the existence of "Q" of questionable scientific value.

The fact that there was a consensus was not self-evident and had to be brought to the consciousness of individual scholars before it could be made the basis for their work together. Sanday above all others performed this function for the English-speaking world of New Testament scholars. It was his eminent success in this role that, as much as any other factor, can be appealed to for an explanation

[8] *Inspiration*, p. 282.

of the otherwise incomprehensible fact of Streeter's oversight with respect to the inconclusive nature of the evidence and arguments he advanced in behalf of the two-document hypothesis.

In this connection it is especially fitting that Streeter dedicated his book to Sanday, for in an important sense Streeter's work originated in and took its point of departure from the consensus which Sanday perceived among the leading German critics of his day.

The influence of Sanday's contribution at this point will be examined at two levels: first, his method of promoting consensus will be documented; and second, the effect of all this upon the individual scholar will be clarified.

In 1891, at the beginning of the last decade of the nineteenth century and at the dawn of a new century of progress, Sanday wrote an influential series of articles for *The Expositor*, under the title "A Survey of the Synoptic Question." This series of articles was very effective in demonstrating Sanday's statesman-like grasp of a wide range of contemporary Synoptic literature and after 1891 he was, on the basis of these articles, widely recognized as an authority on the Synoptic Problem. Therefore, it is especially important to note the way in which Sanday's mediating and consensus-finding *Tendenz* was joined with his practical hope in scientific progress to support a nonscientific sociological function which may be called "consensus-making." Sanday was a consensus *maker*. He not only discovered consensus; he helped create it. He helped create it not by new discoveries supporting the consensus, but by minimizing that which was not in accord with his definition of the growing consensus, and by maximizing the evidence for consensus and exciting hopes for a final solution through the expansion of consensus to cover all aspects of the Synoptic Problem. Sanday's own words tell the story best:

The last two or three years has seen an increased activity in the criticism of the Gospels. . . . I begin by a roll-call of the works of which I shall have to speak.
They are as follows:
  The Rev. J. Estlin Carpenter. . . .
  The Rev. A. Wright. . . .
  Professor J. T. Marshall. . . .
  Dr. P. Ewald. . . .
  Dr. A. Resch. . . .

I do not include in this list the Rev. J. J. Holcombe's *Historic Relation of the Gospels* (London, 1889), because if it were treated at all, it would have to be treated separately; and because, in spite of many scholarly qualities, it seems to me to pursue a line of argument which can only end in disappointment.[9]

After thus eliminating from consideration a work which was not in accord with the consensus he was promoting (Holcombe thought he could prove that John was written first), Sanday discussed briefly the widely diversified work of each of the five authors named, and then wrote:

In the literature which I have been describing there is more than one coincidence which seems to me to *point to the opening*—perhaps only for a time—of what may be called *a new phase* in the criticism of the Synoptic Gospels . . . the opportunity may perhaps first be taken to cast a glance backwards as well as forward, to adjust our bearings in reference to the past, before we decide how our helm is *to point in the future*. Do the works of which I have been speaking indicate any *progress*? Is there any *solid advance* to be recorded apart from the mere ebb and flow of opinion? *The solution* of all great critical problems *moves slowly*. There seems to be an immense expenditure of labour for little positive result. For years, nay, for generations together, there will seem to be only a wilderness of mutually contradictory theories. It is only after a *long and painful struggle*, in which *advance and retrogression* will seem to succeed each other . . . that roads begin to be driven through the thicket *which will be extended until they meet in the end*. The moral is that a sound argument cannot be drawn from these differences. . . . *We may be sure that they will not last for-ever*. . . . By degrees the confusion becomes less, and order is introduced . . . order in one section is followed by order in another; and *the rate of progress is gradually accelerated*.[10] [Italics mine. W. R. F.]

By this time the reader is breathlessly awaiting some assurance that the end is in sight, and that the new day of salvation is about to dawn, when the contradictions and uncertainties of the past and present will be resolved. He is not disappointed (though Sanday qualifies every apocalyptic hope he excites):

Of course opinions will differ as to the outlook of any one subject at any given time. And yet there is reason to think that a number of biblical problems are now nearing the stage when a glimmer of daylight begins to show itself among them. The daylight may still be very partial; it may

9 *Op. cit.*, Part I, pp. 82 ff.
10 *Op. cit.*, pp. 87–88.

be only a faint streak along the horizon; the clouds may come up again and cover it: and yet it *is* daylight, the harbinger of morning and of day. Among the problems which are thus trembling on the verge of discovery— not of final and complete discovery, which no doubt may still be long in coming, but of the first beginnings of a real solution—I believe that we may count this Synoptic Problem as one.[11]

[11] *Op. cit.*, p. 88. Eighteen years later, in 1909, the same year in which Hawkins published the second edition of his *Horae Synopticae*, a Cambridge scholar, Latimer Jackson, contributed an essay, "The Present State of the Synoptic Problem," to the volume *Essays on Some Biblical Questions of the Day*, edited by Henry Barclay Swete. In this essay Jackson took the position that the two-document hypothesis was regarded as an established result by the majority of scholars, and that the relative priority of Mark was taken by the majority of scholars as axiomatic. But Jackson noted that there were unresolved problems, and this led Sanday in his review of the volume to write as follows: "I would not say that the essay is really deficient in perspective. When it comes to such summings-up as on pp. 451, 464 f., the perspective seems to me to be quite right; the facts are put in their place with proper shades and degrees of gradation. And the results, as stated on these pages, are hopeful and encouraging—perhaps as hopeful and encouraging as I fully believe they should be. But I cannot say as much as this for the essay as a whole. It is in view of this that the writer seems to me to be oppressed by the multiplicity and complexity of the problems to be solved, and the comparatively little way that has been made toward the solution of some of them. One might almost think sometimes that his temperament was naturally rather despondent than sanguine. But I suspect that there is something rather more in it than a matter of temperament. It seems to me that the perspective which is so well observed on the pages I have specified is not equally observed all through. It is just the greatest and most fundamental problems that are nearest to their solution; and it is just these which arouse hope and a certain confidence. If we were to treat all questions as of equal value, and all failures to solve them as equally significant, then I admit that the outlook might seem depressing. But I cannot help thinking that the depressing appearance is partly—and even largely—caused by the fact that a good many of the questions that are often put are really insoluble; the data for solving them are insufficient; and it would really be better that they should not be put at all, or only in the way of irresponsible speculation. On the questions that matter most I believe that the progress made, or in process of being made, is really great, and that a few more years will see a large amount of consensus all along the line." (*J.T.S.*, Vol. II, 1909–1910, pp. 176–177.) "Hope," "confidence," "believe," "progress," "process," "consensus" —these are some of the watchwords by which the battle for Marcan priority was won. The victory was not only over the minds but over the hearts of men. It was for many a matter of decision, an intellectual commitment to that which was believed to be the objective result of scientific progress. It is this religious or volitional dimension to belief in Marcan priority that makes it so difficult for many scholars to remain completely open to alternate solutions to the Synoptic Problem, and leads others to make dogmatic statements when to speak with greater caution would be more commensurate with what is actually known about the problem. The fact that eighteen years had passed and Sanday still had to speak in terms of promise—of an imminent fulfillment, yet one that was still clearly in the future, was for one who believed as he did, no cause for being depressed. Despondency had to be checked. Belief in an inevitable scientific breakthrough had to be sustained. This explains why two years later Sanday was led to refer to those members of his Oxford seminar whose essays raised questions about the two-document hypothesis as "dissentients." Their essays Sanday placed after those of Hawkins and Streeter, in part he says, because he thought it an advantage to have his volume begin "with a powerful statement of the views that may be described as generally current—in other words, of the 'Two-Document Hypothesis.'" Sanday went on to

This promise of salvation along the lines of an evolutionary victory of critical labor over all obstacles in the way of a satisfactory solution is followed by a sketch of the development of the two-document hypothesis. This sketch culminated in the work of Holtzmann, after which Sanday writes:

From 1863 onwards the methods of inquiry have not noticeably altered; for heirs to the Tübingen tradition like Hilgenfeld and Keim largely modified their views in this direction, and the return to a more extreme position by Holsten . . . met with little approval and no imitation. On the other hand, a number of very solid works, conspicious among which I would name those by Weiss and Wendt, are constructed upon lines which do not diverge widely from Holtzmann. At the same time Holtzmann has made a number of concessions which have brought him nearer to his fellow workers in the subject.
At the end of this chain of evolution come the five works I have named above. . . . The common postulate of Mr. Carpenter and Mr. Wright in England, and of Dr. Ewald and Dr. Resch in Germany, is what is usually called the Two-Document Hypothesis. . . .
At the present moment there can be little doubt that this Two-Document Hypothesis holds the field. It is however a complex hypothesis, consisting of a number of parts. . . . I shall do my best to distinguish between them, and estimate what appear to be the several degrees of probability attaching to them, so as in some measure to define those lines of investigation on which most has been already done, and also those on which most remains to do. [Italics mine. W.R.F.][12]

How arbitrary and artificial was Sanday's method of creating consensus where no consensus existed in fact may be seen from the words of a contemporary Oxford-trained scholar who was a disciple of Hilgenfeld:

In Germany indeed the old tradition (i.e., priority of Matthew to Mark) . . . has been consistently and uncompromisingly maintained by Professor

---

say that he hoped to show "that the dissent is only partial." He added, "I am myself inclined to mediate between the different positions. It would be a pity if the total margin of difference within the two covers of this book were supposed to be greater than it is. . . . In any case I believe it is not large enough to justify the skepticism which exists in some quarters, as though the whole problem would never be brought to a conclusion —that is, a relatively probable conclusion." *Oxford Studies*, pp. xi-xii. This was the partial vacuum of consensus in the womb of which Streeter's "Fundamental Solution" was formed. It may have been because in those days there *were* skeptics, that Streeter sometimes resorted to dogmatism and sarcasm to strengthen his defense of the two-document hypothesis.

12 *The Expositor*, 4th Series, Vol. III, Part I, pp. 90–91.

Hilgenfeld—to quote his own words recently written, 'The preference at present shown for S. Mark is opposed to the most certain conclusions of science'—but Professor Hilgenfeld is the spokesman of a minority, a minority which Dr. Davidson represents in England almost solitarily. As an exposition of the view now dominant we may conveniently turn to the article "Gospels," by Dr. Sanday, in Smith's *Bible Dictionary*, 2nd edition. Dr. Sanday declares that the greater originality of S. Mark is, "if not an assured result of criticism yet rapidly becoming so," . . . The only essential difference in the situation today from what it was forty years ago is the formidable increase of S. Mark's supporters,—it is apparently their number that convinces Dr. Sanday of S. Mark's approaching triumph—but the significance of this increase may easily be overrated.[13]

These words were written in 1897 by F. P. Badham, M.A., of Exeter College, Oxford. The fact that Badham, instead of holding an academic post, was in residence in the Reform Club in London when he published his book, reflects something of the state of affairs in England by the end of the century.

Sanday did not actually lie about Hilgenfeld's position. In his sketch, however, Hilgenfeld is mentioned only for the purpose of making the point that as a Tübingen scholar he had "largely modified" his view (in some unspecified manner) in the direction of those views resulting from following the methods of inquiry advocated by Holtzmann. This is a definitely misleading statement if it be taken to mean that Hilgenfeld modified his views in the direction of the two-document hypothesis. Hilgenfeld actually abandoned the Griesbach hypothesis in favor of that of Augustine. He never accepted the priority or originality of Mark—a point which is absolutely central to the two-document hypothesis.

Few men had the courage to protest against the developing consensus as Badham did. Those who did protest were treated as was Badham. They were ignored and they placed their scholarly careers in jeopardy.

The kind of pressure felt by scholars in the nineties is reflected clearly in the words of V. H. Stanton in 1893.

It requires some courage to call in question the soundness of a theory which has won the assent of a large number of the most thorough investigators in this field of New Testament criticism, and thus to render oneself

[13] F. P. Badham, *S. Mark's Indebtedness to S. Matthew*, New York, 1897, pp. ix-xii.

liable to the imputation of desiring to impede the progress of criticism and the general acceptance of its conclusions.[14]

In other words, in the last decade of the nineteenth century, *to call the two-document hypothesis into question was to open oneself to the charge of being an obscurantist who wished to impede progress.* Stanton continued:

Nor am I insensible to the attractiveness of the theory. The attempt to reconstruct a lost document by a careful analysis and comparison of later writings which have preserved fragments of it, or otherwise used it, is not in itself illegitimate, and the hope of effecting this has a singular charm for the mind of the critic. More particularly must this be the case when, as in the present instance, we should thus obtain a clearer view of that which is most original and most to be relied upon in the sources of our knowledge concerning the Christ.

In other words, the possibility of being able to reconstruct either of Holtzmann's two primitive sources holds a certain fascination for the critic which is heightened by religious interest in the results.

The very fascination which such a theory must possess is a reason for meeting it with peculiar caution. It is hard to restrict the imagination to its true office in such inquiries. When once we have thought ourselves into a particular theory, a conviction of its truth is apt to be bred in the mind, which is altogether beyond the evidence, while inconvenient facts are ignored.

This is followed by a probing criticism of the notion that Matthew and Luke both copied the *Logia*, concluding in the judgment:

. . . the theory that both St. Matthew and St. Luke used the Logia is open to many and grave objections. . . .[15]

If the philosophical, theological, and psychological factors influencing the intellectual life of Europe and America in the last half of the nineteenth and at the beginning of the twentieth century cannot be appealed to in an effort to understand the critical oversight of Streeter and his generation, then the historian is left with an unexplained mystery. For it is certain that the arguments and

---

14 "Some Points in the Synoptic Problem," *The Expositor*, 4th Series, Vol. III, Part II, p. 181.

15 *Op. cit.*, p. 196. Just how difficult it is "to restrict the imagination to its true office," may be measured by the fact that in due time Stanton, for no better reasons than those which had left him skeptical in 1893, himself accepted the two-document hypothesis.

evidence adduced in support of the two-document hypothesis are logically inconclusive, and that the priority of the canonical Mark to Matthew and Luke was accepted by Streeter and others not only in the absence of compelling proof but in spite of serious literary difficulties for that view.

B. The Labor of the Saints

The only sound historical judgment that can be rendered in a critical review of the history of the Synoptic Problem is that "extrascientific" or "nonscientific" factors exercised a deep influence in the development of a fundamentally misleading and false cónsensus. This is not to suggest, however, that the diligent work of painstaking scholars of the earlier generation who were sincerely convinced of the correctness of their presuppositions did not play a decisive role in preparing Streeter's generation to accept the two-document hypothesis more or less uncritically. The detailed work of men like Hawkins over broad areas of Synoptic material certainly strengthened the idea of Marcan priority. With Hawkins, Marcan priority was a working hypothesis confidently accepted on the basis of Woods' argument from order. With Streeter, however, this working hypothesis was transmuted into an axiom which according to his view could be questioned only by those who had not read and understood the work of Hawkins, or by those who had an "eccentric" view of what constituted evidence.

Another example of highly detailed and painstaking work contributed by the pre-Streeter generation of adherents of Marcan priority is the justly famous *Synopticon* by W. G. Rushbrooke, Fellow of St. John's College, Cambridge,[16] and Abbott's collaborator.

[16] *Synopticon, An Exposition of the Common Matter of the Synoptic Gospels*, London, 1880. This is a 241-page polychrome folio edition of Matthew, Mark, and Luke, including portions of John. The first 133 pages present the complete text of Mark in the left-hand column, with the parallel passages of Matthew and Luke in two parallel columns. Where all three agree the Greek text is printed in red ink. This was done deliberately because Rushbrooke, following Abbott, thought that this material deserved to have concentrated attention as the most reliable form of the earliest tradition. Other agreements are signified by different shapes and spacing of type printed in black ink. The remainder of the volume is made up of three appendices, one including the "double" tradition of Matthew and Luke with the agreements printed in capital letters, and the other two including the "single" tradition of Matthew and Luke, respectively.

The esteem with which Streeter held Rushbrooke's *Synopticon* is suggested by his praise for it in connection with the advice he gave to his readers on the way they should proceed to mark their Gospels in order to objectify the phenomena of verbal agreement and disagreement between the Gospels: "The happy possessor of W. G. Rushbrooke's magnificent *Synopticon* will find the work done for him by the use of different types and colours."[17]

But a contemporary of Streeter told how Rushbrooke's *Synopticon* actually had the power to strengthen the notion of Marcan priority merely by its own intrinsic being.

I used to think before 1916 that I knew enough about the Synoptic Problem to have a right to a definite opinion on the subject. I held, rather dogmatically, that our Greek St. Matthew depends on St. Mark, and (with somewhat less certainty) that Q, the matter common to Mt. and Lk., was the other source; so that I roughly believed what is called the 'two-document' theory. I indicated these views freely when writing on connected subjects. I said somewhere in print (and often in private) that people who were not convinced that Mt. and Lk. had both used Mk. as their principal source had not used Rushbrooke's *Synopticon*. I remember being annoyed when an eminent scholar of very venturesome views once replied that he disliked Rushbrooke precisely because he insisted on one's following Mk. Sir John Hawkins' admirable *Horae Synopticae* seemed to me also fairly conclusive, though less so than the mere study of Rushbrooke.[18]

These views were expressed in 1926 by Dom John Chapman, who between 1916 and 1918 abandoned the two-document hypothesis in favor of that of Augustine. Who the "eminent scholar of very venturesome views" may have been is not known. But he was a remarkably perceptive man, for the most distinguished investigators have been unaware of the true nature of Rushbrooke's *Synopticon*. Hawkins regarded it as "invaluable," and Abbott thought it "indispensable."

That Abbott should be high in his praise of Rushbrooke's work

---

When a parallel passage from John is included the agreements between John and all three Synoptic Gospels are printed in capital letters in red ink. When the agreement of John is only with two of the other Gospels, gold ink is used. Other agreements are signified by different shapes and spacing of letters in black ink.

[17] *F.G.*, p. 161, n. 1.

[18] *Matthew, Mark and Luke. A Study in the Order and Interrelation of the Synoptic Gospels*, London, 1937 (published posthumously by the Very Rev. Monsignor John M. T. Barton), p. 1.

is not surprising. The dedication of Rushbrooke's *Synopticon* reads as follows:

TO
EDWIN ABBOTT ABBOTT, D.D.
THE FIRST SUGGESTER OF THIS WORK
WHO TO SUGGESTION ADDED ENCOURAGEMENT
AND TO ENCOURAGEMENT COUNSEL AND ASSISTANCE
THESE PAGES ARE NOW DEDICATED
BY HIS FORMER PUPIL

After Holtzmann had had an opportunity to see Rushbrooke's *Synopticon* he included it along with the works of von Veit and von Heineke as one of the three synopses best adapted to serve the purposes of serious research.[19] This is no occasion for surprise since the *Synopticon*, conceived by Abbott and executed by Rushbrooke, is but an ingenious large-scale manual designed to facilitate the study of the Synoptic tradition on the terms laid down by Holtzmann in his epoch-making synthesis of 1863.

The *Synopticon* does not contain a single reference to Holtzmann's work, and it is altogether probable that the young Rushbrooke was quite unconscious of the ideological origin of the basic arrangement which Abbott had suggested for his project. But to the historian the dependence is unmistakable. The full title of Rushbrooke's work is: *Synopticon, An Exposition of the Common Matter of the Synoptic Gospels.*

By "Common Matter" is meant those passages in Matthew, Mark, and Luke where it may be presumed that all three have copied some earlier source. But in practice Rushbrooke included the whole of Mark, that is, not merely material Mark held in common with both Matthew and Luke, but also material Mark held in common with either Matthew or Luke, and even that material unique to Mark.

It is clear, therefore, that the idea that the earlier source was an Ur-Marcus, to use Holtzmann's term, has been decisive in the arrangement of the *Synopticon*. For it is reasonably presumed that if the earlier document was an Ur-Marcus, the whole of Mark must be considered as potentially belonging to that Ur-gospel. Thus

---

[19] Cf. *Die Synoptiker*, 3rd ed., Tübingen and Leipzig, in the *Hand-Commentar zum Neuen Testament*, 1901, p. vii.

while Rushbrooke's arrangement is not dictated by Holtzmann's synthesis, it is a logical development from it, which Holtzmann himself would have appreciated. Rushbrooke's own justification for this procedure was as follows:

St. Mark's version, which stands in the left-hand column, apart from other considerations, seemed best fitted by its brevity to be adopted as the standard. It has therefore been printed at full length without deviation from its order; those parts alone of St. Matthew and St. Luke being inserted which are parallel to the narrative of St. Mark.[20]

The decision to follow Mark's order as well as his full text seemed innocent enough on these terms. But such a procedure inevitably strengthened the impression on the mind of readers undisciplined in the history and nature of the Synoptic Problem that Mark was the nearest representation of that earlier document which all three Evangelists had copied.

The next paragraph Rushbrooke wrote gave away the whole procedure which Abbott had suggested to him.

A full index will be printed at the end of the work, by which the reader will be enabled to refer at once to any passage of the three Synoptic Gospels which contains the Common Tradition. If, as is probable, an Appendix be published containing the longer passages common to St. Matthew and St. Luke, and also those peculiar to St. Matthew and St. Luke, the Index will then include references to every part of the Synoptic Gospels.

This seemed fair enough at the time. What could be wrong with an instrument which enabled the student to study "every part of the Synoptic Gospels" according to an arrangement which facilitated minute comparison of passages in this way? Nothing at all, unless there was some reason to question whether or not behind the Synoptic Gospels there were in fact two primitive documents corresponding to Holtzmann's Ur-Marcus and *Logia*. If there is any reason to question the existence of one or both these hypothetical sources, then Rushbrooke's arrangement is absolutely unjustified. For on what other grounds would it be possible to justify the separation of passages common only to Matthew and Luke for comparison without isolating for comparison at the same time the substantial body of material common only to Mark and

[20] *Op. cit.*, p. xii.

Matthew, and the less extensive but not less significant material common only to Luke and Mark? There do not seem to be any other grounds, and, therefore, it is fair to presume that Rushbrooke's *Synopticon* presupposes the two-document hypothesis, and in fact itself promotes the formal idea of a four-document hypothesis. The first document is that presumed to lie behind Mark, the second, that which was copied by Matthew and Luke in passages where there is no Marcan parallel, the third, a document copied by Matthew alone, and the fourth, one copied by Luke alone.

Rushbrooke's titles for these three later groups of material could not have been missed by Streeter.

Appendix A
The Double Tradition of St. Matthew and St. Luke

Appendix B
The Single Tradition of St. Matthew

Appendix Γ
The Single Tradition of St. Luke

Here is the single distinctive difference between the formal imagery fostered by Rushbrooke's *Synopticon* and that promoted by Holtzmann's book in 1863. Holtzmann put his A (Ur-Marcus) and Λ (Logia) on the same level, as two hypothetical primitive documents standing apart from all others by their presumed connection with the two apostolic works referred to by Papias. The material unique to Matthew and Luke was given a secondary status in the format of Holtzmann's presentation.

In contrast, Rushbrooke's formal arrangement tends to suggest to readers that the single traditions of Matthew and Luke have a status more comparable to "The Double Tradition of St. Matthew and St. Luke." That is, whereas in Holtzmann's reconstruction the tradition unique to Matthew and Luke is more or less left in the background, Rushbrooke's arrangement tended to bring it forward and give it equal notice with that of the *Logia*.

Thus there is reason to think that one of the germinal roots of Streeter's four-document hypothesis, and perhaps the most important one, was simply the arbitrary and fortuitous format of Rushbrooke's "magnificent" *Synopticon*.

There is no doubt that Rushbrooke's *Synopticon* was influential within the "Oxford" school of Synoptic criticism in which Streeter was nurtured. In Hawkins' essay on "Probabilities as to the So-Called Double Tradition of St. Matthew and St. Luke" in *Oxford Studies*, he wrote:

In thus beginning by collecting all the parallels for which there is any probability at all of a documentary origin, we cannot do better than adopt as a ground work the very complete and minute statement of them provided in Mr. Rushbrooke's *Synopticon*.[21]

It is also clear from statements in his *Horae Synopticae* that Hawkins regarded Rushbrooke's work as a very important tool, and it may be presumed that it was constantly at hand as he carried out his equally minute and detailed work.[22]

The careful and detailed work of Rushbrooke and Hawkins left a deep impression on students of Streeter's generation. The notion that these intelligent and dedicated scholars would have expended thousands of man-hours' labor developing the highly refined tools necessary to carry forward research into the residual problems left unresolved on the two-document hypothesis, without having virtually unassailable reasons for their belief in the essential correctness of that hypothesis, is a notion that most students of Streeter's generation found unthinkable.

Streeter's highly detailed treatment of the minor agreements of Matthew and Luke against Mark in turn compounded the beguiling influence of this academic delusion, which continued to grow in strength as each successive generation of tireless scholars patiently built upon the foundations laid in the past. Eventually a new argument was to develop which, though it never appeared in print, exercised a greater influence in sustaining belief in the priority of Mark than any that Streeter or anyone else has ever published. This argument may be formally stated as follows: "It is inconceivable that so many scholars could have been so wrong on such a fundamental point for such a long period of time." This is a powerful argument precisely because it is in practice irrefutable. Every scholar respects honest humility and sincere *pietas* in his colleague. The critic who sets his judgment against a consensus endorsed by the vast majority of experts during a long period of time does so at the risk of being guilty of academic arrogance, and of losing the confidence of his colleagues.

[21] *Oxford Studies*, p. 96.
[22] *Cf.* pp. 65 and 81.

Nonetheless, it is only fair to say that this argument is essentially gratuitous and carries no probative value whatever. That it carries any weight at all only witnesses to the absurdity of the situation of impasse which, since Streeter, has immobilized the discipline of source criticism in Gospel studies.

C. Concluding Observations

Chapman's *Matthew, Mark and Luke* was published posthumously in 1937. In that book he pointed out the logical fallacy of the conventional argument from order as did Jameson in 1922. But still New Testament scholarship paid little or no attention. Not until 1951, when Cambridge University Press published Butler's *The Originality of Matthew*, did New Testament scholars more generally begin to take notice of the fallacious character of this much depended upon argument for Marcan priority.

In 1953 Pierson Parker showed convincingly that it was not possible to separate Streeter's "M" material from the material in Matthew parallel to Mark. He also showed that there were very important historical objections to the notion that Mark was the earliest Gospel.[23] But Parker's scholarly work caused hardly a ripple of critical comment.

In 1952 Austin Farrer agreed with Butler that the critical basis for belief in the existence of "Q" was unconvincing.[24] Chapman and Jameson had taken this view long before, as had Ropes of Harvard and his student, Morton Scott Enslin.[25]

All these scholars, however, have been regarded as deviators, and their views on the Synoptic Problem until recently have been sympathetically received by only a very small minority of Gospel critics.

A further cause for concern at the situation of impasse in Synoptic criticism is the fact that these dissenters all in one way or another argue against each other. Thus Farrer believes firmly in the priority

---

[23] *The Gospel Before Mark*, Chicago, 1953.
[24] *See* Farrer's review of Butler's *The Originality of Matthew* in *J.T.S.*, Vol. III, Part I, April 1952, pp. 102–106.
[25] James Hardy Ropes, *The Synoptic Gospels*, Cambridge, Mass., 1934 (republished with new preface by D. E. Nineham, London, 1960). Morton Scott Enslin, *op. cit.*

of Mark, while Parker thinks he has produced evidence supportive of the existence of "Q."[26]

Meanwhile, Monsig. de Solages in 1959 published an 1128-page statistical study of the Synoptic Gospels, in which he purported to prove mathematically the truth of the two-document hypothesis.[27] His work is in fact a monument to the mesmerizing power of the two-document consensus. For what Solages has actually done is to document in exhaustive detail the fact that Mark is in some sense the middle term between Matthew and Luke. The phenomenon which he thought pointed unmistakably to the two source theory as the true solution of the Synoptic Problem is that of the minor agreements between Matthew and Luke against Mark. His argument and procedure, though apparently independently reached, was essentially the same as that set forth by Abbott in his article for the *Encyclopaedia Britannica* in 1879. First he noted that these agreements are virtually negligible. Then he decided to proceed as if they did not exist at all and to solve the problem without taking them into account. Then, having proved the viability of the two-document hypothesis on these unrealistic terms by the use of statistical methods, he returned to the minor agreements of Matthew and Luke against Mark, and explained them as due to "grammatical and stylistic convergence."[28]

The sense of abject poverty and unreal absurdity in the contemporary impasse reached unparalleled heights in Solages' easy explanation of a problem it took Streeter thirty-eight pages of closely argued text to explain away.

All the Hellenists agree in admitting that Mk., in spite of his piquancy, writes an incorrect and clumsy Greek, and that Lk. and Mt. write a more correct and smoother Greek. As two correctors of a pupil's paper, proceeding independently from each other (sometimes), agree in the corrections (so Mt. and Lk. would frequently agree accidentally in correcting Mk.). Hence, for instance, the recurrence of the δέ instead of καί in Mk. (Aramaic) and of the aorists εἶπεν, usual tense of the story in Greek, instead of λέγει or of ἔλεγεν.

[26] Farrer states his belief in the priority of Mark explicitly in his review of Butler's *The Originality of Matthew*, and presupposes it throughout his essay "On Dispensing with Q." Parker's view is based on a statistical study of the vocabulary of "Q," which led him to the conclusion that it was possible to isolate a distinctive "Q" vocabulary.

[27] *A Greek Synopsis of the Gospels. A New Way of Solving the Synoptic Problem* (Eng. ed. tr. from French by J. Baissus), Leyden, 1959.

[28] *Op. cit.*, pp. 1052–1054, and pp. 1085–1086.

Here I only point out how the diagram which we have reached through calculus allows us to explain this literary phenomenon quite easily, which at first sight is rather disconcerting. The detailed development of the explanation belongs, by rights, to an ulterior literary study of vocabulary of the grammar and style of the three Synoptics.[29]

Solages' notion that the Synoptic Problem is first to be solved by calculus and then explained by literary study is only comprehensible in an age which is indebted to a tradition in which the Gospels have been studied as "fossils" are studied. His treatment of the minor agreements illustrates the sanguine expectation the physical scientist holds for the results to be derived from detailed classification of data. The totality of these verbal agreements, including agreements in omission, are neatly catalogued under seven major headings with no less than forty subdivisions.[30]

Even so, agreements in word order are ignored, and, as with Streeter, the reader would never be able to form an accurate impression of the actual nature of the agreement between Matthew and Luke against Mark in a given passage from this highly abstract presentation of the phenomena.

Furthermore, when one turns to the actual context of the Gospels in which the minor agreements occur, he finds that a "literary study" of vocabulary, grammar, and style of the Evangelists fails to support the notion that these agreements can be explained away as Streeter and Solages suggest. They remain as the chief literary stumbling block for the adherents of the notion that Matthew and Luke copied Mark. An adequate hypothesis must provide an explanation for this phenomenon as well as all the other significant literary and historical factors involved in the solution of this most perplexing and highly challenging problem.

[29] *Op. cit.*, p. 1086.
[30] *Op. cit.*, pp. 1055–1065. One does not have to share the presuppositions of this work, nor the conclusions of its author, in order to make good use of it. (*See* Ch. VI, n. 4.) The same can be said for all careful research on the Synoptic Problem, such as for example Hawkins' *Horae Synopticae*.

VI

A New Introduction
to the Problem

The Synoptic Problem is difficult but not
necessarily insoluble. Matthew, Mark, and Luke were almost certainly written in some particular chronological order. Reduced to its
simplest terms the Synoptic Problem sets the task of discovering that
order. However important the part oral tradition and other written
sources may have played in the composition of the Synoptic Gospels,
the problem of determining which was written first, which second,
and which third still persists. One of the three was written before
the other two. One was written after the first, and before the third.
And one was written after the other two.[1]

[1] A critic's conviction of the proper order in which the Synoptic Gospels were
written, however, does not necessarily enable him to prove his beliefs. Even if his
understanding is right, it is not likely that he will be able to settle the question with
finality in the mind of another critic. This is partly because it is not practical for him
to set forth all the arguments and evidence that conceivably could lead impartial
investigators to the conclusion that the question had been settled once and for all.

Certainly, to retrace the history of his own thinking on the Synoptic Problem,
however interesting that might be, and even instructive, would have dubious probative
value.

If a critic, on the basis of his own research, thinks that he knows the order in which Matthew, Mark, and Luke were written, and is asked to write about this question, there are two possible courses of action for him to take: (1) He can attempt to write as if in fact he did not know the truth, and strive to approach the problem with an objectivity that would reflect no particular point of view. In that case, if he set forth the solution he thought to be correct, he would be obligated to treat other possible solutions equally fully. The resulting study would be very extensive, and therefore no such book has ever been written. One reason it has never been written is that the number of solutions which have been propounded is so very great that the human heart and hand falters before a task of such magnitude. (2) Another course he can follow is to write about the problem from his own point of view. In this case he is obligated to disclose to his readers the solution to the Synoptic Problem he accepts, and indicate something of the degree of probability he attaches to his views on the matter.

The latter course is followed in this book. And the time has now come for the reader to know the point of view from which this book has been written.

Matthew appears to be the earliest Gospel, and Luke seems next in order. Matthew was evidently used extensively by the author of Luke, who also may have been the author of Acts. Luke undoubtedly had access to other written materials besides Matthew, and some of

---

But if it is impractical for a critic to set forth all the arguments and evidence that might conceivably lead impartial investigators to the solution of the Synoptic Problem he believes to be correct, what can he do ? If the solution he thinks is the correct one is a solution that has already been proposed, he is first obligated to review the history of the Synoptic Problem to show why this solution was first proposed favorably, and why critical opinion in favor of this solution did not develop into a lasting consensus. But once this has been done, how could he proceed to formulate his argument ? He could next attempt to clarify for his readers the nature of the problem, and then suggest a way to approach the problem which will lead the interested investigator more readily to more fruitful results than any other known way.

It follows from all this that the difficulty of the Synoptic Problem does not justify an attitude of resignation. Attention has been drawn to the complexity of the problem in order to discourage the reader from thinking that the work of another investigator would ever produce in his mind that degree of reasonable certainty and conviction that more justly comes from his own work of verification and further discovery.

Whether a given reader will ever come to the point that he recognizes that there is no longer any reason for him to doubt that a particular solution is the true solution will and should depend upon his own further investigations. There is no substitute for firsthand study of the Gospels themselves.

this material was probably parallel to material which Luke also found in Matthew. But Luke seems to be dependent on Matthew for the general order and form of his Gospel, and in many passages he clearly copied his text from Matthew.

There seems to be no sound literary or historical ground on which to base a denial of the premise that Mark is throughout the whole extent of his Gospel working closely with texts of Matthew and Luke before him.

It is probable that there were other written sources and some kind of oral tradition also available to each of the Evangelists. Matthew and Luke possibly had access to one or more common written sources, but the use of hypothetical written sources (and/or oral tradition) by the Evangelists is not the best way to account for the major phenomena of similarity, and the extensive verbal agreement among Matthew, Mark, and Luke.

On the whole, this view of the matter is not new. Many investigators have held essentially the same view as the best solution to the problem of the Synoptic relationship. The works of critics who have held this view are more cogent than what has been written by those who adhere to alternate views. That is, the arguments of these critics can be verified by an appeal to the phenomena of the Gospels themselves in a way that is not true of other hypotheses.

Arguments against the view that Matthew is the earliest Gospel, Luke second, and Mark third, are unconvincing. On the other hand, it is possible to raise serious objections to alternate views that have been proposed.

Thus it has been possible in Chapters I through V to review the history of the Synoptic Problem in such a way as to help the reader understand that this view was abandoned in favor of another that was less satisfactory, for reasons which scholars would not now justify.

Within this particular historical context, the reader finds himself confronted with a view which calls into question a long-established consensus concerning one of the Gospels, namely, Mark. This view proposes for that Gospel a relationship to Matthew and Luke, that is virtually the opposite to the relationship which it has on the usual view. It may be helpful, therefore, if an effort is made to cut through the whole history of the problem and attempt to follow an argument intended to support the view that Mark wrote after Matthew and

Luke and is dependent upon both, and also that Luke was dependent on Matthew.

Although the particular argument which follows draws upon much that has been done previously, both in form and content, it is to a large extent new. It is intended to encourage a serious reconsideration of a solution which was first formulated in the eighteenth century, flourished in the first half of the nineteenth century, but which for the past one hundred years has been eclipsed by the two-document hypothesis.

The argument is presented in steps. At first it is important to take one step at a time and always in order. But as one advances through the initial steps, it matters little in which order he takes the later steps, some of which indeed may be skipped without serious loss. That is, the cogency of the argument does not presuppose that the separable theses presented .at each step in the argument are like the "links of a chain," which, as a chain, can be no stronger than the weakest link. On the contrary, the cogency of this argument depends upon a web of evidence structured by innumerable arguments, some of which touch only the most minute points, but which, nevertheless, taken together with all the rest, constitute a supportive basis that will bear the full weight of the conclusion: "It is historically probable that Mark was written after Matthew and Luke and was dependent upon both." The destruction of one or more of the strands of evidence which have been woven into this web would not destroy the web. Nor can it be doubted that others in favor of the same conclusion may see ways in which the web of evidence may be strengthened by adding an argument here and by restructuring another one there.

It may be possible to damage the web so that it can no longer hold up the conclusion it has been spun to support. But that will not happen unless one is able to cut one or more of the main strands set forth in the initial steps, or unless one is able to destroy several closely related theses supporting some decisive section in the web of argumentation.

Step I

Thesis: *The similarity between Matthew, Mark, and Luke is such as to justify the assertion that they stand in some kind of literary relationship to one another.*

The nature of this similarity is such as to warrant the judgment that the literary relationship between these Gospels could be one involving direct copying. That is, the degree of verbatim agreement in Greek between any two of these three Gospels is as high or higher than that which generally exists between documents where it is known that the author of one copied the text of the other. The same degree of verbatim agreement could be accounted for on the hypothesis that each Evangelist independently copied one or more common or genetically related sources. But this alternative way of explaining the phenomena of agreement between any two Gospels should not be utilized until after an attempt has been made to explain it on the simplest terms, namely on the hypothesis that one Evangelist copied the work of the other. The reason for this procedure is not that the simplest explanation is necessarily the correct one, but that it is wrong to multiply hypothetical possibilities unnecessarily. There is nothing wrong in hypothecating the existence of an otherwise unknown source or sources, if there exists evidence that is best explained thereby. But for the sake of economy this is not to be done without good reason. This is not an infallible rule, but it is accepted procedure in literary criticism as well as in other disciplines, and one which commends itself by the results achieved when it is followed, compared to those which are achieved when it is ignored.

The following specimens of texts of Matthew, Mark, and Luke are presented as illustrations of the kind of verbal similarity which exists among these Gospels, and which suggests the possibility of direct copying.

Every word underlined is found in the parallel text(s) of the other Gospel(s) printed on the same page. If the underlining is unbroken, the agreement is exact with reference to case, declension, number and gender of nouns, articles, pronouns, adjectives, and participles: and exact with reference to mood, voice, tense, number and person of verbs, etc. Broken underlining indicates agreement as to the word concerned, but where the agreement is not exact in one or more points of grammar. Differences in the endings of words merely occasioned by the circumstance of their position in the sentence, like the movable *nu*, or by the circumstance of the quality of the initial letter of the word following as with the ending of the negative οὐ, are disregarded.

A continuation of underlining between words indicates that the same words not only occur in the other gospel(s) printed on the same page, but that they also occur in exactly the same order. Agreement in word order between the last word in a line and the first word in the next line is indicated by an extension of the underlining into the lefthand margin at the beginning of the second line.

THE FEEDING OF THE FOUR THOUSAND
(Not in Luke.)

Matthew 15:32–39

Ὁ δὲ Ἰησοῦς προσκαλεσάμενος τοὺς μαθητὰς αὐτοῦ εἶπεν· σπλαγχνίζομαι ἐπὶ τὸν ὄχλον, ὅτι ἤδη ἡμέραι τρεῖς προσμένουσίν μοι καὶ οὐκ ἔχουσιν τί φάγωσιν· καὶ ἀπολῦσαι αὐτοὺς νήστεις οὐ θέλω, μήποτε ἐκλυθῶσιν ἐν τῇ ὁδῷ· καὶ λέγουσιν αὐτῷ οἱ μαθηταί· πόθεν ἡμῖν ἐν ἐρημίᾳ ἄρτοι τοσοῦτοι ὥστε χορτάσαι ὄχλον τοσοῦτον; καὶ λέγει αὐτοῖς ὁ Ἰησοῦς· πόσους ἄρτους ἔχετε; οἱ δὲ εἶπαν· ἑπτά, καὶ ὀλίγα ἰχθύδια. καὶ παραγγείλας τῷ ὄχλῳ ἀναπεσεῖν ἐπὶ τὴν γῆν, ἔλαβεν τοὺς ἑπτὰ ἄρτους καὶ τοὺς ἰχθύας καὶ εὐχαριστήσας ἔκλασεν καὶ ἐδίδου τοῖς μαθηταῖς, οἱ δὲ μαθηταὶ τοῖς ὄχλοις. καὶ ἔφαγον πάντες καὶ ἐχορτάσθησαν, καὶ τὸ περισσεῦον τῶν κλασμάτων ἦραν ἑπτὰ σπυρίδας πλήρεις. οἱ δὲ ἐσθίοντες ἦσαν τετρακισχί- λιοι ἄνδρες χωρὶς γυναικῶν καὶ παιδίων. καὶ ἀπολύσας τοὺς ὄχλους ἐνέβη εἰς τὸ πλοῖον καὶ ἦλθεν εἰς τὰ ὅρια Μαγαδάν.

Mark 8:1–10

Ἐν ἐκείναις ταῖς ἡμέραις πάλιν πολλοῦ ὄχλου ὄντος καὶ μὴ ἐχόντων τί φάγωσιν, προσκαλεσάμενος τοὺς μαθητὰς λέγει αὐτοῖς· σπλαγχνίζομαι ἐπὶ τὸν ὄχλον, ὅτι ἤδη ἡμέραι τρεῖς προσμένουσίν μοι καὶ οὐκ ἔχουσιν τί φάγωσιν· καὶ ἐὰν ἀπολύσω αὐτοὺς νήστεις εἰς οἶκον αὐτῶν, ἐκλυθήσονται ἐν τῇ ὁδῷ· καί τινες αὐτῶν ἀπὸ μακρόθεν ἥκασιν. καὶ ἀπεκρίθησαν αὐτῷ οἱ μαθηταὶ αὐτοῦ ὅτι πόθεν τούτους δυνήσεταί τις ὧδε χορτάσαι ἄρτων ἐπ’ ἐρημίας; καὶ ἠρώτα αὐτούς· πόσους ἔχετε ἄρτους; οἱ δὲ εἶπαν· ἑπτά. καὶ παραγγέλλει τῷ ὄχλῳ ἀναπεσεῖν ἐπὶ τῆς γῆς· καὶ λαβὼν τοὺς ἑπτὰ ἄρτους εὐχαριστήσας ἔκλασεν καὶ ἐδίδου τοῖς μαθηταῖς αὐτοῦ ἵνα παρατιθῶσιν, καὶ παρέθηκαν τῷ ὄχλῳ. καὶ εἶχον ἰχθύδια ὀλίγα· καὶ εὐλογήσας αὐτὰ εἶπεν καὶ ταῦτα παρατιθέναι. καὶ ἔφαγον καὶ ἐχορτάσθησαν, καὶ ἦραν περισσεύματα κλασμάτων ἑπτὰ σπυρίδας. ἦσαν δὲ ὡς τετρακισχίλιοι. καὶ ἀπέλυσεν αὐτούς. καὶ εὐθὺς ἐμβὰς εἰς τὸ πλοῖον μετὰ τῶν μαθητῶν αὐτοῦ ἦλθεν εἰς τὰ μέρη Δαλμανουθά.

Often the agreement between Matthew and Mark is more extensive than in this passage, though many times it is less so. This passage, however, is not atypical. Compare Matthew 26:20–29 // Mark 14:17–25 and Matthew 26:36–46 // Mark 14:32–42 as examples where the verbatim agreement between Matthew and Mark is greater than in the specimens cited.

JESUS IN THE SYNAGOGUE AT CAPERNAUM
(Not in Matthew.)

Mark 1:21–28

Καὶ εἰσπορεύονται εἰς Καφαρναούμ. καὶ εὐθὺς τοῖς σάββασιν εἰσελθὼν εἰς τὴν συναγωγὴν ἐδίδασκεν. καὶ ἐξεπλήσσοντο ἐπὶ τῇ διδαχῇ αὐτοῦ· ἦν γὰρ διδάσκων αὐτοὺς ὡς ἐξουσίαν ἔχων, καὶ οὐχ ὡς οἱ γραμματεῖς. καὶ εὐθὺς ἦν ἐν τῇ συναγωγῇ αὐτῶν ἄνθρωπος ἐν πνεύματι ἀκαθάρτῳ, καὶ ἀνέκραξεν λέγων· τί ἡμῖν καὶ σοί, Ἰησοῦ Ναζαρηνέ; ἦλθες ἀπολέσαι ἡμᾶς. οἶδά σε τίς εἶ, ὁ ἅγιος τοῦ θεοῦ. καὶ ἐπετίμησεν αὐτῷ ὁ Ἰησοῦς λέγων· φιμώθητι καὶ ἔξελθε ἐξ αὐτοῦ. καὶ σπαράξαν αὐτὸν τὸ πνεῦμα τὸ ἀκάθαρτον καὶ φωνῆσαν φωνῇ μεγάλῃ ἐξῆλθεν ἐξ αὐτοῦ. καὶ ἐθαμβήθησαν ἅπαντες, ὥστε συζητεῖν αὐτοὺς λέγοντας· τί ἐστιν τοῦτο; διδαχὴ καινὴ κατ᾽ ἐξουσίαν· καὶ τοῖς πνεύμασι τοῖς ἀκαθάρτοις ἐπιτάσσει, καὶ ὑπακούουσιν αὐτῷ. καὶ ἐξῆλθεν ἡ ἀκοὴ αὐτοῦ εὐθὺς πανταχοῦ εἰς ὅλην τὴν περίχωρον τῆς Γαλιλαίας.

Luke 4:31–37

Καὶ κατῆλθεν εἰς Καφαρναοὺμ πόλιν τῆς Γαλιλαίας. καὶ ἦν διδάσκων αὐτοὺς ἐν τοῖς σάββασιν. καὶ ἐξεπλήσσοντο ἐπὶ τῇ διδαχῇ αὐτοῦ, ὅτι ἐν ἐξουσίᾳ ἦν ὁ λόγος αὐτοῦ. καὶ ἐν τῇ συναγωγῇ ἦν ἄνθρωπος ἔχων πνεῦμα δαιμονίου ἀκαθάρτου, καὶ ἀνέκραξεν φωνῇ μεγάλῃ· ἔα, τί ἡμῖν καὶ σοί, Ἰησοῦ Ναζαρηνέ; ἦλθες ἀπολέσαι ἡμᾶς; οἶδά σε τίς εἶ, ὁ ἅγιος τοῦ θεοῦ. καὶ ἐπετίμησεν αὐτῷ ὁ Ἰησοῦς λέγων· φιμώθητι καὶ ἔξελθε ἀπ᾽ αὐτοῦ. καὶ ῥῖψαν αὐτὸν τὸ δαιμόνιον εἰς τὸ μέσον ἐξῆλθεν ἀπ᾽ αὐτοῦ μηδὲν βλάψαν αὐτόν. καὶ ἐγένετο θάμβος ἐπὶ πάντας, καὶ συνελάλουν πρὸς ἀλλήλους λέγοντες· τίς ὁ λόγος οὗτος, ὅτι ἐν ἐξουσίᾳ καὶ δυνάμει ἐπιτάσσει τοῖς ἀκαθάρτοις πνεύμασιν καὶ ἐξέρχονται; καὶ ἐξεπορεύετο ἦχος περὶ αὐτοῦ εἰς πάντα τόπον τῆς περιχώρου.

The verbatim agreement between Mark and Luke is not as extensive as between Mark and Matthew. But the reader can readily see from this specimen and a comparison of the following examples that the verbal similarity between Mark and Luke is quite extensive: Mark 5:1–20 ‖ Luke 8:26–39; Mark 9:37–40 ‖ Luke 9:48–50; Mark 10:17–31 ‖ Luke 18:18–30; Mark 12:38b–44 ‖ Luke 20: 46–21:4.

THE CENTURION'S SERVANT
(Not in Mark.)

Matthew 8:7–10

λέγει αὐτῷ· ἐγὼ ἐλθὼν θεραπεύσω αὐτόν. ἀποκριθεὶς δὲ ὁ ἑκατόνταρχος ἔφη· κύριε, οὐκ εἰμὶ ἱκανὸς ἵνα μου ὑπὸ τὴν στέγην εἰσέλθῃς· ἀλλὰ μόνον εἰπὲ λόγῳ, καὶ ἰαθήσεται ὁ παῖς μου. καὶ γὰρ ἐγὼ ἄνθρωπός εἰμι ὑπὸ ἐξουσίαν, ἔχων ὑπ᾽ ἐμαυτὸν στρατιώτας, καὶ λέγω τούτῳ· πορεύθητι, καὶ πορεύεται, καὶ ἄλλῳ· ἔρχου, καὶ ἔρχεται, καὶ τῷ δούλῳ μου· ποίησον τοῦτο, καὶ ποιεῖ. ἀκούσας δὲ ὁ Ἰησοῦς ἐθαύμασεν καὶ εἶπεν τοῖς ἀκολουθοῦσιν· ἀμὴν λέγω ὑμῖν, παρ᾽ οὐδενὶ τοσαύτην πίστιν ἐν τῷ Ἰσραὴλ εὗρον.

Luke 7:6–9

ὁ δὲ Ἰησοῦς ἐπορεύετο σὺν αὐτοῖς. ἤδη δὲ αὐτοῦ οὐ μακρὰν ἀπέχοντος ἀπὸ τῆς οἰκίας, ἔπεμψεν φίλους ὁ ἑκατοντάρχης λέγων αὐτῷ· κύριε, μὴ σκύλλου· οὐ γὰρ ἱκανός εἰμι ἵνα ὑπὸ τὴν στέγην μου εἰσέλθῃς· διὸ οὐδὲ ἐμαυτὸν ἠξίωσα πρὸς σὲ ἐλθεῖν· ἀλλὰ εἰπὲ λόγῳ, καὶ ἰαθήτω ὁ παῖς μου. καὶ γὰρ ἐγὼ ἄνθρωπός εἰμι ὑπὸ ἐξουσίαν τασσόμενος, ἔχων ὑπ᾽ ἐμαυτὸν στρατιώτας, καὶ λέγω τούτῳ· πορεύθητι, καὶ πορεύεται, καὶ ἄλλῳ· ἔρχου, καὶ ἔρχεται, καὶ τῷ δούλῳ μου· ποίησον τοῦτο, καὶ ποιεῖ. ἀκούσας δὲ ταῦτα ὁ Ἰησοῦς ἐθαύμασεν αὐτόν, καὶ στραφεὶς τῷ ἀκολουθοῦντι αὐτῷ ὄχλῳ εἶπεν· λέγω ὑμῖν, οὐδὲ ἐν τῷ Ἰσραὴλ τοσαύτην πίστιν εὗρον.

The verbatim agreement between Luke and Matthew in this passage is equaled or exceeded at many points. Compare for example: Luke 3:7–9 || Matthew 3:7–10; Luke 4:1–13 || Matthew 4:1–11; Luke 6:41–42 || Matthew 7:3–5; Luke 7:18–35 || Matthew 11:2–19; Luke 11:29–32 || Matthew 12:38–42; Luke 13:34–35 || Matthew 23:37–39.

Not only is there extensive agreement between any two of the Synoptic Gospels, but there are many passages which are characterized by extensive agreement among all three. For example: Matthew 8:2–4 || Mark 1:40–45 || Luke 5:12–16.

THE HEALING OF A LEPER

Matthew 8:2–4

καὶ ἰδοὺ λεπρὸς προσελθὼν προσεκύνει αὐτῷ λέγων· κύριε, ἐὰν θέλῃς, δύνασαί με καθαρίσαι. καὶ ἐκτείνας τὴν χεῖρα ἥψατο αὐτοῦ λέγων· θέλω, καθαρίσθητι. καὶ εὐθέως ἐκαθαρίσθη αὐτοῦ ἡ λέπρα. καὶ λέγει αὐτῷ ὁ Ἰησοῦς· ὅρα μηδενὶ εἴπῃς, ἀλλὰ ὕπαγε σεαυτὸν δεῖξον τῷ ἱερεῖ καὶ προσένεγκον τὸ δῶρον ὃ προσέταξεν Μωϋσῆς, εἰς μαρτύριον αὐτοῖς.

Mark 1:40–45

Καὶ ἔρχεται πρὸς αὐτὸν λεπρὸς παρακαλῶν αὐτὸν καὶ γονυπετῶν λέγων αὐτῷ ὅτι ἐὰν θέλῃς δύνασαί με καθαρίσαι. καὶ σπλαγχνισθεὶς ἐκτείνας τὴν χεῖρα αὐτοῦ ἥψατο καὶ λέγει αὐτῷ· θέλω, καθαρίσθητι. καὶ εὐθὺς ἀπῆλθεν ἀπ' αὐτοῦ ἡ λέπρα, καὶ ἐκαθαρίσθη. καὶ ἐμβριμησάμενος αὐτῷ εὐθὺς ἐξέβαλεν αὐτόν. καὶ λέγει αὐτῷ· ὅρα μηδενὶ μηδὲν εἴπῃς, ἀλλὰ ὕπαγε σεαυτὸν δεῖξον τῷ ἱερεῖ καὶ προσένεγκε περὶ τοῦ καθαρισμοῦ σου ἃ προσέταξεν Μωϋσῆς, εἰς μαρτύριον αὐτοῖς. ὁ δὲ ἐξελθὼν ἤρξατο κηρύσσειν πολλὰ καὶ διαφημίζειν τὸν λόγον, ὥστε μηκέτι αὐτὸν δύνασθαι φανερῶς εἰς πόλιν εἰσελθεῖν, ἀλλ' ἔξω ἐπ' ἐρήμοις τόποις ἦν· καὶ ἤρχοντο πρὸς αὐτὸν πάντοθεν.

Luke 5:12–16

Καὶ ἐγένετο ἐν τῷ εἶναι αὐτὸν ἐν μιᾷ τῶν πόλεων και ἰδοὺ ἀνὴρ πλήρης λέπρας· ἰδὼν δὲ τὸν Ἰησοῦν, πεσὼν ἐπὶ πρόσωπον ἐδεήθη αὐτοῦ λέγων· κύριε, ἐὰν θέλῃς, δύνασαί με καθαρίσαι. καὶ ἐκτείνας τὴν χεῖρα ἥψατο αὐτοῦ λέγων· θέλω, καθαρίσθητι· καὶ εὐθέως ἡ λέπρα ἀπῆλθεν ἀπ' αὐτοῦ. καὶ αὐτὸς παρήγγειλεν αὐτῷ μηδενὶ εἰπεῖν, ἀλλὰ ἀπελθὼν δεῖξον σεαυτὸν τῷ ἱερεῖ, καὶ προσένεγκε περὶ τοῦ καθαρισμοῦ σου καθὼς προσέταξεν Μωϋσῆς, εἰς μαρτύριον αὐτοῖς. διήρχετο δὲ μᾶλλον ὁ λόγος περὶ αὐτοῦ, καὶ συνήρχοντο ὄχλοι πολλοὶ ἀκούειν καὶ θεραπεύεσθαι ἀπὸ τῶν ἀσθενειῶν αὐτῶν· αὐτὸς δὲ ἦν ὑποχωρῶν ἐν ταῖς ἐρήμοις καὶ προσευχόμενος.

Among the other passages which exhibit extensive agreement among all three Synoptics the following may be considered as more or less representative:
Matthew 9:1–8 // Mark 2:1–12 // Luke 5:17–26; Matthew 16:24–28 // Mark 8:34–9:1 // Luke 9:23–27; Matthew 19:13–15 // Mark 10:13–16 // Luke 18:15–17; Matthew 21:23–27 // Mark 11:27–33 // Luke 20:1–8; Matthew 21:33–46 // Mark 12:1–12 // Luke 20:9–19; Matthew 22:23–33 // Mark 12:18–27 // Luke 20:27–40; Matthew 24:4–8 // Mark 13:5–8 // Luke 21 : 8–11.

Step II

Thesis: *There are eighteen and only eighteen fundamental ways in which three documents, among which there exists some kind of direct literary dependence, may be related to one another.*

If the second copied the first, and the third copied the second but not the first, they may be related to one another thus in six different ways:

A	A	B	B	C	C
↓	↓	↓	↓	↓	↓
B	C	A	C	A	B
↓	↓	↓	↓	↓	↓
C	B	C	A	B	A

If the first and second were independent of one another, and the third copied both his predecessors, they may be related to one another thus in three different ways:

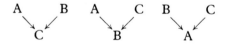

If the second and third independently copied the first, they may be related to one another thus in three different ways:

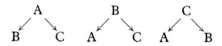

If the second copied the first, and the third copied both his predecessors, they may be related to one another thus in six different ways:

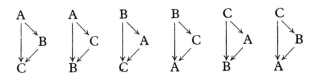

Step III

Thesis: *While it is possible to conceive of an infinite number of variations of these eighteen basic relationships by positing additional hypothetical documents, these eighteen should be given first consideration.*

The reasons for this have been indicated in the discussion of Step I. This does not mean that the investigator should assume that there were no additional hypothetical documents. On the contrary, he should be open to the possibility that such actually existed. There are instances in literary-historical studies where circumstantial evidence requires the investigator to posit the existence of a document for which he has no direct evidence. But a critic should not posit the existence of hypothetical documents until he has made an attempt to solve the problem without appeal to hypothetical documents. Only after the investigator has been unable to understand the relationship between Matthew, Mark, and Luke without appealing to unknown sources is he justified in hypothecating the existence of such sources, in order to explain phenomena otherwise inexplicable.

Step IV

Thesis: *Only six out of eighteen basic hypothetical arrangements are viable.*

This follows from the circumstances that there are agreements between any two of the Synoptic Gospels against the third.

This is a verifiable point, recognized by all careful investigators, and it provides an important clue to the solution of the problem once it is properly understood. For if one does not begin by appealing to hypothetical documents, but rather concentrates his attention on the eighteen basic arrangements set forth in Step II, it follows that where any two Gospels agree, and the third does not (either because the third has something different or is silent), that the Gospel which was written earlier was copied by the author of the later Gospel. The agreement could not be explained otherwise.

But if there are agreements between Matthew and Mark against Luke, and Matthew and Luke against Mark, and Luke and Mark against Matthew, then none of these eighteen basic hypotheses is valid that does not allow for direct literary dependence among all three.

Thus in all six instances where the second Evangelist copied the work of the first, and the third copied the second but not the first, can be eliminated from further consideration. For under such circumstances it would be impossible for the first and third to agree with one another against the second.

The three instances where the first and the second are independent of one another and the third copied both may also be eliminated from further consideration. For under such circumstances it would be impossible for the first and the second to agree with one another against the third.

Similarly, the three cases where the second and third independently copy the first may be eliminated from consideration. For this suggestion would fail to explain how the second and third could agree against the first.

But those six cases where the second writer copied the first, and the third had direct access to both the first and the second, cannot be rejected at this point. For they do afford the opportunity for any two of the Synoptic Gospels to agree against the third. Thus, for example, agreements between the first and the second against the third would result from circumstances where the second copied something from the first which the third did not copy exactly or at all, either from the first or the second. And agreements between the second and the third against the first would result from circumstances where the third copied something from the second which was not in the first. And finally, agreements between the first and the third against the second would result from circumstances where the third copied something from the first which the second had copied less exactly or not at all.

It follows from the above that whichever Evangelist was third faced the problem of working with two Gospels between which there already existed a relation of direct literary dependence, in that the second had copied the first. There are certain definite redactional limitations and possibilities within which a writer under such circumstances is able to function, and this ought to provide a clue for discerning which of the three Evangelists was in the position of being third. A writer in the position of being third can (1) follow the text to which both earlier Gospels bear concurrent testimony; (2) deviate from one, but follow the other, when his sources disagree; (3) attempt to combine them where they disagree; (4) deviate by omission or alteration from both when they disagree; (5) deviate by omission or alteration from both even when they agree.

Isolable and objectively definable categories of literary phenomena are necessary which are more readily explicable when one of the Evangelists is placed third than when either of the other two is placed third.

Step V

Thesis: *There are isolable and objectively definable categories of literary phenomena which have played a prominent role in the history of the Synoptic Problem which when properly understood are more readily explicable when Mark is placed third than when either Matthew or Luke is placed third.*

These are two in number: (1) The phenomena of order and content; (2) The so-called minor agreements of Matthew and Luke against Mark. (*See especially* Chapters III and IV, pp. 94–152.)

There is a third literary phenomenon which has seldom been noted, but which is also more readily explicable when Mark is third than in any other position. This is the strange positive correlation of order and degree of similarity between Matthew and Mark on the one hand and Luke and Mark on the other. That is, Mark tends to agree more closely with Matthew when they follow an order different from Luke, but more closely with Luke when they follow an order different from Matthew.

Step VI

Thesis: *The phenomena of agreement and disagreement in the respective order and content of material in each of the Synoptic Gospels constitute a category of literary phenomena which is more readily explicable on a hypothesis which places Mark third with Matthew and Luke before him than on any alternative hypothesis.*

With very few exceptions, which are no more difficult for one hypothesis than for any other, the order of material in Mark never departs from the order of material common to Matthew and Luke. Therefore, Matthew and Luke almost never agree in order against Mark. If Mark were third, this fact would be readily explained by the reasonable assumption that the Evangelist writing third had no chronological information apart from that which he found in Matthew and Luke, or that if he did, he preferred not to interrupt the order of events to which these two Gospels bore concurrent testimony.

The most striking agreement in order between Matthew and Luke against Mark is the placing of the Cleansing of the Temple on the same day as the Triumphal Entry, whereas Mark places it on the day following. This is not readily explicable on any hypothesis, though on the Griesbach hypothesis it simply entails the recognition that Mark did not slavishly adhere to the order common to Matthew and Luke.

When the order of Matthew and Luke is not the same, the order of Mark tends to be the same as either the one or the other. If Mark was third, this fact would be readily explained by the same assumption stated above, and the recognition that when Mark was confronted by a situation where his sources departed from one another in order, so that there was no longer a common order to follow, he tended to follow the order of one or the other of his sources, rather than depart from both. This cannot be imagined as an unnatural procedure for Mark to have followed under such circumstances. A similar statement can be made concerning the content of Mark. Mark seldom has a story or a saying that is not found either in Matthew or Luke or both. The major exceptions to this statement are two healing stories (Mk. 7:32–35; 8:22–26) and one parable (Mk. 4:26–29).

On the Griesbach hypothesis this is readily explained either by the circumstances that Mark was in fact limited very largely to Matthew and Luke for almost all the stories and sayings found in his Gospel, or that he chose to limit himself to these sources.

While the Marcan hypothesis is not one of the viable six, set forth in Step IV, the phenomenon of order and content has played such a prominent role in the history of that hypothesis that a discussion of this matter on both the Ur-Marcus and the Streeterian form of that hypothesis is in order.

On the Marcan hypothesis, within Streeter's terms, it is possible to explain how Matthew and Luke would sometimes independently reproduce the same order and content for their material through their use of Mark. But this hypothesis would afford no explanation for Luke's following the order and content of Mark whenever Matthew deviated from Mark, and Matthew's following the order and content of Mark whenever Luke deviated from Mark. Since on this hypothesis Matthew has no knowledge of what Luke has done, he could not so consistently have supported Mark's order if he had wanted to, and the same holds true for Luke. The fact that both Luke and Matthew frequently deviate from Mark, either in order or by omission of Marcan material, raises the question of their failure to deviate from Mark's order or to omit his material more often at the same place than they do.

The problem of Marcan order can be posed this way: It is as if Matthew and Luke each knew what the other was doing, and that each had agreed to support Mark whenever the other departed from Mark. Such concerted action is excluded by the adherents of Marcan priority in their insistence that Matthew and Luke were completely independent of one another. Streeter's statement, "The relative order of incidents and sections in Mark is in general supported by both Matthew and Luke; where either of them deserts Mark, the other is usually found supporting him,"[2] was a tour de force, by which a serious problem for the Marcan hypothesis was converted into an argument in behalf of the priority of Mark.

Since it cannot be imagined that Matthew and Luke each consciously decided to support Mark, even when the other deserted him, Streeter's statement on the matter only sharpens the issue. Why *does* Matthew usually support Mark when Mark is deserted by Luke? And, as if to compound the difficulty, why should Luke, in a similar way support Mark when Mark is deserted by Matthew? Since both frequently desert Mark, either by departing from his order or by omitting his material, and since neither knows what the other is doing, why do not their desertions of Mark coincide more frequently?

[2] *Op. cit.*, p. 151.

The Marcan hypothesis on Lachmann's terms, where it is thought that each Evangelist independently copied an Ur-gospel, affords a ready explanation for some but not all the phenomena of order. Thus agreement among all three and between any two against the third would be readily explained by assuming that such agreement derived from the common order given in the Ur-gospel. If an Ur-gospel could be firmly established, then the fact that Matthew and Luke almost never agree with one another against Mark in order could be taken as a sign that Mark had deviated from the order of the Ur-gospel less than either Matthew or Luke.

But one fact still remains unexplained;[3] namely that whenever Matthew deviated from the order of the Ur-gospel, Luke tended to follow that order, and that whenever Luke deviated from the order of the Ur-gospel, Matthew tended to follow that order. Since both Matthew and Luke deviated from the order of the Ur-gospel, and since neither had knowledge of the action of the other, why do not their deviations from the order of the Ur-gospel coincide more often ? Why are there not more instances where neither Matthew nor Luke supports the order found in Mark ? There should be some adequate reason to account for this strange alternation where the order in Mark, when unsupported by both Matthew and Luke, is almost always supported either by one or the other. This fact of alternating support suggests some kind of conscious intention for which the Marcan hypothesis offers no ready explanation on either the terms of Lachmann or Streeter.

Nor does the Augustinian hypothesis afford a ready explanation for this fact. If Mark was second and sometimes followed the order of Matthew, and Luke was third and had access to both, then Luke, by following the order to which Matthew and Mark bore concurrent testimony, would reproduce an order where all three agree. But then it would be necessary to imagine that he not only chose to deviate from the order common to Matthew and Mark on certain occasions, which might not be so difficult to explain, but that whenever the order of Matthew and Mark was not the same, he rather consistently followed the order of Mark. This cannot be explained as due to his preference for Mark's Gospel, since Luke frequently deviated from Mark either in the order that he gave to his

---

[3] Jülicher felt that there was another decisive objection to the Ur-Marcus hypothesis. *See* footnote 33, Chapter III.

materials or in his omission of Marcan material. The problem is this: Why would Luke frequently deviate from Mark either by changing the order of Mark's material or by omitting Mark's stories at times when Mark's order and content were supported by Matthew, but then rather consistently adhere to the order of Mark's material and the substance of his content when Mark's order and content were not supported by Matthew?

This appears to be a rather erratic redactional procedure for a writer, and unless it can be explained by the adherents of the Augustinian hypothesis, it must be counted as an unresolved difficulty for that hypothesis.

A similar argument could be made against a hypothesis which placed Matthew third, for here again there would be no ready explanation for the fact that Matthew's order would then deviate frequently from that of Mark when Mark's order was supported by Luke, but rather consistently follow the order of Mark whenever Mark's order was not supported by Luke.

Thus confining the possibilities to the six viable hypotheses set forth in Step IV, it is possible to say that only the two hypotheses which place Mark third afford a ready explanation for the phenomenon of agreement in order and content among Matthew, Mark, and Luke. Thus:

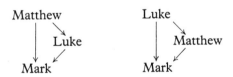

The choice between these two hypotheses cannot be made on the basis of order and content but must be settled on other grounds.

Step VII

Thesis: *The Minor Agreements of Matthew and Luke against Mark constitute a second category of literary phenomena which is more readily explicable on a hypothesis where Mark is regarded as third with Matthew and Luke before him than on any alternative hypothesis.*

In a typical passage where all three Gospels have parallel material there tend to be seven distinguishable categories of literary phenomena: (1) agreements among all three; (2) agreements between

Matthew and Mark against Luke: (3) agreements between Mark and Luke against Matthew; (4) agreements between Matthew and Luke against Mark; (5) words unique to Matthew; (6) words unique to Mark; and (7) words unique to Luke.

Categories (2), (3), and (4) are manifestly distinguishable from (1), (5), (6), and (7). When categories (2), (3), and (4) are compared, it is found that (4) is distinguishable from (2) and (3), in that the agreements in (2) and (3) tend to be more extensive and substantial than those in (4). That is, in passages where all three Gospels are parallel, the agreements between Matthew and Luke against Mark tend to be minor in extent, inconsequential in substance, and sporadic in occurrence, as compared to the corresponding phenomena in categories (2) and (3). This is not true without exception. But it is true in the great majority of cases, and it requires some explanation.[4]

There is no ready explanation for this phenomenon, except on the hypothesis that Mark was third and had access to the texts of both Matthew and Luke. The Augustinian hypothesis offers no ready explanation. For if Luke were third and conflated Matthew and Mark, it would be necessary to think that whenever he copied Mark he frequently compared the parallel passage in Matthew and then allowed the text of Matthew to influence his wording only slightly while he followed closely the text of Mark, frequently copying Mark when Mark deviated from Matthew, but almost never copying Matthew when Matthew deviated from Mark, though departing frequently from both Matthew and Mark in places when they bore concurrent testimony to the same text. Such a redactional procedure would appear to be unnecessarily erratic. On this arrangement, Luke would not show any consistent preference for Mark's text, since he departs readily from the text of Mark when Mark's text is supported by that of Matthew. Furthermore, there are a number of passages, especially in the section of Luke 9:51–18:14, where on the Augustinian hypothesis it would be necessary to say that Luke showed a preference for Matthew, since his text in that section is

[4] It is a merit of Monsig. de Solages' work, *A Greek Synopsis of the Gospels* (p. 1052), that he has isolated this phenomenon, and has recognized it as "the fundamental synoptic problem." It is very clear from his arrangement of the Synoptic material into separate frames that the material he puts in frame #3, namely the agreements between Matthew and Luke against Mark, is significantly less than the material in the frames containing agreements between Matthew and Mark against Luke and agreements between Mark and Luke against Matthew.

closer to Matthew's than to Mark's in passages where all three agree.[5]

Similar difficulties would be faced by any hypothesis in which Matthew was placed third. No such objections can be raised, however, against the view that Mark may have been third, providing it be granted with Burton that it is conceivable that a writer in this situation could have been guided by the literary purpose not to deviate from the text to which his predecessors bore concurrent testimony.[6] It would be inhuman to expect a writer so motivated never to deviate in the slightest degree from the common text in his two sources. It is enough to expect him to depart only when so to do would not affect the sense or the intention of the text to which his sources bore concurrent testimony. This is a fair description of the great bulk of the agreements of Matthew and Luke against Mark. Generally speaking, these agreements do not seriously affect the literary purpose or theological intention of the passages concerned.

On this hypothesis there would also be a ready explanation for the extensive agreements of Mark with Matthew against Luke, and of Mark with Luke against Matthew. These agreements would be created whenever Mark, having reached a point in the texts of Matthew and Luke where they deviated from one another, sometimes followed the one and sometimes the other. In such cases, by departing from both, which would have been quite natural at times, there would have been no agreement at all among the three. Thus, on this hypothesis there is a ready explanation for all seven categories of literary phenomena listed above. The only question which remains unanswered is that of the relationship between Matthew and Luke.

Step VIII

Thesis: *There exists a positive correlation between agreement in order and agreement in wording among the Synoptic Gospels which is most readily explicable on the hypothesis that Mark was written after Matthew and Luke and is the result of a redactional procedure in which Mark made use both of Matthew and Luke.*

---

[5] *Cf.* Hawkins, "Three Limitations to St. Luke's Use of St. Mark's Gospel: The Disuse of the Marcan Source in St. Luke ix. 51–xviii. 14," *Oxford Studies*, pp. 29–59.

[6] *See* Chapter III, p. 78.

When Matthew, Mark and Luke do not all three agree in order, as has been pointed out, either Matthew and Mark will agree, or Luke and Mark will agree. The point is that when Matthew and Mark are following the same order, but Luke exhibits a different order, the texts of Matthew and Mark tend to be very close to one another. And when Luke and Mark are following the same order, but Matthew exhibits a different order, the texts of Luke and Mark tend to be very close to one another. This is quite noticeable in the first half of Mark, and requires an explanation.

This phenomenon is especially difficult to explain on any hypothesis which presupposes that Matthew and Luke independently copied Mark or Ur-Marcus. For, since Matthew had no knowledge of Luke's redactional use of Mark, there is no way he could have known to begin copying the text of Mark more closely where Luke's order was different from that of Mark. Conversely, there is no way in which Luke could have known to begin copying the text of Mark more closely at the point where Mark's order and that of Matthew departed from one another.

The Augustinian hypothesis affords a ready explanation for a part of this phenomenon, but not for the whole of it. For on that hypothesis, although Luke might naturally have followed the text of Mark more closely when he chose Mark's order in preference to that of Matthew, there is no obvious reason why Mark would have copied Matthew more closely when drawing a passage from Matthew while following Matthew's order than when not following Matthew's order.[7]

Therefore, on the Augustinian hypothesis, there is a ready explanation for the positive correlation between agreement in order and closeness of text between Mark and Luke, but not for the similar correlation between Mark and Matthew.

On the Griesbach hypothesis, however, there is a ready explanation for the whole of this phenomenon. For it would not have been

---

[7] It is true that when Mark would have departed from Matthew's order and turned to another place in the text of Matthew and copied out a passage, he would have had to create some kind of ligature of his own to tie in the passage with what he had been copying from Matthew at the previous place, and that this would have sometimes made it difficult for him to copy such a passage closely in its opening verse. This would be a partial explanation for the correlation of order and proximity of text between Matthew and Mark. But the phenomenon of correlation tends to extend to the whole of such passages, and not just the transitional verses. For this there seems to be no ready explanation on the Augustinian hypothesis.

unnatural for Mark to have given some preference to the text of
Matthew when he had deliberately chosen to follow Matthew's
order instead of that of Luke, and conversely, it would not have been
unnatural for him to have given some preference to the text of Luke
when he had deliberately chosen to follow Luke's order in preference
to that of Matthew. One would not expect Mark to follow such a
procedure inflexibly. Indeed the phenomenon is ambiguous enough
to indicate that if in fact Mark was third, he did not follow this pattern
with absolute consistency. Nevertheless a positive correlation does
exist, which was recognized by the advocates of the Griesbach
hypothesis. "When the same facts, which are recorded by the
evangelist whom he (Mark) is following at any time, are narrated
also by the other, he makes use of the latter also, to guide him in his
manner of description, and even of expression, but he keeps mainly
to the former."[8] Assuming Mark to be third and working with
Matthew and Luke, this is a statement which does justice to a
particular literary phenomenon of the Gospels themselves. The point
is that it does not seem possible on any other hypothesis to make a
similar statement which will take into account the same phenomenon
equally as well.[9]

Step IX

Thesis: *It is possible to understand the redactional process through
which Mark went, on the hypothesis that he composed his Gospel based
primarily on Matthew and Luke.*

A demonstration of this thesis is given in Chapter VII. The
reader is further referred to the works of de Wette and Bleek.[10]

[8] Bleek, *An Introduction to the New Testament*, p. 267.
[9] The reader is referred to Chapter VII for the specific confirmation of this thesis.
It is very important not to think that this correlation can be easily verified. There are
places where no correlation seems apparent. But there is generally an understandable
reason for the fact that in some places the matter is ambiguous, that is readily forthcoming on the Griesbach hypothesis.
[10] *See especially* "Erklärung des Verhältnisses zwischen Marcus und den beiden
andern Evangelisten durch die Annahme, dass er sie benutz hat," *Lehrbuch der historisch-
kritischen Einleitung in die kanonischen Bücher des Neuen Testaments*, 5th ed., pp.
167–179; and "Evangelium des Marcus," *Kurze Erklärung der Evangelien des Lukas
und Markus*, in *Kurzgefasstes exegetisches Handbuch zum Neuen Testament*, Ersten
Bandes zweiter Theil, pp. 127–200, by Wilhelm Martin Leberecht de Wette. See also
paragraphs 93–97 in *Einleitung in das Neue Testament*, 2nd ed., by Fredrich Bleek.
In the English translation of Bleek's *Introduction to the New Testament*, in Clark's

It is possible to arrange a presentation of the results of an analysis of Mark on the Griesbach hypothesis in various ways. Therefore, the differences between the ways in which various advocates of the Griesbach hypothesis divide up the Gospel of Mark are not especially important. The point is that it is possible to proceed through the Gospel of Mark on the hypothesis that he based his gospel on Matthew and Luke, and not encounter redactional problems which create serious and peculiar difficulties for that hypothesis. The demonstration of this thesis, given in Chapter VII, is mainly distinguished from the results of previous analyses of Mark on the Griesbach hypothesis by the influence of advances in Synoptic studies which have been made during the past one hundred years in the areas of environmental research and form-criticism.

Step X

Thesis: *The most probable explanation for the extensive agreement between Matthew and Luke is that the author of one made use of the work of the other.*

Such a direct literary dependence between Matthew and Luke is not incompatible with their mutual use of common sources. Where each has material that is similar, but where there is insufficient evidence to warrant the judgment that there was direct copying by one Evangelist of the work of the other, the explanation that a common source has been copied is altogether plausible. But where the evidence for direct literary dependence is strong, the most probable explanation would be that one of the Evangelists had copied the work of his predecessor.

The hypothesis that either Matthew or Luke had the work of the other before him not only affords a ready explanation for the extensive agreement in content between the works of these two Evangelists, but also their remarkable similarities in literary form.

Both Matthew and Luke begin with birth narratives, contain genealogies, begin Jesus' ministry with his baptism by John, record

---

Foreign Theological Library, this section is set forth under the heading: "Dependence of Mark upon Matthew and Luke," Vol. I, pp. 258–275. See also Samuel Davidson's "The Gospel of Mark—'Analysis of Contents,' and 'Relation of Mark to Matthew and Luke,'" *An Introduction to the Study of the New Testament, Critical, Exegetical, and Theological*, 2nd ed., Vol. I, pp. 542–563.

the teachings of John, picture Jesus tempted by Satan in the wilderness, describe Jesus' ministry in Galilee, introduce into their narrative framework large collections of Jewish gnomic and parabolic materials—including primitive sayings reflecting the historical solidarity between Jesus and John, narrate Jesus' journey to Jerusalem with his disciples, his triumphal entry, his cleansing of the Temple, the Last Supper with his disciples, the arrest in Gethsemane, the trial before the High Priest, and before Pilate, and finally the crucifixion, death, burial, and resurrection of Jesus.

The fact that in some parts of this outline Luke introduced different content only indicates that he had ample reason to write a new Gospel, and in no way explains why he follows a literary scheme so similar to that found in Matthew. When compared to other Gospel literature in particular, and to contemporary Hellenistic and Jewish literature in general, Matthew and Luke bear a striking resemblance to one another both in form and content.

The form of Matthew and Luke is unique in literature. It is unlikely that two writers would independently have created such unique and similar literary works. It is altogether probable that one was the original literary creation, and that the author of the other took this orginal work as his literary exemplar, making such improvements and modifications as may have been dictated by his literary and theological purposes.

It is not possible to explain the similarity in content and form between Matthew and Luke by positing their mutual dependence upon either John or Mark, without making appeal to one or more hypothetical sources to explain material held in common by Matthew and Luke not found in either John or Mark. Therefore, as long as one seeks to solve the Synoptic Problem without having recourse to such conjectural sources, he is led to posit direct literary dependence between Luke and Matthew.

Step XI

Thesis: *The hypothesis that Luke made use of Matthew is in accord with Luke's declaration in the prologue to his Gospel concerning his purpose in writing.*

The usual interpretation of Luke 1:1, to mean that at the time Luke wrote there were many Gospels in existence, is linguistically possible though not necessary. Lessing interpreted Luke as meaning that "Many have undertaken to rearrange a narrative," and concluded that this referred to an original narrative, composed by the apostles, which Lessing identified with the Gospel of the Nazarenes.[11] The important point linguistically is that the word διήγησις is singular. Therefore, it would be possible to understand Luke to have referred to a single narrative, which he did not think of as the work of a single individual, but of πολλοί. For it is not necessary to translate ἀνατάξασθαι by "rearrange." The Greek can be rendered "many have undertaken to compile a narrative."

This was a possible way for Luke to have viewed the Gospel of Matthew. For while it is not impossible that a single individual played an important part in the final stage in the redaction of all the tradition which was included in Matthew, the total work of compilation, arrangement and development of the tradition in that Gospel can with justice be viewed as the work of more than one person, perhaps even a school.

When Luke defined the intention of the διήγησις which was compiled by πολλοί as being concerned to set forth "the things which have been fulfilled among us," his words describe one of the characteristic features of the Gospel of Matthew. For in Matthew the motif of the fulfillment of prophecy is prominent.

When Luke referred to the tradition which had been compiled by πολλοί into διήγησις, as having been "delivered to us by those who were from the beginning eyewitnesses," he clearly associated himself with the "many" compilers, in distinction from those who were from the beginning "eyewitnesses."

The Gospel of Matthew seems to have been composed after the eye-witness period, and reflects the results of the very process of composition Luke describes. That is, Matthew can be justly referred to as διήγησις, made up of tradition which had been handed down from an earlier "eye-witness" period.

It is preferable, therefore, on Lessing's terms, where διήγησις is taken to refer to a single narrative, to identify this narrative with the known Gospel of Matthew, rather than an eye-witness "apostolic" Gospel of the Nazarenes, which after all is highly conjectural.

There is no doubt that from the point of view of readers who were sensitive to the prevailing standards of Hellenistic historiography,

[11] *See* footnote 5, Chapter I, p. 4.

the Gospel of Matthew was defective διήγησις. It was not set within an adequate chronological framework, so that readers acquainted with world history could view it within the context of that history. It contained duplicate accounts of certain events, and reported these as if they were completely separated in time and circumstance, when it was clear that they were but different accounts of the same matter. There were defects in the order in which certain material appeared in Matthew. Thus no sufficient reason is given for Jesus to have left Nazareth of Capernaum at the beginning of his ministry in Galilee, though a story of his being rejected by the people of his native place is included later in the narrative. And the call of the disciples after his great Sermon on the Mount is subject to the criticism of being anachronistic, in view of the indications that the sermon was for the disciples.

At all such points Luke's Gospel seems to reflect the results of a prolonged and careful study of Matthew, with a view to the creation of a new διήγησις which would be free of such defects.

In addition, of course, Luke obviously had access to other material which had been compiled and handed down from the earlier period. And Schleiermacher was no doubt correct in perceiving that it was largely out of such earlier compilations of material that both Matthew and Luke were composed.[12] To what extent these briefer compilations could also have been in Luke's mind when he referred to διήγησις having been compiled by πολλοί, remains uncertain. What is certain, however, is that Luke's Gospel is the result of careful study of the work of earlier redactors engaged in the task of producing διήγησις. And it is quite possible that the Gospel of Matthew was in his mind, and in the minds of those for whom he had prepared his work, when he composed the words of his prologue.

Step XII

Thesis: *Assuming that there is direct literary dependence between Matthew and Luke, internal evidence indicates that the direction of dependence is that of Luke upon Matthew.*

In support of this thesis is the fact that passages found in Matthew which express a point of view antithetical to the mission to the

12 *See* footnote 26, Chapter I. p. 18.

Gentiles, such as Matthew 10:5, "go nowhere among the Gentiles," or the continuing importance of Jewish practice, such as Matthew 24:20, "pray that your flight may not be in the winter *or on a sabbath*," are not found in Luke. Words and customs which would have become increasingly less intelligible, as the frontiers of the Christian movement expanded farther and farther from its place of origin, such as *Raca* for fool, in Matthew 5:22, and the wearing of *phylacteries*, in Matthew 23:5, are not found in Luke.

The Semitic parallelism of passages in Matthew, like that in Matthew 7:24–27, is frequently broken in the parallel passage in Luke (*compare* Lk. 6:47–49). The assumption is that during the oral period certain tradition was cast in the form of Semitic parallelism, for purposes of oral communication. When this was included in a written Gospel, the possibility existed for the writer to be conservative in editing his material, and thus to preserve the form of Semitic parallelism. However, to do so was not necessary for purposes of written communication, and in fact to reproduce certain cases of parallelism in all their formal fullness was, in some circles, to make the author's writing subject to the criticism of redundancy. It may be assumed, therefore, that the fact that in Luke Semitic parallelism is frequently broken, whereas in the parallel passages in Matthew it is frequently preserved, indicates that Luke has altered Matthew and not vice versa.[13]

Step XIII

Thesis: *The weight of external evidence is against the hypothesis that Matthew was written after Luke.*

It is not possible to settle with finality the question of the extent to which one should rely upon the unanimous testimony of the Church Fathers that Matthew was written before the other canonical Gospels. But whatever weight is to be given to this external evidence

---

[13] *See* C. F. Burney, *The Poetry of our Lord*, for a decisive study of the bearing of the phenomena of Semitic parallelism on the question of the original form of sayings attributed to Jesus in the Gospels. Burney went beyond the evidence in suggesting that all material cast in the form of Semitic parallelism had come from Jesus. All his work actually proves is that it is possible to recover in many cases the more original form of sayings in the Gospels, by studying them in the light of available knowledge of the formal characteristics of Hebrew poetry. For the purpose of settling the question of whether Luke is more likely to have altered Matthew or vice versa, however, Burney's work provides reliable criteria for a general determination of the probabilities of the matter.

goes against the view that Matthew was written after Luke, and in favor of the view that Luke was written after Matthew.

Although the earliest statements by the Fathers on this matter are quite late, from the third and fourth centuries, they cannot be dismissed as totally irrelevant. These Fathers all came out of the great central, main-line Church which formulated the canon in which Matthew and Luke were included. That Church and its canon were a result of the mission to the gentiles in the apostolic period. As between Matthew and Luke, the latter was more suited for use in the gentile Churches. By comparison with Luke, Matthew still retained features which were peculiarly Jewish, and reflected the interests of the earlier Jewish-Christian mission (see Step XII). Therefore, it is unlikely that a unanimous tradition would have developed in the gentile Church which reversed the true relationship between Matthew and Luke. That is, if Luke had been written before Matthew and had been copied by Matthew, so that Matthew then would have been a later Judaized version of Luke, it would be unlikely for a unanimous tradition to have developed among the gentile Churches which gave pride of place to Matthew. It is historically more probable that attributing pride of place to the more Jewish Gospel reflects a reliable historical memory in the gentile Churches as to the true chronological relationship between these two Gospels.

Step XIV

Thesis: *The weight of external evidence is against the hypothesis that Matthew was written after Mark.*

The same considerations set forth in support of the thesis advanced in Step XIII argue in favor of this thesis. Where the reader finds "Luke" in the discussion of Step XIII, he need only substitute "Mark," and the same conclusions that apply to the relationship of Luke to Matthew apply also to the relationship of Mark to Matthew.

Step XV

Thesis: *That Mark was written after both Matthew and Luke is in accord with the earliest and best external evidence on the question.*

Papias' testimony throws no light on the question of the order in which the Gospels were written. The earliest statement on the question of the order in which the Gospels were written is given by Clement of Alexandria, who stated that he had it from the elders that the Gospels with genealogies were written before the Gospels without them. This statement reflects no critical interest in the technical question of literary dependence, and is likely to have been first formulated in response to some question about the validity or theological significance of the genealogies in Matthew and Luke, or in response to some question about the reliability of Gospels which had conflicting genealogies, as compared with those which had none. In any case, the statement of Clement clearly implies that Mark, which has no genealogy, was written after Matthew and Luke, which do have genealogies.

The value of Clement's statement is uncertain. But it probably takes the investigator back to the middle of the second century, and represents an Alexandrian understanding of the chronological relationship between Mark on the one hand and Matthew and Luke on the other.

In view of the tradition that Mark founded the Church in Egypt, it seems unlikely that Egypt would have been the place for a tradition to develop placing the Gospel of Mark after Matthew and Luke unless there were some foundation for this tradition. The most probable basis for this tradition would seem to have been the historical memory among the Churches of Egypt that the Gospel of Mark had been written after those of Matthew and Luke.

The earliest extant citation of the Gospel of Mark is found in Justin Martyr's *Dialogue with Trypho* (106). There is some question as to whether Justin actually had reference to Mark, though it seems likely that he did. Even assuming that Justin's reference constitutes a bona fide citation of Mark, however, there is no clear external evidence for the existence of Mark before the middle of the second century. Or if it be argued that Justin's citation of Mark implies his acceptance of Mark as an apostolic Gospel, it would be possible to say that Mark was probably known in the Churches of Syria as early as the middle of the first half of the second century, and possibly earlier, that is, between A.D. 100 and A.D. 125. But it would not be possible on the basis of external evidence to place it any earlier than that. This does not mean that it could not have been written earlier. It only means that there is no external evidence that it was.

By way of contrast, there are clear citations of Gospel texts which are distinctive of Matthew and Luke, not only in Justin, but in writings earlier than Justin. In balance these citations seem to constitute reliable external evidence for the existence of the Gospels of Matthew and Luke before A.D. 125, and possibly before A.D. 100 (*compare The Letters of Ignatius* and *The Didache*).

All of this earliest evidence is in complete accord with a view that Mark may have written after Matthew and Luke. Furthermore, if Mark were written as late as A.D. 100 or A.D. 125, Clement's statement would be based upon tradition he had received from elders who in turn had direct access to the living memory of teachers who had lived in the period when Mark was composed.[14]

Step XVI

Thesis: *A historico-critical analysis of the Synoptic tradition, utilizing both literary-historical and form-critical canons of criticism, supports a hypothesis which recognizes that Matthew is in many respects secondary to the life situation of Jesus, and the primitive Palestinian Christian community, but that this Gospel was nonetheless copied by Luke, and that Mark was secondary to both Matthew and Luke, and frequently combined their respective texts.*

A full demonstration of this thesis goes beyond the scope of this book, and rightly belongs to a detailed history of the Synoptic tradition. However, the reader can find a variety of examples of the way in which this thesis may be supported in the criticisms of arguments for Marcan priority given in Chapters III and IV (*see especially* pp. 159–169); and the notes on the Synoptic tradition in Mark, given in Chapter VII. (*See especially* pp. 265–278.)

The canons of criticism utilized in the analysis of the Synoptic tradition referred to in this thesis are as follows:

(1) Assuming that the original events in the history of the Christian movement took place in Palestine, within predominantly Jewish circles, and that by the time the Gospels were written, Christianity had expanded outside of Palestine, and outside of

---

[14] For a further discussion of this matter *see* Chapter VII, pp. 282–283.

circles which were predominantly Jewish in orientation: *That form of a particular tradition found in the Gospels, which reflects an extra-Palestinian, or non-Jewish provenance is to be adjudged secondary to a form of the same tradition which reflects a Palestinian or Jewish provenance.*

(2) "(In the first printing of this book it was assumed that there was a tendency for the Gospel tradition to become more specific. But E. P. Sanders in *The Tendencies of the Synoptic Tradition*, Cambridge 1969, has shown that the opposite happens often enough to vitiate any canon based upon "specificity." For this reason, I have withdrawn the canon that formerly stood in this place. W.R.F.)"

(3) Assuming the redactional tendency to add explanatory glosses, and otherwise to expand tradition to make it applicable to new situations in the churches: *That form of a tradition which exhibits explanatory redactional glosses, and expansions aimed to make the tradition more applicable to the needs of the Church, is to be adjudged secondary to a form of the tradition which is free of such redactional glosses and expansions.*

(4) Assuming the tendency of all writers to use some words and phrases more often than is generally true for other writers when dealing with the same subject: *That form of a tradition which exhibits words or phrases characteristic of a redactor whose hand is clearly traceable elsewhere in the same Gospel is to be adjudged secondary to a form of the same tradition which is free of such words and phrases.* And, as a corollary to this: *That form of a tradition which exhibits words or phrases characteristic of a redactor whose hand is only traceable in another Gospel is to be adjudged secondary to the form of the parallel tradition in the Gospel where the redactor's hand can be clearly traced, provided the characteristic word or phrase occurs in the former Gospel only in passages closely paralleled in the latter, where the verbatim agreement indicates direct literary dependence.*

No one of these canons of criticism is decisive in any given instance. Only when they combine to reinforce one another in indicating that one particular form of a tradition is clearly secondary to another form of the same tradition can the critic with confidence render a judgment between primary and secondary material.

These canons do not exhaust all the literary and form-critical guides available to the student of the Gospels. The first canon, however, is especially inclusive and is intended to cover all such valid considerations as pertain to the presence or absence of Semitic parallelism in the formal structure of Gospel material, and the presence or absence of such literary forms as may be distinctive of the Hellenistic world.

These four canons supplement the six set forth by Ernest De Witt Burton in his monograph, *Some Principles of Literary Criticism and Their Application to the Synoptic Problem* (p. 198). Burton stated that in questions of literary dependence between two documents, that document is to be adjudged dependent which contains features of a secondary character. The following he regarded as evidences of a secondary character: "(1) manifest misunderstanding of what stands in one document on the part of the writer of the other; (2) insertion by one writer of material not in the other, and clearly interrupting the course of thought or symmetry of plan in the other; (3) clear omission from one document of matter which was in the other, the omission of which destroys the connection; (4) insertion of matter the motive for which can be clearly seen in the light of the author's general aim, while no motive can be discovered for its omission by the author if he had had it in his source; (5) vice versa omission of matter traceable to the motive natural to the writer when the insertion (of the same matter in the other Gospel) could not thus be accounted for; (6) alterations of other kinds which conform the matter to the general method or tendency of the author."

The six evidences of the secondary character of a document, outlined by Burton, together with the preceding four canons for the analysis of Synoptic tradition, provide the most important guides necessary for a study of the history of the redaction of the Synoptic tradition at the hands of the canonical Evangelists.[15]

Considerations which sometimes have influenced students of the Gospels in their statements about the Synoptic Problem, but which are either irrelevant or inconclusive, and therefore have little or no probative value in settling a question of literary dependence, may be listed as follows:

---

15 There are additional canons of criticism which must be observed when the critic attempts to trace the history of a tradition back to its beginning, and to make a judgment about its probable authenticity considered as a saying of Jesus, or its reliability considered as tradition about him. These, however, do not play a decisive part in the study of the Synoptic Problem, and therefore are not set forth here.

(1) *The relative length of a given passage.* Since writers sometimes enlarge, and sometimes condense, their sources, the relative length of a given passage, by itself, offers no criteria by which it may be adjudged primary or secondary to another.

(2) *The grammar and style of a writer.* Since some writers improve the grammar and style of their sources, while others spoil it, such considerations provide no objective basis by which one document may be adjudged primary or secondary to another. There is no provable correlation between style and chronology in matters involving the question of literary dependence between documents of the same general period and class of literature.

(3) *The christology of a given passage.* Since the letters of Paul disclose the fact that christology was already both complex and highly developed in some circles in the period before the Gospels were written, and since our knowledge of christological developments in the Churches in the post-Pauline period depends upon a correct solution to the problem of the chronological and literary relationship between the Gospels, and not vice versa, the christology of a given passage in the Gospels affords the critic no reliable criteria by which to adjudge it primary or secondary to its parallel in another Gospel.

This is not to deny the fact that the life situation of Jesus can be distinguished from that of the later Church. The tendency of the later Church was to modify the tradition from Jesus in the light of the post-Easter faith in him as the risen Lord. The nonchristological statements of Jesus can therefore be distinguished from the christological traditions of the early Church.

But there is no reliable way in which to adjudge the christology of Mark as earlier or later than that of Matthew or Luke. All three Gospels came from the post-Pauline period of the early Church, about which very little is known apart from inferences derived from the Gospels themselves. Apart from the Gospels there is no objective basis upon which to reconstruct a scheme of christological development in this period against which to measure the relative date of a specific christological reference in the Gospels. For this reason, the christology of a given passage offers no secure criteria by which it can be judged primary or secondary to a related christology in a parallel passage. Neither can the omission, nor the insertion, of such a detail offer proof of the relative primary or secondary character of a given passage, unless it be connected in some way with one of the objective canons of criticism listed above or some other valid canon of criticism.

One classic example of the inconclusiveness of the christological, or "theological," argument will suffice to illustrate the lack of probative value in such considerations. It is sometimes argued that Mark is earlier than Matthew or Luke because the latter two with their birth narratives have clearly been written after the time when the idea of a virgin birth of Jesus had been accepted, whereas Mark, with no such birth narrative, is more likely to have been written before this idea had been accepted in the Church. In response to this view of the matter Samuel Davidson wrote:

> The absence of that history which records the conception, birth and childhood of Christ, should not be adduced as a proof of the gospel's early origin, as it is done by some, for the writer presupposes it as the (other) synoptics, and develops it even to its negative consequences. Instead of Matthew's "Is this not the carpenter's son? Is not his mother called Mary?" Mark has "Is not this the carpenter, the son of Mary?" which agrees better with birth from a virgin than the genealogical registers, where Joseph intervenes in order to deduce the Davidic descent of Jesus. (*Op. cit.*, pp. 564–565.)

The implication of Davidson's reply to those who would appeal to the absence of the Virgin Birth stories in Mark as a sign of its primitivity is that if the acceptance of the Virgin Birth of Jesus be made a canon by which a Gospel can be dated, Mark would be dated after Matthew, since Mark's Gospel represents Jesus as the son of Mary but not of Joseph, whereas Matthew, even with the Virgin Birth story, elsewhere in his Gospel represents Jesus as the son of Joseph.

In truth, however, the matter is inconclusive, so long as the outcome of the debate hinges on some preconceived idea of development of dogma in the early Church. For there is no way in which it can be known in which Churches, and at what times, any particular idea about Jesus came to be regarded as an article of faith.

This is not to be taken to mean that christology is of no importance in a study of the Synoptic Problem. For example, in the case above, once it is recognized that it was not the custom of Jews to identify a man by referring to him as the son of his mother, it can be seen that, as between Matthew and Mark, the text of Mark is the least Jewish, and therefore the most likely to have been influenced by a secondary factor, in this case possibly a developing doctrine concerning the birth of Jesus to a virgin. In balance, then, this consideration would weigh in favor of dating Mark at a time, and locating its place of origin in a region, where the Virgin Birth stories were known and understood in such a way as to preclude the idea of a human father for Jesus.

If it could be proved that in the different churches where Matthew and Mark were written, the dogma that Jesus could not have had a human father was accepted at about the same time, then it would be possible to interpret this consideration by itself as weighing in favor of a date for Mark after this development, and a date for Matthew before this development. But precisely the information upon which any such proof would rest is not available to the critic, and for that reason he will find very little, if any, probative value in such considerations.

CHAPTER **VII**

Notes for a History
of the Redaction
# of Synoptic Tradition
in Mark

A. Introduction

The notes in this chapter are by no means complete. Only a commentary on Mark would afford an adequate scope for a full scale treatment of all the questions of critical interest. The intention of these notes is to deal generally with the more serious redactional questions which a critic faces in working with the text of Mark on the Griesbach hypothesis. A secondary purpose of these notes is to demonstrate that in a variety of passages it is possible to explain the history of the Synoptic tradition more adequately on the Griesbach hypothesis than on any hypothesis which posits the priority of Mark.

Notes on chapters 14 and 15 of Mark have been purposely omitted in line with the stated aim to reopen the question of the Synoptic Problem, and not to attempt to settle it with finality. The reader is thus afforded the opportunity to test for himself the adequacy of the

233

Griesbach hypothesis in these chapters, uninfluenced by critical notes reflecting another's judgment.[1]

The redactional problems in the final chapters of Mark are not particularly complicated, and can be explained on any hypothesis which recognizes some kind of direct literary relationship among the three Evangelists, and acknowledges Luke to have edited with considerable freedom one or both the other Gospels. The reader should not, therefore, expect the Griesbach hypothesis to be strikingly superior to all other hypotheses in that section of Mark. The question to be asked, for the purpose of testing the thesis in Step IX, in the argument set forth in Chapter VI, is whether one encounters redactional problems in that section of Mark which cannot be understood on the Griesbach hypothesis.

In comparing the relative merits of the Griesbach hypothesis with those of other hypotheses, while working critically with the Synoptic tradition in the passion narrative, the reader should be mindful of the fact that the most advanced critical treatment of that section of Synoptic tradition, on the Marcan hypothesis, leads to the conclusion that in the churches where Mark's Gospel was intended to be read, there was an oral tradition which is best preserved in the parallel texts of Matthew.[2]

On neither the Augustinian nor the Griesbach hypotheses would it be necessary to place such heavy reliance upon the hypothetical existence of such a particular fixed form of oral tradition. In this instance, oral tradition is held to explain Synoptic phenomena, which at an earlier period in the history of the Marcan hypothesis, could have been explained without such an appeal, by conjecturing that Matthew and Mark were copying an Ur-gospel, and by concluding that Matthew had preserved the more original form of the text of that primitive Ur-gospel. That solution had the advantage over the present view of the matter on the Marcan hypothesis, in that it allowed the critic to acknowledge freely that the probable provenance of Mark was some distance removed from the geographical and ethnic beginnings of the church. Whereas, if one is led

---

[1] If for any reason it is desirable to know how these final chapters of Mark would be analyzed on the Griesbach hypothesis by critics disposed to accept this hypothesis, the reader is referred to the works of de Wette and Bleek listed in the discussion of the thesis set forth in Step IX, n. 10.

[2] N. A. Dahl, "Die Passionsgeschichte bei Matthäus," *New Testament Studies*, Vol. II, 1955, pp. 17–32. *See especially* p. 24.

to conjecture that the intended readers of Mark's Gospel could be expected to be acquainted with an oral tradition which has been faithfully preserved in Matthew, he is thereby constrained to consider seriously a provenance for Mark not too far removed from that of Matthew, and in so doing is left with the critical problem of explaining the phenomena in Mark which dispose most critics to propose a provenance for Mark as far away as Rome.

It is important, therefore, in working with the final chapters of Mark, to keep in mind that serious problems remain unresolved for the adherent of the Marcan hypothesis, which, as in this case, largely disappear on other hypotheses.

In the notes which follow, it is presupposed that the reader has at least worked through Steps I–IX in the argument in behalf of the Griesbach hypothesis outlined in the preceding chapter. Otherwise there is the likelihood that he may misjudge the probative significance of these notes and misconstrue their very limited purpose in this book. That purpose is merely to demonstrate that it is possible to understand Mark's redactional process on the hypothesis that he based his Gospel on Matthew and Luke. The extent to which this attempt to support the thesis in Step IX will be convincing to the reader depends, of course, upon the adequacy of these notes; but it also depends upon the degree to which the reader's mind has been disposed (by what precedes these notes in this book, including the whole of what is reviewed in the first five chapters) to give serious consideration to the Griesbach hypothesis. The reader is privileged, of course, to read any part of any book in whatever order he chooses. But he should know that if, before reading these notes, he has not given serious attention to what precedes them in this book, he has not read them in the context in which they were intended, and thus the possibility exists that he will misinterpret their purpose. That purpose is a very limited one, and is clearly determined by the place held by the thesis set forth in Step IX of the argument in behalf of the Griesbach hypothesis presented in the preceding chapter.

B. Mark 1:1–20 // Matthew 3:1–4:22

On the Griesbach hypothesis, there is evidence in this section of Mark that the Evangelist compared the parallel materials in Matthew and Luke and conflated Luke's text with that of Matthew—especially in verses 2-4 and 7-13. But he seems to have followed the order of Matthew, and adhered closely to his wording throughout this section.

The decision concerning the way to begin any literary work is of great importance. It is not possible to know all the factors which might have influenced Mark to begin as he did. It is not unlikely, however, that Mark was influenced in his decision by the fact that this is the place where Matthew and Luke begin to agree in their accounts. He may also have been influenced by the statement of Peter in Acts 1:22: ". . . beginning from the baptism of John." Certainly his decision against beginning his Gospel with a narrative of Jesus' birth, including his human genealogy, cannot be viewed as unique. For the Evangelist John made the same decision.

Mark included a brief notice of Jesus' temptation and then related the call of the first disciples, following the order of Matthew and adopting in the call of the disciples almost the same words.

In Matthew an introduction to the Sermon on the Mount immediately follows—which sermon Mark apparently associated with Luke's sermon on the plain (Lk. 6:20 ff.). In any case, Mark then began following Luke and continued to follow him to the introduction to his sermon on the plain. Mark seems to have thought of Matthew's Sermon on the Mount and Luke's sermon on the plain as marking two clearly distinguishable and quite comparable literary transitions in his sources. He began by following Matthew up to his Sermon on the Mount, and thereafter proceeded to follow the order of Luke up to his sermon on the plain. In this way Mark deviated from his sources as little as possible, following their common order whenever possible, adhering first to the order of Matthew up to a distinguishable point of literary transition and thereafter the order of Luke up to the corresponding point in Luke's narrative. This is a perfectly intelligible redactional procedure for any writer to follow if he were faced with the task of combining Matthew and Luke, without doing unnecessary violence to the interests and proprietary concerns of the adherents of either of his sources.

Mark's redactional procedure reflects no sense of slavish dependence on either Matthew or Luke. Mark is a new form of the Gospel, characterized by a distinct measure of literary freedom, but distinguished above all for its representation of tradition that for the most part would have been familiar to its readers or hearers through their acquaintance with either Matthew or Luke. What would have been new tradition in Mark for those acquainted only with Matthew would have come primarily from Luke, and what would have been new for those acquainted only with Luke would have come primarily from Matthew. That the Evangelist, Mark, added two new miracle stories and one new parable to his Gospel only underlines the fact that he was not slavishly dependent upon Matthew and Luke and that his work is a *new* form of the Gospel. Within this redactional context the opening words of his Gospel become more pointed: "The beginning of the Gospel of Jesus Christ." In the light of the different ways in which the other Gospels begin, the peremptory tone of this introductory formula has an authoritative ring that is probably ecclesiastical in origin and/or sponsorship. If so, the apostolic justification for such a judgment would most probably have been the words attributed to the Apostle Peter in Acts 1:22.

C. Mark 1: 21–3: 19 // Luke 4: 31–6: 16

In this section Mark deviated from the order of Luke only to omit Luke's account of the miraculous catch of fish (Lk. 5:1–11), and to invert the order of the call of the Twelve (Lk. 6:12–16 // Mk. 3:13–19) and the healing of the multitudes (Lk. 6:17–19 // Mk. 3:7–12). Mark's omission of Luke's account of the miraculous catch of fish is explained by his having already included the loosely parallel account of the call of the first disciples from Matthew (Mk. 1:16–20 // Mt. 4:18–22). His inversion of the call of the Twelve and the healing of the multitudes is explained by his con-flation of Luke and Matthew (Lk. 6:1–19 // Mt. 12:1–21). Matthew did not have the call of the Twelve at this point in his Gospel. Therefore, Mark simply conflated what was in Matthew with the Lucan parallels, omitting the call of the Twelve until he finished his expanded version of the healing of the multitudes (Mk. 3:7–12 // Lk. 6:17–19 // Mt. 12:15–21), after which he added the call of the Twelve that he had just omitted from Luke, and very largely in the wording of Luke (Mk. 3:13–19 // Lk. 6:12–16).

It should be noted that while it cannot be said that Mark followed the exact order of Luke in including the call of the Twelve, the place he gave to his literary unit is closer to the order it is given in Luke than to the order it is given in Matthew. And in this connection, it is significant that the wording of Mark's account of the call of the Twelve is closer to the account in Luke than to that in Matthew.

It is further to be noted that Mark 2:1–22 constitutes a subsection of Mark in which, for three successive literary units, he conflated passages from Matthew and Luke where both of these Gospels contained the same literary units in the same order (Lk. 5:17–26 ∥ Mt. 9:1–8; Lk. 5:27–32 ∥ Mt. 9:9–13; Lk. 5:33–39 ∥ Mt. 9:14–17). Since in this subsection it cannot be said that Mark has departed from the order of Luke, it has been treated as but a part of the larger section of Mark 1:21–3:19, where Mark basically followed Luke 4:31–6:19. However, while in the first of these three literary units, the healing of the paralytic, Mark followed Luke's account more closely than that of Matthew, in the second and third, the call of Levi, and the question about fasting, Mark's text is a conflation of the parallel accounts of Matthew and Luke in which there is no clear preference for either the one or the other.

This is an example of a phenomenon that occurs elsewhere in Mark. Whenever Mark comes to a series of passages in Matthew and Luke where they both have the same literary units in the same order, his text does not tend to be uniformly closer to that of one of his predecessors than it is to that of the other. In other words, Mark's text tends to be closer to that of the Gospel whose order he is following, only when the other Gospel has the same material in quite another order. Thus in this section, Mark's text is significantly closer to that of Luke in Mark 1:29–31; 1:40–45; 2:1–12; 2:23–28. This, however, does not mean that Mark's text cannot be closer to that of one rather than to that of the other of his predecessors whenever all three have the same literary units in the same successive order. Note that Mark is significantly closer to the text of Luke in his account of the healing of the man with the withered hand (Mk. 3:1–6 ∥ Lk. 6:6–11 ∥ Mt. 12:9–14).

Luke 6:17–19 actually constituted his introduction to his sermon on the plain (Lk. 6:20 ff.). Therefore, having followed Luke up to his sermon on the plain, Mark next shifted back to the text of Matthew as the guide for his narrative, and began copying material found in Matthew 12:22 ff. This is perfectly intelligible, since in following Luke after reaching Matthew's Sermon on the Mount,

Mark had in effect moved forward through the parallel sections of Matthew to exactly this point, that is, Matthew 12:22.

D. Mark 3: 20–4: 34 // Matthew 12: 22–13: 35

The redactional history of this section of Mark is more complex, but not unintelligible. Mark 3:20–21 is a Marcan introduction to the tradition in Mark 3:22–35. Mark 3:22–30 follows closely the wording of the story about Jesus when he was charged as an agent of Beelzebub in Matthew 12:24–32. Mark 3:31–35 in a similar manner follows closely the wording of Matthew 12:46–50. This brought Mark to another large body of sayings in Matthew 13:1–53. This time, however, he was faced with a different problem. Whereas Matthew's Sermon on the Mount and its Lucan parallels presented almost insuperable redactional problems for satisfactory conflation (consider, for example, the difficulty of combining the Matthean and Lucan forms of the Beatitudes), the problems for Mark in using material from Matthew 13 were less difficult. Moreover, it is clear from the fact that Mark introduced into his Gospel a parable unique to him concerning a seed growing secretly that he had a special interest in the seed motif of Matthew 13.

It is a striking phenomenon that Mark has no parables parallel to Matthew that do not also have a Lucan parallel. Mark's use of the parabolic material in Matthew 13 is no exception. Mark 4:1–9 follows closely Matthew 13:1–9. Mark 4:10–12 is closely paralleled by Matthew 13:1–15, with two exceptions: (1) Matthew 13:12 is omitted, and (2) the quotation from Isaiah is omitted. This is very interesting because it also defines the relationship of the Lucan parallel to Matthew 13:10–15 found in Luke 8:9–10.

The influence of Luke 8:9–10 upon Mark 4:10–12 is apparent not only in Mark's omissions from Matthew but in Mark's wording. Mark allowed Luke to guide him in the matter of order in this section where he was otherwise following Matthew as his chief source. Thus he followed Luke (1) in passing over Matthew 13:16–17 (which Luke actually used at a later point in his Gospel [10:23–24]); (2) in taking Matthew 13:18–23 // Mark 4:13–20 // Luke 8:11–15 (one could say he took Luke 8:11–15 and conflated it with Matthew 13:18–23); (3) in following Luke 8:16–18 // Mark 4:21–25 (after which Mark inserted his parable of the seed growing secretly, which is appropriate in this context); (4) by omitting Matthew 13:24–30. Mark's reason for omitting Matthew 13:24–30, however, may have been more related to his desire to follow his parable of the seed growing secretly with the parable of the mustard seed. In any case, Mark next took up Matthew's parable of the mustard seed (Mt. 13:31–32) in Matthew's order (Luke has it in a different order in Luke 13:18–19), and then omitted Matthew's parable of the leaven (Luke has it with its sister parable in 13:20–21), and closed with words based on Matthew 13:34 ∥ Mark 4:33–34. At this point Mark turned to Luke where he left off copying him at Luke 8:18.

In 8:19–21 Luke has the story about Jesus' true relatives, parallel to Matthew 12:46–50, which Mark had already incorporated into his Gospel earlier (Mk. 3:31–35) while following the order of Matthew. Therefore, he began following Luke in the succeeding passage, namely the story of the stilling of the storm (Lk. 8:22–25 ∥ Mk. 4:35–41 ∥ Mt. 8:23–27), which Mark had bypassed in Matthew along with other Matthean material, while following the order of Luke after reaching Matthew's Sermon on the Mount.

It is noteworthy that in this section just discussed (Mk. 3:20–4:34), where Mark does not simply or consistently follow the order of either Matthew of Luke, though he is covering material which as a whole is found in one particular section of Matthew, the degree of verbal kinship between the text of Mark and Matthew on the one hand and the text of Mark and Luke on the other is correspondingly ambiguous as compared to those sections of his Gospel where he unambiguously follows the order of either Matthew or Luke.

E. Mark 4:35–5:43 ∥ Luke 8:22–56

In this section Mark took up three successive literary units from Luke 8:22–25, the stilling of the storm; 8:26–39, the Gerasene Demoniac; and 8:40–56, Jairus' daughter and the woman with the hemorrhage. There are Matthean parallels to all three in Matthew 8:23–27; 8:28–34; and 9:18–26. It is clear that these Matthean parallels have influenced the wording of Mark's text. But it is also unmistakably clear that the text of Mark in this section is significantly closer to the text of Luke than to the text of Matthew. This is particularly so in Mark 5:1–20, the story of the Gerasene Demoniac, and 5:21–45, the story of Jairus' daughter and the woman with the hemorrhage. This is a very clear example of the phenomenon of a positive correlation between agreement in order and agreement in wording which was set out in Step VIII.

F. Mark 6:1–6 // Matthew 13:53–58

At this point Mark took up Matthew 13:53–58, the story of Jesus' rejection at Nazareth, which Luke recorded much earlier in his Gospel (Lk. 4:16–24). Mark thus preserved the relative order of Matthew in this particular instance. Mark located the incident in time as happening on the Sabbath as in Luke 4:16, which indicates that he either turned to, or had in mind, the Lucan parallel. Otherwise, however, Mark followed the wording of Matthew very closely. The Lucan and Matthean rejection stories are very different. But the point is that Mark chose to copy closely the form of the rejection story as it lay before him in his copy of Matthew rather than copy it from Luke where it occurs in quite a different order. The close agreement between Mark and Matthew at this point is to be compared with Mark's close agreement with the text of Luke in the preceding passages, where in following Luke's order he had to deal with Matthean parallels which were in quite a different order.

This is strikingly in keeping with a pattern of alternation in agreement of wording, where Mark agrees closely now with one of his sources and then suddenly just as closely with the other; an alternation which corresponds positively with an alternation in agreement in order occurring at exactly the same place where the agreement in wording shifts.

G. Mark 6:7–16 // Luke 9:1–9

At this point Mark took up Luke immediately after the place where he had previously left off following him, and recorded the story of the sending out of the Twelve: Mark 6:6–13 // Luke 9:1–6 // Matthew 10:1–14 (the agreements in wording between Mark 6:6b and Matthew 9:35 and Luke 13:22, if not deceptive, are probably from memory). The influence on Mark of Matthew's wording in this passage may be seen especially in verses 7, 8, 10 and 11. But on the whole, Mark's text is conformed to the shape of Luke's shorter version of the incident, including, for example, among many omissions, that of the admonition of Jesus to his disciples not to go into the way of the Gentiles, nor any city of the Samaritans, but to the lost sheep of the house of Israel (Mt. 10:5–6).

Mark continued to follow Luke in recording next the tradition concerning the notion that Jesus was John the Baptist redivivus (Mk. 6:14–16 // Lk. 9:7–9 // Mt. 14:1–2). Mark, however, clearly turned to the Matthean parallel, for his account is a blending of Matthew's account with that of Luke. Furthermore, Mark then took up the fuller account in Matthew 14:3–12, and thereafter followed the order of Matthew in the succeeding sixteen literary units of his Gospel, without omitting a single story from Matthew (though, of course, he omits parts of some stories), and without interrupting the order of Matthew except twice to introduce two healing stories from some other source (Mk. 7:32–37 and Mk. 8:22–26).

H. Mark 6:17–9:32 // Matthew 14:3–17:23

The main difference between Luke and Matthew in this section of Mark is that Matthew has the feeding of two multitudes, whereas Luke has only one. Mark follows Matthew not only by including both feeding stories, but by incorporating all the material Matthew had included in between: five separable literary units in all. None of these five literary units is in Luke.

Mark's account of the feeding of the five thousand is the result of a conflation of the texts of Matthew and Luke, although his text is somewhat closer to that of Matthew (Mk. 6:30–44 // Mt. 14:13–21 // Lk. 9:10–17).

Mark followed the wording of Matthew very closely in the story of Jesus walking on the water. He apocopated the story in Matthew, however, by omitting the second half. He thereby changed a story created to serve the needs of Christian preaching (emphasizing the point that doubt and fear lead to death, but that faith in the lordship of Jesus saves), and converted it into a wonder story concentrating attention on Jesus' lordship over nature. (Mk. 6:45–52 // Mt.

14:22–33). Mark followed the wording of Matthew a little less closely in the story of the healings at Gennesaret (Mk. 6:53–56 ‖ Mt. 14:34–36).

I. THE SYNOPTIC TRADITION CONCERNING UNCLEANNESS

Mark's account of the story of defilement (Mk. 7:1–23 ‖ Mt. 15:1–20) follows Matthew's account rather closely with one very striking exception. Mark's account includes a lengthy explanatory gloss (Mark 7:3–4) concerning the customs of the Pharisees, which all commentators agree was added for the benefit of Gentile readers unacquainted with the practice of Palestinian Judaism.

From the following considerations it is clear that Mark's version of this tradition is secondary to that of Matthew:

(a) In Matthew the point is that to eat with unwashed hands does not defile a man. The appropriate question is set forth in verse 2, and the answer fittingly comes at the end of the literary unit in verse 20. In Mark, however, the point is that Jesus declared all foods clean (19b), a point of special interest to Gentile churches.

(b) Mark has rearranged and expanded Matthew's list of evil thoughts (Mt. 15:19 ‖ Mk. 7:21–22). Mark's list of vices includes the addition of five words which are found in similar lists in Paul's letters and two others unique to Mark. Furthermore, the distinctively Jewish vice (forbidden in the Decalogue) of bearing false witness, though found in Matthew, is omitted in Mark. Once again, then, Mark's version reflects the transformation of the tradition into a form better suited to meet the needs of the Gentile church. Matthew's list by comparison is much closer to the life situation of the earliest church, which was presumably Jewish-Christian in orientation and Palestinian-Syrian in locale.

(c) Mark has omitted the polemic against the Pharisees in Matthew 15:12–14. This polemic meant little to the later Gentile church, far removed from the continuing annoyance of hostile attitudes and activities of the Pharisees. This hostility, however, had been very real to Christians in Palestine and Syria during the first decades of the church.

In the story of the Syrophoenician woman, Mark's text varies considerably from that of Matthew, although there are also striking verbatim agreements (Mk. 7:24–30 ‖ Mt. 15:21–28).

The redactional summary in Matthew 15:29–31 is expanded in Mark by the insertion of a healing story characterized by the use of spittle (Mk. 7:31–37).[3]

Mark's account of the feeding of the four thousand adheres very closely to Matthew's (Mk. 8:1–10 ∥ Mt. 15:32–39). Mark continued to follow Matthew's order in recording the story of the Pharisees seeking a sign, traces of which are also found in Luke in a different order (Mk. 8:11–13 ∥ Mt. 16:1–4 ∥ Lk. 11:16).

2. THE SYNOPTIC TRADITION ON THE SIGN OF JONAH

Matthew 16:1–4 is a doublet of Matthew 12:38–39, a parallel to which is found in Luke 11:29. Mark 8:11–13 is a conflation of Matthew 16:1–5 with Luke 11:16 and Luke 11:29.

Only the Griesbach hypothesis enables one to unravel satisfactorily the redactional history of Mark 8:11–13. Luke tended to avoid doublets (*compare* his avoidance of a second story of a miraculous feeding of the multitudes); therefore, while he has a parallel account of Matthew 12:38–42, there is only a trace of the influence of the doublet in Matthew 16:1–4 upon his text (Luke 11:16). Mark included Matthew 16:1–4 in a section of his Gospel where he was incorporating something of all the literary units in the parallel section of Matthew. But in so doing he compared the Lucan parallels in Luke 11:16 and 29, and conflated the first part of Matthew's text with Luke 11:16 and the second part with Luke 11:29, ending with Matthew's transitional sentence leading to the saying about the leaven of the Pharisees (Mk. 8:11 ∥ Mt. 16:1 ∥ Lk. 11:16; Mk. 8:12 ∥ Mt. 16:1b ∥ Lk. 11:29; Mk. 8:13 ∥ Mt. 16:4a, 5a).

It is very difficult to place Mark at the beginning of this redactional process, making his account the source of all the Synoptic parallels. Streeter (*Oxford Studies*, p. 177) appealed to the notion of Mark's knowledge of Q to explain Mark 8:12. He rightly regarded Luke 11:29 as the proper parallel to Matthew 12:39, but he was mistaken in making Mark 8:12 parallel to Matthew 12:39. In that particular verse the agreements are deceptively equal between Mark and Matthew 12:39 on the one hand and Mark and Matthew 16:4 on the other. But outside that verse, it is quite clear that the literary

---

[3] For the probable significance of the presence of ἐφφαθά, see discussion of Mark's Aramaisms, Chapter IV, pp. 172–174.

kinship of the Marcan passage is closer to Matthew 16:1–5. So the problem is more complicated than Streeter presented it.

On Streeter's terms it would be necessary to imagine that there was a "Q" version of this passage in addition to Mark 8:11–13, and that Luke in 11:29 conflated the "Q" version with the Marcan version, and that Matthew copied the "Q" version in 12:39, and the Marcan version in 16:1–5. But there are close verbal agreements between Luke 11:16, Matthew 16:1, and Mark 8:11, which would require even further explanation on Streeter's terms. One would have to imagine that in 11:16 Luke copied Mark 8:11, neatly separating what he was taking from Mark's version at this point from what he was going to take from Mark's version a few verses later when he was to conflate the Marcan version with that of "Q." It must further be imagined on Streeter's terms that Luke, in copying Mark 8:11, in some way managed to agree at minor points with Matthew 16:1 against Mark 8:11 in word order and in the use of the preposition ἐκ instead of ἀπό.

Only if on other grounds it were virtually certain that Mark was a source for Matthew and Luke would one with any sense of confidence assert that this was the probable explanation of the redactional history of the sign of Jonah tradition in the Synoptic Gospels.

Mark 8:14–21, the discourse on leaven, is parallel to Matthew 16:5b–12. At this point Mark introduced a second story of miraculous healing, once again characterized by the use of spittle (Mk. 8:22–26). Then, continuing to follow the order of Matthew, Mark took up the story of the confession at Caesarea Philippi and the first prediction of the passion (Mk. 8:27–33 ‖ Mt. 16:13–23 ‖ Lk. 9:18–22). Though Mark's wording is closer to that of Matthew than to Luke, it is clear that he shaped his account under the influence of Luke, both in its wording and in its extent. Like Luke, Mark omitted the section in which Peter is given the keys to the kingdom (Matthew 16:17–19). It is notable that Mark in including the anti-Petrine tradition in Matthew 16:22–23, not found in Luke's account, softened Jesus' rebuke to Peter by the omission of the words "you are a scandal to me."

Still following the order of Matthew, Mark next took up the passage on the conditions of discipleship (Mk. 8:34–9:1 ‖ Mt. 16:24–28 ‖ Lk. 9:23–27). Once again Mark's wording is closer to that of Matthew, but Mark 8:38 was clearly formed under the influence of Luke 9:26. There are other agreements between Mark and Luke in Mark 9:1, which indicate that the accounts by Matthew and Luke have been conflated by Mark.

Mark then conflated Matthew's account of the transfiguration with Luke's (Mk. 9:2–8 ∥ Mt. 17:1–8 ∥ Lk. 9:28–36), though following Matthew's wording more closely than Luke's. Mark then continued to follow Matthew in giving the discourse about the coming of Elijah, which is not in Luke (Mk. 9:9–13 ∥ Mt. 17:9–13).

Next Mark conflated Matthew's story of the healing of the epileptic with Luke's, though expanding it far beyond the length of either Matthew or Luke (Mk. 9:14–29 ∥ Mt. 17:14–21 ∥ Lk. 9:37–43a).

Those who first fought the Griesbach hypothesis were quite sure that the details in Mark 9:20–25a were evidence of the primitive eye-witness character of Mark, which proved that Mark could not be the late Gospel the Tübingen scholars held it to be. But the picture of the lad rolling on the ground foaming at the mouth would not generally be regarded today as a detail due to the eye-witness character of Mark, and many critics are quite prepared to agree with the judgment of Schleiermacher that such a detail is to be regarded as due to a literary effort at verisimilitude.

This passage marks a transition point in the redactional history of Mark. For while the verbal agreements of Mark with Matthew and Luke are about equal in this passage, Mark's account is actually closer to Luke's due to his agreement with Luke in omitting Matthew's saying about having faith as a grain of mustard seed, to which Luke has another parallel in his Gospel (Mt. 17:20 ∥ Lk. 17:6). As a matter of fact, however, Matthew 17:20 has a doublet in Matthew 21:21, and Luke 17:6 is a conflation of the two. Mark copied Matthew 21:21 in Mark 11:23.

The next passage in both Matthew and Luke concerns a prediction of the passion, and Mark's text is a conflation of the two in which the verbal agreements between Mark and Matthew and Luke are about equal (Mk. 9:30–32 ∥ Lk. 9:43b–45 ∥ Mt. 17:22–23).

I. Mark 9:33–40 ∥ Luke 9:46–50

In this section Mark clearly followed Luke in omitting Matthew's story of the temple tax (Mt. 17:24–27). In the next literary unit concerning the dispute about greatness, it is quite clear that Luke was Mark's main guide, for he omitted with Luke Matthew's saying about becoming like little children (Mk. 9:33–37 ∥ Lk. 9:46–48 ∥ Mt. 18:1–5). Immediately thereafter Mark copied Luke's account of the strange exorcist (Mk. 9:38–40 ∥ Lk. 9:49–50), adding as an explanatory gloss, perhaps from memory, a saying which has a close parallel elsewhere in Matthew (Mk. 9:41 ∥ Mt. 10:42).

It should be noted that ever since Mark 8:27 ff., Mark had been working with Matthew and Luke in a section where these Gospels followed the same order. At first Matthew continued to be Mark's main guide in this section, which is natural enough, since Mark had been following Matthew exclusively in the preceding section, where there were few Lucan parallels and none of these in the same order as Matthew. But gradually Mark's text begins to indicate that in following Matthew and Luke where they had material in the same order, he tended to agree about equally with both, and before shifting to the order of Luke in this section, Mark as early as 9:14 had begun to shape his material as much (or more) under the influence of Luke as of Matthew. For this reason, it should not be expected that between Mark 8:27 and 9:37, a section of Mark where all three Evangelists have followed the same basic order, there should be any striking and consistent positive correlation between agreement in order and agreement in wording. Indeed there is none.

Wherever Matthew and Luke followed the same order over several passages, Mark's task of combining their accounts was facilitated, and any practical need to adhere more closely to the text of the Gospel which at the moment would seem to be serving as Mark's main guide would be considerably minimized, if not completely obviated. Thus the Griesbach hypothesis offers an explanation for the fact that Mark's text is rather equally close to that of Matthew and Luke from Mark 8:27–9:37, whereas no ready explanation for this is forthcoming on alternate hypotheses. An adequate explanation would require that this relative equality be explained in the light of the alternately unequal closeness in the earlier parts of Mark. There seems to be no ready explanation for this on the Marcan hypothesis.

Having copied Luke's account of the strange exorcist, Mark arrived at a point in his text of Luke where Jesus was presented as going with his disciples into Samaria on his way to Jerusalem (9:51 ff.). This introduced a very long section of material including many parables unique to Luke, a few parables paralleled in Matthew, and also a great deal of gnomic material, much of which is closely paralleled in Matthew. This would have posed for any writer faced with the task of combining Matthew and Luke a redactional problem of the greatest magnitude.

Mark was not averse to incorporating material which he found only in Matthew, or only in Luke. Nor was Mark averse to taking a parable or gnomic saying from Matthew and conflating or combining it in some way with its parallel in Luke, or vice versa. But whenever Mark undertook to conflate or combine material from one of his sources with parallel material from another, he tended to confine himself to literary units between which there already existed a close relationship of literary dependence. This is in notable contrast to the Fourth Evangelist who combined similar stories between which there was no close literary connection (*compare* story of anointing in John 12:2–8).

Mark, for example, never conflated parables from Matthew, which, though found in Luke, reached Luke independently from Matthew, having had a different history of transmission than their parallels in Matthew (*compare* parables of the great supper, Lk. 14:15–24 ∥ Mt. 22:1–10; lost sheep, Lk. 15:4–7 ∥ Mt. 18:12–14; talents, Lk. 19:11–27 ∥ Mt. 24:14–30). The only parables Mark conflated from Matthew and Luke were those Luke had copied from Matthew. The parable of the wicked tenants (Mt. 21:33–46 ∥ Mk. 12:1–12 ∥ Lk. 20:9–19) is an excellent case in point.

I. THE SYNOPTIC TRADITION CONCERNING THE PARABLE OF THE WICKED TENANTS

The reason Mark's form of the parable of the wicked tenants is shorter than that of Matthew and Luke is not that it is earlier but that it was difficult, or rather impossible, to conflate the clearly secondary addition found at the end of Matthew's form of the parable with Luke's substitute ending. Thus Mark, by omitting these two quite different endings to the parable, inadvertently recreated the parable in a form which in outward shape is closer to the original. It is clear from an analysis of the internal structure and content of the parable that Mark's form of this parable is secondary both to Matthew and Luke.

The view that Mark conflated Matthew's form of the parable with Luke's finds support from the following considerations:

(1) Matthew's form of the parable depends for its effectiveness upon a progressively dramatic intensification of the rebelliousness of the tenants, building up to that climax of confrontation between the householder and the tenants which is previewed in the question: "When therefore the owner of the vineyard comes what will he do to those tenants?" This progressive intensification depends on the messengers sent, not upon their treatment. Thus, first the owner sends some servants, then a larger number, and finally he sends his own son. In Oriental terms, the murder of the man's son obligated the owner and all his relatives to spend their lives seeking revenge upon the tenants. Therefore, though the son was only one, he fittingly represented the climax in the series of those sent.

(2) Luke's form of the parable depends for its effectiveness upon a similar progressively dramatic intensification. But unlike Matthew, Luke's progressive intensification of the rebelliousness of the tenants depends upon the reception of the messengers. The fact that it was the owner's son who was murdered and not just one of his servants is important, but the progression leading up to the murder of the son is based on the progressively more shameful treatment meted out to a series of three successive servants. (In Matthew, murder marked both the beginning and the end of the progression.) In Luke, servants were sent out one at a time until finally the son was sent. The first servant was beaten and sent away empty-handed; the second was beaten, treated shamefully, and sent away empty-handed; the third was wounded and cast out; finally the son was cast out and killed.

(3) Mark describes a servant beaten and sent away empty-handed; then another wounded in the head and treated shamefully; the third servant was killed; then there were many other servants sent, some of whom were beaten, while others were killed; finally the son was sent and he was murdered and cast out of the vineyard.

It seems clear that Mark took the progressive series of three servants in Luke and conflated it with the parallel series in Matthew, but with a loss in dramatic effectiveness. Mark's account has no proper climax. There was first the progression from the first to the third man who was *killed*. Then many were sent, some of whom were beaten and some *killed*. Then the son was *killed*. As a text for a parable, Mark's wording is atypically pleonastic. Mark does not simply have an intensification according to the messengers sent or the treatment received, but both, with a consequent loss of the economy of thought and clarity of expression so characteristic of parables of Jesus.

That Mark conflated from Matthew and Luke only parables that Luke copied from Matthew does not mean that Mark gave no consideration to his use of the great body of parables and gnomic material in Luke's central section until he actually reached this point in the redactional process of composing his Gospel. He probably knew in principle the way he would handle this important matter even before he began the actual task of writing his Gospel. The matter was undoubtedly of great importance because of the importance of the material concerned.

The parables unique to Luke contained in this central section are so complementary to the theology of Paul that some critics have explained them as later creations of the church made under the influence of the Pauline theology. There is no reason to doubt that to those Christians for whom Luke was a well-known and favorite Gospel these parables would have constituted a distinctive point at which they could claim that Luke's Gospel enjoyed a superiority over all other Gospels, including that of Matthew. On the other hand, adherents of Matthew could rightly feel that the parables in that Gospel were equally important, and no less representative of Jesus.

A decision not to take any parable from Matthew or Luke which could not be found in the other, under the circumstances may have been a matter of great practical consequence. In any case, having reached this point in Luke's Gospel, Mark would have been given further reason to pause.

One of the sharpest discrepancies between Matthew and Luke is found in Jesus' instructions to his disciples with reference to Samaria. In Matthew he admonishes them not to enter any town of the Samaritans (Mt. 10:5). Whereas in Luke he sends messengers ahead of him into a Samaritan village (Lk. 9:52), passes through the middle of Samaria (Lk. 17:11), and ministers to a Samaritan leper (Lk. 17:12–19).

This sharp discrepancy did not exist in Matthew, since there was no reference to Jesus or his disciples going to or through Samaria in that Gospel. Luke avoided creating a discrepancy for his readers by omitting from his Gospels the words from Matthew forbidding the disciples to enter a Samaritan town. But in churches where both these Gospels were known, at least in the period before they were canonized and had to vie with one another as well as with other Gospel literature for their survival, this discrepancy is likely to have been a bone of contention in the rivalry between the advocates of each respective Gospel.

Mark had already followed Luke in omitting the Matthean dominical prohibition against the disciples going into Samaritan towns. Now he also omitted the reference to Jesus sending messengers into a Samaritan village, and the reference to his going through Samaria, and the story of his ministry to the leper, and everything recorded by Luke in between, which is the greater part of this central section of Luke's Gospel.

Luke 17:11 reads literally "he passed through the middle of Samaria and Galilee." In any case, in churches far removed from Palestine where exact geographical and topographical knowledge concerning Galilee, Samaria and Judea was not current, it would have been possible to understand Luke not only to have represented Jesus going through Samaria, but since he sent messengers into a Samaritan village at the time he first set his face steadfast toward Jerusalem, at 9:52, it would have been possible to claim that the commissioning of the seventy in Luke 10:1 was for a mission which took place in Samaria, and all the teaching from 9:52 up until Jesus entered Jericho in 18:35 was given by Jesus to his disciples while in Samaria. In any case, Mark did not again work with the Gospel of Luke until Luke began paralleling Matthew in 18:15 (Mk. 10:13 ǁ Mt. 19:13 ǁ Lk. 18:15).

Hawkins, in his essay, "The Disuse of the Marcan Source in St. Luke ix. 51—xviii. 14," in *Oxford Studies*, argued that the parallels between Mark and Luke in this section of Luke are not "sufficient to prove any *direct use* of one of these Gospels by the other [p. 52]." These parallels, which Hawkins admitted were difficult to explain on the Marcan hypothesis, are readily explained on the Griesbach hypothesis.

Hawkins discussed three passages—Luke 10:25-28; 11:15, 17-23; 13:18, 19. In each case there is both a Marcan and Matthean parallel. And in each case the Marcan and Matthean passages are in the same relative order in the respective Gospels. In each case, Mark so carefully conflated the Lucan version with its Matthean parallel which he took up in Matthew's order, that the verbal agreements between Luke and Mark against Matthew, or Mark and Matthew against Luke, are rather slight. So slight indeed are they that they led Hawkins to conclude that there was in this section of Luke no clear evidence of direct literary dependence between Mark and Luke. Mark was able to conflate these sayings so carefully, mainly because he was working with sayings Luke had initially copied from Matthew.

Careful analysis of these three sayings dealt with by Hawkins indicates that Mark did make use of material from this great central section, but the circumstances under which he did so are notable. First, Mark took nothing from Luke in this great central section for which he did not have a Matthean parallel. Second, he conflated the material he used with the Matthean parallel. And, third, he tended to give the saying a place in his Gospel corresponding to its order in Matthew.

There are seven passages where the degree of verbal agreement between Luke and Mark is great enough to warrant these passages being considered in this connection.

(1) Luke 10:25–28 ∥ Matthew 22:34–40 ∥ Mark 12:28–31;
(2) Luke 11:14–23 ∥ Matthew 12:22–30 ∥ Mark 3:22–27;
(3) Luke 12:10 ∥ Matthew 12:32 ∥ Mark 3:28–29;
(4) Luke 13:18–19 ∥ Matthew 13:31–33 ∥ Mark 4:30–32;
(5) Luke 14:34 ∥ Matthew 5:13 ∥ Mark 9:50;
(6) Luke 16:18 ∥ Matthew 19:9 ∥ Mark 10:11–12;
(7) Luke 17:2 ∥ Matthew 18:6–7 ∥ Mark 9:42.

In every case, except Luke 14:34 and 16:18, there are sufficient agreements between Mark and Luke against Matthew to warrant the judgment that Mark probably consulted the Lucan parallel to each passage in Matthew. Luke 14:34 is a saying which all three Evangelists have in a different order. In the other six cases, Mark and Matthew have the saying in the same relative order in their Gospels.

Under these circumstances it is evident that Mark's redactional procedure with reference to Luke's great central section is intelligible on the Griesbach hypothesis. There was a great deal more sayings material which Luke had copied from Matthew in this section, some of which Mark probably could have conflated successfully. The question, therefore, remains: why did Mark omit material he presumably could have incorporated into his Gospel? But this question of omissions is never completely answerable on any hypothesis. There are always certain unresolved questions as to why any particular Evangelist omitted the material he did. Streeter's words are a proper reminder of the attitude to be taken on this question in the light of the actual circumstances under which the modern critic works: "Very often we can surmise reasons of an apologetic nature why the Evangelists may have thought some things less worth while reporting. But, even when we can detect no particular motive, we cannot assume that there was none; for we cannot possibly know either all the circumstances of churches, or all the personal idiosyncrasies of writers so far removed from our own times." (Underlining mine—W.R.F.)[4]

J. Mark 9:42–10:12 ‖ Matthew 18:6–19:12

At this point in the redactional history of Mark, the Evangelist turned from Luke and took up the saying on temptations from Matthew 18:6–9, having not long before incorporated the material in Matthew 18:1–5, in copying its Lucan parallel (Luke 9:46–48).

Matthew 18:6–9 is one of the six passages discussed above, where Luke has a significant parallel in the great central section of his Gospel (Luke. 17:1–2). Mark's version is a conflation of the texts of Matthew and Luke. That Mark followed Matthew is clear from the fact that he continued to the end of the literary unit of Matthew, thus including material not found in Luke (Mk. 9:43–47 ‖ Mt. 18:8–9).

That Mark's form of this tradition is secondary to that of Matthew is clear from the following considerations: In Matthew the carefully structured Semitic parallelism in verse 8 is preserved in verse 9, whereas Mark's version is expanded, glossed and altered. In Matthew the balance is between sins of the "hand or foot" on the one hand, and sins of the "eye" on the other. In Mark this twofold parallel structure is expanded unnecessarily and pendantically into a prosaic threefold admonition concerning sins of the "hand," of the "foot" and of the

4 *The Four Gospels*, p. 169.

"eye." In Mark the Jewish technical term *Gehenna* which Matthew used as if it were understood by his readers (5:29–30, 18:9) is commented on in an explanatory gloss (9:44). This gloss "is best explained as a comment of Mark based on Isaiah 66:24 . . . for the benefit of his Gentile readers" (Taylor, *op. cit.*, p. 412). In fact, Isaiah 66:24 is added by Mark at the end of this literary unit as a gloss to *Gehenna* in Mark 9:48. Finally, the parallelism between "to enter life" in verse 8 of Matthew is preserved by "to enter life" in verse 9. Whereas in Mark this parallelism is altered by the substitution of "to enter the kingdom of God" for "to enter life" in Mark 9:47. Mark's substitution is clearly interpretive, and therefore secondary.

Mark 9:49 presents a textual problem. But it is evidently an additional explanatory gloss on the material that precedes it in Mark, and serves as a transitional sentence, leading into the saying about salt in Mark 9:50, which may have been added at this point from memory, or it may have been the result of careful conflation. The Matthean and Lucan parallels, as has been indicated above, are in a different order from Mark's and from one another.

The next literary unit in Matthew concerns the lost sheep, to which there is a parallel in Luke (Mt. 18:10–14 ‖ Lk. 15:3–7). The verbal agreements between these two different forms of this parable are as great as in some passages which Mark has conflated from Matthew and Luke. But this verbal agreement is deceptive. Actually there is no evidence here of literary dependence between Matthew and Luke. The words that are the same are natural to the content of the parable. The parable as it is preserved in Luke makes the point that there is more joy in heaven over one sinner who repents than over ninety-nine righteous men. Whereas the parable as it is preserved in Matthew reflects a modification in the use of the parable to exhort church members to seek out those of the flock who have gone astray. The fact that the intention of the tradition is somewhat different in each case presented a special difficulty for a writer who wished to combine them. But if similar sayings from Matthew and Luke could not be combined, they were not to be taken into Mark's Gospel. That seems to have been a procedural policy followed fairly consistently by Mark in his redaction of the material he drew from these Gospels in composing his own.

At this point, then, Mark was once again confronted with his major redactional problem, i.e., what to do with the great wealth of parabolic materials in Matthew and Luke. For the parable of the lost sheep is but the beginning of a long section of sayings material in Matthew, including the parable of the unmerciful servant (Mt. 18:10–35). Mark, in a manner commensurate with his treatment of Luke, passed over all this sayings material and moved forward to a passage in Matthew which has a parallel in Luke's central section (Mk. 10:1–12 // Mt. 19:1–12 // Lk. 16:18). That Mark was following Matthew as his guide rather than Luke is confirmed by the fact that Mark's text includes the first eight verses of Matthew's literary unit, which are absent from the Lucan parallel.

I THE SYNOPTIC TRADITION ON DIVORCE

To trace the history of the Synoptic tradition on divorce on the Griesbach hypothesis affords the reader an excellent opportunity to see how a somewhat confused interpretative problem on the Marcan hypothesis can in fact be made quite intelligible.

To begin with, Matthew 19:9 "Whoever divorces his wife, except for unchastity, and marries another, commits adultery," has a doublet in Matthew 5:32 "everyone who divorces his wife, except on the ground of unchastity, makes her an adulteress; and whoever marries a divorced woman commits adultery." In both Matthean passages, divorce is accepted in the case of fornication according to the Halakhah of the school of Shammai (Gittin IX:10). Matthew 5:32 is secondary to 19:9 in the redactional history of Matthew, and complements it so that the adulterous effect of divorce is made more inclusive.

The first part of the saying in Matthew 5:32 seems to be based on two assumptions: (1) that the woman will be forced into another marriage, which will be an adulterous arrangement, since (2) the woman is still bound to her first husband in the sight of God. That a woman would be forced to seek another husband was a natural assumption under the circumstances, since there were few alternatives for such a woman in contemporary Jewish society. Matthew 5:32, therefore, was probably formulated at the latest while the interests of the Jewish Christian community were still quite strong.

Luke 16:18 represents a conflation of Matthew 19:9 and 5:32.

Luke accepted the teaching in Matthew 19:9 "everyone who divorces his wife and marries another commits adultery." He also accepted the second part of Matthew 5:32 "whoever marries a divorced woman commits adultery." But Luke apparently could not assume that a divorced woman would necessarily remarry, and therefore he omitted the opening words in Matthew 5:32 which make the point that to divorce a woman forces her into adultery. These words would not necessarily apply in churches which took seriously the tradition on divorce preserved in I Corinthians 7:10, which discouraged the practice of remarriage for divorced women in the church.[5]

The first half of Mark's form of the saying (10:11), "whoever divorces his wife and marries another commits adultery against her," is closer in verbal agreement to Matthew 19:9 than Matthew 5:32, or Luke 16:18. But the qualifying words, "except for unchastity" may have been omitted under the influence of Luke's version from which they are absent. Mark's addition of "against her" is ambiguous, leaving unclear whether the antecedent is the first or second wife. Jewish law does not provide for a man to commit adultery against his wife.

The second half of Mark's version could reflect the influence of the second half of Luke 16:18, or Matthew 5:32. It clearly represents an interpretation of the tradition to meet a situation in the church where the possibility existed for women to divorce their husbands: "if a woman divorces her husband, and marries another, she commits adultery." This was not possible under Jewish Law.[6] New Testament critics, therefore, often explain Mark 10:12 "as a secondary addition or modification based on Roman Law."[7]

There is no difficulty, therefore, in seeing Mark at the very end of the history of the redaction of this Synoptic tradition, which is where Mark is placed on the Griesbach hypothesis. On the other hand some adherents of the Marcan hypothesis have no difficulty placing Mark early. Burkitt dissents from the general view: "I venture to

---

[5] This had apparently become quite a problem in the church with the continuing delay of the parousia, and by the time of Luke's Gospel posed a serious economic problem, which may partly explain Luke's concern for χῆραι. Though usually translated "widow," this word can stand for any bereft woman left without the support of a brother, father, or husband. Such a woman could be bereft of her husband either through death, separation, or divorce.

[6] Cf. Josephus, *Antiquities*, 15. 7. 10 (259–260).

[7] Taylor, *op. cit.*, p. 420.

think such a view mistaken, and that so far from being a secondary addition it is one of the really primitive features of the Gospel of Mark. . . ." [8] Burkitt based his opinion on the fact that Herodias left her husband, and he suggested that it was Jesus' reference to this historical incident which was the origin of Mark's form of the saying. Such a suggestion, however, is a sheer guess, and the historical probabilities on the Marcan hypothesis are on the side of those critics like ,B. Weiss, J. Weiss, Schmiedel, Wellhausen and others, who regard the second half of Mark's version of the saying as a secondary addition reflecting the life situation of churches where divorce laws are administered in Roman courts, or where the laws administered by the local courts in cases of divorce were based on Roman Law.

It would only be with the greatest difficulty that one could explain satisfactorily the history of the Synoptic tradition on divorce by a redactional process in which Mark is placed first. Furthermore, the division of opinion among adherents of the Marcan hypothesis as to whether tradition in Mark is early and historical, or late and unhistorical, is a clear sign that the Marcan hypothesis has not provided scholars reliable ground on which to base a Synoptic criticism that can issue in a dependable and fruitful scientific consensus.

K. Mark 10:13–12:37 // Matthew 19:13–22:46 // Luke 18:15–20:44

In order to understand Mark's redactional activity in this section of his Gospel, it is helpful to know two things about Luke's relationship to Matthew. First, Luke at this point, that is 18:15 (after having introduced into his Gospel a great body of sayings material which he worked together with sayings material taken from Matthew or a source common to Matthew—making up the great central section of his Gospel) began to follow Matthew's narrative once more, and continued to do so with certain exceptions, through the story of the empty tomb. Second, the material preserved in Matthew 23, 24 and 25 presented Luke with very special problems which he handled in ways which consequently complicated the redactional problems for Mark. In effect, this section of Mark covers material in Matthew and Luke which occurs between the place where Luke resumed

[8] *The Gospel History and Its Transmission*, p. 100.

copying the narrative of Matthew's Gospel and the place where Luke's redactional problems became more complicated upon reaching Matthew 23:1 ff.

In this section, then, since Matthew and Luke followed the same general order, and since Mark almost never departed from their common order, the redactional problems for Mark were relatively simple. Whatever Matthew and Luke had in common Mark included, sometimes following Matthew's account more closely than that of Luke, and sometimes Luke's account more closely than that of Matthew, but always showing the influence of both.

Mark omitted all of the material peculiar to Luke (the story of Zacchaeus, 19:1–10; the parable of the pounds, 19:11–27; the prediction of the destruction of Jerusalem, 19:39–44). He also omitted most of the material peculiar to Matthew (the parable of the laborers in the vineyard, 20:1–16; the parable of two sons, 21:28–32; the parable of the marriage feast, 22:1–14). The only Matthean literary units without any kind of Lucan parallels which Mark included in this section were those concerning the cursing and withering of the fig tree (Mk. 11:12–14 // Mt. 21:18–19, and Mk. 11:20–25 // Mt. 21:20–22).

I. THE SYNOPTIC TRADITION ON CLEANSING THE TEMPLE

In Mark 11:11–25 there is a phenomenon which indicates that Mark was not unwilling to exercise his freedom to create a discrepancy between his Gospel and both Matthew's and Luke's. It is possible that he did this under the influence of some other source. Whatever the cause, after following both Matthew and Luke reporting Jesus' entry into the temple after his entry into Jerusalem (Mt. 21:12 // Mk. 11:15 // Lk. 19:45), Mark represented Jesus as leaving the city without having cleansed the temple. Both Matthew and Luke agreed, however, that this was the occasion of his cleansing the temple. But Mark did not simply omit the cleansing. He agreed with Matthew in reporting Jesus' departure to Bethany for the night; then the next day after cursing the fig tree on his way back to Jerusalem, Mark represented Jesus as re-entering the temple and cleansing it. Then, according to Mark, Jesus went out of the city again, and the following morning, while passing by the fig tree, Jesus' attention was

called to the fact that it had withered, and he made his pronouncement concerning faith.

In Matthew, the story about the fig tree is in one literary unit.
The fig tree withered immediately after Jesus cursed it. It has been
suggested on the Marcan hypothesis that Matthew made the fulfillment of the curse follow immediately after its pronouncement in
order to heighten the miraculous power of Jesus. But on form-critical
grounds, it is more likely that both parts of such a story were originally contained in a single literary unit.

In general, it may be said that the separation of two related acts
(in this case (1) the curse, and (2) what happened in consequence of
the curse), by the narration of an unrelated incident or incidents,
represents a later stage in the redactional history of tradition.

That would be the proper form-critical solution to the problem of
the pre-Synoptic history of Matthew 9:18–26 || Mark 5:21–43 ||
Luke 8:40–56. In that section of Synoptic tradition, Jesus responded
favorably to a request from a man to come and heal his daughter. But
the related action which followed, namely the actual healing, was
separated from the first part of the story by the narration of another
unrelated healing. In the earliest stage of this tradition the story of the
woman with the hemorrhage probably had no connection with the
story of the healing of the ruler's daughter. Then at some later stage
in the history of the transmission of this tradition, one story was inserted into the other with a consequent separation of the first part of the
latter story from its sequel by the narration of an unrelated incident.

The literary analogies in these two cases are not exact. But the
general principle is clearly illustrated in both cases. That principle
may be stated as follows: since related acts are originally conceived
together, their separation in narration is the result of a conscious
literary decision. On the basis of this literary principle, the story of
the fig tree in Matthew 21:18–21 seems more original than the Marcan form of this tradition where one part of the story is separated
from its sequel by the narration of unrelated events.

Certainly no one would deny, on the basis of form-critical considerations, that the story of the cleansing of the temple is an incident
which is in no way related to either part of the story of the fig tree.
The main purpose of Mark in narrating the story of the cleansing of
the temple on the second day seems to be related in some way to his
purpose in providing an interval of time between the cursing of the

fig tree and the subsequent reaction of Peter to the fulfillment of the curse. The pronouncement of Jesus has no more meaning in the one case than in the other.

\The agreement of Matthew and Luke against Mark in fixing the time of the cleansing of the temple on the same day as the triumphal entry, in balance, argues against their dependence on Mark.\There is no reason why these two Evangelists should agree against both Mark and John in this matter (whenever these Gospels were written) unless there was some genetic relationship between them that existed independent of their relationship to either of the other two Gospels. That relationship could have been through an Ur-gospel, or it could have been direct.

Mark's dependence upon Matthew and Luke in his account of the cleansing of the temple may be seen to be probable from the following considerations: Luke 19:47–48 is a Lucan redactional construction based upon the words of Jesus recorded in Matthew 26:55. There Jesus says to the crowd sent out by the chief priests and elders of the people to arrest him: "Have you come out as against a brigand with swords and staves to seize me ? I sat daily in the temple teaching and you did not take me. . . ." \As a dramatic achievement Matthew's text is unimpeachable in this instance. But as history it is defective in that the basis for Jesus' claim that he was daily in the temple teaching had not been previously established in Matthew's Gospel.\

Luke abstracted from Matthew 21:15 the information that the "chief priests and the scribes" were opposed to Jesus' activity in the temple, and conflated this with two items of information from Matthew 26:47–55;[9] to produce 19:47–48, which he substituted for Matthew's account of Jesus' healing activity in the temple following its cleansing.

This redactional summary which serves the purpose of establishing the historical basis for Jesus' condemnation of the cowardly and unjustified manner of his arrest in Luke 22:52, reads as follows: "And he was teaching daily in the temple, and the high priests and scribes were seeking to destroy him, and the leaders of the people as well; but they couldn't agree on a course of action, for all the people listened to him attentively."

---

[9] (1) that "the chief priests and elders of the people" sent an armed posse out to find Jesus, and (2) that Jesus had been "daily in the temple teaching."

In 11:15 Mark began by conflating Matthew's and Luke's accounts of the cleansing. In 15b he continued to copy Matthew in recording (what could be viewed as) the irrational violence of Jesus (which is omitted from Luke's account). Then in verse 16 he added the information that Jesus would not allow anyone to carry a vessel through the temple, which indicates that Mark either did not know the topographical situation of the temple in Jerusalem, or that he wanted to present Jesus' action in the light of the kind of scandalous abuse of sacred precincts for commercial purposes which prevailed at pagan places of worship known to his readers.[10]

In verse 17 Mark, in agreement with Matthew and Luke, recorded with reference to Jesus, "and he said to them." But he conflated this with Luke's redactional summary in Luke 19:47, namely that Jesus was teaching in the temple (which Luke had originally copied from Matthew 26:55). So that Mark 11:.17 reads: "And he taught and said to them: 'Is it not written, My house shall be called a house of prayer for all the Gentiles? But you have made it a cave for brigands.'"

The words "for all the Gentiles" actually belong to the text of Isaiah 56:7, which is being cited here. But these words are omitted in both Matthew and Luke.ᴺSince the Gentile mission is endorsed in both Matthew and Luke, their agreement against Mark in the omission of these words is difficult to explain on the Marcan hypothesis.[11]ᵥ

---

[10] It is striking that commentators in appealing to historical parallels for this abuse cited in Mark's text are reduced to passages which are quite inconclusive. Thus, Josephus' statement that "it is not so much as lawful to carry any vessel into the temple" (*Contra Apionem* II. 7. 106), has reference to going into the interior of the actual temple building where all the religious furniture was housed, and does not refer to passing through temple grounds. And the reference in the Mishnah to the prohibition against making the temple mount a short by-path (Berakoth ix. 5), makes no reference to carrying vessels.ᴺMark's text presupposes a practice in Jerusalem for which there is no evidence, and which on topographical grounds is unlikely to have obtained.ᴶ Unlike some pagan temples which are on the same level with the rest of the city and allow easy access to temple precincts from all sides, the temple in Jerusalem was situated on a site elevated above the rest of the city, and out of the normal line of commercial traffic.

[11] Stendahl in *The School of St. Matthew*, pp. 66–67, noted that Mark's inclusion of these words from the LXX text of Isaiah "most clearly shows that this Gospel's quotation is primary and that Matthew left it out as less important in the context." This is conceivable, and on the Marcan hypothesis it may be the best explanation. But Matthew's text could well be original. For the LXX goes beyond the Hebrew text in translating לְכָל־הָעַמִּים (all the People) as πᾶσιν τοῖς ἔθνεσιν (all the nations, or Gentiles). It is a translation which reflects a theological interpretation which need not have been

Mark 11:18 is a conflation of the redactional summary in Luke 19:47–48 with Matthew 22:33—which is itself an editorial transitional statement made by the final redactor of Matthew (*compare* Matthew 7:28–29 *et al.*). It would be very difficult indeed to explain the redactional history of Luke 19:47–48 on the Marcan hypothesis because of its verbal agreements with Matthew 26:55. Mark 11:19 is a redactional transition made by the Evangelist.

To place Mark 11:15–19 at the beginning of the history of the redactional process of the Synoptic tradition concerning the cleansing of the temple would create very serious difficulties. On the other hand, the whole of this Synoptic tradition is readily explicable on the Griesbach hypothesis.

2. THE SYNOPTIC TRADITION ON TRIBUTE TO CAESAR

The question concerning tribute to Caesar affords a clear-cut test of the Marcan hypothesis as over against that of Griesbach. In Mark 12:14 Jesus is addressed in the following way: "Teacher we know that you are true, and care for no man; for you do not receive men on the basis of their official standing, but truly teach the way of God." There are four clearly distinguishable phrases in this address: (1) Teacher, we know that you are true; (2) and care for no man; (3) for you do not receive men on the basis of their official standing; (4) but truly teach the way of God.

On the Marcan hypothesis, Matthew has faithfully copied the text of Mark with two exceptions: (a) he transferred the final phrase

---

in the mind of all first century interpreters. In any case, this interpretation is not necessary to the point being made in this context, where the contrast is between the right and wrong use of the temple. This contrast is somewhat blunted by Mark's "for all the Gentiles." But it is not difficult to understand why Mark, or some earlier Gentile Christian redactor of his copy of Matthew or Luke, would have added these words. They are in the LXX, and they make a theological point favorable to Gentile Christians. The point that God intended his temple to be a house of worship for the Gentiles, *all* the Gentiles, was well worth making in the interest of the Gentile Mission.

On the Griesbach hypothesis, Matthew's text is best understood as a result of Jewish Christian exegesis, where there was a modification of the text of Isaiah by omission of the words "for all people," for the purpose of heightening the contrast essential to the particular context in which it was used in the developing tradition concerning Jesus. This is in accord with the discoveries of Stendahl concerning the exegetical methods current in his "school" of Matthew. The text of Luke is readily explained as due to Luke's dependence upon Matthew. And the text of Mark is explained as a later development in which the increasing preponderance of Gentile Christian influence in the Church has led to the recovery of the full LXX text of Isaiah, but at the cost of blunting the original point of the story about Jesus.

to a place between the first and second of Mark; (b) he reworded that phrase slightly. On the other hand, Luke maintained the same order of phrasing as Mark, but omitted the second phrase entirely, reworded the first and third, and copied faithfully only the final phrase. There is no obvious explanation for Matthew's changing the order of Mark's phrasing, or for his slightly altering the wording of one phrase after copying three faithfully. Although if he had changed the place of phrase four, some slight rewording of that phrase would not have been unnatural.

But on the Marcan hypothesis, Luke's changes in the wording of phrases one and three, and his complete omission of phrase two, in contrast to his faithful preservation of the order of Mark's phrasing, and the exact wording of phrase four, defy critical analysis.

On the Griesbach hypothesis, however, Luke freely reused the text of Matthew in this instance, as he characteristically did: omitting a phrase here, rearranging the order of a phrase there, and frequently rewording the whole in a rather free manner. Luke sometimes copied Matthew quite closely. But in this instance, there is no faithful preservation of Matthew's content, order or wording; and the whole is freely recast in a typical Lucan fashion. Furthermore, Luke's transfer of the phrase "and teach the way of God truthfully" to the end of the sentence is in accord with the purpose of the Evangelist to emphasize the Christian faith as "The Way of God."[12] Luke, by giving that phrase the final place in the sentence, makes it serve as a climax to the whole. In comparison, Matthew's text gives the phrase only a subordinate place in the sentence. Luke's omission of the phrase, "and care for no man," presents no problem, since it is to a certain extent redundant in meaning compared to the following phrase ("for you do not receive men on the basis of their official standing"). It is characteristic of Luke to omit certain phrases in order to avoid the appearance of redundancy.[13] The text of Luke, therefore, on the Griesbach hypothesis presents no special difficulty to the critic. It is understandable to him in terms of a modification of the text of Matthew according to Luke's known theological purposes and literary tendencies.

[12] William C. Robinson, Jr., "The Theological Context for Interpreting Luke's Travel Narrative (9:51 ff.)," *Journal of Biblical Literature*, Vol. LXXIX, Part I, March, 1960, pp. 20–31.
[13] Henry J. Cadbury, *The Style and Literary Methods of Luke*.

So, also, the text of Mark is perfectly comprehensible on the basis of the Griesbach hypothesis. Having both the texts of Matthew and Luke before him, Mark often combined them when the respective wordings of their texts were close enough to make some kind of combination feasible. This is a case in point. Mark followed his texts of Matthew and Luke faithfully, making no unnecessary deviations. As between the ordering of the respective phrases of Matthew and Luke, Mark chose that of Luke. As to the difference in content between Matthew and Luke, Mark chose the fuller text of Matthew, including the phrase omitted by Luke. As to the wording of his text, Mark followed faithfully the text of Matthew, until the final phrase where he deemed it preferable to follow that of Luke, which is quite understandable, since he took that phrase in the order presented by Luke and not that of Matthew.

Such behavior on the part of Mark will seem strange to those unacquainted with the phenomenon of conflation in textual criticism, or to those unacquainted with the history of Synoptic criticism and the fact that there is no solution to the Synoptic Problem that does not entail some conflating activity on the part of one or more of the Evangelists. The Griesbach hypothesis entails the greatest degree of conflation. But a careful analysis of Mark's Gospel on the Griesbach hypothesis discloses nothing irrational or unintelligible about the redactional activity of Mark. And not infrequently, as in this instance, the Griesbach hypothesis affords the most intelligible solution to otherwise difficult redactional problems.

L. Mark 12:38–13:37 || Luke 20:45–21:38 || Matthew 23:1–25:46

The redactional activity of Mark in this section of his Gospel was fundamentally determined by the disjunctive relationship between the corresponding parts of Matthew and Luke. Though Mark in this section sometimes copied the text of Matthew very closely, his material was basically shaped under the influence of Luke's omission of most of Matthew 23, a large portion of Matthew 24, and the whole of Matthew 25.

To understand what Mark did with the texts of Matthew and Luke in this section, it is first necessary to understand what Luke did with the text of Matthew.

I. THE SYNOPTIC TRADITION ON THE WOES TO SCRIBES
AND PHARISEES

Having composed his Gospel up to 20:45, Luke, in working with Matthew, at this point arrived at the long section of woes against the Pharisees (Mt. 23:1 ff.). Having already utilized much of this material (or material parallel to it) back in 11:39–52 of his Gospel, Luke here only took two verses from a section he had previously omitted, i.e. he took verses 6 and 7 from Matthew 23:5–7. These two verses from Matthew are parallel to Luke 20:46.

In verse 47 Luke added further charges against the scribes: (1) they devoured widows' houses, and (2) for pretense made long prayers. Then Luke added a moralizing judgment: they would receive the greater condemnation. There is no reason to doubt that Luke 20:46–47 is an altered and expanded version of Matthew 23:5–7, since it reflects a definite Lucan interest in widows (*compare* Luke 2:37; 4:25, 26; 7:12; 18:3, 5; 21:2, 3. Also Acts 6:1; 9:39, 41), and since the evidence for literary dependence between Matthew and Luke is clear, and the text of Matthew is more Jewish and Palestinian in provenance.[14]

Luke's form would have been immediately comprehensible to Gentiles, as Matthew's would not. The first woe was against those who were ostentatious in their dress. Few Gentiles outside of Palestine would have understood Matthew's text: "they make their phylacteries broad and their fringes long." Luke's version: "they walk around in long robes," referred to an ostentatiousness understood by his readers which he thought corresponded to the ostentatiousness of the scribes and Pharisees. The Palestinian Judaism which conditioned Jesus' historical existence was Torah-centric— Law centered. And the law was the Law of Moses. Every pious Jew conscientiously sought to obey all the commandments of Moses. Some of these commandments affected external dress. The two most famous of these were the command to bind the words of the Lord to the arm and the head, and the command to wear fringes on the borders of garments.

In recent years a number of phylacteries have been recovered in Palestine. They are tiny parchments upon which are written passages of scripture in very fine script, which, when rolled tightly, could fit

---

14 *See* canon number 4 in Step XVI, and 4 and 6 of Burton's six evidences of a secondary character, Chapter VI, pp. 229.

into small leather capsules which then could be bound to a band on the upper arm or the head. When so worn the pious Jew believed that he was thereby protected from evil—thus these little leather capsules came to be associated with protective charms called phylacteries.

To make broad these phylacteries or the bands around the upper arm or head to which they were attached was to draw attention to the fact that the wearer was observing the Mosaic Law, and that he was not ashamed of being an observant Jew, and no doubt in some cases proud of it. Jesus' stricture was against this kind of piety— done to be seen by men. It is obvious that the Lucan form of this tradition in Matthew has lost something in the process of being translated into Gentile terms. And it should be equally obvious that the Lucan form is secondary to that of Matthew (*compare* Chapter VI, p. 227).

Mark 12:38–40 is almost word for word the same as Luke 20:46– 47. There is no evidence in this instance that Mark did anything other than copy the text of Luke.

2. THE SYNOPTIC TRADITION ON THE WIDOW'S MITE

The next literary unit in Luke was introduced from some special source available to the Evangelist. It was originally formulated as a biographical apophthegm or *Chreia*.[15]

The definition of a *Chreia* given by Dibelius (*op. cit.*, pp. 150–151 [152–153]) is worth quoting: "It is a reproduction of a short pointed saying of general significance, originating in a definite person and

---

[15] R. O. P. Taylor, in *The Groundwork of the Gospels*, Oxford, 1946, has conveniently collected the most important texts from the Greek Rhetores (translated by T. Nicklin), pp. 82–90. These texts are prefaced by an important introduction to the *Chreia*, pp. 75–81. The Greek texts are accessible in the Teubner series, collected by Spengel, under the title *Rhetores Graeci*. *Chreiai* themselves may be conveniently found in (1) Lucian's *Life of Demonax*, 12–67; (2) Plutarch's *Life of Marcus Cato*, vii–ix; (3) Diogenes Laertius' *Lives of Eminent Philosophers*: Socrates II, 30B–37; Aristippus II, 127–30; Plato III; Xenocrates IV, 8–10; Diogenes VI, 32–69; Antisthenes VI, 3–9; Crates VI, 89–91; Metrocles VI, 95; Zeno VII, 17–26; Ariston VII, 163; Cleanthes VII, 171–4; Sphaerus VII, 177; Chrysippus 182–3; Heraclitus IX, 12; Xenophanes IX, 20; Zeno of Elea 27–39; Protagoras IX, 56; Anaxarchus IX, 58–60; Pyrrho IX, 64–9; Timon IX, 113–15; (4) Xenophen's *Memorabilia of Socrates* III, 13. Important bibliographical references will be found in Martin Dibelius's discussion of the *Chreia* in his *Die Formgeschichte des Evangeliums*, 3rd ed., Tübingen, 1959, pp. 150–164; English trans. of 2nd ed., with same discussion of *Chreia* as in 3rd ed. *From Tradition to Gospel*, New York, 1935, pp. 152–164. Robert Grant treats the *Chreia* in *The Earliest Lives of Jesus*, New York, 1961, pp. 17–18, 99–101.

arising out of a definite situation." "In the age of the Gospels," writes Dibelius, "rhetoricians called such a small literary unit a *Chreia*, as also did the Stoics in the first century B.C."

Some *Chreiai* are very concise, as for example this one concerning Antisthenes: "One day when he was censured for keeping company with evil men, he replied, 'Physicians attend their patients without getting the fever themselves'" (Diogenes Laertius, VI, 6). Sometimes the *Chreiai* include action, as in the *Chreia* concerning Anaxagoras: "When someone inquired, 'Have you no concern for your fatherland?' he replied, 'I am greatly concerned with my fatherland,' and pointed to heaven" (Diogenes Laertius, II, 7). In other *Chreiai* the sayings are more developed and involve both a question and answer construction, as for example those quoted by Xenophon in his *Memorabilia of Socrates* (III, 13).

The *Chreia* form as developed and used by the rhetoricians was admirably well adapted to meet the needs of early Christian preachers. Dibelius was correct in noting the similarity between the Hellenistic *Chreia* and his Marcan paradigms. He was also correct in noting that in the Synoptic tradition peculiar to Luke there are true *Chreia* forms. He was wrong, however, in regarding these as the result of a literary tendency of the Evangelist to cast tradition which came to him in the form of paradigms into the more concise *Chreia* form. It happens that in the Hellenistic literature in which *Chreiai* are found (notably in the lives of various famous men) the pattern is not for the authors of these works to create *Chreiai*, but rather to incorporate them into their accounts from earlier collections of *Chreiai*. On the basis of a comparative study of the nearest parallels in contemporary literature, it seems likely that the *Chreiai* in Luke have been incorporated into that Gospel from some earlier source or sources. The attempt by Dibelius to show that the *Chreia* forms in Luke are Lucan on the basis of Luke's assumed practice of reducing some of the Marcan paradigms to a more concise form falls short of its goal. Sound procedure requires that we carefully examine each *Chreia* in Luke to see whether there is evidence of Lucan composition.

The *Chreia* first of all was designed to be easily committed to memory; for once committed to memory it could then be recalled and thus constituted a well-structured text which thereafter could be quoted, paraphrased, illustrated, expounded, etc., at will, leaving the speaker (or preacher) free to concentrate upon his task without either the encumbering handicap of written notes or the embarrassing fear of being "lost for words." The gifted public speaker might find such helps unnecessary, but for the majority they proved to be very useful.[16]

The original form of the *Chreia* in Luke 21:1–4 can be reconstructed by the omission of verse 4:

Looking up Jesus saw rich people casting their gifts into the temple treasury. And he saw a needy widow casting in two very small coins. And he said: Truly I say to you, "This poor widow cast in more than all of them." (Luke 21:1–3)

Verse 4 following is what the rhetoricians termed an *aitia*, or "reason." It was one of the standard acceptable additions to attach to a *Chreia*, and had as its purpose to explain the general principle incorporated in the *Chreia*. The reason why it could be said that the

---

[16] The use of *Chreiai* in the schools of rhetoric was so widespread, and had such a firmly fixed place in the educational system of the empire in the first century that Quintilian, though writing in Latin, refers to the composition of *Chreiai* as a rudimentary activity for pupils who are preparing for the school of rhetoric (The *Institutio Oratoria* of Quintilian, Book I, ix, 3–6). Quintilian's dates are c. A.D. 35–100. He implies that this discipline was included among the first essentials of general education. Although writing about the situation in Rome, Quintilian describes a situation which also prevailed at the eastern end of the Mediterranean. *Cf.* the second century A.D. inscribed "school texts" Ostraka published and discussed by Grafton Milne in the *J. Hellenic Stud.* xxviii, 1908, 121–32. An excellent example of the way in which the copying of *Chreiai* was made a part of the schoolboy's written exercises is provided by a papyrus notebook (dated third and fourth centuries—but assumed to be representative of educational practice in the Graeco-Roman period from at least the time of Quintilian), in which the *Chreiai* are preceded by written exercise in syllabification and followed by the copying of moral maxims. See Papyrus Bouriant N. I—to be conveniently found as N. 29 in Erich Ziebarth's *Aus der Antiken Schule* (Bonn, 1910), in the Hans Lietzmann *Kleine Texte* series. *Cf.* also in Ziebarth's collection, the third-century wooden tablet on one side of which is declined a *Chreia* concerning Pythagoras, published originally in the *J. Hellenic Stud.* xxix, 1909, 11. The point is not that as public orators they would be called upon to create *Chreiai*, but rather, having written *Chreiai* themselves, they would better understand the principles governing their composition, and thus be better prepared to make the most effective use of those collections of *Chreiai* of philosophers and famous men, whose example and words would carry weight in the minds of their hearers. To have invented such *Chreiai* would have defeated the speaker's purpose, since it was essential that his hearers acknowledge the authenticity of the *Chreiai* he used. For all *Chreiai* contain the words or refer to the actions of known historical persons. It follows, therefore, that just as *Chreiai* concerning Jesus are not to be regarded as having been invented by the Evangelists while writing their Gospels, neither are we to think of them as having been created by early Christian preachers. But rather we should imagine these early preachers drawing upon previously prepared collections of *Chreiai*, in which sayings or actions of Jesus have been provided historical settings and against the background of which the respective sayings or actions are to be understood and interpreted.

two very small coins of the widow were more than the gifts of all the rich was that: "They gave to the treasury out of their abundance; but she, out of her want, cast in the whole of her substance" (Lk. 21:4). This *aitia* then opened up the possibility for the rhetorician or preacher to expatiate on the subject of sacrificial giving, making practical application of the principle under the illumination provided by the picture of the needy widow giving her two tiny coins, and in the power and with the authority of the man to whom the saying in the *Chreia* was attributed.

Bultmann was right in terming the Marcan form of this story a Biographical Apophthegm. But it is clearly an expanded version of the more original form in Luke, and clearly secondary to the Lucan form. There is first of all the completely unnecessary threefold repetition of the term used for "temple-treasury" in Mark 12:41 and 43. The Marcan introduction to the *Chreia* in verses 41–42 is not concise, and the added detail that he "called his disciples to him" in verse 43 is but a literary effort at verisimilitude, which adds nothing to the *Chreia*.

The clearest sign of the secondary character of the Marcan form of this tradition as compared to that of Luke is found in the interpretative gloss added to verse 42, in which it is explained to Mark's readers that the two *lepta* in terms of Roman coinage amounted to a *quadrans*. Attention is not called to this gloss in order to make the point that Mark is a Roman Gospel. This interpretative gloss is no more proof of a Roman provenance for Mark than the use of *quadrans* in Matthew 5:26 is proof of a Roman provenance for Matthew. But in its original form the *Chreia* required the concise use of terms and images immediately comprehensible to hearers. Therefore, when the most original form of the Marcan *Chreia* (or Bibliographical Apophthegm, to use Bultmann's term), is reconstructed by the elimination of the clearly secondary accretions, that reconstructed form is found to be closer to the text of Luke than to the text of Mark.

It is gratuitous to argue that Luke could have made Mark's form of this tradition more concise. On the Marcan hypothesis, at least on Streeter's terms, one is forced to this as an explanation. But on strictly form-critical grounds, Luke's form is clearly more original. Therefore, since the verbal agreement is so extensive in this instance, and leaves little ground on which to base a doubt that there was direct literary dependence between the two, the burden of proof rests upon the shoulders of the critic who agrees that the evidence for Marcan priority is inconclusive, and yet wants to maintain that Luke is secondary to Mark. He must show by appeal to the style and vocabulary of Luke that Luke's form of Mark 12:41–44 is of Lucan construction. This would be difficult to do convincingly.

One final consideration concerning the relationship of Mark to Luke in this section has to do with a matter of *Tendenz*. Widows are never mentioned in Mark, except in this section of his Gospel, where there is clear evidence of literary dependence. The simplest explanation for these facts is to imagine that the presence of references to widows in Mark's Gospel is due to his having copied Luke. To reason otherwise, and to argue that the established tendency of an author through the whole of his work affords no clue as to his authorship of a part, would be to subvert the integrity of literary criticism. Luke mentions widows in Chapters 2, 4, 7, 18, 20, and 21. Furthermore, this concern for widows is but one aspect of a special interest in women in his Gospel. Thus there can be no doubt that the interest and concern of the tradition in Luke 20:47–21:4 is in accord with a well-established and characteristic *Tendenz* of the Evangelist. In the history of Christian tradition, it is most likely, therefore, that these verses, that is, the woe against those who devour widows' houses (Lk. 20:47a), and the *Chreia* concerning the needy widow, first came into the Gospel tradition through the special tendency of Luke to be mindful of the interests and concerns of women.

This consideration of *Tendenz* does not constitute proof of the priority of Luke to Mark. For Luke's interest in widows would have led him to take this tradition into his Gospel from Mark if Mark was one of his sources. But it is a literary phenomenon which is readily explicable on the Griesbach hypothesis, whereas, on the Marcan hypothesis, there is no ready explanation for the presence of these two, and only these two references to widows in Mark. The fact that these two references to widows are back to back in the Gospel of Mark, and that they are the only references to widows in his Gospel, suggests that they have come into his Gospel from a source which featured tradition concerning widows. Therefore, in whatever direction one moves, he is led back around to the hypothesis that Luke was a source for Mark as the simplest explanation of the literary phenomena in this section of the Synoptic tradition.

3. THE APOCALYPTIC DISCOURSE

Mark never actually made direct use of material from Matthew 23. His parallel to that chapter of Matthew seems to have been completely determined by Luke's use of Matthew. In the case of Matthew 24, once again it is not possible to understand the relationship between Matthew and Mark without first understanding what use Luke made of Matthew. However, in this case, Luke's use of Matthew 24 is such as to lead Mark to work with both Luke and Matthew, and to produce one of the most interesting and complicated redactional problems in the whole of Synoptic criticism.

The correct solution to the redactional history of Mark 13 must take into account the fact that there are not only parallels in Matthew 24 and Luke 21, but that there are, in turn, significant parallels to these materials in Matthew 10, Luke 12 and 17.

At 21:5 Luke began following Matthew 24:1 ff., utilizing Matthew 24:1–7; 15–19; 29–35. Luke thus utilized a considerable portion of the material in Matthew 24, and always in Matthew's order. However, there are significant omissions and one major insertion which require explanation. Luke 21:11b marks a transitional point in Luke's text. Up to this point Luke had been following Matthew 24:1–7. But the next literary unit in Matthew contains the words: "but he who endures to the end will be saved (Mt. 24:13)." These words constitute a doublet to the identical phrase in Matthew 10:22b. At this point Luke evidently turned back to Matthew 10 to compare the material there with what he found in Matthew 24. For some reason Luke preferred Matthew 10:17–22 to its parallel, Matthew 24:9–14. Perhaps Luke preferred the reference to Christians "being hated by all" in Matthew 10:22a to their "being hated by *all the Gentiles*" in Matthew 24:9b. In any case, Luke 21:12–19 ‖ Matthew 10:17–22, and since Luke in 12:11–12 had already copied Matthew 10:19–20, he is led to paraphrase those words at this point (Luke 21:14–15)—presumably in order to avoid creating a doublet, which would leave the appearance of redundancy in his work. It is to be noted in this connection that he did the same thing in 21:22, where he was dependent on Matthew 24:16–17, part of which he had used previously in Luke 17:31. This is a perfectly comprehensible literary device, and lends support to the hypothesis that Luke was using Matthew as his source (or a source similar to Matthew which has material in the same order as does Matthew). For it is the natural practice of a writer making use of a narrative source to move in general in a forward direction through the source. And when a writer using a narrative source skips forward in the source to copy material out of order for some special reason, then later, when moving forward through the source he reaches material he has previously used, it is natural that he either skip that material or utilize it in the light of the fact that he had already made some previous use of it.

After substituting Matthew 10:17–22 for Matthew 24:8–14, Luke returned to Matthew 24, and began copying at verse 15 (Lk. 21:20–24 ∥ Mt. 24:15–22). The difference between Luke and Matthew can be explained as follows: (a) Luke 21:20, 23b–24, are Lucan modifications reflecting a post-70 A.D. situation where the readers of Luke's Gospel could be expected to be acquainted with historical accounts of the destruction of Jerusalem and the treatment of its captives by the Romans; (b) Luke 21:22, 24 contain Old Testament references which indicate that Luke may have been utilizing other tradition in his modification of Matthew in these verses; (c) Luke 21:21a is identical with Matthew 24:16. But Luke 21:21b is a paraphrase of Matthew 24:17–18. Luke had previously used these verses of Matthew in editing Luke 17:23–37. That section of Luke constitutes a special problem. In all probability Luke had access to a special source which contained apocalyptic material parallel to material in Matthew 24. Luke 17:26–30 exhibits synonymous parallelism and is probably in a more original form than its parallel in Matthew 24:37–39. But it is quite possible that Luke drew from Matthew 24 some or all of the other material in 17:23–37, which is paralleled in Matthew 24. In any case, in Luke 21, material in Matthew 24, which is paralleled in earlier sections of Luke, is either omitted or, as in the case of Matthew 24:17–18, paraphrased. There are no exceptions. There is no verbal overlap between apocalyptic material in Luke 21 and corresponding material elsewhere in Luke. In other words, apocalyptic material which is presented as a whole in Matthew 24 is found in Luke, neatly divided and presented in different parts of his Gospel. And whenever there is an overlap in content, as for example between Luke 17:31 and Luke 21:21b, the neatness of this redactional division is preserved through the literary artifice of paraphrase.

Luke 21:25–27 is parallel to Matthew 24:29–30. Luke had previously drawn from Matthew 24:23–28 in his editing of Luke 17:21–24, 37. Therefore, he omitted this portion of Matthew's text in his editing of Luke 21, and began working with Matthew 24:29 ff. Luke 21:25–33 is parallel to Matthew 24:29–35. Luke had already incorporated material parallel to Matthew 24:36–42, back in Luke 17:26 ff., and he therefore omitted this section from his account in Chapter 21. Furthermore, in Luke 12, the Evangelist in editing material on the theme of "the folly of postponing repentance" (Luke 12:35–13:9) took the material in Matthew 24:43 –51 and joined it with a parable from his special source material which enjoyed the common motif: "Blessed be the servant who is ready when his master comes" (Lk. 12:37 // Lk. 12:43). Therefore, in Luke 21 the Evangelist also omitted this closing section of Matthew 24.

In the above manner, it is possible to explain all the significant redactional differences between Luke 21:5–33 and Matthew 24:1–51. All the Lucan parallels to material in Matthew 24, which are found outside Luke 21, occur in the great central section of Luke. It has been shown that Mark made no direct use of this section of Luke's Gospel. This explains the striking fact that the Marcan version of Matthew 24 in Mark 13:1–32 is limited to the sections of Matthew 24, which are found in Luke 21. There are instances where Mark, having been led to compare a Matthean parallel to a section in Luke 21:5–33, copied Matthew's text more closely and fully than had Luke. And in one instance, Mark continued to copy Matthew's text beyond the point where he might have stopped, had he slavishly limited himself to those passages in Matthew 24 which he found in Luke 21 (*compare* Mk. 13:21–23 // Mt. 24:23–25). Nevertheless it cannot be disputed that the literary units of Matthew 24, which are not found in Mark 13, are also not found in Luke 21, but are found in the great central section of Luke. These literary units are three in number: (1) Matthew 24:26–28 // Luke 17:23–24, 37; (2) Matthew 24:37–41 // Luke 17:26–37; (3) Matthew 24:43–51 // Luke 12:39–46.

These redactional phenomena are afforded a ready explanation on the Griesbach hypothesis. They constitute a difficulty for the Augustinian hypothesis, since there is no apparent reason why Mark should have omitted these three literary units from his Gospel, in view of the fact that he otherwise copied the text of Matthew 24 very closely indeed. Similarly on the Marcan hypothesis, since there are minor but significant agreements between Matthew and Luke against Mark in Matthew 24:1–7 and 24:30–35, which (on Streeterian terms, at least) require these verses, as well as 24:26–28; 24:37–41; and 24:43–51, to be attributed to "Q," it is difficult to know why Mark would have omitted from "Q" exactly those literary units which Luke does not have in common with Matthew 24, in Luke 21, but does include elsewhere. Since Mark would have no preknowledge of how Matthew and Luke would arrange material they independently drew from "Q," it does not seem possible to explain why Mark's selection from "Q" would have followed the pattern it does. Furthermore, one would be expected on the terms above to imagine the following redactional procedure on the part of Matthew: (1) In 24:1–7 Matthew conflated Mark and Q; (2) In 24:8–25 he copied Mark, though he may have conflated verses 17–18 with a closely parallel passage from "Q"; (3) In 24:26–28 he returned to "Q" for three verses; (4) In 24:29–35 he conflated Mark and "Q"; in 24:36 he copied Mark; (5) but in 24:37–51 he copied "Q" again. He furthermore probably interrupted this use of Mark and "Q" by inserting passages from M at 24:10–12 and 24:30.

It may not be possible to deny categorically that a writer would have proceeded to edit material in this fashion. But it is incumbent upon those who think that Matthew so proceeded to consider the possibility that instead of being added by the Evangelist to what he found in Mark and "Q," the following verses were an organic part of the material available to him when he composed his Gospel: (1) "And then many will fall away, and betray one another, and hate one another. And many false prophets will arise and lead many astray. And because wickedness is multiplied, most men's love will go cold" (24:10–12). (2) "The sign of the Son of Man shall appear in heaven, and then all the tribes of the earth will mourn" (24:30).

Even more likely to have been an original part of the apocalypse is the Matthean text: "Pray that your flight may not be in the winter or on a sabbath" (24:20). The parallels in Luke and in Mark have no reference to the Sabbath. It is difficult to dismiss the suggestion that the reference to the Sabbath in Matthew's text is a sign of the original Palestinian provenance of the materials in Matthew 24, and that the absence of this reference in Luke and Mark is a sign that these Gospels were written for churches in which the Sabbath had lost its importance. Only on the hypothesis that Matthew copied

Mark (by which the critic is forced to make an Evangelist committed to the universal mission to the Gentiles responsible for Judaizing sections of his Gospel), would one deny that this reference to the Sabbath was an indication of the primitivity of the tradition in Matthew 24, taking the critic back to the time when Christians had not yet consciously disassociated themselves from Judaism and its practices. There is no sound reason to doubt that most of the material incorporated by the Evangelist into Matthew 24 is Jewish-Christian in origin and Palestinian in provenance, nor that Matthew's version of this material is closer to the original than Luke's or Mark's. It has been possible to explain Luke's redactional use of this material from Matthew. It is now necessary to show that it is possible to explain Mark 13:1–32 as a conflation of Matthew 24:1–36 with Luke 21:5–33.

On the Griesbach hypothesis, Mark 13:1–8 is a conflation of Matthew 24:1–8 with Luke 21:5–11. The verbal agreement among all three is quite extensive. The agreement between Matthew and Mark against Luke is considerable. The agreements between Luke and Mark against Matthew are minimal and sporadic, being of the same order as the agreements of Matthew and Luke against Mark. This indicates that while Mark has rather carefully combined the closely related texts of Matthew and Luke, he has tended to follow the fuller text of Matthew.

All three Gospels agree in including the exhortation to be "watchful" (Mk. 13:5 // Mt. 24:4 // Lk. 21:8). But in 13:9 (and 13:23) Mark heightens this motif of "watchfulness," which is to climax in and dominate his ending of the apocalyptic discourse in 13:33–37. A linguistic analysis of that ending indicates that it is a Marcan construction based upon the Lucan and Matthean endings to the discourse and related passages from Matthew 25 (Lk. 21:34–36; Mt. 24:42–44; 25:13–15). Therefore, the agreement of Matthew and Luke against Mark in the omission of the exhortation to "watch" found in Mark 13:9 (and 13:23 as well) is an indication of the secondary character of this feature of Mark's text, and also its probable Marcan origin.

At that point, Mark reached the place in the text of Luke where Luke had shifted back to Matthew 10:17–22, as a substitute for its parallel in Matthew 24. Mark evidently perceived that Luke had made this shift, and followed his redactional lead in doing the same.

When Mark turned to Matthew 10:17–22, the true parallel to Luke 21:12–19, he not only conflated these two passages, but once again adhered more closely to the text of Matthew than to the text of Luke. For understandable reasons mentioned above, Luke had paraphrased Matthew 10:19–20 in Luke 21:14–15. Luke in 21:18 had also introduced into his version of Matthew 10:19–20 an idea from Matthew 10:30, "But not a hair of your head will perish." Luke's wording represents an interpretation of the exact words of Matthew's text: "But even the hairs of your head are all numbered," which Luke copied rather closely while following Matthew 10:26–33 in Luke 12:2–9. In any case, Mark followed the text of Matthew closely at the point where Luke paraphrased and agreed with Matthew against Luke in omitting the saying from Matthew 10:30 which Luke had reworded and introduced into his text.

In that part of Luke's text which is paralleled in Mark 13, it is striking that at all three places where Luke's text indicates that he paraphrased sentences from Matthew which he had copied faithfully earlier in his Gospel, Mark adhered closely to the text of Matthew. These three places are Luke 21:14–15, 18, and 21. The point is that Mark was on perfectly safe ground in following closely the texts of Matthew in all these places, since Luke had testified against the originality of his text at these points by elsewhere in his Gospel having preserved the text which Mark found before him in Matthew. From this point of view, Mark's Gospel is superior to that of Luke at those points in this section where Luke makes positive deviations from the text of Matthew. Mark's Gospel in this section would not completely satisfy adherents of Matthew's Gospel. But it would especially commend itself to those adherents of Luke's Gospel who were sensitive to the charge that their Gospel had unnecessarily departed from a wording of the tradition to which Luke elsewhere testified. No one would want his Gospel to be inconsistent. This would have been especially true for adherents of Luke.

Mark was not produced for readers who would appreciate the literary finesse of Luke in avoiding redundancy. Mark wrote his Gospel for a church which knew more than one Gospel, and was tired of unnecessary bickering over the rival claims and counter claims of the adherents of different Gospels; the chief rivals and contenders for general acceptance apparently being Matthew and Luke. Mark 13 is a revision of Luke 21, in which Mark recognized the superior claim of the parallel texts in Matthew 10 and 24 on the ground that Luke elsewhere in his Gospel supported the text of Matthew 10 and 24 against the Lucan parallel texts in Luke 21.

At the end of Mark 13:9 the reference to "bearing witness" which he found in both Luke 21:13 and its parallel, Matthew 10:18, was associated by Mark with the reference to "a witness to all the Gentiles" in Matthew 24:14, and Mark therefore incorporated the substance of that tradition in 13:10.

In 13:11–13 Mark conflated Luke 21:14–17 with Matthew 10:19–22 (Huck-Lietzmann is misleading in its arrangement of the parallel materials at this point), omitting Luke 21:18 and adhering more and more closely to the text of Matthew. Mark then returned with Luke to Matthew 24:15 ff. From that point in the text of Matthew, Mark adhered so closely to the text of Matthew that Marsh could write: "there is such a close verbal agreement for twenty verses together, with the parallel portion in Matthew's Gospel, that the texts of St. Matthew and St. Mark might pass for one and the same text, in which a multiplication of copies had produced a few trifling deviations. At least they do not differ more from each other than each differs from itself in different manuscripts." (*Op. cit.*, Vol. III, Part II, p. 170.)

What Marsh failed to note, however, was that although the differences between Mark's text and that of the *parallel* passages of Matthew seemed trifling, there were four significant passages in Matthew's apocalyptic discourse for which Mark had no parallel: (1) Matthew 24:10–12; (2) 24:26–28; (3) 24:30; and (4) 24:37–51. These same four passages are missing from Luke 21:5–33. These common omissions, together with the minor and sporadic agreements between Mark and Luke against Matthew in Mark 13:14–32, indicate that Mark was not only following the text of Matthew as closely as a copyist might, but that he was also shaping his version of the apocalyptic discourse in the light of the parallel version in Luke 21:5–33.

Wherever the text of Luke followed that of Matthew, Mark copied the common text so closely that the agreements between Matthew and Luke against Mark were reduced to insignificance. Likewise, whenever the text of Luke deviated from that of Matthew, Mark followed the text of Matthew so closely that the agreements between Mark and Luke against Matthew were reduced to insignificance.

This is why it is possible to describe Mark's version of the apocalyptic discourse as a revision of Luke's, in which the general shape of Luke's version of the discourse was preserved, but in which the text was revised to bring it into accord with the text of Matthew, from which Luke's text was originally derived, and which Matthean text was significantly supported elsewhere in Luke's Gospel, even supported in some cases in such a way as to testify against the authenticity of the text of Luke's version of the discourse.

Mark's ending of the discourse affords further evidence of the secondary character of his Gospel in comparison with Matthew and Luke.

M. Mark's Ending for the Apocalyptic Discourse and the Purpose of His Gospel

If there is any part of Mark which provides a reliable hint of the original use for which it was intended, it would be Mark's ending to the apocalyptic discourse in 13:33–36. The fact that Mark heightened the motif of watchfulness in his version of the apocalyptic discourse by the insertion of admonitions to be watchful in 13:9 and 13:23 has been noted.

Mark's introduction to his end for the discourse, "Take heed! Watch!," is a combined version of the watchwords at both the beginning and close of Luke's ending to the discourse (Lk. 21:34–36). Furthermore, the warning to "Watch!" at the beginning of Mark 13:35, following as it does the warning to the doorkeeper to be on the watch at the end of verse 34, reemphasized the existential urgency of the admonition which found its climax in the closing words of Mark's ending: "And what I say to you I say to all: Watch!" Taylor noted that Mark made an application of the saying concerning the man who left home and put his servants in charge, in which the relationship between the man and his servants in verse 34 was made to refer to the relationship between Christ and his church in verse 35. "In the application the change . . . reveals the standpoint in Mark's day. The Church is in daily expectation of the return of its Lord."[17] Taylor thought of the whole of Mark 13:34–36 as "a homiletical

---

[17] Op. cit., p. 523.

echo of several parables."[18] Bleek thought that Mark had "manifestly endeavored briefly to give the substance of the various parables in Matthew xxiv. 37–xxv. 30."[19] Many commentators agree that Mark intended that his readers (and those who hear his Gospel read) feel themselves addressed directly by Jesus as their risen Lord, in the closing words: "what I say to you [the disciples on the Mount of Olives], I say to all [namely all the faithful in the Church who in daily expectation await his promised return]."

If this be true, it is difficult to resist the thought that Mark's work has a distinct cultic orientation—in which an account of the Gospel was formulated in such a way as to bring worshipers hearing it read in church to a fever pitch of eschatological expectation precisely at the point where Mark began his account of the Passion narrative. Whatever liturgical use may have been made of Mark's Gospel in the church or churches for which it was prepared, it seems peculiarly well adapted for use in connection with some important liturgical event in the life of the Church in which the whole of the Gospel of Mark was to be read, and in which the worshiper's powers of concentration and his eschatalogical expectations were sharply focused on the words of the Lord of the cult: "What I say to you I say to all: Watch!," followed immediately by a dramatic representation of the final acts in the redemptive drama of universal salvation through the Passion of the Son of God.[20]

Although it is true that Matthew and Luke may have been used in a similar way in the churches where they originated, it is obvious that Mark's Gospel would have enjoyed certain advantages: (1) In situations where for one reason or another a shorter version of the Gospel was more practical, Mark was easily the choice; (2) It was serviceable for mixed congregations. By "mixed" congregations is meant churches which included as members Christians who had come from different places where different Gospels were read in church.

There is no reason to doubt that the Gospels of Matthew and Luke

---

[18] *Op. cit.*, p. 524.

[19] *Op. cit.*, p. 273.

[20] This is not to imply that Mark 14:1 ff. is the script for a Passion drama, but simply a new and somewhat more dramatic version of the familiar Gospel account of the Passion story. There is no reason, however, to think that the dynamic idea of "the stations of the cross," for example, was a late invention in the church. It is intrinsically probable that on special occasions in the early church the reading of the Gospel account was interrupted and/or accompanied by supplementary liturgy exhibiting dramatic as well as musical features.

would have been very popular in the churches for which they were originally written. But in places like Alexandria or Rome, or in any place where no one Gospel was clearly recognized as *the* Gospel to be read in church, the question of which Gospel to read on any given occasion would have been a very practical question of no little moment. Lectionaries were finally developed to guide the Church in just these matters. But in the period before there was a formal canon which gave official recognition to certain Gospels which was denied to all others, the problem had to be met in other ways. Undoubtedly, different solutions were tried at different times and places.

Even Tatian's *Diatessaron* can be viewed from this perspective as a contribution to the solution of this problem. But Tatian's work reflects a later situation in which four Gospels needed to be worked together on the principle of "inclusiveness"—that is, not only does Tatian include what all four have in common, but he also includes most of what is common to three or two, and even most of what is unique to each. This inclusive principle is not followed slavishly by Tatian. There are a few parts of the fourfold Gospel tradition which seem not to have been included in Tatian's *Diatessaron*. Nevertheless, in general Tatian accomplished the remarkable work of harmonizing the greater part of the contents of Matthew, Mark, Luke, and John.

But in the earlier period, after the first Gospels had been written, but before all four of the canonical Gospels were in existence, another possibility was very real. This was the possibility of creating a new Gospel out of existing Gospels on an "exclusive" principle. Such a Gospel would only have been possible where there was a very close literary relationship between two or more of the existing Gospels. But to the extent that this condition prevailed, it would have been possible to make a significant contribution to the practical problem of deciding which Gospel to read on a given occasion— especially on those high liturgical occasions where it would have been particularly important to the adherents of the various existing Gospels for their favorite Gospel to be read—by creating a new Gospel largely out of existing Gospels concentrating on those materials where their texts bore concurrent testimony to the same Gospel tradition. The Gospel of Mark to a considerable extent could be understood as just such a work, providing it be assumed that two of the most popular and highly regarded Gospels in use in the church or churches for which Mark's Gospel was intended were the Gospels of Matthew and Luke.

It would only be with the greatest difficulty that an adherent of the Gospel of Matthew could convincingly argue that Mark was in balance unduly partial to the Gospel of Luke. Similarly, an adherent of the Gospel of Luke would have had little success in attempting to justify a complaint that Mark's Gospel was unduly partial to the Gospel of Matthew. This is a very important point. For in the beginning of the life of any Gospel produced under these circumstances there would have been a period during which the future of such a Gospel would have remained uncertain. Unless a Gospel like this could have served certain needs in some important church better than any existing Gospel, it could never have gained a place for itself in any canon of the Catholic Church.

The degree to which protests against the use of such a new Gospel could be successfully disregarded by ecclesiastical authorities would have been dependent upon the degree to which that Gospel was successful in reproducing the great core of the undisputed tradition common to the most highly regarded of the existing Gospels, and the degree to which it maintained some over-all semblance of impartiality, vis-à-vis points of dispute between partisans of these Gospels. From this point of view, Mark could have been viewed as a remarkably successful form of the Gospel, by practical-minded church authorities who were more concerned with finding the common ground on which all Christians could stand together than in defending or perpetuating the special interests of any particular group, including their own. For such authorities to acknowledge the peculiar practical advantages of Mark's Gospel would not have entailed their repudiation of existing Gospels. On the contrary, the genius of Mark lay in its implicit endorsement of the existing Gospels. Mark could never have successfully replaced Matthew and Luke except under very temporary, special and limited circumstances. In any church where Mark was used, it would have been necessary, for example, to use one of the other Gospels for a fuller presentation of the teaching of Jesus. At the most, Mark would have had but a supplementary value even in those churches where it received maximum use.

Only at a later time, after the use of Mark in some influential church like Alexandria or Rome had disposed ecclesiastical authorities to find for it a place in any Catholic canon which was ever to be formed, would it be needful to imagine for Mark an origin befitting its actual status in the Church.

But once Mark, along with a limited number of other Gospels, was included in a canon, then arose the very practical possibility of solving the problem which Mark may have been created to solve, by the production of church lectionaries based upon the four canonical Gospels. This development would have entailed the eventual eclipse of Mark even in the church which first obtained for it a place in the canon. For in church lectionaries based upon the four-fold Gospel canon, Mark obviously had less to contribute than any one of the other three. Therefore, it would be a mistake to argue that the provenance of Mark is to be traced to a church in which later traditions concerning its origin would most naturally have developed. For that would have been the church which played the dominant role in forming the canon and therefore the church which had to bear the burden of defending it, including the decision to include any particular Gospel.

There is no way in which to settle the question of the provenance of Mark on the basis of Mark's Gospel alone. A hint of Mark's provenance is given in the tradition of Clement of Alexandria (which implies that Mark was written after Matthew and Luke). That tradition, which Clement received from the elders, and which therefore takes the historian back to the middle of the second century, was, even by the time of Clement, in competition with the tradition of Papias, and it was implicitly rejected by Origen when Origen wrote that Mark was next after Matthew. The best way to account for Clement's tradition is to acknowledge that it was based on reliable information still available to the elders of the church in Alexandria in the middle of the second century. But the memory that Mark was written after Matthew and Luke could have been most readily retained in the church for which Mark was originally produced.

This is by no means a decisive consideration. And it is not possible, for example, to rule out Rome for very serious consideration as a likely place of origin for Mark.

The mystery of Mark's provenance is not solved by the considerations set forth above. These considerations do, however, make it possible to understand better two points which have troubled many scholars concerning Mark's Gospel: (1) how it ever got into the canon; and (2) why, in view of the fact that it did get in, it had so little influence in the life of the churches which accepted that canon.

APPENDIX $\overset{*}{\mathbf{A}}$

I have purposely kept to the last the most remarkable of all the minor agreements, as it illustrates in a peculiarly interesting way the extent to which the problem we are considering belongs to the sphere, not of documentary, but of textual criticism.

Mark 14:65	*Matthew* 26:67–68	*Luke* 22:64
... καὶ ἤρξαντό τινες ἐμπτύειν αὐτῷ [καὶ περικαλύπτειν αὐτοῦ τό πρόσωπον] καὶ κολαφίζειν αὐτόν ... καὶ λέγειν αὐτῷ προφήτευσον.	Τότε ἐνέπτυσαν εἰς τὸ πρόσωπον αὐτοῦ καὶ ἐκολά- φισαν αὐτόν, οἱ δὲ ἐρράπισαν λέγοντες, προφήτευσον ἡμῖν, χριστέ, τίς ἐστιν ὁ παίσας σε;	καὶ περικαλύψαντες αὐτὸν ἐπηρώτων λέγοντες, προφήτευσον τίς ἐστιν ὁ παίσας σε;

The words χριστέ, τίς ἐστιν ὁ παίσας σε occur in Mark also in some MSS.; but, if one merely looks up the authorities in Tischendorf, the list is not imposing. But it takes on quite a different complexion when one discovers that the addition is found also in W, Θ, 13 &c., 579, 700. It then becomes apparent that the addition in Mark is influentially supported in each of three main streams of textual tradition: by the later Egyptian Δ, X, 33, 579, Sah. cod., Boh.; c. A.D. 400 by the African father Augustine (expressly, in a discussion of "The Agreements of the Evangelists"); by the Caesarean Θ, W, 13 &c., 565, 700, N, U, also by Arm., Syr. H^{cl}. In the face of this evidence only two conclusions are open to us. *Either* the reading is correct and the words have accidentally dropped out of the text of Mark both in ℵ B L and in D *k, or* the passage is one which has specially invited assimilation, and this to such an extent that it has taken place independently along three different lines of transmission. The second alternative I believe to be correct. But the MS. evidence suggests that at any rate a certain measure of assimilation has infected the ℵ B L text also in this particular context. For the words describing the veiling,

* This appendix is a quotation from Streeter's *The Four Gospels*, pp. 325–328, and should be read in connection with the discussion of it given above in section A. 6 of Chapter IV.

which I have bracketed in Mark, are omitted by D *a f*, with the substitution of τῷ προσώπῳ for αὐτῷ. Further, Θ, 565, Arm. have this substitution *in addition* to the ordinary reading—a conflation of two types of text which shows clearly that originally they agreed with D *a f*, the conflation being due to a reviser. Syr. S. agrees with D in the omissions, but makes the guards slap "his cheeks" instead of "him." This looks as if in the text from which the Syriac was translated the words τῷ προσώπῳ had been slightly displaced—a hypothesis confirmed by the reading "slapped his face" in some MSS. of the Sahidic. Further, it is to be noticed that the omitted clause does not occur in Matthew; but he would have been unlikely to omit such a striking point, if it had occurred in his source, more especially as the whole point of the taunt *"Prophesy* who it is that struck thee" depends upon the fact that He was prevented by the veil from *seeing* who did it. Indeed this last consideration leads up to what I believe is the true solution—that the original text of Matthew and of Mark omitted *both* the veiling and the words "Who is it, etc." These two stand or fall together. In Luke they are both original; and from Luke the first has got into the Alexandrian (but not into the earliest Antiochene and Western) text of Mark; the second has got into all the texts of Matthew.

The view that τίς ἐστιν κτλ. is an interpolation into Matthew from Luke was originally suggested to me by Prof. C. H. Turner, and at first I demurred to the view. But a consideration of the evidence that in Mark assimilation has been at work both in B ℵ and *fam.* Θ has removed my previous hesitation to believe that these MSS. have suffered interpolation in Matthew also. Further, the view argued in Chapter VIII., that Luke had an account of the Passion which was quite independent of, and in certain ways very different from, that of Mark, affects our judgment on this issue. Luke inserts the incident of the Mocking *before* the Trial by the high priest, instead of *after* the Trial, as in Mark and Matthew. This alteration of order in itself suggests he was following a different source. If, then, we accept the shorter text in Mark and reject τίς ἐστιν κτλ. in Matthew, we shall find that Matthew as usual is substantially reproducing Mark, but that Luke has an entirely different representation. In Mark the mockers spit on His face and slap Him and cry, "Play the prophet now!" In Luke they veil His eyes and then, striking Him, say, "Use your prophetic gift of second sight to tell the striker's name." Each version paints a consistent picture; but, if one half of Luke's picture is pieced on to Mark and the other half to Matthew (as in the ℵ B text), both are blurred, with the result that in the accepted text Matthew's version dulls the edge of the taunt in Mark, but does not succeed in substituting the quite differently pointed taunt in Luke.

Assimilation of parallels is a form of corruption which can result, and, as I have shown, has often actually resulted, in producing an *identical* corruption along more than one *independent* line of transmission. I suggest that for once this has happened along all lines. I should say, rather all lines for which evidence is extant, for *k*, *e*, and Syr. C. are not here extant for Matthew. I will conclude with a quotation from Hort (Vol. I, p. 150)—the italics are mine. "It must not of course be assumed to follow that B has remained unaffected by *sporadic* corruption. . . in the *Gospel of Matthew*, for instance, it has occasionally admitted widely spread readings of very doubtful genuineness." I suggest that the insertion of τίς ἐστιν ὁ παίσας σε is one of these.

Since Streeter in 1924 made no reference to Jameson's work, and proposed his fundamental arguments as if their logical fallacy had not already been publicly exposed, it is necessary to document Jameson's refutation of Streeter's arguments carefully.[1]

Jameson was anxious to disclaim any reactionary bias so he wrote as follows:

There are two great stumbling-blocks in the way of an appeal for the reconsideration of any accepted critical theory. One of them is more or less personal. It is probably true that the attitude of critics today is less affected by religious prejudice than at any former period of history. But notwithstanding this any attempt at reconstruction which happens to be associated with such names as St. Augustine or Dr. Lightfoot is apt to be labelled at once as 'reactionary,' and to be suspected of some ulterior motive. The present writer has no prejudice at all against the Two-document theory. For many years he contentedly accepted it, as so many others have done, as a working hypothesis, and it was only in the course of trying to work it out that he became convinced, not that it was objectionable, but simply that it was not true. The other obstacle consists in the great difficulty which we all experience in realizing even the existence of any point of view different from the one to which we are accustomed. The majority of students today start with the Two-document hypothesis at the back of their minds. They look at every difficulty, and seek for its solution, from the point of view of Mark and Q. It does not even occur to them that their problem might wear a different aspect if approached from some other point, and any suggestion to this effect is at once put aside. No doubt it is necessary to start somewhere, and to assume something, in approaching any kind of problem, but it is also advisable from time to time to go back and examine the foundations on which our inquiry ultimately rests. With regard especially to the Two-document hypothesis I have tried to show in this chapter that many commonly accepted arguments in its favour are so inconclusive or fallacious, and that the difficulties in connection with the Q theory are so confessedly

---

[1] All quotations of the words of Jameson are taken from *The Origin of the Synoptic Gospels*, Oxford, 1922. Page references are given in brackets at the end of quotations.

great, that there is substantial ground for demanding a reconsideration of the whole question [16–17].

That scholarly consensus is no reliable avenue to truth is another point Jameson was careful to make.

It must be admitted that the Two-document hypothesis holds a strong position at the present time. It has the support of a majority of critics, and it has met with little serious opposition, partly no doubt owing to the fact that it tends to support rather than to detract from the historical validity of the Gospel narrative. It is commonly referred to in such a manner as to convey the suggestion that any doubts as to the priority of Mark, or the existence of Q, have now at last been finally settled for all time. But, after all, there have been other theories—the 'Tübingen hypothesis,' 'Ur-Marcus,' 'Oral transmission'—which have been as confidently upheld in their day, and those days were not so very long ago! Less than forty years have passed since it was possible for Dr. E. A. Abbott to write (*The Common Tradition of the Synoptic Gospels*, p. vi), with regard to the accepted opinion of critics at that time, 'Few reasonable sceptics now assert . . . that any one of the three first Evangelists had before him the work of either of the other two.' Criticism has made a real advance in these latter days, and no one would wish, of course, to put the clock back; but it may well be remembered that, while the clock perforce goes *on*, it has also a disconcerting way of going *round*, and many who are still working at this subject have seen more than once such revolution of opinion. [7]

Jameson, with reference to the usual arguments for the priority of Mark wrote:

. . . even so cautious a critic as Dr. Sanday himself asserts . . . that the modern inversion *both of the view of St. Augustine and that of the older Tübingen school* 'is due mainly to two arguments: (1) an examination of the order of the narrative in all the Gospels; (2) an examination of their language.' . . . Dr. Sanday refers to the well-known essay by F. H. Woods, *On the Origin and Mutual Relation of the Synoptic Gospels*, where they were enunciated; and seeing that these arguments of Woods are either reproduced or referred to as conclusive by nearly all later writers (including Streeter in Peake's *Commentary*) who have supported the Two-document hypothesis, it must be assumed that they have regarded them as valid. . . . [8–9].

Jameson then proceeded to point out the inconclusive character of these two arguments from the point of view of the Augustinian hypothesis.

The argument from common contents and language. Woods enunciates it thus:—'With but few exceptions we find parallels to the whole of St.

Mark in either St. Matthew or St. Luke, and to by far the greater part in both.' Canon Streeter somewhat amplifies this by pointing out that the substance of approximately two-thirds of Mark is found in *both* Matthew and Luke, and the remaining one-third, except for thirty verses, is found in *either* Matthew or Luke; and further that most of the actual words used by Mark occur in both Matthew and Luke, and most of the residue in either one or the other. Now seeing that Luke, as is generally agreed, reproduces rather closely all except a small portion of Mark, and that, on the other hand, the greater part of Mark is also to be found in Matthew, the above result must necessarily follow. There remains only the question as to what is to be inferred from the parallels between Matthew and Mark. Obviously they imply one of two things—either Matthew copied them from Mark, *or* Mark copied them from Matthew. But the facts here stated (and they are all that concern us in this argument) do not give even a hint why one of these alternatives should be true rather than the other. The argument, that is, does not bear either for or against the priority of Mark *as regards Matthew*, and therefore does not affect St. Augustine's theory at all.

The argument from relative order. Woods gives this as follows:—'The *order* of the whole of St. Mark, excepting of course what is peculiar to the Gospel, is confirmed either by St. Matthew or St. Luke, and the greater part of it by both.' This state of things, again, is the natural result of the two familiar facts, (1) that Matthew and Mark after the dislocations of order in the early chapters, agree throughout the rest of their course, and (2) that Luke, when he is following Mark, scarcely ever deserts his order at all except towards the close. It is evidently very unlikely, under these conditions, that variations in order in (1) and (2) should coincide. It is a little difficult to see, however, why Canon Streeter (among others) should so insist on this point. He gives one exception, but otherwise, 'wherever Matthew departs from Mark's order, Luke supports Mark; wherever Luke appears to depart, Matthew supports Mark, . . . and in no case do Matthew and Luke agree together against Mark in a matter of arrangement.' These are really quite *insignificant* facts. The only thing which could give them any significance would be the absurd supposition that Matthew and Luke had *agreed together* that one or other of them would always 'support' Mark, even if the other deserted him. Here, as in the previous argument, the only thing with which we are really concerned is the relative order of Matthew and Mark, and any light which it may throw on the question as to the priority of one or the other. But it is evident that, while the *nature* of the dislocations of order found in the early chapters might give some hint as to which was the earlier of the two, the mere fact of their *existence* (which is all that we are concerned with here) leaves the question quite open. As before, therefore, there is no argument either for or against St. Augustine's theory. [9–11]

These words were published in Oxford in 1922. In the same year Burkitt's review of Jameson's book in *J.T.S.*, without questioning the logic of these paragraphs, carried as its closing comment: "... Mr. Jameson supposes that Mark wrote with Matthew before his eyes. I find it frankly incredible."

Two years later Streeter wrote:

A century of discussion has resulted in a consensus of scholars ... that the authors of the First and Third Gospels made use either of our Mark, or of a document all but identical with Mark. The former and the simpler of these alternatives, viz. that they used our Mark, is the one which I hope in the course of this and the following chapters to establish beyond reasonable doubt. [*F. G.*, p. 157]

Then, without mentioning Jameson by name, Streeter continued:

The attempt has recently been made to revive the solution put forward by Augustine, who styles Mark a kind of abridger and lacky of Matthew, "Tanquam breviator et pedisequus ejus." But Augustine did not possess a Synopsis of the Greek text conveniently printed in parallel columns. Otherwise a person of his intelligence could not have failed to perceive that, where the two Gospels are parallel, it is usually Matthew, and not Mark, who does the abbreviation. ... Now there is nothing antecedently improbable in the idea that for certain purposes an abbreviated version of the Gospel might be desired; but only a lunatic [*sic*] would leave out Matthew's account of the Infancy, the Sermon on the Mount, and practically all the parables, in order to get room for purely verbal expansion of what was retained. On the other hand, if we suppose Mark to be the older document, the verbal compression and omission of minor detail seen in the parallels in Matthew has an obvious purpose, in that it gives more room for the introduction of a mass of highly important teaching material not found in Mark.

Then followed a complimentary reference to Professor Burkitt's recent book, *The Earliest Sources for the Life of Jesus* (1922), where Burkitt protested against the idea that Matthew and Luke both used Mark in the same way. Streeter stated that he planned to build on the suggestion of Burkitt in that book, and then wrote:

Partly in order to clear the way for a more thorough investigation of this point, partly because this book is written for others besides students of theology, I will now present a summary statement of the main facts and considerations which show the dependence of Matthew and Luke upon Mark. Familiar as these are to scholars, they are frequently conceived of in a way which tends to obscure some of the remoter issues dependent on them. They can most conveniently be presented under five main heads.

Streeter then presented the same five arguments he had set forth for the priority of Mark in his article on the "Synoptic Problem" in Peake's *Commentary* in 1920, merely reversing the order of the fourth and fifth arguments.

These five arguments were conveniently abstracted by Streeter and set forth at the beginning of his chapter on the "Fundamental Solution" as "Five reasons for accepting the priority of Mark."

The first two reasons were those treated together by Jameson as *The Argument from Common Contents and Language.* That there may be no doubt that Jameson and Streeter were referring to the same phenomena, Streeter's words will be quoted so that they may be compared with the arguments which Jameson refuted:

(1) Matthew reproduces 90% of the subject matter of Mark in language very largely identical with that of Mark; Luke does the same for rather more than half of Mark.

(2) In any average section, which occurs in the three Gospels, the majority of the actual words used by Mark are reproduced by Matthew and Luke, either alternately or both together.

Streeter's third reason for accepting the priority of Mark was the one treated by Jameson as *The argument from relative order.* Streeter's abstract of this argument was as follows:

(3) The relative order of incidents and sections in Mark is in general supported by both Matthew and Luke; where either of them deserts Mark, the other is usually found supporting him.

These are precisely the same arguments which Jameson refuted in 1922. Streeter, in 1924, first acknowledged that a recent "attempt" had been made to "revive" the Augustinian hypothesis. Then he ridiculed this view by assuming that anyone who held it was committed to think that Mark had "abbreviated" everything he took from Matthew, which in all probability Augustine himself knew to be false. Streeter's rhetoric in saying that only a "lunatic" would have acted as Mark is assumed to have acted on the Augustinian hypothesis in his omissions from Matthew was in especially bad taste in view of his own dictum in connection with the problem of explaining omissions. "But, even when we can detect no particular motive, we cannot assume that there was none (that is, we cannot assume lunacy on the part of the writer concerned); for we cannot possibly know, either all the circumstances of churches, or all the personal idiosyncrasies of writers so far removed from our own time."

Then, after ridiculing Jameson's view, Streeter makes a flattering reference to Burkitt's book of 1922, which was largely gratuitous since Streeter had already worked out the essentials of his theories concerning Proto-Luke in his article, "Fresh Light on the Synoptic Problem," in the *Hibbert Journal* for October 1921.

Then, without further qualification, as if Jameson's exposure of Streeter's arguments as *non sequiturs* had never been made, Streeter repeated them in essentially the form he had given them for his article on the Synoptic Problem in *Peake's Commentary*.

There is one curious example of academic bravado that deserves documentation. Jameson, in connection with his discussion of the "Q" hypothesis, wrote:

Canon Streeter, reviewing Lummis' *How Luke Was Written*, writes, "If there were nothing else against it, the theory that Luke derived his Q matter solely and directly from Matthew makes shipwreck on one single fact. . . . Go through St. Mark's Gospel in a Greek Testament and put a mark against the exact point in the Markan outline in which a 'Q' saying is inserted by either Matthew or Luke, and note the result. With the exception of the Q additions to the Markan version of John's preaching and the Temptation (the context of which, of course, is fixed by their subject matter) it will be seen that there is not a single case in which Matthew and Luke insert the same 'Q' saying at the same point in the Markan context. Now this is exactly what one would expect to happen if Matthew and Luke were *independently* incorporating another source or sources in the Markan outline. It is, however, incredible that, if Luke knew this 'Q' matter only as it appears already incorporated by Matthew in the Markan outline, he should, in *every single* case have removed it from its context in Matthew to put it into a different one—the more so as the contexts into which Matthew inserts his additions are as a rule extraordinarily appropriate, which is by no means the case with Luke."[15]

To this Jameson responded:

Now this looks very convincing, until we remember the well-known fact, which Canon Streeter himself calls attention to in more than one place, that, except in the chapters dealing with John the Baptist and the Temptation (where the contexts agree), *Luke does not attempt to insert his "Q" matter into the Marcan context at all,* but collects it all into some three or four large sections, which are interposed between similar large sections of Marcan matter. . . . [15–16]

This observation draws attention to a fallacious proposition in Streeter's argument where he wrote: ". . . there is not a single case in which Matthew and Luke insert the same 'Q' saying at the same point in the Marcan context." The fact is that few 'Q' sayings have a Marcan context in Luke's Gospel. Luke works these sayings together with sayings from his special source material, so that they seldom if ever have a so-called *Marcan* context.

In spite of the fact that Jameson's insightful observation nullified the cogency of this argument which Streeter said was first suggested to him by Hawkins, Streeter repeated it unchanged in 1924. Only its tone was altered:

If then Luke derived this material from Matthew, he must have gone through both Matthew and Mark so as to discriminate with meticulous precision between Marcan and non-Marcan material; he must then have proceeded with the utmost care to tear every little piece of non-Marcan material he desired to use from the context of Mark in which it appeared in Matthew—in spite of the fact that contexts in Matthew are always exceedingly appropriate—in order to re-insert it into a different context of Mark having no special appropriateness. A theory which would make an author capable of such a proceeding would only be tenable if, on other grounds, we had reason to believe he was a crank. [*F. G.,* 183.]

Sarcasm was an effective weapon in the hands of Streeter. After presenting the evidence and arguments in support of his fourth reason for accepting the priority of Mark, Streeter wrote:

The examples adduced above are merely a sample given to illustrate the general character of the argument. But it is an argument essentially cumulative in character. Its full force can only be realised by one who will take the trouble to go carefully through the immense mass of details which Sir John Hawkins had collected, analysed and tabulated, pp. 114–153 of his classic *Horae Synopticae.* How any one who has worked through these pages with a Synopsis of the Greek text can retain the slightest doubt of the original and primitive character of Mark I am unable to comprehend. But since there are, from time to time, ingenious persons who rush into print with theories to the contrary, I can only suppose, either that they have not been at pains to do this, or else that—like some of the highly cultivated people who think Bacon wrote Shakespeare, or that the British are the Lost Ten Tribes—they have eccentric views of what constitutes evidence. [*F. G.,* 164.]

Indexes

Subject Index

Abbott, Edwin A.: argument against Griesbach, 74ff., 75, 76, 77, 78, 85, 89, 90;
article in *Encyclopaedia Britannica,* 70,
72, 74, 78, 88, 94, 99, 103, 121, 159,
178n., 180n., 197
Abbott-Streeter argument for Marcan primitivity, 159ff.
Acta Pilati, 122, 123, 123n., 173
Acts of the Apostles, 4, 30, 31, 33, 39, 41,
236, 237, 265
Aieteia, 268, 269
Apocalyptic material, 272, 277, 278
Apocryphal Gospels, 15, 179n.;
tendency to make more specific, 228;
written after canonical Gospels, 228
Aramaic, Gospels in, 4, 5, 10, 14, 34
Aramaic oral Gospel, 31
Argument from omission, 13, 14
Argument from order, fallacy of, 50, 196,
289;
for Marcan priority, xi, 23, 49, 50, 50n.,
64n., 65, 66, 67, 91, 99, 153, 190, 291
Augustinian hypothesis, xii, 1, 6, 7, 13, 37,
49n., 63, 65, 86, 88, 89, 113, 122, 129,
136, 137, 141, 143, 144, 153, 176,
182, 188, 191, 214, 215, 216, 218,
234, 273, 289, 290, 291, 292

Bampton Lectures in 1893 (Sanday), 60,
73, 183
Baur, F. C.: attacked by Ewald, 28, 29, 46;
radical criticism of, 59
Berlin school, 9, 73
Biographical apopthegm. *See Chreiai*

Burkitt, F. C.: lectures of 1906, 90ff., 91

Chreiai, 266, 267, 268, 269, 270
Christ-myth school, 59
Christian faith, historical foundations of, 18,
19
Christian theology, 37
Christianity, dogmatic interests of, 19
Christology, 230ff.
Church, 58, 59, 254, 256;
christological traditions of, 230;
first decades of, 243;
Gentile influence in, 243, 262n.;
history of, 86;
irreconcilable traditions of, 1, 2;
Jewish-Christian, 243;
liturgical usage in, 174;
origins of, 18, 234;
in post-Pauline period, 230;
tendency to make tradition specific, 171;
use of Lectionaries in, 280, 282
Church Fathers, 2, 39, 224, 225;
traditions of, 2, 3, 32
Clement of Alexandria's Tradition, 1, 8, 282
Consensus, xi, 36, 37, 38, 47, 51, 52, 161,
183, 184, 186n., 187n., 188, 195, 197,
201, 257, 288, 290;
falsity of, xii, 190;
making, xi, 184;
of twentieth century, 178;
on Marcan hypothesis, 44, 77, 78, 89
Criticism, assured results of, x, xii, 46, 51,
60n., 140, 177, 186n., 188;
canons of, xiii, 228;

294

Index of Names

Index of Synoptic References